LEGAL THEORY, POLITICAL THEORY, AND DECONSTRUCTION

LEGAL THEORY, POLITICAL THEORY, AND DECONSTRUCTION

Against Rhadamanthus

MATTHEW H. KRAMER

Indiana University Press
BLOOMINGTON AND INDIANAPOLIS

Publication of this book was aided by grants from Trinity College (Cambridge) and the British Overseas Research Fund.

The paper used in this publication meets the minimum requirements of American National Standard for Information Sciences—Permanence of Paper for Printed Library Materials, ANSI Z39.48-1984.

∞™

Manufactured in the United States of America

Library of Congress Cataloging-in-Publication Data

Kramer, Matthew H.
Legal theory, political theory, and deconstruction : against Rhadamanthus / Matthew H. Kramer.
p. cm.
Includes bibliographical references.
ISBN 0-253-33148-X (alk. paper)
1. Law—Methodology. 2. Law—Philosophy. 3. Deconstruction.
I. Title.
K212.K73 1991
340′.1—dc20 89-46347
CIP

1 2 3 4 5 94 93 92 91 90

Contents

Preface

This book aims to reach three principal audiences: (a) those people interested in jurisprudence and political theory in the Anglo-American tradition; (b) those people who are without much knowledge of Continental philosophy—above all, of deconstruction—and who wish to know more; and (c) those people who are well versed in Continental thought, particularly in deconstruction. Balancing the needs of these groups is a precarious enterprise, and some portions of this book will undoubtedly prove more interesting or more comprehensible to one group than to another. On the whole, however, I seek to blend clarity with sophistication. I sometimes expound points at greater length than people in the first or the third group might need, but I also have intervened unstintingly in the most complex discussions carried on by such people. Conversely, some of the arguments and individual sentences in this book may remain obscure for anyone hitherto unfamiliar with deconstructive philosophy, but in general I have tried to write in a fashion that will not exclude or alienate such a reader. If one keeps in mind the ideas developed in the first chapter, one should not meet with undue difficulty while following what is said in the later chapters.

While striving to eschew needless obscurity, I have not endeavored to forsake jargon entirely. Complete avoidance of jargon would be impossible and would in any event be undesirable, for jargon can nicely obviate stilted circumlocutions. What I have done, however, is to define all my important jargon—sometimes briefly, sometimes at length. People not already conversant with the language of deconstructive philosophy (and some other modes of Continental philosophizing) should not herein feel *tout dérouté*, except insofar as even the most informed reader should when deconstructionist methods are highlighted. (Incidentally, *ça va sans dire* that a reliance on jargon is in no way unique to Continental philosophy; *every* subdiscipline has its own argot[s] which will formulate its inquiries and which will exclude or disadvantage outsiders. No one can escape altogether from jargon, but I can strive to keep it illuminating and unrepellent. If the trumpet gives an indistinct sound, who bothers to get ready for battle?)

I can clarify one question of terminology at the outset: I use the words "paradox," "antinomy," "aporia," and "double bind" interchangeably.

Chapters 2, 3, and 4 highlight deconstructive readings of particular works, but one should not expect therein to discover aridly single-minded treks leading to conclusions that have paid little note to textual specificities. Deconstruction, as will be emphasized in my first chapter, must entail scrupulously close readings of the discourses and activities and phenomena that it shows to be incoherent. Incoherence elaborates itself in endlessly varied patterns, to which a deconstructive approach has to attend with rigor if its demonstrations of incoherence are to achieve cogency. No reading is impartial, but some readings are much more careful than others. A single-minded trek would fail to provide the subtlety and attentiveness that are needed to discern paradoxes in a profound and convincing way. Much of the analysis in my middle three chapters, then, will not directly be highlighting and wielding deconstructionist methods, but will be undertaking the sort of scrutiny that in time can bring such methods to the fore with due verve. In those middle chapters, the sections that are explicitly and sustainedly deconstructive are but the second half of Part Two in Chapter 2, the second half of Part Two in Chapter 3, the initial half of Part Two in Chapter 4, and the second half of Part Three in Chapter 4. Other sections will now and then—and to varying degrees—be informed overtly by problems and maneuvers and themes of deconstruction, but such maneuvers and problems will become the focus primarily in the sections that I have just referred to. Some sections, notably Part One of Chapter 2 and Part One of Chapter 3, will have stirred more interest among members of my first audience (whose prime concern is analytic philosophy) than among members of my second and third audiences (whose major concern is deconstructive philosophy), for those Parts undertake an exacting scrutiny of abstruse arguments put forward by analytic philosophers, and the scrutiny does not highlight deconstructive techniques and goals very often. Yet those Parts deserve serious attention from people in the second and third audiences as well, since—as has just been maintained, and as will be further argued in Part Two of my Introduction—a careful interrogating of arguments and highlighted patterns is an indispensable dynamic in any cogent deconstructive critique; without a meticulous recountal of a perspective's seeming coherence, one cannot persuasively track its *in*coherence.

Throughout this book, I refer to insights of deconstruction in many ways: as methods, techniques, strategies, theses, standpoints, approaches, doctrines, positions, tactics, and so forth. In my view, deconstruction amounts to all these things and ergo does not amount to any of them univocally or conclusively. Its strategies and procedures flow from its substantive ideas, and its substantive insights flow from its methodological acuteness. A reference to deconstructive philosophy as a method will imply that it also is a position, and a reference to it as a position will imply that it also is a method. Indeed, even this useful way of presenting the relationship between deconstructionist theory and deconstructionist practice will have played down the vibrancy and disturbingness of such a relation; deconstructive philosophy has highlighted the paradoxes of structures-and-their-events, and those paradoxes must apply to the theory/practice of deconstruction itself.

I have used the term "deconstruction" quite frequently in this volume, though I am by no means entirely comfortable with it. My discomfort stems partly from the slipshod use of the term by many theorists to denote skepticism or indeed any type of dissatisfaction, and partly from the closeness of "deconstruction" to "destruction"—a closeness which provides a strategic leverage for displacing and redefining the latter term, but which nonetheless has encouraged the unfortunate and pervasive tendency to confuse deconstructive philosophizing with skepticism. In my future work I shall be moving away from "deconstruction" and cognate terms, and shall be pointing up a vocabulary of "enjoining." But in the present volume I have retained the more familiar vocabulary, for two principal reasons that are closely connected. First, by attaching to itself the label of "deconstruction," this book has signaled its place and its allegiances in current philosophic disputes; and, in particular, it has thereby flagged its indebtedness to the work of Jacques Derrida. Second, this study has resolved not to take its place too submissively in the current disputes, and has sought to overturn and disrupt theories that have highlighted tamely anodyne construals of texts by Derrida. In that way, I have tried to re-emphasize the deconstructive uncanniness and power of deconstruction—a goal which has militated in favor of preserving the tag of "deconstruction" in order to point out the domesticating discourses (self-announced as "deconstruction") that will here be impugned.

In my first and fifth chapters (and to some extent in the other chapters), I recount several of the routes by which my analyses will try to dislodge the common modes of deliberately or inadvertently draining Derrida's work of its immense power. Such modes of domestication will have indeed been shown to frustrate themselves. For now, let me emphasize just one point. In my discussions of paradoxes, especially in Part One of Chapter 1 and Part Three of Chapter 4, my approach will underline the futility of attempts to characterize the poles of the difference/presence divide (or of cognate dualisms) as somehow equiprimordial.[1] Reciprocal prioritization, not a blandly coeval juncture, is the relationship that presence and difference have enjoined; differences have to antecede presences *because* presences have to antecede differences. Each moment of prioritization will have led to its own reversal, which will of course have led back. A key to understanding reciprocal prioritization—as opposed to equiprimordial coexistence or, rather, as that which has compelled and debarred all such coexistence—is to realize that *anything*, no matter how involuted or basic, is entirely due to its differences from all other things and is therefore due to its wholly self-determining presence. *Every* unit of reality has succumbed to paradoxes of differentiation, which are indeed paradoxes from the precise fact that *every* unit always succumbs to them. And, because every such unit will be going through paradoxes, coeval junctures of presences and differences are ruled out. Differences and identities require each other completely and forbid each other completely; but unless there is some unit that can escape this paradoxical interaction, the interaction will never cease—as it would have had to if the equiprimordial coexistence of poles in dyads were possible. Equiprimordial co-occurrence would demand baselines in distinction from which ostensibly coeval networks and things would have emerged. Yet neither dyadic poles nor anything else can ever play the part of a baseline, since aporias of differentiation engulf all. It is the all-encompassing scope of difference/presence paradoxes that makes them paradoxes. Or so I argue in Chapters 1 and 4 (where the import of what has just been said will become much clearer).

In regard to the all-encompassing scope of paradoxes, one additional point deserves brief emphasis here. When Derrida writes that some or another doctrine will perforce lack a stable center that can arrest its play, he is hardly casting his lot with schools of anti-foundationalism, which have become fashionable in recent years. He is not simply denying the existence of any ultimate ground on which our knowledge and action might be based. His aim, rather, is the much more venturesome one of highlighting the paradoxical flows and counterflows that embrace both groundedness *and* ungroundedness. Infinite regresses of enjoining (that is, of the interplay between absolute necessitating and absolute proscribing), rather than some infinite series of impermanent grounds, are what a deconstructive critique must always bring to the fore. To insist emphatically on the all-encompassing reach of difference/presence aporias—to insist upon the absence of any units that can escape and halt the seesaw between thorough autonomy entailing complete dependence and complete dependence entailing thorough autonomy—is not to espouse a vulgar anti-foundationalism, but is to highlight the utter lack of toeholds without which neither anti-foundationalism nor foundationalism can achieve thinkability and coherence.

Finally, I should say a few words here about what I have not said—a few words, that is, about some people who have not been discussed at length in this volume: (1) This book does not refer very much to Hegel, and it refers even less to Kant, but the importance of both of those great thinkers for the traditions that have shaped my approach can hardly be overestimated. Indeed, as I shall observe, the critical impetus of the present study amounts to the interrogating and upheaving of the Hegelian dialectic by the Hegelian dialectic. The dearth herein of express remarks on Kant and Hegel should not obscure the implicit presence of their philosophies throughout this book's challenging of presence. In a future work I shall be discussing them, and their highly complex relation to deconstructive analyses, in depth. (2) Chapter 5's perusal of theories that attack reification will ignore some of the leading work on the topic, as the chapter focuses no attention on such figures as Lucien Goldmann and Joseph Gabel. Theodor Adorno receives only some glancing references, and Hegel's brilliant anticipation of Marx's work on fetishism goes unanalyzed. (I initially wrote a section on Hegel, but—because I felt I could not abridge it, and because it made Chapter 5 much too long—I have deleted it here.) My focus on Marx, Lukács, and Sartre has been determined by two considerations: those three writers deal, in various ways, with all the basic patterns of conduct that I describe as "reification"; and it is the analytical frameworks of those three writers that have established the terms in which the scholars of the American critical legal movement have assailed reification. Thus, given that Chapter 5 aims to transform the critical legal scholars' analyses, a restriction of my focus to Marx and Lukács and Sartre should provide reasonable comprehensiveness at a manageable length. (3) Ronald Dworkin enjoys nearly as much prominence in current Anglo-American legal theory as does H. L. A. Hart, yet I comment very little on Dworkin while devoting a long chapter to Hart. Dworkin's criticisms of Hart seem to me telling and astute, but I think they can be accommodated by a more subtle version of Hart's theory (with a shifting of emphasis from the fact/value distinction to the uncontroversial/controversial distinction). Further, Dworkin's account of law—like a more sophisticated version of Hart's account—can best be interpreted as a mode of relativism,[2] though a mode which lays heavy stress on the presumed univocality of each major outlook. As a mode of relativism, Dworkin's theory must run afoul of the paradox that my fifth chapter has highlighted in neo-pragmatism.

This book is a considerably revised form of my Ph.D. dissertation at Cambridge University. I wrote the book between the autumn of 1985 and the spring of 1988, when I put it aside in order to begin a new book, *Critical Legal Theory and the Challenge of Feminism*. (In the latter work, I develop some of the current book's main themes at much greater length than I have developed them here, and I discuss many topics—such as the nature/culture dichotomy and the politics/metaphysics relation—that the current book has treated only in passing [or not at all].) In February 1989 I began the extraordinarily grueling task of revision, which I completed in July 1989.

Part of Chapter 2, in a different form, has been published as "G. A. Cohen's Conception of Law: A Critique" in *Ratio Juris*. Another excerpt from Chapter 2, in a different form, has been published as "The Specter of Communism" in *Political Theory*. Part of an early version of Chapter 3 has been published as "The Rule of Misrecognition in the Hart of Jurisprudence" in the *Oxford Journal of Legal Studies*. Part of Chapter

4, in a different form, has been published as "The Deferral of Nature in Hume's Theory of Justice" in the *Canadian Journal of Law and Jurisprudence*. Some sentences from Chapter 1 and from Chapter 5 have been published in "Critical Legal Theory and Deconstruction" in *Textual Practice*. I am very grateful indeed to all these journals, though my piece in *Political Theory* is to some extent marred by mistakes of printing that were uncorrected despite my having called the attention of the publisher to them when I proofread the galleys.

Scholarships and grants from Trinity College (Cambridge) and from the British Overseas Research Fund helped to make the writing and publication of this book possible. I thank both institutions. I am obliged as well to Darwin College (Cambridge), which has provided a friendly home at the stage of final corrections.

While in Cambridge, I have enjoyed remarkable hospitality from Norman and Jean Murray and their family. I deeply regret that Norman Murray did not live to see the completion of this book.

The following people helped me greatly by reading some or all of this book at various stages of its evolution: Philip Allott, Jack Balkin, Nathaniel Berman, Richard Bronaugh, Christiane Burgi-Schmutzler, William Connolly, Martin Greig, Mark Kramer, Sandy Levinson, Raun Rasmussen, Armin Schmutzler, an anonymous reader for *Political Theory*, and several faculty members at the University of Michigan Law School (whom I do not single out, for fear of omitting someone). My special thanks go to Bernard Jackson and Christopher Norris, who examined me on my work for my Ph.D.

Jerry Cohen provided long, perceptive, and generous comments on Chapter 2. He is wary of deconstruction, and he differs with me on several points, but he has sharpened my thinking in regard to his brilliant work.

My thanks extend as well to the staff of Indiana University Press, and especially to the reader for the Press whose detailed and penetrating comments induced a number of redeeming amplifications.

My profoundest thanks are reserved for seven people, five of whom have read some or all of this book at earlier stages. Isaac Kramnick was the professor who first instilled into me a love for political theorizing, and he has supported me in numerous contexts since my freshman year at Cornell. Jerry Frug, David Kennedy, and Duncan Kennedy have all helped to shape my thought with their remarkable teaching, writing, and intellectual camaraderie. They have also supported me without fail in many ways. Demonstrating their excellence as teachers, they have enabled me to question key aspects of their own views. Nigel Simmonds was my Ph.D. supervisor at Cambridge, but he is also my friend and intellectual comrade. I could not have wished for a more careful and astute reader of my dissertation; every chapter has profited from his trenchant scrutiny. I also have learned a lot from our many conversations on sundry issues.

The last two people whom I shall mention are the people to whom this text is devoted. My parents' ceaseless encouragement and love were the most important factors of all in my ability to write this book. Though my parents have not yet read my work, they are its true authors. To them I devote this study with all my love.

Cambridge, England
August 1989

LEGAL THEORY, POLITICAL THEORY, — AND — DECONSTRUCTION

CHAPTER 1

INTRODUCTION

This book's subtitle contains the paradox that is my principal thesis. I trade on the semantic fecundity of the first word of the subtitle and thereby turn it *against* itself. Rhadamanthus, so we are told, was incorruptibly and unfailingly just, both as a lawgiver and as one of the three Judges of the Dead. He has come down to us as one of the great symbols of objectivity in judgment. This book will therefore have set itself *against* Rhadamanthus in two ways that are wholly incompatible but reciprocally constitutive: it proceeds in opposition to Rhadamanthus, but it also relies on him and submits fully to him as the inevitable background against which strategies that oppose him must take their shape.

Each chapter will be explicitly informed and structured by the first way in which this book is against Rhadamanthus. One of the dominant contentions throughout the book is that analytic philosophy—more precisely, the analytic approach to jurisprudence and political theory—has systematically privileged objectivity over subjectivity in a number of forms (sometimes expressly, sometimes implicitly). The elevation of objectivity over subjectivity is perhaps most apparent in the analytic philosopher's conception of legal rules and judicial decision making, as we shall observe squarely in Chapter 2; but the yearning for objectivity goes well beyond juristic conceptions narrowly defined. A similar elevation of objectivity pervades analytic philosophy's self-conception. Each of the philosophers to be studied in this book has few doubts that his own judgments partake of the objectivity that has eluded competing theories. Each has pretensions to an objectively valid perch for analyzing the fields of action and discourse that he is examining, for each presumes to have come upon a solid foundation for his stance. Foundations can range from the materiality of production to the observable patterns of legal discourse to the particularities of sense data, but in each case the overriding goal is to match Rhadamanthus in the objectivity of one's judgments. In this respect, even theories that privilege individual agents are thereby striving to be objective. Analytic philosophers struggle to achieve what Barbara Johnson describes as the supreme *telos* of every judgment, be it a general cognitive judgment or a specifically legal judgment—*viz.*, the transformation of indeterminateness into decidability.[1] But the fulfillment of such an aspiration will at a bare minimum require a fundamental coherence in the projects directed thereunto; and since this book will be bringing out the stark incoherence of the theories that it considers, I shall be writing here against Rhadamanthus as an opponent.

When a critique of judgment is fully generalized and is thus not limited to judicial determinations, it has immediately raised vast problems of self-reflection and self-criticism. After all, every such critique will involve countless acts of judgment and argument. Problems of self-criticism indeed turn out to be central in every chapter of this book, and are therefore encapsulated in the second principal meaning of this volume's subtitle—the second of the two ways in which this book is written against Rhadamanthus. As has been noted, the ideal of objectivity looms not merely as the "target" of the critiques that follow, but equally as their indispensable precondition. Those critiques cannot stand outside the sway of the paradoxes they highlight; hence, whatever they might tear down will have always already been rebuilt, for here we are waging war against concepts as resilient as boomerangs that return even before they can be ejected. It is the very essence of paradox to produce failure as a necessary concomitant of success, which is why this book will serve Rhadamanthus through the sheer action of fighting him. Objectivism will have to be joined in battle, ceaselessly, only on its own terrain, as there is no enemy force that it cannot conquer amid its own defeat. It will always act as the formidable background *against* which its own undoing proceeds.

As has been stated, then, the two meanings of this book's subtitle are inextricably interwoven as well as mutually exclusive. This unthinkable paradox in no way precludes a certain measure of triumph for the critiques that are undertaken herein; indeed, it will render the critiques all the more uncanny and more effective, even as it renders their political implications more slippery. But their success will ground itself through and through on their failure and will thus offer irresistible leverage for their own downfall (which will in turn offer irresistible leverage for their reviving, and so forth). In this dizzying tumble, wherein analyses draw their life from their own subversion, my critiques will not distinguish themselves from the orthodox approaches they target—except, perhaps, in a joyful resignation that stems from their highlighting of the paradoxes that generate and disrupt them.

For those not familiar with the more arcane pathways of recent French philosophy, the preceding paragraphs may be somewhat obscure. It is the aim of this introductory chapter, and indeed of this whole book, to start to gain wider currency for the insights of French scholars among jurisprudes and political theorists in the Anglo-American tradition. Most of what remains in this first chapter will be devoted to explicating the chief strategies and ideas that this book has appropriated—with all the violence which that verb would imply—from recent French thought. Similar strategies have been developed in other philosophic traditions, as will be observed presently, but the themes that suffuse this book have attained their most sophisticated expression in French, particularly in the deconstructive writings of Jacques Derrida.

This does not mean, of course, that deconstructionist insights have been incorporated mechanically as a fixed body of thought. Rather, they have been amplified and appropriated in ways that should prove most fruitful for political theory and jurisprudence. (For instance, the vexed relation between deconstructionism and politics will receive special attention, most notably in my fifth chapter.) Moreover, deconstructionist strategies of reading will demonstrate their verve in areas of political and legal philosophy that hitherto have attained but little self-conscious interaction with the frontiers of Gallic thought. Nonetheless, it is quite possible that the highly structured approach of this first chapter will lead to the impression that deconstructive theories are rigidly systematic. That, alas, is a risk which must be accepted for the sake of providing an overview of deconstruction that will do more than convince exclusively the convinced. However, one would do well to keep in mind that, although this chapter will be attempting to furnish a broadly integrative account of this book's motifs, the chapter's main purpose is to evoke a certain orientation or mood that can assist in one's reading of Chapters 2–5. In other words, this initial chapter's theoretical framework should not arouse expectations that the ideas elaborated herein will be "applied" neatly to the analytical questions in the succeeding chapters. The movement of those ideas is far more elusive and open-ended than any typical model of the application of theory would suggest. Most of the themes articulated here will turn up in express forms only now and then in the chapters that follow. They generally play more furtive roles in determining what counts as significant and in shaping methodologies of disruption. Deconstructive analyses pay scrupulously close attention to texts, and develop abstract critical themes from specific moments of discourse (which are themselves highlighted, of course, by the abstract themes). In addition, and even more important, one of the prime messages of the deconstructive approach adopted here is that efforts to "apply" structures in order to produce concrete results will always have already exploded into double binds of regression without surcease. With the structure/event paradox as one of its mainstays, a self-critical project must avoid conniving at any vulgar notions of the dichotomy between structure and practice—even though such notions cannot be once and for all jettisoned.

Part One of this chapter will introduce the three basic strategies that work themselves out in diverse ways all through the arguments of this volume. A number of brief examples flesh out much of the abstract discussion of the book's themes. Part Two of the chapter, which is markedly shorter than Part One, will delineate the overall structure of the book by supplying a crisp summary of each of the last four chapters and by explaining how those chapters are closely interrelated. Suffice it for now to say that Chapter 2 is a deconstructive critique of a renowned Marxist; Chapter 3 is a deconstructive critique of a renowned liberal; Chapter 4 is a critique of an eminent conservative; and Chapter 5 examines what might remain of jurisprudence and political theory if one concedes the trenchancy of the foregoing critiques.

Part One. Deconstructive Themes

This Part is divided into three sections, all of which will elaborate the main themes that inform my resistance to Rhadamanthian objectivity: paradoxes, iterability (or sunderability), and framing (or the frustration of closure). Of these sections, the first—on paradoxes—is by far the longest and is itself constituted of four subsections: problems of differentiation, paradoxes relating to infinity, structure/event antinomies, and problems of self-referentiality.

Though French deconstruction holds pride of place in sustaining a high degree of sophistication while probing the aforementioned themes, many other texts must share in the credit for a rigorous exploration of several of the problems that will concern us. One should cite, at a minimum, the texts of Critical Theory, post-structuralism (apart from Derrida's work), feminism, and neo-pragmatism (or post-analytic philosophy). As will be emphasized hereafter, these discourses are not at all just "saying the same thing"—at the level of overt thematization—but they have all contributed to the evolution of insightful techniques of reading. Their importance will be acknowledged continually throughout the notes to this volume, especially in the fifth chapter (where abundant citations aim to provide a context for a rewriting of jurisprudence and political theory).

The themes which follow are but part of a wider network of strategies and ideas amounting to a critical legal theory (i.e., a critical theory of law and politics). Indeed, a crucial component of the theoretical strands that have been woven into this book is the American critical legal studies movement. In articles dating from the early 1970s to the present day, critical legal scholars have been challenging mainstream views of jurisprudential issues by drawing upon some of the discourses that were mentioned (and applauded) in the preceding paragraph.[2] What this book will suggest is that the critical legal movement has not gone far enough and has taken aboard a host of orthodox preconceptions far too uncritically. Of course, one cannot banish the orthodox assumptions conclusively, for banishment will require a simultaneous immigration. While not hoping for an absolute ouster, nonetheless, one should strive explicitly to impugn the orthodox scheme of values by turning its own bases against themselves (in a torsion that has always occurred already). It is precisely here, in mounting a staunchly paradoxical contestation, that the critical legal studies movement has been deficient, no matter how much it has opposed traditional faith in Rhadamanthus. One of the leading purposes of this book, then, is to commence a redefining of critical legal scholarship. Especially in this first chapter and in Chapter 5, but in other chapters as well, the themes of this book will enter into a dialogue and a confrontation with critical legal scholars.

A. Paradoxes

Though the four types of paradoxes distinguished here are ultimately collapsible into one another—at times in fiendishly complicated ways—they can usefully be divided, in a provisional and flexible manner.

1. *Problems of Differentiation*

If there is one theme that activates every part of this book, it is the problem of differentiation, which Derrida most often adverts to as *différance*.[3] In the last section of Chapter 4, the paradoxes of differentiation will be treated at greater length than they can be here, but for now they can be roughly stated as follows: presence requires yet must exclude difference in order to become present. On the one hand, difference serves as the *sine qua non* of presence. The identities of words, concepts, and objects—i.e., of all the earth and the fullness thereof—are determined wholly by the relationships in and through which they function. Until each thing has been at least vaguely separated or marked off from everything which is *not* it, it can never achieve the status or presence of a thing in any form whatsoever. Self-contained essences can arise only by way of mutual delimitation, for the specific nature of any unit is founded by its place (and thus by its boundaries) within a pattern or network. Without difference, in short, no plenitude can present itself. Because identity is a product of relationality, there can be no units and indeed no world unless differences have played their defining role. Until borders—even incipient or ambiguous borders—have appeared, no presences will have made their way into being, since nothing at all would separate each of them from what it is not. Entities can emerge as such only by being cordoned off from all other entities; if the world does not display definition, then it does not display anything whatsoever. Unless differences have become established, the world and all the fullness thereof will have remained completely devoid of form, like Schelling's Absolute, which (as Hegel wittily saw) was absolutely nothing.[4]

Precisely by not becoming what it is not, each thing has become what it is. Within a pattern or world or system, the role of each of the units will be determined fully by what the other units necessitate *and* leave out (i.e., by what they have presupposed but have themselves not included). Each thing will hence amount to a by-product of the needs and omissions of all the other units in the relevant structure. Each thing, that is to say, will ensue from the imperatives of the structures in and through which it gains its slot. Such imperatives, which obtain in endlessly varied forms in all structures (ranging from the entire fabric of the universe to the most trifling substructures thereof), will have derived from the givenness of synchronic relations. At every moment in time, from the point of view of each item in a configuration of presences, the rest of the units in the configuration and their interlinkages with the specified item will act perforce as a given and a determinant in whatever forms those units might take. Being exactly what the specified thing or unit is not, no matter how closely similar that unit may be to some or all of the other units, the remaining constituents of the structure endow the specific unit with its identity—by differing from it and by providing it with something from which to differ. They not only make possible the emerging of presentation in general, by having led *generally* to difference and individuation, but they also determine the precise nature of the specified unit because they differ from it *in particular ways*. In order to exist as they do, the other elements must constrain the specific unit to be of a particular kind. Their functioning and arrangement will have presupposed that the unit differs from them, and therefore stands in relation to them, in a unique and fully determined way. Through their own givenness at each moment in relation to that which they are not, structural elements will have marked out a place for every one of themselves. Each unit will differ from the rest of the units in the ways that those other units have established (by diverging from *it* along exactly those lines). Hence, each unit must receive the identity that the other units require it to have—through its differences from them, which of course mirror *their* differences from *it*, and which thus make each unit into what all the other units have presupposed and left out.

Yet, on the other hand, presence is not only a by-product but also a precondition of the divergences among units. Differences set bounds to identities and thus make them possible, but differences must themselves have been given birth by identities. Without beings of some sort that differ from one another, difference will have been extirpated along with presence; to kill the latter is likewise to kill the former. An undifferentiated Absolute is precisely that: undifferentiated. Distinctions cannot exist unless there are entities among which they can obtain. If nothing has been distinguished in any way from anything else, then, patently, no distinctions exist. A configuration of differences can arise only if the identities of some or all of its units have become settled into place.

But because *every* element of any configuration must have emerged by way of differences, there can be no foothold or *point d'appui* that would break the uncanny circle of differences chasing after themselves and trying to pull themselves up by their own bootstraps. *All* units are sheer outcomes of differences, and, exactly for that reason, no units can act as benchmarks that could relieve differences from having to operate as their own foundations. Every unit has to mark itself off from every other unit in order to become present; but squarely because this proposition must apply fully to *all* the units, there cannot be anything present from which anything else can differ. Every apparent presence can only fail to give the requisite toehold, because each such presence will have turned out to be a quotient produced by differences. That is, each unit is as unnervingly and wholly reliant on its differences from all other units as is each of the other units, and accordingly no presence can function as a baseline or starting point against which differences may emerge. (*Mutatis mutandis,* entering into play here are considerations not wholly unlike those that induced Wittgenstein to observe that "[i]f you tried to doubt everything you would not get as far as doubting anything. The game of doubting itself presupposes certainty."[5] All that needs to be added here is that we *must* do what we cannot do.) Since differentiation requires presences, furthermore, its role as a precondition of presences may now best be seen as the foremost way in which it has barred itself (and so barred the presences to which it has given rise). What makes presence possible is exactly what rules it out altogether, as identity and relationality call forth and preclude each other. In this light, no entities can attain to simple presence or absence, but must attain in full to both and to neither.

Aporias of differentiation likewise afflict temporality, as is demonstrated with most force by Zeno's Paradox of the Arrow (which is briefly recounted in the next subsection). More generally, such aporias constitute and subvert the array of dualisms on which Western philosophers have relied. In legal philosophy and political philosophy, some of the most important dyads have been form versus substance, nature versus society, action versus discourse, factuality versus normativity, male versus female, generality versus particularity, subjectivity versus objectivity, and structure versus dynamics. Philosophers have traditionally wielded one or more of these dualisms throughout their arguments and, in doing so, have adopted either of two principal tactics: the prioritizing of one pole of a dyad over the alternative pole, or the blending of the two poles in some felicitous balance. As subsequent chapters of this book will attempt to show—and as should be manifest from what has been said thus far—neither of the aforementioned tacks can ultimately succeed, for both of them have to disregard the paradoxes that overturn them. Attempts to prioritize one pole of a dualism will take place in an endlessly frustrating to-and-fro, whereby each act of prioritizing will always have already undone itself and thus will have turned into an act of devaluation (which will have already evolved into an act of prioritizing). Poles of philosophical dyads have to be differentiated, and are hence caught up in the aporias of differentiation that have been outlined here; thus it is that each act of prioritizing has constantly turned against itself, since prioritizing consists in differentiation. Each pole has to rely through and through on the presentness of the other for its own presence, because its own presence comes about by way of its differences from the other presence. Yet, through its having to depend unreservedly on the other, each pole debars the other from becoming present, since the other pole will in turn be looking to the first pole as the baseline that the other pole cannot and does not constitute. Theorists who endeavor to strike a happy balance between the poles of dichotomies will fare just as badly. As we have seen in this subsection's account of demarcations and presences, differentiated poles are *completely* reliant on each other at all times (while they launch devastating pre-emptive forays against each other), and—we may now add—the completeness of their relationship will inexorably hold sway and make itself felt. Attempts at eluding this uncanny reliance, by construing it as reciprocal but partial, will thus unwittingly rive themselves in two directions at once. Splitting the difference will not fend off aporias but will have mired itself in them with particular naiveté.[6]

At great cost, these problems of differentiation must be distinguished from the results of the quasi-structuralist methodology that informs critical legal scholarship. (This is undertaken "at great cost" because any such distinction may seem inadvertently to bolster the claims of the quasi-structuralist approach.) What critical legal scholars maintain is that inveterate conflicts within the goals, categories, and argumentative patterns of legal discourse must willy-nilly confute the widespread belief that judicial cases can have "correct" or thoroughly reasoned outcomes. Critical legal scholars see judges as engaged in a hopeless quest for a way to mediate contradictory aspects of human life in a principled, apolitical manner. These scholars hold that choices between mutually exclusive outcomes will always be indeterminate and will merely reproduce at a new level the conflicts they purport to resolve. The following passage from an essay by Gerald Frug, on the ideology of bureaucracy in American law, is an apt example of the general line of assault taken by nearly everyone in critical legal studies:

> [E]very attempt to separate objectivity and subjectivity in bureaucratic thought has instead resulted in a relentless intermixing of them. . . . In an attempt to overcome the combination of subjectivity and objectivity, legal theorists have sought new lines between subjectivity and objectivity. . . . But this line-drawing enterprise has reproduced the same relentless intermixture of subjectivity and objectivity. . . .
>
> . . . [T]his relentless attempt to divide and redivide subjectivity and objectivity has produced a form of legal doctrine that restates the very problems of bureaucratic domination and personal self-expression that it was created to solve. Instead of providing a way to decide whether a concrete bureaucratic activity should be approved or condemned, legal doctrine simply presents a structure that lawyers can use to formulate arguments for and against the activity under review. Because every aspect of bureaucratic life that must be objective also must be subjective, lawyers can argue endlessly over which of these conflicting yet essential ingredients should be focused on. The law either oscillates between seeing the subjective or the objective side as the more important or offers alternative, but inconsistent, schemes for combining-yet-separating both sides. Legal doctrine thus provides a justification for both a particular course of action and its opposite.[7]

This quotation brings out two closely connected weaknesses of the quasi-structuralist approach that Frug and his colleagues favor. In the first place, Frug sees mixture rather than paradox as the chief thorn in the flesh of mainstream legal theory; the reason that all efforts to mark off subjectivity from objectivity are doomed to fail is not that the two categories determine and decompose each other *in toto*, but that such categories are *partially* and unsiftably intermixed. Frug's view of legality and society takes much the same course as that staked out by his conception of objectivity and subjectivity:

> Neither society-without-law nor law-outside-of-society seems a meaningful possibility in the world; the use of one of these terms always seems to imply the existence of the other. . . . If so, one can see why the task of "drawing a line" between law and society becomes an incoherent, meaningless task. Society is constituted, *in part*, by law, and law is constituted, *in part*, by society.[8]

Now, as one ought to deduce from my preceding paragraph, these attempts to interpret paradoxes as mere tensions or intermixtures will fall prey (on closer examination) to the very aporias that Frug recklessly disregards. For example, in the following passage we may glimpse Frug's train of thought derailing itself:

> [O]nce one understands the relationship between subjectivity and objectivity, it should . . . . be clear that we can never draw a line between them. . . . . I suggest that we should abandon the attempt to understand the world in terms of the subjective/objective dichotomy; we should deal with the problems of human association in other ways. It is impor-

> tant to realize that we need not understand the world in terms of subjectivity and objectivity—that this dichotomy, like so many other categories through which we experience the world, is a human creation and not a reflection of what the world "is really like."[9]

The boomerang has always returned already. Frug's renunciation of the subjective/objective dichotomy—in favor of a free-floating mixture of the two categories—is itself thoroughly dependent on the continuation of that dichotomy. We are called upon to eschew the subjectivity/objectivity dualism on the precise ground that it is subjective (i.e., "a human creation") rather than objective (i.e., "a reflection of what the world 'is really like'"). Key methodological assumptions have left Frug blind to what the flow of his argument cannot but tell us: the dimensions of subjectivity and objectivity are always totally present *just because* they are always totally absent, and their complete inclusion and complete exclusion will disrupt any balancing or mixing, no matter how flexible the blending may be.

A second weakness of Frug's approach is a bit more subtle, though very closely related to the first problem. (Indeed, in many respects, this point is the first problem discussed from a different angle.) When Frug argues—along with most of his comrades—that traditional legal discourse fails to mediate conflicts and instead merely displaces them, he concedes far too much uncritically. In accord with his perception of dualisms as mixtures (rather than as antinomies), he contends that striving to draw lines between clashing elements of juridical structures will *restate* rather then *resolve* classificatory questions: once a line has been arbitrarily drawn, each side of the structure that is demarcated by the line will turn out to manifest the same mixture of subjectivity and objectivity that the line had seemingly separated. At each level of Frug's analysis, we discover a repetition of an utterly indissoluble blend that would have foiled even the ants who aided Psyche. Subjectivity and objectivity constitute each other in part, Frug holds, and therefore they can never be disentangled completely, even if one were to go on separating them *ad infinitum*. Unfortunately, however, Frug's analysis of displacement and repetition stems from his focus on partial mixing or partial interaction, and it is just that focus which has already been challenged here. Frug sees an interpenetration of subjectivity and objectivity which is only partial (and thus unparadoxical) but which reproduces itself at each new level of one's inquiry. A deconstructive account of differentiation proceeds more boldly. Not only does it lead us to view interpenetration as total (and thus as fully impossible—though still necessary), but also it unremittingly questions Frug's entire analysis of displacement and levels. When deconstructionist tactics are put to work, they wrench processes of displacement in two directions that entail and oppose each other: displacement will always have been occurring already, and it will always have not yet come about. On the one hand, paradoxical dislocations are already proliferating incessantly in each stratum of one's inquiry, and are hence putting the very notion of "strata" into doubt. Dislocations collapse levels by having at once undergone all of them, again and again. Paradoxical positions will have always undone the analytical strata through which they pass; for every position will have torn away from itself and will have accordingly rendered problematic the levels that have sited its "self." Aporias of differentiation can hardly leave the differences among levels simply intact. But, on the other hand, those aporias have always yet to take place through acts of interpretation that can somehow elaborate themselves while undermining themselves. (Lest this use of "interpretation" appear to smack too much of anthropocentric leanings, one should construe that word—i.e., interpret "interpretation"—in the extremely broad sense that is assigned to it in the fifth chapter. Under that broad usage, the term will here have applied to every interrelationship between things, including but *not confined to* every interrelationship between people or between people and other things.) No act of interpreting can ever begin, for it would then need the starting points that its own articulation must reject as completely indefensible. If it is true that each paradox has always been inconceivably overwhelming itself in oscillations, then it is also true that each paradox cannot strictly lay claim to the coherence that it requires for presenting the exact difficulties which induce its uncanny shuttling. Frug's approach necessarily fails to highlight this mind-bending double movement, through which "levels" are continuously receding into a pure anteriority and are just as much driving forward into an indefinite delay. With some expansion of settled meanings, we may denominate this movement as "leveling," since that word can neologistically capture both the consolidation *and* the proliferation of self-disordering tiers. Critical legal scholars tend, at best, to propose a soothingly watered-down version of this movement—a version that might appear to uphold a comforting mixture (that is, a partial mixture) of subjectivity and objectivity. Heuristic models put forth by critical legal scholars have done their best to remain essentially static, for a dearth of self-criticism blinds those models to their vertiginous disarray.

Paradoxes of differentiation, in short, diverge fundamentally from mere contrasts or oppositions,[10] even when the conflicting poles of an opposition are viewed not as simple exteriorities *vis-à-vis* each other, but as reciprocally constitutive in part. Paradoxes make clear that the reciprocal constitution is perforce total and therefore inconceivable (because there is no place to begin). But to draw a sharp distinction like this—between deconstruction and quasi-structuralism—is to invoke the very model of dualisms and conflicts from which we are supposed to be distancing ourselves. Unable to avoid acting out the weaknesses that have here been censured, my last two paragraphs have transferred a vulgar picture of dualisms from the "targets" of deconstruction and structuralism to the methods thereof. It would thus seem that, in order to be articulated, the difference between structuralism and deconstruction will have to have been effaced. Among the conclusions that we might draw from this, two are most noteworthy and most fruitful. First, the very failure of all attempts to separate deconstruction from quasi-structuralism, where those attempts can but privilege structuralism in the course of getting away from it, is itself a victory (by way of defeat) for deconstruction. A paradoxical interplay of abandonment and embracement is precisely what deconstructionist thinking has prodded us to expect when confronted with efforts to establish borders. With a practical and discoursive economy that turns each loss into triumph—and each triumph into loss—a deconstructive critique regains its mastery by resuming its servitude. We may indeed do well to take notice of a remark on Derrida by Gayatri Spivak: "[I]f we respect Derrida's discourse, we cannot catch him out so easily. What does it show but that he is after all caught and held by the metaphysical enclosure even as he questions it, that his text, as all others, is open to an interpretation that he has done a great deal to describe?"[11] A second conclusion to be drawn at this point is equally defiant and sanguine. Given the difficulty of marking off aporias from conflicts, it is safe to presume that critical legal scholars have been *unwittingly* doing what they have been accused here of not *explicitly* doing. If we were to analyze the work of critical legal scholars suitably, in order to highlight strains in their writing that they have left in the background, we might find that they are to deconstruction what Monsieur Jourdain was to prose.

2. *Paradoxes Relating to Infinity*

A. THE PARADOXES EXPLICATED

Paradoxes relating to infinity are peculiarly striking instances of the problems bred by differentiation. These paradoxes received their most brilliant treatment at the hands of an Eleatic writer named Zeno, whose arguments on motion have come down to us largely through Aristotle's *Physics*.[12] Zeno elaborated at least four paradoxes of motion (as well as forty arguments relating to pluralism), but we shall examine only three: the Dichotomy, the Achilles, and the Arrow. Since the Paradox of the Arrow is discussed further in Chapter 5, and since I have considered Zeno at some length elsewhere,[13] the account here will be terse.

Aristotle provided a laconic description of the Dichotomy Paradox: "Zeno formulated four arguments about motion which worry those who try to solve them. According to the first, 'nothing can be in movement, since whatever is in local movement must arrive at the half-way stage before it arrives at the end.'"[14] Consider, for example, a person who attempts to traverse some or another distance *d* from an initial point *A* to an end point *B*. Before reaching *B*, the person will have had to move through the midpoint *M* of *AB* at a distance of *d*/2. Before reaching *M*, however, the person will have had to move through the midpoint of *AM* at a distance of *d*/4, and so forth *ad infinitum*. A person must always cross an infinity of points before he or she can move from the initial point *A* to the end point *B*, even if *A* and *B* are but a tiny distance apart. And because the points must be crossed sequentially, we are forced to conclude that even the slightest motion will be forever disqualified from occurring, as each step has become a never-ending futility.

Zeno launched an equally devastating blow with his Paradox of Achilles. Aristotle gave a curt summary:

> The second argument, known as "the Achilles," is to this effect: "The slowest runner will never be caught by the swiftest, since the pursuer must first reach the point from which the fleer has in the meantime escaped; so that the slower runner must always be some distance ahead." This is the same argument as that from repeated bisection; but with this difference that ever-prolonged paths are to be analyzed into segments in different relations [*Physics*, 239b.]

Suppose that Achilles is pursuing a tortoise that is at point *P*, some distance *d* ahead of him. By the time Achilles can get to *P*, the tortoise will have arrived at *P′*, which lies at a distance greater than the original distance *d* from Achilles' starting position. This process of deferral will be repeated at every point of Achilles' chase, and—because an infinity of points will lie between the initial perch of Achilles and the spot where he finally catches the tortoise—the chase will never end, even if Achilles starts out only a tiny distance behind his prey. We have therefore come up against the same basic movement of unceasing deferral that we met in the Dichotomy Paradox.

Aristotle at first tried to dispel these paradoxes by pointing out that the feature of infinite divisibility is just as characteristic of time as it is of space; Achilles must indeed cross an endless number of points before he can catch the tortoise, but he enjoys an endless number of moments in which to do so (*Physics*, 233a). But, as Aristotle himself soon came to realize, he had not *solved* the paradoxes but had merely *rephrased* them: "Suppose one were to leave out the reference to distance in the question whether an [infinity of points] can be covered in a finite period of time and one were, instead, to ask the question about the time itself, which is infinitely divisible. The solution given would then no longer be adequate" (*Physics*, 263a). Jonathan Barnes has made this point nicely: "Instead of one infinity to traverse, we have two: if *AB* is impenetrable, *T* [i.e., the time it will take to move from *A* to *B*] is unendurable."[15]

By no means had Zeno disregarded the paradoxical flows and counter-flows that produce time. He focused on temporality in his third paradox, which was summarized with disdain by Aristotle:

> There is a fallacy in Zeno's way of arguing: "If anything is at rest or in motion when it is where it is, and such is invariably the case with a moving body at any moment, then a flying arrow cannot start moving." This is wrong because time is not made up of indivisible moments any more than any other magnitude is made up of indivisible parts. . . . "The flying arrow continues at rest." This conclusion depends upon taking time as composed of moments; if this is not granted, the conclusion does not follow. [*Physics*, 239b.]

It seems obvious that a flying arrow moves, yet if we attempt to figure out *when* it moves, things become curiouser and curiouser. At every instant, the arrow will occupy a space equal exactly to its own volume, and it will therefore not move from one location to another location. Hence, there appears to be no time whatsoever through which the arrow *could* move, for any span of time will itself be divisible into further motionless instants. A paradox looms: the arrow is always *moving*, yet it can never *move*.[16] (If it be maintained that the arrow does in fact move at each instant, over an infinitely minute stretch of space, then we shall encounter once again the problems that underlie the first two of Zeno's paradoxes. However one might interpret the Paradox of the Arrow, it will disrupt the progress of time.)

What these three paradoxes bring out is what the *Physics* suggested: portrayals of reality as a field of self-same atoms will render motion impossible. The wish of Faustus will have held true, as time will have ceased and midnight will never come. On the one hand, groups of atomic presences across time would be utterly inconceivable without motion. Presences require differentiation, and temporal differentiation requires movement (that is to say, change of any sort), as Aristotle observed: "[I]t is by reference to the moving body that we recognize what comes before and after in the movement, and it is in so far as the 'before' and 'after' can be counted that there is a present" (*Physics*, 219b). On the other hand, motion will have perforce been stymied by the sequence of present atoms that it enables. It turns out that motion can occur only if seemingly basic atoms—instants in time and points in space—are not present at all in any straightforward way, but are instead shot through with differences. Only if every point in space is inhabited by what foregoes and succeeds it, does the Dichotomy's range of points become a continuum throughout which motion is possible. Likewise, every instant of time must willy-nilly partake of what it is not, if the flying arrow is ever to gain a chance to move. Infinitely small units will have to subsist outside themselves as their only possible mode of being.

Basic atoms of time and space must hence prove exterior to themselves. Unnerving as this fact may appear already, it will also lead into the gnarled aporias that must plague all attempts to demarcate present units of any size. Because *every* unit must receive its identity from what comes before and after it, there can be no "before" and "after," for there are not any starting points or coherent keystones in relation to which the past and future can determine themselves. No seeming benchmark can escape the paradoxes of differentiation. One must appeal to an unalloyed alterity that could ground all units—but that appeal is as keenly problematic as trying to put everything into doubt. One would be invoking a pastness that must recede without ever *being* present and a futurity that cannot cease to postpone itself from ever *becoming* present. Yet, as has been argued, otherness without presences will be as dauntingly incoherent as presences without otherness. Unless some units can be taken for granted as purely self-same and already in place, invoking alterity will remain out of bounds forevermore.

Zeno thus succeeded in demonstrating a twofold paradox in our ordinary conceptions of time and space. First, he showed that infinitesimal components of space and time will unavoidably dwell beyond their limits as precisely what they are not. Every such atom cannot emerge unless it is somewhere else than it is; to affirm each atom as what it is will entail affirming it as what it is not. Such are the paradoxes of infinite divisibility. Furthermore, infinitely minute atoms will succumb to more general paradoxes of differentiation. Not only must all such units be composed through and through of what they are not, but—because *every* unit is in exactly the same position—there cannot be any thing(s) whatsoever that each unit is not. Each item depends wholly on other items for its grounding and, as a consequence, is wholly unable to ground *them*. Baselines will have always already dissipated because *every* baseline will have relied completely on the flow of recursive processes that can never get started until a baseline has already come forth.

Here we have arrived at the second way in which points and instants can only gain being as precisely what they are not. Each infinitesimal component of space and time must on the one hand acquire its mode of existence solely as a result of its divergences from the rest of the components; yet, on the other hand, the creation of *all* identities through differences will have straightaway disrupted all *points d'appui* and will thus have thwarted itself before it can have commenced. This breakdown of differences as the ground of presences will have pulled us back to a view of infinitely small monads as completely autonomous and self-same. But because every "autonomous" and "self-same" unit will derive its nature through its assorted differences from all other "self-same" units—in other words, because autonomy and self-sameness are (entirely and necessarily) functions of delimited borders—any model of time and space as enclosing self-defined atoms will have always already pushed us yet again to embrace the incompatible view of presence as a function of difference. That alternative scheme will of course have crumbled and will already have driven us again to the other view, and so forth. In this way, then, instants of time and points of space must always hold the exact status of what they can never be; as self-sufficient presences they turn out to be mere offspring of differences, and as mere quotients of differences they have to arise as fully self-contained presences.

This uncanny oscillation, this second way in which points and instants are always what they are not, will by no means bear uniquely on problems stemming from infinite division. On the contrary, what has just been described is the relentless and paradoxical seesaw of differentiation, a seesaw that is potently generalizable to units of any size and intricacy. Zeno's aporias are hence best viewed as paradoxes of differentiation with a remarkable twist.

B. PARADOXES REFUTED?

Before we move on to the next subsection, a few words ought to be said about the flurry of work in recent decades on Zeno's various paradoxes. Based on certain developments in modern mathematics, especially on the writings of Georg Cantor, numerous essays have purported to show how Zeno's arguments go awry.[17] Some of this work is highly sophisticated indeed, though much of it teems with straw men and with begged questions. Even the most potted overview of this work would lead us too far afield, but, happily, one can here raise a fundamental objection without first having to pause for an overview. All of the most advanced "refutations" of Zeno's paradoxes are founded on the acceptance of Cantor's Theorem, which holds (roughly) that the set of all subsets of any set has more members than does the set itself, even if the latter is infinite.[18] Cantor's Theorem is in turn founded on the acceptance of the so-called Power Set Axiom, which holds that for every set there exists the set of all of its subsets. This axiom and the theorem built upon it by Cantor have proved enormously fruitful for subsequent mathematics and logic, and it is certainly not my purpose here to attack the broad reliance on Cantor's Theorem within those fields of inquiry.

But what *will* be contested is the blithe assumption that Cantor's work can refute the paradoxes of Zeno. If we pay no attention to the underpinnings of Cantor's Theorem, then Zeno's problems may seem to have been defused; yet it is precisely those underpinnings that cry out for attention. When applied to infinite sets, the axiom that underlies Cantor's Theorem does not in any way overcome Zeno's paradoxes, but instead assumes them away—or, rather, it embraces them and systematizes them. What makes Zeno's arguments into paradoxes is the unthinkability of somehow getting beyond what is endless, but the method devised by

Cantor to support his theorem shows that we *must* go exactly where we can *never* go. With compelling rigor, the theorem beckons us to surpass the utterly insurpassable, and it therefore reproduces the structure of Zeno's arguments. Like modern physics, the mathematics derived from Cantor's Theorem has seen fit to take certain paradoxes as given (and has immensely benefited therefrom). As a result, then, Cantor's work can provide no succor to those who wish to resolve Zeno's aporias. Challenges to Zeno can make some headway only "if the concept of super-denumerable infinity is itself free from contradictions,"[19] as one of the leading challengers has conceded. But that essential concept takes aboard what it should be excluding; refutations of Zeno's line of argument presuppose the antinomies they profess to have done away with. (Apart from the foregoing remarks, we could have responded to the latest assaults on Zeno by making clear that his arguments can be revamped to avoid reliance on infinite division. That is, his aporias can be made into paradoxes of differentiation that do not uniquely pertain to infinitesimal components of space and time. As has been noted, the aporias described by Zeno are special instances of the more general problems of differentiation. But if this were our only means of replying, there would have been no point to establishing this second genus of paradoxes.)

3. *Structure/Event Antinomies*

Structure/event antinomies will emerge in the fourth chapter and in the fifth chapter and most saliently in the second chapter. In each case, we shall be dealing with a tenacious circle of prioritization and disruption. If one is focusing on the structures of rules and systematized differences that govern events within a patterned activity such as discourse, one will be led to accord priority to those structures over the individual events. Events can never come into being till the conditions of their occurrence have been established by the prevailing structures. Without the categories and rules and underlying relationships that structures afford, events cannot possibly come about; for they would have to enter a universe which could not accommodate them in any way and which could have no place whatsoever for their arising. Until a course has in some manner been staked out for any particular events, those events quite plainly will have no course to pursue. If no rules and no exceptions to rules have made an event possible by dealing with its emergence, then its emergence has been ruled out—not really owing to its unlikelihood, but to its sheer inapplicability. If a branch abideth not in the vine, it bears no fruit.

Yet if one turns one's attention to the specific acts governed by structures, one will find that events assume priority over structures. Not only must rules and patterns originate in the particularized events that compose them gradually, but they will depend at every moment thereafter on the concrete realization of their abstractness. Problems of genesis are also problems of continuity. Until the universalities of rules and classifications have been distilled into series of particulars, they remain undefined and indeterminate. Every structure and every rule—as a result of its generality—can unfold in countless ways at each point in time, and only in retrospect will it have compelled a certain pathway or set of pathways of evolution. What a pattern or rule *is* cannot be precisely answered before we know the particularized applications that determine its course. It is not the ambiguity of the rules and patterns, but their generality or universality, that must keep them undecidably open till the events that constitute them have occurred. Detecting patterns and rules among events will perforce involve looking at those events from one or another angle, which entails departicularizing the events and absorbing them into a general structure that overarches them. Yet it is exactly this process of departicularization that structures produced by past events can never finally constrain, since efforts to determine future instantiations will have to be departicularized themselves when other events are. No factors can gain control over processes within which they must be ultimately subsumed. That is, as Wittgenstein stressed over and over, rules and patterns cannot have the final say regarding their own continuation in a specific manner, because any instructions they might lay down would forever be subject to interpretation and would hence stand in need of further instructions (which would stand likewise in need of further instructions, and so forth).[20] Neither the outside analyst nor the inside participant can educe future events from structures that have been constituted by past events, for structures are being re-created perpetually with each new instantiation. (Though the outside perspective of the analyst has here occupied center stage, the bizarre circle of the structure/event paradox will apply with as much strength, *mutatis mutandis,* to the internal vantage of the participant—even when the "participation" is carried out by an inanimate force or substance.)

The structures and the events of patterned activity thus engage in an unstoppable interplay that disqualifies them from coming to be established. Novelty is both irreducible and impossible, both absolutely required and absolutely excluded. Structures can come about, both at their time of origin and in all their subsequent workings, only through the events which form themselves into patterns and which thereby engender structurality. But the structures will always have to obtain already if the events are to be made possible. Unless relevant differences have already become operative, events will not have been made realizable—for there would never have come forth anything in contrast with which they would be able to manifest their emergence and their results by staking themselves off. And this means that structurality has to precede events, since structures consist precisely in the establishment of germane differences. In a never-ending cycle of dislocations, that is to say, the inception of events must presuppose structures, and the inception of structures must presuppose events. Like a man who is taller than himself, each point of inception enjoys priority with regard to the other point, to which it is also secondary. At once productive and paralyzing, the interaction between structures and their events will prove unmasterable and ceaseless.

Structure/event antinomies involve more or less the same flows and counterflows that subvert and constitute presence in "hermeneutic circles" (as we shall observe in Chapter 2), and, more generally, they partake of largely the same problems that have always characterized the relationship between universals and particulars in Western philosophy. Consider, for instance, Hegel's treatment of that relationship:

> [I]n speaking of some definite animal we say it is (an) animal. Now, the animal, *qua* animal, cannot be shown; nothing can be pointed out excepting some special animal. Animal, *qua* animal, does not exist: it is merely the universal nature of the individual animals, while each existing animal is a more concretely defined and particularized thing. But to be an animal—the law of kind which is the universal in this case—is the property of the particular animal, and constitutes its definite essence. Take away from the dog its animality, and it becomes impossible to say what it is. All things have a permanent inward nature, as well as an outward existence. They live and die, arise and pass away; but their essential and universal part is the kind; and this means much more than something *common* to them all.[21]

Here Hegel was driven both to deny that universal types can exist beyond their embodiments *and* to hold that animality is a "permanent inward nature" and "definite essence" that is absolutely prerequisite to the intelligibility of particular embodiments. These incompatible urgings of his analysis point not to a dialectical resolution but to a maelstrom of deferrals that always outlaw what they demand. Nevertheless, for reasons to be explored in the second half of my final chapter, we are here prudent to adopt a vocabulary derived from structuralism rather than to embrace the more traditional argot of "particularity" and "universality."

4. *Problems of Self-Referentiality*

Some thinkers have held that all true paradoxes consist in one or another form of self-referentiality.[22] As was noted at the beginning of this section, the four kinds of antinomies that have been distinguished here can be ultimately collapsed into one another; in that way, the focus by logicians and other theorists on self-referentiality will be justified, for all paradoxes can be construed as self-referential. Nonetheless, without simply discarding the traditional standpoint, one can equally well offer an alternative view. One need not strain too hard to preserve the categories that have been outlined hitherto, and to mark off a separate category for problems deriving from self-reference (albeit the separateness of this fourth category will be as frail as the separateness of the first three categories). Let us, then, define self-reference as an explicit statement concerning the explicit statement itself or the class to which it belongs or the agent who articulates it. With this definition, we can readily muster several renowned paradoxes, such as that of the Cretan liar. If Epimenides avows that all Cretans never make truthful statements, and if he is himself a Cretan (and if all Cretans thitherto have indeed been chronic liars), then his pronouncement will be true only when false and false only when true. A similar situation crops up when we consider the potential for words to characterize themselves. Some adjectives (such as "short" and "sesquipedalian") describe themselves nicely, whereas most adjectives (such as "long" and "purple") do not do so. If one has labeled the second group of adjectives as "heterological," one will face profound difficulties when one attempts to categorize this new label: the word "heterological" can be heterological if and only if it is not heterological.[23]

Paradoxes evoked by certain kinds of self-reference, then, have exhibited with a telling clearness the structure of dependency-cum-exclusion that every paradox has displayed. In each case, the fundamental dynamic is a whirlpool of incoherent positions that can take us out of themselves only by having doubled back on themselves. Each answer to a paradoxical problem will have gutted itself by resting on a sharply opposed answer, which always will in turn have been resting on the sharply opposed answer that has led into it. Answers undo themselves by having reversed themselves again and again. An unrestrained oscillation will have subsumed and subverted every possible standpoint; for each standpoint will have twisted itself into precisely the opposite of what it is, by virtue of being what it is. In each case, then, an antinomy will comprise ungraspable interfoldings of stark dependence and stark rejection. Each position will have called forth what it must not call forth, as each will always have already turned out to rest on what it avoids and to compel what it bars. In a paradoxical quandary, solutions that are completely irreconcilable are also insistently intertwined. No choice between solutions is possible, for every solution will have collapsed into being its own antithesis—which will always have already collapsed back. The logic of a true double bind is "not-A if and only if A."

B. Framing as Frustrated Closure

In the course of the argument concerning structure/event antinomies, the preceding section adverted to the problem of framing, on which this section will focus. Certain processes, such as processes of interpretation, will always frustrate their own closure by producing uncontained elements in the act of finishing and encompassing themselves. The totalizing flow of classificatory or analytical discourse will ineluctably leave behind new layers of incompletion; as it tries to yield a comprehensive account of its own unfolding, such discourse mires itself in an infinite regression of self-referential attempts at closure and mastery. In this way, the condition for total analytic success is also the condition for endless analytic failure. One example of the frustration of closure was described briefly in our account of structure/event paradoxes (and will be discussed further, with relevant citations, in Chapter 2): the Wittgensteinian insight that rules can never seal themselves up, because devices for gaining closure cannot settle the means by which they themselves are to be closed off. Each rule is subject to an endless array of (mis)interpretations, and each new layer of interpretive guidance—designed to narrow the range of possible exegeses for any given rule—will be likewise subject to a proliferation of readings that will necessitate still more guidance. Hermeneutic closure will thus postpone itself endlessly, as each specification has in turn to be specified. Nor will self-encompassing clauses be of any avail. That is, one cannot achieve interpretive closure and escape the problem of framing through a norm that is made to fall within its own scope by means of a special clause: "All rules of such and such a type, *including this rule,* should be construed and applied in such and such a manner." That a norm can point to a certain manner in which it should be construed does not help us one whit to construe that pointer. In this respect, one is not in even a slightly firmer position than one would occupy without any self-encompassing clause, for the self-embracement of an interpretive standard will have *per se* done nothing to incorporate what has been left out of the standard—namely, a full specification of the ways the standard and its self-reference should be applied. For a full specification, we must still resort to an infinitely receding chain of guideposts. Every part of that chain always will have reintroduced the lack that it fills. None of this is to say, of course, that rules cannot function if they cannot manage to close themselves. As Wittgenstein happily observed,[24] everyday modes of discourse often appear to go ahead quite nicely without the security of a closed grounding. All we need maintain here is that the everyday functioning of rules will be strictly unjustifiable.

A second example of deferred closure arises within the cardinal problem faced by liberal political theory: the pressing need to control the violence of institutions that prevent violence. In any liberal theory of politics, the authority of the state is viewed as both necessary and dangerous—necessary because it serves as the only means of taming the conflicts that would wrack civil society, and dangerous because officials who wield the mighty power of government may be prone to commit outrageously brutal actions. Moreover, governmental effectiveness in subduing turmoil can be guaranteed only through the governmental prerogative to employ violence. As Barbara Johnson observes: "The legal order, which attempts to submit 'brute force' to 'forms, measured forms,' can only eliminate violence by transforming violence into the final authority."[25] What this means is that state mechanisms can potentially introduce more coercion than they remove (or, at any rate, more coercion than needed for eliminating the worst strife that would ravage civil society). Though ventured in quite a different context, a query by Juvenal directly bears on the point at hand: "But who is to keep guard over the guards themselves?"[26]

Undue state violence can take at least two chief forms, aside from that of belligerence between states. On the one hand, a state's officials may impose brutal discipline on the general public beyond what is necessary to quell glaring disturbances. On the other hand, state officials may war among themselves while establishing their control over the general public. The first of these outcomes will consist in tyranny of a greater or slighter noxiousness, while the second will lead to tyranny (as each branch of government strives ruthlessly to outpace all the other branches) or to ineffectiveness or, most likely, to the worst of both worlds: a tyrannical mode of ineffectiveness, with overweening state-imposed violence accompanied by a large amount of uncurbed oppression in the social and economic spheres. (A structure of checks and balances—one of the most ingenious attempts to tackle the first problem of tyranny *tout court*—will foster the second problem of intragovernmental strife and concomitant ineffectiveness.[27] Even more important, a system of checks and balances will at times malfunction and then do little to halt the advent of tyranny *tout court*.[28] Any such system can be guaranteed its effectiveness only if it is supervised, but the supervisor will then have to be supervised, and so on.) Of course, neither the first problem of tyrannical violence nor the second problem of intragovernmental strife will occur *ineluctably*, but each of them always *can* occur, and every effective means of warding them off will prove to be just as vulnerable to a like degeneration. There can never emerge a supervisor—personal, systemic, or corporate—that will not be in need of still further supervision. Those who hope for assurance that a tyranny cannot ever arise will have to plummet into an infinite regress, wherein each ground for encouragement has reproduced all the insecurities that evoked it. Each layer of supervision will provide assurance about everything but itself. Liberal theories of politics hence turn out to be structured by incompleteness, as they enact the impossibility of achieving full and rigorous closure.

Perhaps the best way to clarify the idea of framing is to conclude this section with a lengthy counterexample. Helpful will it be to study a doctrine which may seem at first glance to lend itself to the basic sort of approach that has here been outlined, but which will be seen on closer examination to differ markedly from the two foregoing instances of deferred closure. We may thereby understand better how and when the problem of framing comes about. Let us, then, look at the apparently self-refuting power of skepticism, which gained a hold on the attention of Plato in his *Theaetetus*.[29]

Through Socrates, Plato argued against the relativism championed by Protagoras and his followers, who held that each person is the "measure of all things." Plato seized on the fact that most people disagree with relativism, and he concluded therefrom that relativism is a false doctrine. He claimed that Protagoreans had implicitly granted that a relativist view is false for most people, given that most people do not believe in it, and given that each person's beliefs are—according to Protagoras—determinative of what is true for each person. This presumed concession, so Plato argued, should in turn have obliged Protagoras to admit that relativism is false for everyone (including Protagoras himself).

Now, as many expositors have seen, Plato's argument is clearly invalid. To avow that relativism will be untrue for *some* people does not commit one to holding further that relativism will be untrue for *all* people. A simple movement of self-subversion will not apply, for Plato was dealing with a relativistic rather than nihilistic version of skepticism. Nihilism, which seeks to have us renounce truth altogether, leads straightaway to a conspicuously self-referential mode of unraveling; nihilistic pronouncements cannot rightly lay claim to truth at all, since their trueness would disallow their trueness. But relativist views will not succumb quite as blatantly and will therefore have to be approached far more subtly.[30] For the relativist, truth always or almost always has meaning, though each meaning will be specific to a person or context. A simplistic turning of relativist doctrines against themselves will uphold the significance of those doctrines by describing their truth in starkly relativist terms. To concede that relativist statements do not have to be true for every person is to abide by relativistic standards of truth.

Nevertheless, it may appear that the general insight advanced by Plato is sound and salvageable, for it may appear that relativistic theses will frustrate their own closure and will have hence constrained themselves to become grounded in an unrelativized conception of truth. If we examine the dictum by Protagoras that each person is the exclusive judge of truth for herself, we can inquire at once into the exact status of this skeptical proposition. Presumably, he who offered this maxim would reply that it was true for him only (and for anyone else who found the maxim convincing). But we should then have to ask about the status of this reply and of subsequent replies, *ad infinitum*. Every means of framing the skeptic's argument as a finished doctrine, through successive replies, will have again opened up the argument by virtue of closing it. Every Protagorean attempt to find a home for truth in self-presence will either tumble into objectivism or embark on a never-ending regress.

A reply to questions about the status of earlier replies will present itself as categorically true, until a further reply can state that its predecessor is true in only a relativized fashion. Replies will be hoist with the petard of linguistic generality, which postpones the siting of truth in individual viewpoints. Until we are told to use a relativistic standard of truth for each reply, we shall be forced to construe each one as an ordinary constative statement. Absent qualifiers, descriptive language inevitably presents itself as imparting truth *tout court*, even when the truth it conveys is a report of an individual person's outlook. As Paul de Man has maintained: "[T]o the extent that [it] is necessarily misleading, language just as necessarily conveys the promise of its own truth."[31] Qualifications must be inserted to make ordinary constative statements into statements that are true relativistically. Only thus can we know that what appears to be general truth (however narrowly focused) is being offered as something very different, and only then can relativists avoid implicitly trading on the non-relativistic tenor of normal constative discourse, which they cannot help using. But if qualifications perforce demand still further qualifications, then we have plunged into an infinite regress. Every new response must come forth in language that will have to be qualified by yet another response. Each layer of one's response will commend itself *prima facie* as the objective truth (i.e., the objective truth regarding subjective facts and the metaphysical consequences associated therewith), and therefore every such layer will necessitate a new layer by which it can become relativized.

Thus far, skepticism appears to be as incapable of framing itself as is guidance on interpreting rules. But here we must take account of an ingenious device with which the skeptic can overcome this predicament. He or she can have recourse to some self-encompassing words, for words of that type will here have gained success where they earlier could but fail. Suppose, for example, that Protagoras had resorted to the following motto: "Each person is the measure of all things, which include this sentence and this clause." A vast number of alternative formulations are possible; for instance, Protagoras could have claimed that "all truths are relative, and this sentence will apply to itself as much as to every other truth." In exchange for dispensing with the laconic beauty of his original formulation, Protagoras could have found a way to elude the infinite regress of unqualified qualifiers. The situation here is quite different from the circumstances regarding the interpretation of rules. When we sought interpretive closure through a self-referential caveat, we found that any such move would never bring about closure, since it would have failed to establish just how it should apply to itself (or, thus, how it should apply to the other rules) and would ergo fail to help us at all in getting interpretation started. Here, however, we do not find a corresponding conundrum, for—if we temporarily disregard interpretive problems, which must finally prevail but which will not be unique to relativist doctrines—a self-encompassing clause within the Protagorean maxim will indeed encompass itself. What the revised version of the maxim declares is that its own truth is relative *and* that the relativization of its own truth is relative. As a result, no endless train of qualifications will be needed to make the latter point, because the self-referential group of words will have always relativized its own inclusion already. A relativizing clause can treat of itself and limit itself in ways that a self-encompassing hermeneutic guideline cannot.

This analysis of relativism has decidedly not been meant to avouch that relativist doctrines can withstand all critical scrutiny. Paradoxes of differentiation will generalize themselves unremittingly, and will thus have drawn any relativist standpoint into a disruptive interrogation of its grounding in absolutist standards of truth. A Protagorean view must appeal to the self-presence of individual agents, whose subjectivity is exalted as the sole measure of truth. Such a view will hence carry with it the aporias that deconstruction has highlighted in countless species of present-ation. (Thus, a leading form of relativism—neo-pragmatist philosophy—will be deconstructed in Chapter 5.) Our purpose, then, is *not* to uphold relativist doctrines, but to make clear why they are not susceptible to critiques of framing. If one hopes to demonstrate that an instance of framing can but lead to the deferral of closure, then the doctrine being considered must prove unable to encompass its own tenets inside a clause that governs the act of framing as well as that which is framed. When such a clause is available, the critique of framing will not apply. For the frustration of closure, an interminable regress (of instructions, qualifications, reassurances, or the like) must always and implacably loom. Only in contexts where no self-referential guideline can obviate the need for an endless flow of modifications, will every step toward closure and mastery have pushed its ultimate aim still further from being realized.

C. Iterability as Sunderability

1. *Variations on a Theme.*

Like the themes of paradoxes and framing, the theme of iterability in signification is an idea based on a strategy and a strategy deriving from an idea.[32] It builds upon the fact that communicative exchanges must at all times proceed in a conventionalized, codified manner. Conventions are of course variegated throughout history and geography, but a convention of some sort *must* prevail whenever communication arises. Without some established categories and rules of meaning, no signified messages could be transmitted at all, since we would have lost any way of recognizing and classing the particular signs as such. A background of assumptions and understandings must have emerged already if people who receive messages are to know how to make even the slightest glimmer of headway in interpreting the significance of that which they have received. However, because meaning depends entirely on hermeneutic conventions, the received meaning and the transmitted meaning of any particular occurrence can always fail to agree. Rules and categorial frameworks that underlie the *reception* of some event may differ remarkably from the rules and categorial frameworks that have shaped the *production* or *transmission* of the event. Many basic presuppositions will almost certainly perform crucial roles in just about any scheme of categorization, but countless beliefs and attitudes can vary from one scheme to another. Whenever a substantial divergence has arisen between the codes of intentionality and the codes of construability (*viz.*, between the codes that give rise to an event and the codes that form the reception of the event), we shall encounter one of the following misjudgments: a meaning or set of meanings will be mistakenly interpreted as another meaning or set of meanings, or an unmotivated action will be perceived as intentional (i.e., unmotivatedness will wrongly be viewed as motivatedness), or a motivated occurrence will be regarded as unintentional (i.e., motivatedness will be mistaken for an absence of motive). No misjudgment *has* to crop up, for there does not *have* to be a significant divergence between codes, but it always *can* crop up. Furthermore, this potential for mistakes will inhere in every act of communication not just as parasitic on "normal" functioning, but *en plus* as prerequisite to that functioning. Any communication will need some rules of classifying and structuring in order to go ahead, and thus all communication implies the possibility of a mismatch between codes. Were there no possibility of a mismatch, there would be no possibility of a match (and thus no communication whatever), since the coordination of codes is always liable to go astray. If we seek to protect ourselves from ever going astray, we shall be led into a problem of framing—a problem quite like the never-ending regress that haunts liberal political theory. That is, the only way to eliminate the potential for mismatched codes is to thwart communicative activity altogether; the convention-shaped workings of communication beget an inextirpable chance that truth will have been sundered from meaning in any given instance. Figs can well be gathered from thorns, and grapes can be picked from bramble bushes. (The foregoing exposition has been evolved in terms that characterize human discourse, but no particular limitations should be inferred. What has been said here will apply, with only some minor shifts of focus, to the interpretation and interaction of natural processes and events.)

Another, more Hegelian way of articulating this theme would highlight the generality or universality of linguistic units and other signifiers. Everything becomes manifest through diverse modes of categorization which partake of universal applicability in several ways, most notably inasmuch as the categorizations will provide meaning in the absence of any item or process to which they are supposed to refer. Should generalized categories not obtain, nothing would ever be communicated or understood, for everything would be radically disjoined from everything else. The beliefs of any person could not be shared at all with another person, and even the individual agent would be devoid of continuity, since each bit of experience would be totally unrelated to other bits. (To define what counts as a "bit" would be hopelessly unfathomable.) Linguistic units and other signifiers must, then, display a generalized scope. But precisely on account of their generalized purview, signifiers can be unloosed from the grounding of particular referents; signifiers are at all times repeatable—iterable—despite a lack of conditions that would have made them true. Thus, for example, sentences like "I feel a sharp pain" or "There is a tall man near the window," if they are to become knowable and communicable at all, will have to be understandable by those persons who are not at the present undergoing any experiences that might occasion or justify such statements. For any interpersonal dialogue, each agent will have to have some basic ability to know what sentences like these mean when the person who has employed them is not the agent herself. Much the same can be said about the individual person's knowledge: a potential divide between veracity and significance will forever lurk, because what breeds the potential for a split of this type is general categorization, and categorization is the *sine qua non* of integrated experience. Without understandability (i.e., repeatability) in the *absence* of motivating intentions, no signifiers could manage to convey the *presence* of motivating intentions, for we would thus be trapped in a completely disjointed universe. As Derrida writes:

> My nonperception, my nonintuition, my *hic et nunc* absence are expressed by that very thing that I say, by *that* which I say and *because* I say it. This structure will never form an "intimately blended unity" with intuition. The absence of intuition—and therefore of the subject of the intuition—is not only *tolerated* by speech; it is *required* by the general structure of signification, when considered *in itself*. It is radically requisite; the total absence of the subject and object of a statement—the death of the writer and/or the disappearance of the objects he was able to describe—does not prevent a text from "meaning" something. On the contrary, this possibility gives birth to meaning as such, gives it out to be heard and read.[33]

The unavoidable generality of signifiers will have allowed them to bear meaning without regard to the existence or nonexistence of the things and activities they denote. A generalized ambit perforce leaves room for a certain vagrancy of the signifier.

A third way of developing this idea can be derived from the work of Wittgenstein (among others), and will point out that something can never signify *truly* if it can never signify *falsely*. If lying and mistakes and deception cannot arise, then neither can anything that might be perceived as truthful signification. When falsehood is completely ruled out as a *possibility* in some or another instance, truth will similarly have gone by the wayside—for the very status of truth will not be any longer endowed with meaning, which it acquired by virtue of differentiating itself from what it is not. Wittgenstein made this point most clearly while criticizing the idea of a "private language": "[I]n the present case I have no criterion of correctness. One would like to say: whatever is going to seem right to me is right. And that only means that here we can't talk about 'right.'"[34] If truth is guaranteed absolutely, it will have done away with itself. By expunging that which delimits truth, an absolute guarantee will render the whole concept of "truth" vacuous. (As has been seen, difference *qua* delimitation will always have become difference *qua* antinomical interfolding. But I can formulate my third variation on the theme of iterability without highlighting the paradoxical energies of difference-and-presence. Those energies will indeed make themselves felt in time, however, which means that an analysis of iterability must be comprehended and dislocated in the seesaws of double binds. Some aspects of the ineluctable comprehension-and-dislocation will be highlighted shortly.)

To the Wittgensteinian argument for iterability one might respond that a tautological statement will be true in every possible world, and that this condition holds without having disabled us from referring to the statement as true. Such an objection is misconceived. We may grant that, once a specific sentence has been construed as tautological, its fallaciousness has been entirely ruled out; but this does not mean that the construction placed on the sentence will be necessarily true or proper. A sentence of the form "*A* equals *A*" can signify any number of things, determined by its particular contexts. A person adhering to a special code may use such a sentence to transmit claims that are (at best) contingently true, such as the proposition that the speaker is hungry. In that case, someone who has evaluated the sentence "*A* equals *A*" as necessarily true will come to an erroneous judgment (in regard to the truth-value of "*A* equals *A*") when the pertinent state of things—e.g., the speaker's esurience—does not obtain. That a group of signifiers is necessarily true according to one code will in no way decide its status or its meaning in other codes.

Thus, signifiers regarded as a tautological statement can indeed signify falsely, in at least two principal ways. First, their incontestable truth according to one batch of assumptions may decide an interpreter to suppose that they will remain true from all perspectives in any circumstances, and that the context of their articulation is hence irrelevant. This surmisal, we have found, will occasion incorrect judgments in certain instances. Second, when seen to be a contingent truth a sentence will prove liable to all the mishaps and the mendacious stratagems to which any contingent truth is vulnerable; and the vulnerability will have not at all been diminished by the fact that a sentence is of a form which makes it a necessary truth within many codes. In short, we can come up with interpretations of a specific sentence that will rule out its falsehood, but we can never rule out the falsehood of those interpretations. We would cast ourselves into yet another problem of framing if we tried to achieve the latter goal. Because signifiers are always subject to recontextualization, because "[e]very sign—verbal or otherwise—may be used at different levels, in configurations and functions which are never prescribed by its 'essence,'"[35] a chain of signifiers amounting currently to a definitional truth will perforce lie open to a resituating of its functions and consequences within a code that identifies the chain as a merely contingent truth (or, for that matter, as a falsehood). One cannot forestall the use of the sentence "*A* equals *A*" as something other than a tautology, because one cannot forestall the transplanting of the sentence from relatively familiar contexts into much less familiar contexts. Thus, as Umberto Eco observes, no signifiers can guarantee their own functioning; precisely because of recontextualization, even tautologies can be made to lie.

> A sign is everything which can be taken as significantly substituting for something else. This something else does not necessarily have to exist or to actually be somewhere at the moment in which a sign stands in for it. Thus *semiotics is in principle the discipline studying everything which can be used in order to lie.* If something cannot be used to tell a lie, conversely it cannot be used to tell the truth: it cannot in fact be used 'to tell' at all.[36]

2. *Displaced Positions*

None of these ways of pointing up the sunderability of signs from their motivating intentions will amount to a stable and coherent outlook on meaning. Some commentators have recently proclaimed that Derrida's emphasis on iterability involves an adherence to a conventionalist account of linguistic functioning. They hold that "Derrida's denial that meaning can be determined by intention . . . depends on the claim that language is essentially conventional," and that Derrida "accepts the mistaken view that speech acts are essentially conventional acts." Under Derrida's theories, "[c]onvention, not the author, determines what the author has done."[37] Such assertions, though by no means unrepresentative of the anodyne and hasty reductionism practiced by writers who have sought to domesticate or eviscerate deconstructive philosophy, are nonetheless particularly misleading since they earn for themselves a measure of plausibility through tendentious quotations and a truncated exposition. Paradoxical dislocations have stirred no little uneasiness among scholars, and so even the most sophisticated thinkers may have convinced themselves through a partial reading—in both senses of the word "partial"—that a text highlighting such dislocations is in fact up to something else, something much more tame.

In the case at hand, an interpretation of Derrida's account of iterability as a conventionalist account of meaning will find some obvious support in what has been said thus far. Throughout this section, we have appealed to contexts (or conventions or codes) as generators of meaning in activities such as discourse. If one were to stop there, one could be charged quite justly with conventionalism. But neither the present volume nor Derrida's work stops at a conventionalist position, as if such a stop were feasible; rather, appeals to contexts are undertaken only as strategies that disrupt themselves in the end. As a critical device, conventionalism will explode conceptions of meaning that endeavor to cast aside the structure/event antinomy (and to discount the importance of contextuality) through the privileging of events in the individual consciousness as the sites of meaning-production. Conventionalism overturns these conceptions by decisively showing that they must situate the events of consciousness in transindividual assumptions and categories. In demonstrating that collectively fashioned rules and structures must set the stage completely for individual acts, conventionalism will have highlighted moments of self-upheaval and self-expropriation in all intent-based theories of semantics. Here the force of conventionalism is inescapable; but analyses cannot terminate here. Just as a conventionalist critique will have undermined the discourse of anyone who hopes to prioritize the individual grains of consciousness, so it must finally topple its own prioritizing of structures and collectively shaped practices. Indeed, the emphatic aim of Derrida's writing on the iterability of signs—if we may be allowed to ascribe purposes to it—has been to elaborate the incessant overturning of *all* efforts at prioritization.

One can highlight the bizarre "logic" of prioritization in an endless variety of ways. Chapter 5 of this book, for instance, will deconstruct neo-pragmatist philosophy, one of the chief forms of modern-day conventionalism. But one of Derrida's own critiques of discourse that emphasizes a privileged role for conventions is particularly apposite here because it follows upon his clearest and most telling account of iterability, in the essay "Signature Event Context."[38] Having argued at some length that the iterability of signs will disrupt theories of communication which privilege intentionality, Derrida proceeds to underline a "perhaps paradoxical consequence of the recourse I am taking to iteration and to the code: the disruption, in the last analysis, of the authority of the code as a finite system of rules; the radical destruction, by the same token, of every context as a protocol of a code" (SEC, 316). He deconstructs the writings of J. L. Austin, who essayed to work out a purely structural or conventionalist understanding of speech acts, but who had to rest all his hopes on the presumption that agents who perform standard speech acts will have been harboring "serious" intentions. As Derrida concludes: "For a context to be exhaustively determinable, in the sense demanded by Austin, it at least would be necessary for the conscious intention to be totally present and actually transparent for itself and others, since it is a determining focal point of the context" (SEC, 327).

Thus, Derrida's projects are much more bold and unsettling than some commentators would have us think. Derrida does not *simply* claim that meaning derives wholly from conventions; rather, he claims both that it does do so and that it derives not at all therefrom. On the one hand, a conventionalist attack can show quite persuasively that exalting the discrete bits of consciousness as the privileged sources of meaning is untenable. As the initial half of this section has maintained, the boundless potential for the relocation of signifiers into new contexts will have entailed that each signifier is not essentially linked to any specific states or acts of the mind. Originarily set adrift, each signifier *can* somehow stay at dock, but it *need* not do so. Its meaning arises elsewhere. On the other hand, as the deconstruction of speech-act theory (and my later deconstruction of pragmatism) would indicate, the transparent presence of subjectivity is invoked by the very discourses that are most aware of the stark opacity of intentions—an opacity due, of course, to the endless iterability of signs. A conventionalist outlook must finally ground its explanation of meaning in a tacit or explicit reliance on intentions as the decisive factors, even while it purports to give them a markedly subservient role. Insights regarding iterability are not concerned with the location of meaning, but are concerned with the location and *dis*location of meaning. At once decisive and powerless, intentions fail to have any impact on what they always determine fully. Meaning must have emerged precisely where it can never sprout. Whatever the critics may assert, only through a perilous disregard of structure/event problems could one employ the theme of iterability in an effort—a simple effort—to locate meaning. A deconstructionist discourse will avoid such complacency, for it knows that "simple" efforts will have undone themselves through paradoxical blind spots. Though even the most tenaciously self-critical text cannot fully escape blind spots, it can try to relinquish the naive hope that it enjoys vision clear enough to discern where meaning resides. In antinomical oscillations, meaning defers a si(gh)ting.

D. Some Concluding Remarks

Before we move on to a brief overview of this book's structure, a few remarks may highlight some of the most important and most frequently misinterpreted aspects of the ideas that have just been sketched. First, in line with what the preceding section has argued, the themes of iterability and framing are provisional tactics (i.e., tactics for developing and articulating aporias) rather than self-contained positions. They disrupt theories which have sought to privilege intentionality or which profess to attain closure, but they should not depict themselves as any more stable or secure than what they impugn. They confound themselves while upturning other doctrines, for they cannot stand aloof from the aporias they generate. Each of these two themes is hence nothing but a tentative strategy, with enormous critical power, that has hurtled itself against its own theses. Each can be set to work with great penetration against various dogmatic theories, but each must ultimately take part in the to-and-fro of paradoxical interfolding as each one wrenches itself away from its starting points. We ought to have expected as much, in light of the arguments and concepts that have been marshaled here to elucidate the problems of deferred closure and iterable signifiers. To account for these problems, we have had to depend on well-tried notions (such as conventionality, self-presence, and differentiation) which have been explicitly placed in doubt and which will be challenged further as this volume proceeds. Of course, this does not mean that we ever can or ever should flatly do away with such notions once and for all time. Those notions are irrepressible; they must undergird any theory that deconstructs them. Rather than fool ourselves into striving for a simple obliteration of key strategies and concepts, then, we should seek to turn those concepts—and the critical strategies they inform—mercilessly against their own implications. In showing that the ideas of iterability and frustrated self-completion do not emerge unscathed by the lines of force they engender, we have inscribed them into a paradoxical to-and-fro that subverts them without stripping them of effectiveness.

A second point relates closely to what has just been said. Both critics and proponents of deconstruction have classed it frequently as the latest version of skepticism. Derrida is time and again pictured as a relativist or nihilist who has been seeking to overcome the Western tradition of philosophy and its grim fixation on truth. Thus, one leading observer has declared that Derrida "wants to do better than Heidegger the job of 'overcoming the tradition of Western metaphysics' which Heidegger attempted."[39] Now, as was maintained earlier, a nihilistic renunciation of truth will have consigned its own verdict to a self-referential falseness of a peculiarly vulgar and unreflective sort; the intensely self-critical maneuvers of deconstruction cannot brook any such sloppy thinking. A relativistic form of skepticism, which is what Rorty has in mind, will not display the gross shortcomings of nihilism—as we have already noted—but it dismantles itself in any case through its stark need to incorporate self-presence (i.e., the self-presence of the perceiving subject) into its overall account. In the critique of pragmatism in Chapter 5, we shall discover that the principal modern line of relativistic thought has depended fully on just the type of absolutism that it purports to have vanquished. Once again, skepticism turns out to be far more lax than a deconstructionist discourse, which highlights its own antinomies to the greatest extent possible (rather than try in vain to elude them). The basic point is that anyone who endeavors to collapse deconstruction into some kind of skepticism is aiming to elide what is most unsettling *and* most exhilarating about deconstructionist methodologies: the countless ways in which paradoxes can be brought to the fore, not least through the examination of writings that may seem to disregard or escape them. Interpreting deconstruction as skepticism is an otiose means of turning uncanny flows and counterflows into reassuringly stable paths. Skepticism inverts all orthodox hierarchies and values without taking account of its dependence on what it overturns, and it thus appears to render itself thinkable (though perhaps maverick). Because a skeptical credo focuses scant attention on its underlying aporias, it might seem to evade them and to offer thereby a settled and coherent view of philosophy, however iconoclastic. As Hegel astutely realized, however, any simple distrust of orthodox metaphysics will not at all transcend the antinomies from which it averts its gaze.

> Zeno, who first showed the contradiction native to motion, concluded [or is frequently thought to have concluded] that there is no motion; and the ancients, who recognized origin and decease, the two species of Becoming, as untrue categories, made use of the expression that the One or Absolute neither arises nor perishes. Such a style of dialectic looks only at the negative aspect of its result, and fails to notice, what is at the same time really present, the definite result, in the present case a pure nothing, but a Nothing which includes Being, and, in like manner, a Being which includes Nothing.[40]

Like other theories, skeptical arguments will have torn themselves from the grip of their own conclusions and will have always already caused themselves to crumble away in order to be articulated. Skepticism may beguile its proponents into thinking that its unorthodox views are somehow free of the double binds that afflict mainstream philosophy, yet it will prove merely to want the bold and implacable awareness of its own problems that a deconstructionist theory tries to sustain. When faced with a paradox, such as "The present sentence is completely untrue," one may find comfort in trying to adhere to some negative position (e.g., that the sentence quoted—along with everything else—is indeed untrue); but such a position will be as woefully incoherent as will any contrasting outlook (e.g., that the sentence is in fact true). As surely as the "yes" of traditional metaphysics, the "no" of skepticism will be caught up and endlessly displaced in the unthinkable movement of aporias. Deconstruction can never leap through an exit from the whirlpools of paradoxes by insistently saying "no," but must forever bring out that saying "no" entails saying "yes" (and, conversely, that saying "yes" entails saying "no").

Finally, major themes of the introductory framework sketched in this Part—the analysis of structure/event aporias and the account of paradoxes of differentiation, above all—have been advanced in broad terms that stress the general applicability of deconstructionist insights to every sort of process and thing. Furthermore, as has been mentioned, other parts of the introductory framework can easily be rewritten to make clear this same point, i.e., that the categories at work in natural and social processes are as liable to deconstruction as are the categories at work in discourse. (For example, in describing iterability we can substitute an appearance/reality disjuncture for the disjuncture between signs and intentions, and we can substitute the contexts of physical interaction for the codes of discoursive meaning.) Paradoxes are both ontological and epistemological, both generative and structured, and they deconstitute everyday events as much as they ravage philosophical discourse.[41] Having noted this much, however, we do not now *have* to conclude that deconstructionist tactics will enjoy outstanding persuasive power in *every* line of inquiry, no matter how mundane. It seems not unlikely that deconstructionist strategies will amount to overkill when articulated and set to work in discussions of quotidian problems. In such contexts, deconstructive approaches may lack efficacy—*not* because deconstruction is inapplicable, but because the glaring contrast between the humdrum nature of given problems and the sophistication of the techniques brought to bear on them may produce a laughable incongruousness that drains the techniques of critical trenchancy. (There obtains a partially analogous situation regarding Einstein's theory of special relativity, which applies in full to every possible motion, but which deals in most ordinary contexts with speeds too slight to impair Newtonian measurement significantly.[42]) To be sure, one can never tell *a priori* whether a split between the applicability and the usefulness of deconstructive techniques will emerge stubbornly in particular situations. Each set of circumstances must lie open to countless readings, some of which may prove able to achieve a deconstructionist rigor without bathos. For each set of circumstances, that is, we must confront strategic questions of reading that permit no categorical answers, either for individual cases or *(a fortiori)* for general types of such cases. In many instances, deconstructive readings of quotidian matters may felicitously avoid the appearance of heavyhandedness. Certainly, one can have no warrant beforehand to rule out such readings unqualifiedly as oversophisticated and preciously out of place. Nonetheless, it is far from improbable that deconstructionist methods will seem overrefined in numerous mundane situations, and that those situations will hence not be unsettled as powerfully by a deconstructive critique as will sophisticated philosophical doctrines. Though deconstructionist insights are as applicable to commonplace problems as to rarefied theories, the involutions and subtlety of a deconstructive approach may limit its usefulness for pondering everyday questions. One can only hope that future analyses of such questions will prove one's fear of bathos and overkill to be unfounded.

Part Two. A Guide for the Perplexed

A. Some Orienting Remarks

In the four chapters that follow, the ideas elaborated in the preceding Part will unfold themselves and refold themselves, as they explicitly or implicitly structure many of the chief arguments. With misleading crudeness, one might describe the basic course of this book as follows: the first chapter has introduced a framework of themes, the middle chapters "apply" those themes to various texts, and the final chapter draws out the themes' programmatic potential. This description, with its facile acceptance of a theory/practice dichotomy, is glib and more than a bit wooden but not wholly unfair. On the one hand, as Derrida has maintained, "[i]t is . . . evident that in the field of a deconstruction of philosophical oppositions, the opposition *praxis/theoria* first is to be analyzed, and may no longer simply govern our definition of practice."[43] Structure/event aporias will assail texts that have relied too complacently on oppositions between theory and practice; though such aporias cannot and should not ever be circumvented, their disquieting energies must be carefully considered and thematized if they are to figure less as a plague than as a boon. Moreover, apart from any general considerations, a vulgar theory/practice distinction is peculiarly out of place in any synopsis of this book's arguments, for the middle chapters herein do at least as much as the first chapter to outline, shape, and develop the ideas that they are exemplifying. Even if a formalist's dream of mechanically applying theories to texts were free of devastating aporias, it would be decidedly inappropriate here. On the other hand, however untenable the theory/practice split may remain, it is unobliterable and irreducible, and nothing can be written without it. One can radically and successfully controvert the logic of exemplariness—the logic of "the example"—but one can never escape that logic conclusively. Any escape would itself have to exemplify what it had deemed possible, and would therefore seal itself in the very pattern it had renounced. If, then, we regard this book's middle three chapters as exemplifying the topics and strategies laid out in the first chapter, we shall not be approving of a merely contingent form of argument that could (in its broadest contours) be surpassed once and for all. Every argument must be focused in some way or another, and every focus constitutes an example, of a greater or lesser richness. Thus, while declaring that the notion of "the example" is "not acceptable within my argument," and while asserting that the justification for an argument's foci "can . . . never be absolute and definitive," Derrida acknowledges that he cannot simply skirt the gesture of focusing his contentions: "Since I am about to deal with what, using . . . much caution, I call an 'example,' I must now justify my choice."[44] In the present work, we shall follow a like path. Chapters 2, 3, and 4 do indeed flesh out and sharpen the ideas adumbrated in this opening chapter, and the texts that are scrutinized in those middle chapters have been singled out as "exemplary."

Chapter 2 concentrates on the Marxist account of law and history developed by G. A. Cohen; Chapter 3 directs its attention to the positivist form of liberal jurisprudence evolved by H. L. A. Hart and others; and Chapter 4 scrutinizes the conservative view of legal and moral discourse propounded by David Hume. To a not inconsiderable degree, then, the main texts to be studied in those chapters have been selected deliberately to embrace a wide grouping of political stances. Such an approach is bound to be more persuasive than a study addressing itself just to Marxism or just to liberalism. But two additional factors are even more important. First, the texts under consideration will force us to delve deeply into some crucial topics that have preoccupied jurisprudes and political theorists: the distinction between public and private, the origins of society, the relation between law and morality, the interaction of material forces and sociopolitical relations, and so forth. All of these problems will be tackled in unconventional ways, most of which will rely expressly on deconstructionist insights. A second reason behind the choice of specific texts is the intractable split between analytic and Continental modes of philosophy. Thus far, most Anglo-American philosophers have sedulously ignored the recent French thought that has induced so many upheavals in other disciplines. Moreover, the few attempts to find common strategies within French insights and analytic developments have by and large been less than rewarding, for deconstruction has generally been portrayed as little more than a neo-pragmatist theory.[45] In this situation, a book attempting to mount a deconstructive critique of analytic philosophy should take pains to encounter some of the leading analysts, whose rigor of thought would be acknowledged even by diehard critics. (Rigor is what the analytic philosophers most prize, and is what they see as a truly distinctive virtue of their own style of philosophizing.) If I were to look only at minor thinkers, my analyses could too easily be dismissed as having little to do with more refined discourses. Hence, the theorists on whom this book will be focusing in its middle chapters—G. A. Cohen, H. L. A. Hart, and David Hume—are generally viewed as epitomizing the rigor that supposedly characterizes Anglo-American philosophy. Cohen and Hart have been widely hailed for bringing new vigor and new preciseness to their respective fields, while Hume is frequently dubbed the greatest philosopher in the English language. If this book can advance cogent deconstructive analyses of such rigorous and enormously influential philosophers, it can go a long way toward realizing its ultimate aim: *viz.*, to highlight the inescapable force of deconstruction within a mode of discourse that gives little or no thought to deconstructionist insights. Those insights need not and should not be confined to discourses (such as Continental philosophy and literary theory) that have long been taking the paradoxes of deconstruction into account.

As has just been stated, this book's principal aim is to make clear the relevance and power of deconstruction for analytic philosophers. Readers may hence be rather puzzled to learn that sizable portions of the middle three chapters—especially the first half of Chapter 2 and the first half of Chapter 3—do not draw (in any manifest way) upon the themes enunciated so far, but are devoted to extensive and fine-grained criticisms of the texts that are being scrutinized. For the most part, my deconstructive analyses take place only after the germane works of Hart, Cohen, or Hume have been closely read and dissected, along lines that often will not involve the highlighting of deconstructionist themes. Far from being extrinsic to the deconstructive analyses, however, the meticulous readings that forego those analyses will be vital means of gaining a purchase on the dynamics of the relevant texts. By patiently working through a text and by criticizing it on its own terms and within its own logic (i.e., within the exact logic and on the exact terms that it seeks to privilege), one can achieve the intimate comprehension of it that one will need in order to demonstrate its *in*comprehensible *il*logic. Deconstructive critiques require painstaking attention to structures in the texts being examined, as Paul de Man has observed: "[I]t is a common and productive gesture of [deconstructive critiques] to outdo the closeness of reading that has been held up to them and to show, by reading the close readings more closely, that they were not nearly close enough."[46] In this book, all of the middle chapters will essay to act out the operations of close reading that made them possible. To preface deconstructive analyses with trails of close commentary will serve to orient readers to the subtle patterning of the texts under consideration, and will accord nicely with the rigor and strangeness of this book's methodology. Because the paradoxes of deconstruction so fundamentally challenge all conceivable modes of thought, a critique that highlights those paradoxes must *think through* what it is doing, with great care. Close reading amounts to a decisive prerequisite of such a critique, for the radically unsettling nature of the arguments will oblige them to meet high standards of meticulousness if they aspire truly to be convincing. As Derrida notes, the relentless unthinkability of a deconstructive critique can make one "uneasy and uncomfortable,"[47] and it is for exactly this reason that the analyses in this book must be especially painstaking if they are to win acceptance. Deconstruction is not an easy method that can be taken up on a whim, but is instead a demanding process of highlighting aporias—aporias that would escape detection by those who are not willing to feel uncomfortable and uneasy.

B. Synopses of the Remaining Chapters

Chapter 2 begins with a detailed summary of the main strands of G. A. Cohen's Marxism, interspersed with important critical observations. These criticisms will not only advance the purposes outlined near the end of the last section, but will in their own right tell very deeply against key arguments that Cohen puts forward. However, the second half of the chapter is more venturesome and wide-ranging. It challenges Cohen's theory of law, which will turn out to rest on naive assumptions about rules, and which will have to embrace the interpretative style of analysis that Cohen hopes to transcend and that he presumes to denigrate as unscientific. During this discussion of Cohen's jurisprudence, we shall consider at length his crucial distinction between the private realm (of the economic base) and the public realm (of the legal superstructure). Then, in the most important section of the whole chapter, Cohen's historical materialism—with its privileging of the forces of production over relations of production—will invert its priorities in the very course of establishing them at all. In more than one way, and quite unwittingly, Cohen's texts will exalt language as an implacable and disruptive force that overturns Marxist hierarchies. Because Cohen undoubtedly is the most acclaimed exponent of Marxism in the analytic tradition, a critique of his work carries far-reaching implications for a whole school of philosophers, not least because Cohen's theory will be shown to undo the article of faith that unites almost all Marxists: a prioritizing of material forces over social relations.

The next chapter will probe the jurisprudential thought of H. L. A. Hart. Like Chapter 2, Chapter 3 will offer a partial overview of the texts that are being studied, along with some critical remarks. The chapter then moves on to consider two intractable difficulties in Hart's work: a vicious circularity that prevents his model of law from living up to his own basic requirements for any theory, and an ultimate incoherence stemming from his positivist separation of factuality and normativity. While focusing on Hart's theories, the chapter will have cause to interrogate some views broached by other eminent champions of legal positivism—Neil MacCormick and Hans Kelsen—as well. Among the questions that will arise in the third chapter is the existence or nonexistence of a fundamental dichotomy between primitive and modern legal regimes. Very likely, however, the most important and most unsettling contribution of the third chapter is its deconstructive derangement of the Hartian split between facts and norms, for such a wholesale critique will throw implicitly into question the wide array of jurisprudential theories which base themselves on that fact/norm split.

Chapter 4, which studies the work of David Hume, diverges from Chapters 2 and 3 in that it does not start with a compendious overview of the texts it is scrutinizing. Instead, its first Part examines various ideas about language that can be teased out from Hume's principal texts on human nature and human understanding. Part Two highlights the infinitely receding abyss into which Hume's theory of the foundation of social life will have plunged us. In addition, Part Two urges that Hume's claim to have ferreted out a natural bedrock in people's psyches will have been disallowed by his own conception of human faculties; moreover, the same Part challenges Hume's distinction between the natural power of moral norms and the artificial status of legal norms. Part Three begins by flushing out certain tensions between Hume's brilliant psychological narratives and his epistemological pronouncements. The chapter ends with a deconstructive critique of Hume's empiricist doctrines, which will be shown to have given rise to a remarkable paradox of differentiation that will engulf all types of empiricism.

Chapter 5 is the longest, most ambitious, and most difficult of the chapters. It amounts to a manifesto for a critical legal theory, with a somewhat hortative tone and a frequent use of first-person plural pronouns. As has been noted, this final chapter stakes out one of the countless and fruitful paths that offer themselves to jurisprudence in light of the deconstructionist themes that earlier chapters have developed. Chapter 5 takes as given the strategies and maneuvers of deconstructive philosophy—rather than reassemble the arguments that have already been made for them—and it seeks to illustrate how one might engage in jurisprudential discourse while trying to keep in view those strategies and maneuvers as far as possible (by directing them forcefully and repeatedly against one's own discourse). In its barest outlines, the chapter traces the career of a pregnant concept and argues for transmuting the ways in which the concept has hitherto been discussed. Specifically, Chapter 5 expounds the theme of "reification," as it has intricately evolved in Marxist and existentialist writings and in the work of the critical legal studies movement. After surveying relevant works by Marx, Lukács, Sartre, and Peter Gabel, the chapter takes up some general methodological concerns and reflections. These include a thoroughgoing critique of pragmatism, which is so frequently and slackly equated with deconstruction by its proponents as well as by its critics. From there, the chapter goes on to analyze and reorient standard discourses on reification. That topic will attract our sustained attention for at least three reasons. Most generally, it girds us with a device for focusing the analyses, arguments, proposals, and exhortations that constitute Chapter 5. To be written at all, within manageable proportions, the arguments therein have had to be made to cluster round a relatively precise set of issues. Moreover, aside from narrowing the range of discussion in their role as a guiding thread, problems concerning reification will afford opportunities for the clarifying and sharpening of critical legal discourse. Most critical legal scholars who advert to reification are in that way denouncing several forms of social congealment, but these scholars tend to collapse the different types of rigidification with alarming insouciance. Though distinctions among those types will not ultimately stand firm, a reckless effacement of them will lead simply to muddled crudeness. Thus, one of the principal objectives of Chapter 5 is to ferret out what "reification" means. Implicitly doing battle with those scholars who conflate several meanings of the term, much of the second half of the chapter will attempt to sort out the medley of definitions that have at some time or other been assigned to "reification." Such a task will not only help in eliminating unnecessary confusion, but should allow analysts to opt more deliberately and incisively for some definitions over others.

A third reason for focusing on the theme of reification is that it touches on many of the key problems within critical legal theory. Like the rest of the book, the final chapter aims above all to highlight the acuteness and analytical power of a deconstructive approach in areas of philosophical thought that heretofore have looked most askance at deconstruction. This the chapter accomplishes not by putting forth full-scale deconstructive readings of texts (like those advanced in previous chapters), but by trying to pay full heed to the paradoxes of such readings while taking stands on several points of debate among the critical legal scholars. That is, this book will strive to begin elaborating a jurisprudence informed by deconstruction as well as a deconstruction of jurisprudence. For this purpose the theme of reification will serve admirably, since it will lead the fifth chapter to confront a number of crucial problems in legal and political theory, and will ergo induce us to explore how a deconstructionist critic might view those problems. Thus, the chapter receives its guidance from a motif suitably narrow to make the arguments feasible, but suitably ramified and far-reaching to inspire a good introduction to some unthinkable ways of thinking about jurisprudence.

In combination, the five chapters attempt to realize three principal objectives. First, they bring out the forcefulness and rigor of deconstructionist tactics for the consideration of problems and the interpretation of thinkers whose philosophical background may at first seem alien to the concerns of deconstructive philosophy. In a move that defies commonsense notions of spatiality, deconstruction will be made to extend to where it already reaches. Second, the detailed studies of some major philosophers will be emphasizing aporias that place in question far more than the specific texts under scrutiny. Through detailed readings, this book launches a general challenge to Marxists, legal positivists, and empiricists; for the paradoxes it highlights are unavoidably intertextual. Third, the book tries to amplify deconstructive tenets in fresh and notably piquant ways that should prove to be of great interest even for long-time Derrideans (not least, for example, in regard to the highly troubled relation joining deconstruction and politics—a relation that is depicted here as free-floating and markedly indirect, but vital). Critical legal theory should be playing a major role in the most advanced philosophical inquiries as well as learning a great deal from them.

CHAPTER 2

THE SPECTER OF COMMUNISM

Is Marxist thought a miasma from which leftists should boldly distance themselves? Does Marxism take for granted too many key starting points of the doctrines that it purports to be rejecting? In his best writings, was Marx but little more than a talented epigone of Hegel? Should Marx be assigned a not insignificant share of blame for the ruthless dictatorships that revere him as their guardian saint? Is the dogmatism of most Marxist groups less a fortuity than a readily predictable by-product of the linking of political ambitions to philosophical speculation?[1]

My inclination is to reply to each of the above questions with a provisional but general "yes." In the process, each question would be rendered grammatical (rather than rhetorical); the very proffering of an answer to each question denies that each answer is *self-evidently* affirmative. Responding to the above queries thus becomes one way of insisting that the whole legacy of Marxism be considered with great care. Indeed, pursuing full answers to such queries will doubtless be an interminable task. It should in any event preoccupy those who still aspire to be leftist in the face of the crushing disillusionment that has accompanied Marxism's horrid failures.

Though perhaps generative of infinite controversy, the above questions surely need to be answered; they are too pressing to be merely rhetorical. If there exists a future for leftist social criticism, it may well lie in the tenacious candor with which present-day radicals supply the needed responses to those questions. Nevertheless, one would be rash to think that Marxism can or should be *simply* abandoned *tout court*. Two considerations should give pause to anyone fashionably eager to plunge into a post-Marxist world. First, much of the best writing within the Marxist tradition has prepared the way for whatever might engross us once Marxism is de-emphasized. One should scarcely deny the fruitfulness and profundity of the "Economic and Philosophic Manuscripts" of Marx, the "negative dialectics" of Adorno, the questioning of capitalism's "second nature" by Lukács, the challenge to technocratic ascendancy by Marcuse, the later social theory of Sartre, or even the frequently annoying prose of Althusser.[2] A tradition that can lay claim to such a stellar array of theorists—as well as a host of others not mentioned here—cannot be lightly abjured, even if many of its best works stretch its limits well past the breaking point. Marxism may indeed guide us toward a more sophisticated and self-critical future, though the works most likely to do so are just barely recognizable as Marxist.[3]

Second, an abrupt renunciation of Marxism would have to take as given the coherence and self-sameness of Marxist texts. To "go beyond" a certain body of thought requires the establishment of clear boundaries past which any transcendence must occur. If it can be shown, however, that Marxism distinguishes itself from *itself* as much as from any other discourses, the whole notion of "boundaries"—which would of necessity be determined on the basis of clear self/other distinctions—must be thrown radically into doubt. In that event, Marxism will be seen as a mode of thought at war with itself in ways that preclude the closure of its identity. Marxism will present not a unitary doctrine that can be readily surpassed, but the (dis)location of its own unraveling. One cannot flatly renounce Marxism, for something that will always remain in question is just what "Marxism" is.

> To impose this prudence upon oneself is to take seriously the difficulty, and also the heterogeneity, of the Marxist text, the decisive importance of its historical stakes. . . .
>
> . . . [T]he entire text and conceptuality of Marxism cannot be *immediately given*. To believe so would be to erase the specificity of these fields and to limit their *effective* transformation. . . .
>
> . . . In saying this, I am not advocating anything contrary to "Marxism," I am convinced of it. These texts are not to be read according to a hermeneutical or exegetical method which would seek out a finished signified beneath a textual surface. Reading is transformational. . . .
>
> No more than I have dealt with Saussure's text, or Freud's, or any other, as homogeneous volumes (the motif of homogeneity, the theological motif *par excellence*, is decidedly the one to be destroyed), I do not find the texts of Marx, Engels, or Lenin homogeneous critiques.[4]

If we cannot entirely leave Marxism behind, that is because Marxism—with its bizarre heterogeneity—is always already leaving itself behind. Scarcely should it come as a great surprise that the subversive theory *par excellence* may, in the end, have been subverting itself as much as it subverts other positions.

Full substantiation of claims made in the preceding paragraph would entail a vast project of meticulous deconstructive readings. Such a project would take in not only the works of Marx and Engels, as well as all the main texts of their sundry intellectual heirs, but also the writings of the giant thinkers—such as Kant and Hegel—who figured in the philosophical atmosphere with which Marx so fruitfully interacted. Quite likely is it, indeed, that we should have to broaden the scope of any thorough inquiry to embrace much of Western thought. "[O]ne must not only go back to Marx, or at least to an entire stratum of the text he opened up, but much further back, as Marx himself knew, as far as the 'Greek materialists,' traversing problems of reading and 'translation' that are indeed difficult, and whose results are difficult to anticipate in our lexicon" (*Positions*, 75). And since coming to grips with Hegel's *oeuvre* alone "in a certain way is interminable, at least if one wishes to execute it rigorously and minutely" (*Positions*, 43–44), a thoroughgoing deconstruction of Marxism would be a daunting task.

Fortunately, my aims in this chapter are a bit more modest. Far from being a full-scale deconstructive survey of Western metaphysics, this chapter focuses on a set of writings grouped under the signature of G. A. Cohen. Chief among these texts is *Karl Marx's Theory of History*,[5] a *tour de force* of the analytic style of philosophizing that has prevailed in Great Britain and the United States for the better part of this century. Cohen's book has been hailed as "a more sophisticated interpretation of historical materialism than any we have had before,"[6] and its publication in 1978 brought its author into the front rank of Anglo-American exegetes of Marx. Even those reviews that are strongly critical of Cohen's theory have lavished praise on its virtues. Above all, his book has been saluted for its limpidity and its brilliance, yet these two qualities do not coexist in quite as untroubled a relation as one might think. My reading of Cohen's work will cut across his lucidity and his brilliance; the brilliant glare and powerful exuberance of his prose may generate blindness, blindness that will put into question the supposed luculence of his analytical scheme. This uneasy relationship between insight and clarity will take an especially acute form in light of Cohen's fierce rigor—another quality of his book that has been highly commended. It is the care and the scrupulous precision with which the book is argued that should make its blind spots all the more dazzling.[7]

Like a modern Ezekiel, Cohen hopes to breathe life into the dry bones of "an old-fashioned historical materialism" with the bracing winds of analytic philosophy (KMTH, x). In restating Marx's theory of history, Cohen eschews reliance on any dialectical modes of interpretation; he employs the word "dialectic" only a few times and always with condescending quotation marks.[8] With the exception of a few words on the anti-Hegelian Althusser (KMTH, x, 280 note 1), Cohen wholly ignores the Marxists whom I mentioned four paragraphs ago. In Cohen's view, all such thinkers fail to attain the virile clarity of the analytic tradition. Theirs is the more effete task of demonstrating "how elegantly—and evasively—the French [or German] language [can] be used" (KMTH, x).

(Lest the focus on gender in the preceding two sentences appear unkind or *ad hominem*, it should be mentioned that Cohen's book is overwhelmingly masculine in tone. Cohen invariably employs male pronouns, and virtually all his illustrative examples involve men. His few examples involving women pertain to marital relations or to sexual intercourse [KMTH, 90, 93, 182]. When, in a later essay, Cohen denounces "the sexist personification of humanity which Marxists have not always avoided" ["Materialism," 232], he sounds not unlike Oedipus condemning the man who murdered Laius.)

Cohen's work merits lengthy consideration here not only because of its general brilliance but also owing to its incisive treatment of one relatively neglected topic in Marxism: the "problem of legality" (KMTH, 216–48). As will shortly become evident, law can play a major subversive role in the elaboration of a critique of Cohen's arguments. Of much less interest here is the "faithfulness" (or absence of "faithfulness") achieved by Cohen in his interpretation of Marx. Although Marx's writings are occasionally consulted, this chapter is not primarily concerned with questions of so-called accurateness—the accurateness of Cohen's re-presentation of important Marxian ideas.[9] Such questions are not completely inconsequential; after all, the more faithful Cohen's writings have been, the more far-reaching will be the implications of my critique. Marxism more generally could be placed in question. Be that as it may, however, the whole issue of faithfulness or accuracy seems largely devoid of meaning and out of place, for reasons hinted at in my hyphenating the word "representation." To *represent* something accurately is to *present* it once again, to recapture its original presence in a signified form. But, as was postulated above, Marxism can never come to be present in a straightforward or unproblematic way. It must obscure itself in the very motion of presenting itself. This chapter will try to show, moreover, that what holds for the referent holds too for the signifier. Cohen's argument is no more identical to itself or free of aporias than is the entire Marxist tradition. Questions of faithfulness will be indefinitely postponed.

Nor shall we explicitly render judgment—except once, *en passant*—on the adequateness of Cohen's Marxism as an account of human history. His book has been subjected to often powerful criticisms on this score, in particular to the charge that Cohen has generalized unduly from the dynamic structure of capitalist society to sweeping theses about the whole of human development.[10] Such criticisms, however cogent, feed too comfortably off the metaphysical tradition that has informed Cohen's work. Because "there is nothing outside the text," because, that is, the "general text" of all history is a "fabric of traces referring endlessly to something other than itself" and "overrun[ning] all the limits assigned to it,"[11] we should not expect to unearth a bedrock of hard facts in socioeconomic life against which Cohen's ideas could be assessed. If Cohen's stance does indeed approximate that which we call "reality," it perhaps most strikingly does so when it most uncannily works to undermine itself.

Most of this chapter is divided into two Parts. The first gives an outline of Cohen's major arguments, as they have been formulated in his book and in several related essays. My exposition will of course be tendentious—as are all expositions—but it will not be unfair. Critical remarks on specific matters are interspersed throughout Part One. No full-scale critique is ventured until Part Two, however, which will investigate the clashes and tangles bred by Cohen's mode of expression (or the way his text *works*) and his prime substantive themes (or what his text *says*). Along the way, Part Two will cast doubt upon the solution offered in Cohen's text to the aforementioned "problem of legality." The basic conclusion of Part Two, and of this entire chapter, may be pointedly summarized as follows: if Marxism is profoundly unsatisfying, that is because it stays unattuned to its own aporias.

Part One. Cohen's Defense of Marxism

Cohen begins his book, significantly, with a denigration of reading. Near the end of his introductory chapter on images of history in the writings of Marx and Hegel, Cohen compares Marx favorably to Hegel, in striking terms:

> [W]e may attribute to Marx, as we cannot to Hegel, not only a *philosophy* of history, but also what deserves to be called a *theory* of history, which is not a reflective construal, from a distance, of what happens, but a contribution to understanding its inner dynamic. Hegel's reading of history as a whole and of particular societies is just that, a *reading*, an interpretation which we may find more or less attractive. But Marx offers not only a reading but also the beginnings of something more rigorous. [KMTH, 27.]

The full import of these assertions will presently become clearer. For now, suffice it to point out that Cohen here undertakes one of the classic moves of the orthodox tradition of metaphysics (in either its philosophical or its theological form): the elevation of signifieds over signifiers. Unlike Hegel, who was content with a "reflective construal . . . of what happened," Marx went beyond clever interpretations to penetrate the "inner dynamic" of the progress that he discerned in history. Marx, according to Cohen, could not rest satisfied with a detached *reading* of social forms, since the point was to *explain* the world (as a prelude to changing it).[12] For anyone interested in gaining a theoretical grasp of the mechanisms of history, it would be essential to pierce signifying epiphenomena and to win an unmediated access to the hard facts that lie behind, at the very core of all social change. What would be needed is a "reduction of the opacity of the signifier [as] the origin of what we call presence."[13] It is Marx's efforts at achieving just this sort of reduction to which Cohen gives voice.

A. Definitions

1. *Productive Forces and Production Relations*

To set the stage for his main argument, Cohen starts (after his introductory chapter) with a series of definitions. His first aim is to distinguish productive forces from production relations. Articulating his view that "a force or power . . . is not a relation" (KMTH, 28)—a view that would evoke a derisive laugh from Nietzsche[14]—Cohen argues that the productive forces do not form any part of the "economic structure." Productive forces will underpin all or almost all aspects of society as a whole, including the economic structure, whereas the economic structure will underpin all or almost all aspects of society as a whole, excluding the productive forces (KMTH, 28–31). Development of the forces of production is thus primary and autonomous, even though it requires vast reinforcement from whatever economic relations it brings about.

As an aside, it should be mentioned that Cohen seals off productive forces from economic structures on the slim basis of a single pronouncement in Marx's "Preface" to *A Contribution to the Critique of Political Economy:* "The sum total of [the] relations of production constitutes the economic structure, the real basis, on which rises a legal and political superstructure."[15] Cohen argues that because Marx adverted only to the relations of production (and hence not to the forces of production) in defining the economic base, "we conclude *ex silentio* that production relations alone serve to constitute the economic structure" (KMTH, 28). To be sure, Cohen's argument is persuasive. Nonetheless, as Wittgenstein taught us, inferences *ex silentio* are never immune from contestation.[16] Cohen thus seems presumptuous when he writes that "Marx *unambiguously* excludes [the productive forces from economic structures]" (KMTH, 29). This is but one of many times that Cohen resorts to highly coercive adverbs and adjectives—such as "clearly," "plainly," "patently," "surely," "of course," "conclusive," "undeniable," "natural,"[17]—to underscore points that are not always as convincing as the one here.

Let us return to the main thread of our discussion. What, then, are the productive forces and the production relations? Productive forces, Cohen maintains, can be identified through several criteria: (1) They must be capable of being used in some process that, partly as a result of their being so employed, brings about the production of useful goods; and it must be someone's intention that the forces contribute in this way to productive activity (KMTH, 32). (2) If a substance, a device, or a form of labor is necessary for a given productive process, then—if the thing is to be counted as a productive force—it must be necessary because of the material aspects (rather than social aspects) of the productive system (KMTH, 32–34). Thus, for example, measures to improve social discipline will not qualify as "productive" in the relevant sense. (More will be said shortly regarding the material/social dualism). (3) Something can be deemed a productive force only if effective control (or lack of control) over the thing contributes to establishing the place occupied in the economic structure by the person enjoying such control (or by somebody lacking such control) (KMTH, 41). (4) The productive forces *develop* in history, at least over the long run (KMTH, 41). (5) The development of productive forces can be promoted or fettered by the relations of production. At least over the long term, Cohen holds, the productive forces tend to enwrap themselves in productivity-boosting economic structures (KMTH, 41, 134–74).

Production relations are defined more easily than productive forces. They are either (1) relations of effective control by persons over productive forces or other persons, or (2) relations presupposing relations of effective control (KMTH, 34–35). What Cohen dubs "effective control" is a supposedly pre-juridical power to determine the fate of a particular resource (KMTH, 219–20).

2. *Critical Comments*

A. PRODUCTIVE FORCES

We shall not follow all the intricate details of the classificatory game Cohen plays as he decides whether to include certain types of resources in the category of "productive powers." Instead, four brief criticisms will here be made regarding the general definitions that Cohen advocates. i. *Professions and Services.* It is unclear what role services and professions play in Cohen's taxonomy. Cohen seems very clearly to have in mind the production of concrete, tangible goods whenever he speaks of economic production as a whole. At one point, for example, he considers the possibility of comparing two overall productive outputs by measuring the volume and the weight of each output (KMTH, 58). (He dismisses the possibility, but only by pointing out that such parameters are "beside the point" [KMTH, 58], rather than by additionally noting that a large portion of each of the two outputs would have no weight or volume.) If, as seems likely, Cohen equates total output with industrial output, he gives no reason for assuming away professions and services. At least some professions might be considered superstructural, but to consider them so here without any argument is to beg the question.

For at least three reasons, the division Marx saw between productive labor and unproductive labor will not help matters here.[18] First, as Marx repeatedly maintained, the productive/unproductive dichotomy does not coincide with any industry/services diremption. Industry can be unproductive, and services can frequently be the opposite. Second, Marx's distinction, which assumes the generating of surplus value, can retain pertinence only in the age of capitalism. Yet Cohen's version of Marxism is a "theory about epochs" that requires comparisons across ages ("Materialism," 228). Intra-epochal dyads therefore tend to lose their significance. Third, and most important, the distinction between productive and unproductive labor will always presuppose one or another version of the labor theory of value, which Cohen quite properly eschews.[19]

ii. *Sociality and Materiality.* Cohen's dichotomy between social and material aspects of production will not hold up. Let us pose the example of religion used as a stimulus to production. Any number of things can take the place of religion in this example, from restraining walls to work breaks to tasty food (KMTH, 47, 53–55). In Cohen's view, all such cases that involve *willingness* to work, rather than the *ability* to work, must lie outside the sphere of productive forces. That is, if religious discourse (say) is used to promote workers' enthusiasm for their lot without bolstering their strictly physical capabilities, then Cohen will not regard it as a productive force, even if it boosts productivity (KMTH, 47, 53–55). How does Cohen defend this seemingly arbitrary restriction? With a coercive adverb in tow, he writes that classing religious discourse as a means of production "plainly contradicts the intent of Marx's theory" (KMTH, 33). Though here Cohen is probably on solid footing, his loyalty to the master does very little to ward off charges of arbitrariness. Nor are his further statements of much avail. For instance, he says that "nothing is materially produced out of or with" religious discourse (KMTH, 33). Now, even if one ignores the problem of services and professions, one can see that the quoted phrase will apply to virtually any factor that has not been combined with other productive agencies. That religion alone will not manufacture goods is not any more relevant than is a similar absence of productive power in most other uncombined forces of production.

Equally unavailing is the contention that religious activity is a "means not of production but of motivating producers. . . . [Its] necessity is [not] grounded in the physical facts of the situation" (KMTH, 32, 34). (This contention is not made specifically for religious practices, but it will apply or fail to apply thereto in an exactly similar way.) If religious activity spurs producers to arrive at a higher output than they otherwise would, then the activity must be needed (in the absence of other stimulants) for creating that extra output. Moreover, it is not at all difficult to characterize this necessary relationship—between the religious discourse and the extra production—in a way that clashes with Cohen's argument. One merely has to assert that the need for the religious practices will be obviously tied to "the nature of the . . . technology . . . [and] the physical facts of the situation" (KMTH, 33–34). Specifically, if religious practices are a necessary condition for obtaining a certain level of output, that is because the current technology cannot yield such a level in the absence of religious beliefs or some fitting substitute. Suitably altering the description of our hypothetical set of facts can shift the provenance of necessity—or the perceived provenance of necessity—from social considerations to the "physical facts." Limited attainability of a given level of output can invariably be traced to technical factors, just so long as we give the right focus to our explanatory account. Cohen himself is hardly unaware that "an explanation of a phenomenon succeeds or fails relative to some finitely specific description of it, not irrespective of how it is described" (KMTH, 163). Who sets the tone calls the tune.

iii. *The Productivity of Potentiality.* Cohen leaves unresolved the problem of classifying knowledge as a productive force. In particular, he seems to head down a very dangerous path in his discussion of so-called work relations. These are the relations that join workers directly on the job or within their producing units. (In passing, we might note that Cohen places himself on shaky ground when he writes that work relations are "conceptually independent of the social roles [workers] occupy" [KMTH, 111]). At most, they are only partially independent, for if some person consistently gives orders to other persons, we may safely infer therefrom that the social relationships among such persons are not egalitarian—even if the exact form of *in*egalitarianism cannot be specified.) While holding that work relations are not part of the economic structure, and that they "belong alongside the productive forces as substratum [*sic*] of the economic structure" (KMTH, 113), Cohen does not wish to classify these relations as belonging to the productive forces proper. He therefore argues:

> We agree that *something* in this conceptual area is a productive force, but not the work relations themselves. On our account, knowledge of ways of organizing labour is a productive force, part of managerial labour power, but the relations established when that knowledge is implemented are not productive forces. It is necessary to distinguish the blueprint for the set of relations from the relations themselves, and it is the first which is a productive force. A principle for allocating tasks in a certain fashion is *used* in production, and it is *owned* by whoever owns the labour power which includes knowledge of it. Relations obtaining when tasks are divided as it prescribes are neither used nor owned. [KMTH, 113–14.]

Cohen thus brings to the fore a problem that will pervade his definitional enterprise. Having in this case admitted "blueprints" into the select group of productive forces, he may find it extremely difficult to exclude them in other cases. Arguments parallel to the one just quoted could apply to the major concepts behind *all* productive stimuli—*including* those stimuli that Cohen regards as superstructural.[20]

iv. *The Divisibility of Agents.* Cohen does not include human beings under the rubric of "productive forces" (KMTH, 43–45). He justifies this exclusion on the ground that it is a person's labor power, not anyone herself or himself, that is a productive force; what an employer buys is not people as such, but people's capacities to create valuable goods. Except in bizarre cases, it is such capacities, rather than the bodily mass of anyone, that gets used in processes of production. Cohen explains: "Production is an intentional activity in which men use productive forces, and they do not use themselves, but their strengths and skills" (KMTH, 44). (In a footnote, he adds: "Or, of course, their muscles and limbs" [KMTH, 44 note 1].) Once again, Cohen seems headed down a very dangerous path. His distinction between people themselves and the diverse skills that they exercise would appear applicable in full to other productive forces (such as machines and land), which can be analytically separated from the productive potency marshaled by them. To be sure, if we altogether renounce the agent/capacity distinction because it can so clearly be generalized, then people "have to be treated as instruments of production, and no one would claim Marx thought they were that in the labour process" (KMTH, 44). Still, Cohen has furnished no convincing argument for declining to extend his analysis to nonhuman productive agents. His reference to "intentionality" (KMTH, 43) is beside the point, for the distinction that he erects is between people and their general productive faculties (or appendages), not just between people and their intentionality. Even if—as Cohen presumes—intentionality were uniquely human, the same could scarcely be said about the power to transform objects.

B. PRODUCTION RELATIONS

Cohen's account of the relations of production is far less involuted than his masterful survey of the productive forces. Only two brief observations need be made here.

i. *The Emptiness of Structurality.* Cohen wants to define class membership in a purely structural sense. He declares:

> A person's class is established by nothing but his objective place in the network of ownership relations, however difficult it may be to identify such places neatly. His consciousness, culture, and politics do not enter the *definition* of his class position. Indeed, these exclusions are required to protect the substantive character of the Marxian thesis that

> class position strongly conditions consciousness, culture, and politics. [KMTH, 73.]

With the above passage in mind, let us look at another passage, this time from an early essay by Cohen:

> For Marx, then, a person's social existence is the economic role he occupies. And though role-defined behaviour, the *performance* of a role, may . . . involve the use of ideas in a causation-excluding sense, the same cannot be said for a man's *occupancy* of a role. . . .
>
> . . . [O]ne can occupy a role without playing it, for one naturally speaks of occupying rather than playing a position. People occupy roles without playing them when they lack the will or ability to play, or when obstacles prevent their doing so. They retain their rights and duties, but they do not exercise and fulfil them. The distinction between occupancy and performance helps us to see how the first may causally explain the second ["Roles," 91, 93.]

Cohen apparently does not realize just how much his argument works against itself. Even if we do not invoke straightaway the antinomies of events and structures, we can hurl at Cohen a charge often made by Hegel in his critiques of Kantian moral theory: substance can never be derived from pure abstract form (even if we assume, *pendant un moment*, that these are meaningful concepts).[21] By attempting to draw an undialectical disjuncture between performance and occupation (or consciousness and networks), Cohen disqualifies himself from attaining his own goal—the goal of bolstering "the Marxian thesis that class position strongly conditions consciousness, culture, and politics" (KMTH, 73). In his schema, there is no interplay between the intentionality of performance and the structurality of occupation. There is no interplay, because subjectivity (of performance) has been banished from objectivity (of occupation). Ideas have no function in the establishing of formal class statuses; but this means that they will never function at all, at least insofar as they are supposed to be "conditioned" by roles, for nothing could bridge the gap that Cohen hopes to maintain between nonintentional roles and the intentionality of role-playing.[22] Ideas could be acquired only through the *performance* of roles, or through some outside source or outside activity, but never through the formal *occupancy* of roles, which—as Cohen stresses—must ground itself on a radical exclusion of all intentionality. Until occupancy is somehow given effect, it must be incapable of forging specific modes of consciousness, for it is equally detached from all such modes. Sealed off from what instantiates it, occupancy has no effect on its instances.

This argument can then be carried a step further, to performance: performance, which is supposed to generate the ideas that form no part of occupancy, always presupposes the very outlook of which it is a prerequisite. If the effectuation of roles must implicate consciousness, it must always previously have done so, since there cannot be any originating moment that is not grounded and recognized as such through concepts deriving from an earlier moment. Genesis recedes forever because intentionality—whether in a specific form or in general—cannot provide its own grounding. Thought must always remain concealed in the dark realm of the unthinkable; it can become active and manifest only through the categories and concepts to which supposedly it gives rise. (A lengthier version of the argument in this paragraph will inform Chapter 5's displacement of neo-pragmatism.)

ii. *Legal Generality and Legal Particularism.* One other point merits attention here. Though not in itself of great importance, it does permit some degree of insight into the naiveté with which Cohen conceives of law. He argues at one point, in the course of a discussion of "possible and impossible ownership positions of producers" (KMTH, 66), that no one can own all means of production that she uses *and* none of her own labor power. This class position is the reverse of that of the proletarian, who owns all of her own labor power but no means of production. Since there is no shortage of proletarians, the impossibility of the reverse position may evoke some surprise. But, Cohen assures us, "there is a genuine disparity between the roles of labour power and means of production in [his analysis]." He elaborates:

> The proletarian may do anything he wishes with his labour power, short of violating the general laws of society, and nothing may be done with it without his contractual consent. He may not, of course, work with whatever means of production he chooses, but this follows from the exclusion of illegal behaviour in general. For parity, the person [who owns all means of production that he uses but none of his own labor power] should, in virtue of his supposed ownership of means of production, be able to do whatever he wishes with them within the law, yet this is excluded by his being forbidden to work with them as he wills, which is not a general law, but a legal feature of his particular situation. [KMTH, 66.]

Once again Cohen seems to have overlooked the importance of the characterizations on which his arguments rest. By characterizing the inability of a person to dispose of her labor power as "a legal feature of [her] particular situation" and thus "not a general law," Cohen makes his argument hold up. We might, however, view the situation in quite a different manner. A lack of control over the disposition of one's labor power can be construed as resulting from a "general law" that prevents those who own the means of production from compelling those who own labor power to make such power available for use on or with a certain productive factor. (After all, it is through just such a "general law" that "nothing may be done with [a proletarian's labor power] without his contractual consent.") The reverse of proletarianism then would become perfectly conceivable, though improbable and—most likely—unstable.

B. The Material and the Social

Before moving to the heart of his lengthy argument, Cohen takes some time to distinguish carefully between the material and the social aspects of production. He points up the advisability of a painstaking division between the social and the material sides of life by adducing some passages from Marx that ostensibly show needless confusion in identifying the chief constituents of productive processes (KMTH, 88–90). At some points, Marx described productive forces (within specific forms of society) as relations; in other places, he described them as things. Capital, for instance, was sometimes represented as a "social production relation," and at other times as things (or a thing) "*in* certain relations" (KMTH, 89, 88; emphasis added).

For a post-structuralist, these clashing formulations present no grave difficulty that has to be clarified or resolved. They should be regarded as the self-unraveling poles—poles of identity and difference—between and within which all social theory must pendulate. Capital exists, necessarily, *both* as an effect of social relations that precede it in a logical sense as well as in a temporal order, *and* as an element, or a set of elements, that precedes and (in combination with other elements) brings forth the relations that construct social life. Shuttling between accounts of capitalism that highlight *elements* and other accounts that highlight *structures*, and giving prominence to the stark complicity between such accounts, would be the only way to do justice to the aporias that constitute and derange them.

Cohen, however, takes a different view. He chides those who would adopt a stance similar to the one just outlined. As was remarked earlier, Cohen flinches from anything that smacks of dialectical thought.

> On entering production relations, persons and productive forces receive the imprint of the form those relations constitute: a Negro becomes a slave, a machine becomes a portion of constant capital. Those who favour 'dialectical' language might say: a Negro is and is not a slave, a machine is and is not capital. But these are evasive declarations. The right course is to try to express Marx's distinction as clearly as possible.[23]

Cohen concludes that Marx was simply in error when he sometimes described capital as a set of social relationships. Correctly viewed, capital is a "set of means of production . . . which has assumed a certain social character" (KMTH, 90).

Cohen backs up his favored definition by pointing to a dichotomy that received pride of place in most of Marx's theoretical schemes: the social versus the material. It is by keeping a sharp disjuncture between these spheres that we can avoid further bemusement in analyzing capitalism. Cohen formulates the disjuncture through the following definition of sociality: a description of a social phenomenon or event will attribute to a person or set of persons—whether specified or not—formal rights or effective powers (over assets of any kind) *vis-à-vis* other persons. Accounts of some aspect of society that do not involve ascription of rights or powers can refer only to the material side of life (KMTH, 94).

Cohen's sociality/materiality dyad can translate smoothly into a form/substance or culture/nature diremption. Each of these can be mapped easily onto the well-tried Marxian distinction between productive forces and production relations (KMTH, 98). Not analogous, however, is the perceived split between mind (or mental life) and matter (or the physical world); Cohen subsumes most branches of scientific knowledge—every branch, that is, which "contributes to production in virtue of the material character of production"—into the broader group of productive forces, which are all material in the sense relevant here, "though they are of course not [all] material in a more familiar sense of that term" (KMTH, 47). Nor are all types of economic relationships to be categorized as social. Cohen classifies work relations as material—notwithstanding his view that such relations do not qualify for a place in the elite company of "productive forces" (KMTH, 113). In addition, he invites us to take account of "material relations between producing units," on which he provides this gloss: "Thus it is a material fact that shoes produced by A protect the feet of B who produces a shirt to be worn by C who produces wheat consumed when A eats a bun, whatever may be the social mechanism (market, plan, custom, etc.) mediating these material connections" (KMTH, 111).

Cohen realizes, of course, that material production cannot take place without social forms, any more than a piece of granite can exist with no shape (KMTH, 99). He also recognizes—indeed, insists—that one cannot draw deductive inferences from material conditions to social frameworks. In other words, no set of productive forces ever *entails* any specific social constellation (KMTH, 92 note 1). Nonetheless, even if "content cannot exist without form, . . . that does not diminish its importance. . . . [C]ontent may be described in illuminating abstraction from the form with which it is integrated" (KMTH, 99). And even if the productive forces cannot settle the exact lineaments of an economic structure, there remain "important non-deductive [i.e., nonnecessary] inferences from material to social properties" (KMTH, 92). Here we come to the central argument of Cohen's book.

C. The Primacy Argument

Cohen's chief purpose in starkly separating life's social dimension from its material dimension is to assert the dominance of the latter over the former. He does this with two closely related theses: a "Development Thesis," which postulates that productive forces tend to develop during the course of human history; and the "Primacy Thesis" proper, which contends that the basic form of the production relations in a given society is traceable to the stage of evolution—and to the need for further development—of the society's productive forces (KMTH, 134).

Productive forces perform two key roles in Cohen's Primacy Thesis.[24] On the one hand, the level to which the forces have developed will cause specific networks of production relations to be more suitable than other possible networks for promoting further development. On the other hand, as was just stated, it is the further growth of productive power that commands most attention in the Primacy Thesis; if *existing* levels of forces tend to make only some sets of relations optimal, then the *future* level of forces is precisely that in regard to which judgments of optimality are made. Both the level and the continuation of productive development must be taken into account. As we might have anticipated, the second factor—that of enhancing or maximizing the rate of change of productive forces—receives the bulk of Cohen's attention throughout *Karl Marx's Theory of History*. Very little is argued there, save in Chapter VII and (to a lesser degree) in Chapter XI, with regard to the first factor: that of the relation between levels of development and the optimality of particular economic structures for continued development.

By "development" of productive forces Cohen means that ever more surplus is producible as time marches on. An equivalent way of expressing what he means is that "less direct labour is required in order to make a larger product [of essential goods]" (KMTH, 55). (The actualized level of basic products does not have to expand, so long as the ratio of possible labor time to necessary labor time is increasing.) Cohen does not commit himself to defending the proposition that the potential surplus product grows constantly. There exists only a *tendency*—affirmed in the Development Thesis—for the productive forces to move ahead; any number of circumstances may thwart the realization of such a tendency. Nor does Cohen insist that changes in the means of production inevitably produce corresponding changes in economic regimes. Some mutations are far too limited to have such an effect. All Cohen affirms is that "for any set of production relations, there is an extent of further development of the productive forces they embrace which suffices for a change in those relations, and . . . that further development tends to occur. But how large the development must be will vary from case to case" (KMTH, 135).

How then, does Cohen argue for his two theses? Having tried to amass evidence that each thesis played a prominent role in Marx's "mature" writings, Cohen then proceeds to "a more venturesome and perhaps foolhardy business, namely, to assemble some reasons for thinking the theses are true" (KMTH, 150). We shall begin, as Cohen does, by looking at the Development Thesis.

1. *Human Nature, Rationality, and Development*

Cohen grounds his argument in a specific theory of human nature and human rationality. He knows that his belief in a transhistorical "human nature" will disconcert many Marxists, but he declares: "It *must* be agreed that there are enduring facts of human nature" (KMTH, 151; emphasis added). Though he makes a half-hearted attempt to lend this statement some argumentative backing, his main source of support is the conviction that no sensible person could disagree with him: "[T]he contribution of biology *will have to be* acknowledged" (KMTH, 152; emphasis added).

Having laid down the law on the acceptability of "human nature," Cohen explains the pertinence of this concept for the claim that productive forces tend to progress through history. He presents us with what he calls "three facts" (KMTH, 152): (1) People are rational, in the sense that they know how to fulfill their needs by appropriating and utilizing productive forces. (2) The history of humankind is characterized by scarcity. What Cohen means by this is that people can satisfy their wants only if they expend a great deal of time and effort in work that is not thought of as a good in itself. (3) People can reflect and build on the knowledge that has been bequeathed to them by their predecessors. Gains in knowledge frequently lend themselves to productive use, and are very often perceived as being useful in this respect.

Taken together, Cohen's three facts lead us to conclude that some version of the Development Thesis must be true if we are to uphold human rationality. Or so it appears. As Cohen points out, his argument "has weaknesses, which are noted. . . . The resulting defence of the development thesis is not conclusive" (KMTH, 150–51). Two weaknesses, which Cohen does not espy, deserve brief attention.

First, it is not clear that Cohen can justifiably speak of "progress" or "development" in the flow of history. His defense of Marxism is not tied to any principle of unchangingly manifested wants; he emphasizes, in fact, that "what people need or want is not constant in history. . . . [I]t is a Marxian insistence, and a sound one, that needs expand in history, and undergo changes of character" (KMTH, 59). (Subsequently, he states that "man is a mammal, with a definite biological constitution, which evolves hardly at all in some central respects" [KMTH, 151]. However, he is thus writing about general need rather than the specific instantiations thereof—i.e., about "[h]uman need, whatever may be its historically various content" [KMTH, 152].) But as soon as the expression of basic needs is relativized, we cannot confidently rank periods according to their greater or lesser productivity, since comparing the productivity of one age with that of a much earlier or later time requires a steady background—of *particular* needs—against which products take on the character of "goods." When the backgrounds become too disparate, the productive outputs will become largely incommensurable. Even if one knows that a society *A* can produce greater quantities of most services and things than a society *B*, one cannot with certitude know where the productive forces are more advanced. For the latter determination, we must make an additional assessment that would enable us to pin down, in each society, those things and actions that can rightly be deemed productive. Any such assessment would base its findings on the needs that characterize each one of the social systems. If the societal sets of needs do not extensively overlap, and if the differences in the needs do not all occur within lines of output where society *A* enjoys the upper hand, we shall be disqualified from making a neat quantitative judgment of economic superiority, for we must then take into account the space within which goods (and thus productivity) are defined. To be sure, as Cohen declares in his response to a partly similar criticism (KMTH, 59–62), the present point will most likely not attain much practical import. Nonetheless, a more thoroughgoing and more sophisticated variant of this problem—which will be explored in the second half of Part Two—could have grim consequences, not least of which is a challenge to the dichotomy between practical and conceptual importance.

Chief among the remaining weaknesses of the argument that Cohen propounds is its attempted divorce of blindness from insight. In Cohen's schema, the validity of self-knowledge (and the efficacy of actions based on such knowledge) must be construed as something that we can presuppose generally. However problematic this view may be in the case of an individual agent, it becomes even more clearly so when we consider collective actions. Even within the analytic philosopher's unpacked view of subjectivity, "there seems no reason to expect 'invisible hands' to predominate over 'prisoner's dilemmas' or other structural arrangements that generate undesirable outcomes from individually rational actions."[25] Aside from the problems of collective action, one always must take into account the fervid resistances of entrenched groups. As Jon Elster maintains, "the general interests of society do not create their own fulfillment."[26]

Cohen does recognize the problem of unintended consequences

(KMTH, 153)—though he remains complacent about dislodging entrenched groups (KMTH, 158–59, 292–93)—and he admits that a straightforward response would ultimately lead him to beg the question when he argues for the Primacy Thesis (KMTH, 153). As a result, he opts for a rather curious *in*direct reply by stating that very few societies replace good productive forces with forces of inferior quality (KMTH, 153–54). Regression occurs only in extreme instances, such as natural calamities, whereas progress has occurred much more frequently. This, says Cohen, should induce us to re-evaluate the significance of his explanation, which had seemed to be left in doubt by the lurking "shadow between what reason suggests and what society does" (KMTH, 153). (Quite appropriate is his choice of metaphors; the shadow represents the inevitable elusiveness of that which subjectivity tries to master.) Cohen argues that if we credit his assumptions as weighty, we shall have "a superior account of the marked lack of regression in productive power we have just been emphasizing." Cohen concludes from this that his explanation "ha[s] more weight than we came to fear" (KMTH, 154). Hence, his proposal of the Development Thesis has in large part been vindicated.

If we may have recourse to a standard criterion of analytic parlance—the criterion of validity—we may pronounce Cohen's argument invalid. The crucial step in his latest strategy is the following conditional premise: if his explanatory model is deemed weighty, it will amount to a better explanation of productive development than an explanation that focuses on people's inertia. When one infers from this premise that we again have good grounds for trusting in the veracity of Cohen's explanation, the inference will have opened the door to every explanation that one might care to suggest. Consider, for example, a theory that an omnipotent evil genius controls our minds and impels us to enhance our productive power incessantly. If that hypothesis is deemed weighty, then *ipso facto* we have affirmed as true a powerful explanation of the progress that Cohen sees. But most people would nonetheless shrink from looking upon the evil-genius supposition as weighty. They would distinguish weight or *credibility* from explanational *power*. In other words, the credibility of the antecedent in a conditional premise of the aforesaid type—"if *X* is true, then *Y* can readily be explained by *X*"—cannot ever be deduced from (or even slightly affected by) the status of the conditional as a whole. So long as the consequent is true, the truth of the antecedent cannot have any bearing upon the truth of the whole claim. Cohen cannot escape from having to wrestle with the query posed by one of his more astute critics: are invisible hands more common and more important than prisoners' dilemmas?[27] The truth of Cohen's explanatory model—which will turn, in large part, on the solution to that query—must be established on its own merits, for it can scarcely be derived from a conditional claim whose truth does not depend on the truth of any part of the explanation.

2. *The Primacy Thesis*

Cohen employs two major starting points to ground his Primacy Thesis. In addition to the Development Thesis, which "provides the needed supplementation" to his other starting point, he takes as a central premise the view that "a given level of productive power is compatible only with a certain type, or certain types, of economic structure."[28] Enough has been said already about the "gaps" in the Development Thesis.[29] Let us look at the other premise, which concerns what I previously referred to as the connection between stages of development and the optimality of particular economic structures. Cohen tries to resolve the difficulties which surround that connection (KMTH, 175–215), though he confines himself to a study of the capitalist economic structure; as he admits with disarming frankness (KMTH, 199–201), his approach has distinctly limited application to bygone eras.

We shall not examine the details—or even the broad outlines—of Cohen's chapter on "The Productive Forces and Capitalism." Rather, four very brief remarks may serve to highlight the inconclusiveness of Cohen's pronouncements. (1) Cohen appears to be at odds with himself about the standard of argument that he would approve as sound for the type of explanation he is proposing. On the one hand, he concedes that "[n]o abstract proof will show that slavery and production for the expansion of exchange-value are opposed in tendency. . . . There would be no incompatibility between capitalism and docile slaves at work on advanced productive forces: twentieth-century dystopian fantasies are internally consistent" (KMTH, 190, 192). For the most part, Cohen adheres to the relaxed standard of argument implied in these sentences. His accounts of the unique tendency of capitalism to promote free labor and economic growth are clever, sweeping, highly conjectural, and (to some extent) self-doubting, in the manner of high-quality newspaper editorials.[30] On the other hand, Cohen criticizes Max Weber for offering a surmisal about the conflicts between capital accumulation and slavery; the soundness of Weber's argument, according to Cohen, "depends on circumstances. But nothing so circumstantial can provide a reason of principle against a union of slavery and capital accumulation" (KMTH, 191). Readers may be excused for wondering where this animadversion leaves Cohen's own hypotheses.

(2) Cohen's often persuasive reasons for finding an inconsistency between large-scale economic development and unfree labor are open to a huge counterexample, one to which Cohen—as a loyal Marxist—remains blind. From the late 1930s to the mid-1950s, the Soviet Union underwent often rapid growth in some lines of output with a regime

of work that was much closer to slavery than to free contract (even if we acknowledge the brutal force that, in a manifest or a latent form, will suffuse and undergird every system of "free" contract).[31] Not always does Marxism in practice square with Marxism in theory.

(3) Cohen moves at times from attacking one position to attacking another, in a way that leaves him vanquishing straw men. For example, when trying to explain the coexistence of serfdom and the accumulation of capital within Eastern Europe at the end of the Middle Ages, Cohen insists that the reduction of Eastern peasants to serfdom "embarrasses thesis (h) [i.e., the thesis that 'if production is for the sake of accumulating capital, the producers are free labourers'] only if [the reduction of the peasants] was largely due to a heightened pursuit of exchange-value" (KMTH, 188). Here Cohen commits an *ignoratio elenchi*. What he has to discredit is not a causal claim—that serfdom was largely *due* to the heightened quest for exchange-value—but a more modest view that serfdom did not *rule out* an expanded level of capital accumulation. By trying to force his critics into defending causal theses, Cohen diverts attention from the issue at hand: whether accumulation of capital may consort with multiple forms of labor. One can assume, *pace* Cohen, that a multiplicity of such forms are indeed possible, without hoping to account for specific forms by reference to the accumulation itself.

(4) Cohen makes assumptions about human behavior that are not easily reconciled with each other. To see this, we must first look at one of his thought experiments. While arguing that a system of free labor requires capital accumulation, he pictures a society in which landlords compensate proletarians not with money but with part of the product of their labor (e.g., rations of dairy products and meat) as well as with some sort of abode. In such a state of affairs, each laborer is in essence a horizontally mobile serf; each works for whichever landlord she pleases, yet each is paid not in cash but in kind, and nothing is produced for exchange. Cohen declares that these arrangements will not last very long:

> [T]he landlords will seek good workers at minimum sacrifice to the consumption of their households. A tendency to compete for workers will arise. The rations consist of meat and wheat, and, at the outset, all farms produce both, for there is, *ex hypothesi,* no trade between them. But farms with a 'comparative advantage' in wheat and meat production respectively will be disposed to swap products, if only in order to offer an enhanced basket of rations, and thus tempt good labour away from other farms. With enough development of such trade, production with a view to expanding the stock of exchange-value would become the norm. [KMTH, 184.]

This scenario sits uneasily with remarks made a dozen pages later. There Cohen seeks to demonstrate that pre-capitalist economic structures will not promote development systematically in the same way that a capitalist structure will. He contends that, in a pre-capitalist social form, "production will not be for the accumulation of value . . . , and the only point of wealth will be 'enjoyment.' The exploiter will want the producer's surplus for the sake of its use-value." He then maintains that the pre-capitalist exploiter "will, accordingly, be content to extract a limited surplus only, since there is a ceiling to the amount of use-value he may sanely desire and feasibly dispose of" (KMTH, 195). Insatiable desire is now viewed as exceptional and extravagant, whereas it amounted earlier to a natural drive that would always make itself felt. Despite Cohen's theory of a transhistorical human nature, one cannot avoid gaining the impression that in his work there *are* shifts in the basic features of human life—whenever his argument is served thereby.

3. *Primacy and Mutual Influence*

Among Cohen's great accomplishments, none of them is more brilliant than his laying to rest confusion over the combined Marxian theses that (1) the productive relations in a given society are explained, for the most part, by the level of its productive forces, and (2) productive relations exercise a vast influence on productive forces in everyday life. A tempting reaction to these claims is to judge them mutually exclusive and to disallow one of them (more often the first). Such is the tenor of remarks made by Sidney Hook that "social relations of production . . . cannot . . . be regarded as the automatic reflection of technology. On the contrary, the development of technology is itself often dependent upon the system of social relationships in which it is found."[32] Cohen makes clear how oversimplified such a response is. He argues that the prime link between productive forces and the productive relations is a functional one; that is, relations crop up as a particular scheme *because* that scheme suits the further development of the forces. He explains:

> The proposition that the production relations condition the development of the productive forces is, it should now be clear, not only compatible with, but entailed by, what we assert as the most important way in which the forces determine the relations. The effect of the relations on the forces is emphasized in our reading of the primacy thesis. It is that effect which explains the nature of the relations, why they are as they are. The forces would not develop as they do were the relations different, but that is *why* the relations are not different—because relations of the given kind suit the development of the forces. [KMTH, 161.]

Cohen thus seemingly transfigures what had been viewed by some people as one of Marxism's glaring faults into one of its great strengths. Far from sapping the primacy of the forces, the influence of relations will be a part, an integral part, of any such primacy.

D. The Problem of Legality

The last portion of Cohen's book to be outlined here is his treatment of the base/superstructure relation. Specifically, we shall explore his analysis of the interfolding between legal systems and economic structures; this intertwining raises the so-called problem of legality, which Cohen sets out to solve in the eighth chapter of his book (KMTH, 216–48). Since his treatment of law will be criticized presently at some length, only its most general contours will at this point be limned.

Cohen starts, as he elsewhere does, with some definitions. He brands as "superstructural" all noneconomic institutions whose workings can be explained by the needs and workings of the productive relations (KMTH, 216). He then asserts that noneconomic institutions are largely superstructural—which means, of course, that noneconomic institutions can largely be explained by the needs of the productive relations that underlie them (KMTH, 217). (Note the ambiguity, which will not be of direct concern here, between [1] the claim that *most* noneconomic institutions are *wholly* called forth by the needs of the productive relations and [2] the claim that *all* noneconomic institutions are *in large part* called forth by the needs of the productive relations. Cohen generally seems to opt for the milder half of each claim, and he therefore "views with comparative equanimity the possibility that art [along with certain other noneconomic practices] is out of step with the economy."[33])

Given the premise that most noneconomic institutions are largely superstructural, one might think to discover unidirectional causation tying the economic arrangements to the rest of society. Yet for at least one noneconomic institution, unidirectional causality seems very much out of place. Since the legal system is the provenience of the rights that make up the economic structure, one can scarcely deny legal institutions some sort of causal role. Indeed, the problem can be pushed even a step further: not only must legal practices be assigned a substantial causative role, but it is far from clear that one can even distinguish them, satisfyingly, from the economic base on which they supposedly have grounded themselves. As Cohen asks: "[H]ow can [legal systems and economic structures] fail to be mixed up when the economic structure is *defined* in legal terms? And is not such a definition mandatory, since the structure of an economy is (or at least includes) a structure of ownership?" (KMTH, 218).

To his own questions Cohen gives an ingenious answer. He proposes to substitute a new argot for the legal terms that are usually employed in describing the production relations. This matching language, which must be free of all juridical words, then can be employed to characterize economic structures that will be separate, in principle, from their carapaces of law.[34] Here, then, is Cohen's formula for the substitution of a nonlegal vocabulary: "[W]e can transform any phrase of the form 'the right to ϕ' into a phrase which denotes a power by dropping the word 'right' and replacing it by the word 'power.' Let us call the power the new phrase denotes a power which *matches* the right denoted by the original phrase" (KMTH, 219). All talk of "rights" or "ownership" is hereafter to be jettisoned and replaced with a vocabulary of "powers" and "control." Only the latter terms may be applied to the economic structure (in contrast with the juridical superstructure, which is of course still composed of rights).

Cohen's powers do not entail the rights that they match, nor do the rights entail the powers. Only the enjoyment of a *legitimate* power will comprise the enjoyment of its matching right, and only the enjoyment of an *effective* right includes the enjoyment of the power it matches. Cohen elaborates the distinction as follows:

> [A] man has the power to ϕ if and only if he is able to ϕ, where 'able' is non-normative. 'Able' is used normatively when 'He is not able to ϕ' may be true even though he is ϕ-ing, a logical feature of legal and moral uses of 'able.' Where 'able' is non-normative, 'He is ϕ-ing' entails 'He is able to ϕ.' [KMTH, 220.]

Having pried loose the facts of economic relationships from the norms of legal systems, Cohen proceeds to argue that those facts and those norms are functionally intertwined, very much like productive forces and production relations. Modes of property rise and fall insofar as they promote or hinder the evolution and stability of productive relations (which are in turn demanded by the productive forces). Legal structures take certain shapes because their economic foundations have obliged them to do so. Cohen specifies the exact way in which law serves to bolster the productive relations:

> In human society might frequently requires right in order to operate or even to be constituted. Might without right may be impossible, inefficient, or unstable. Powers over productive forces are a case in point. Their exercise is less secure when it is not legal. So, for efficiency and good order, production relations require the sanction of property relations. [KMTH, 231.]

It is the so-called legitimating effect of legal systems to which Cohen adverts here. Because the authoritativeness of law tends to generate acquiescence, and because gulfs between law and fact can breed cynicism and unrest, the stamp of legality is a clear boon for anyone hoping to initiate or entrench a given set of relations.[35] (Somewhat strangely,

Cohen declines to add that enforcement mechanisms of the state will uphold relations far more effectively when aligned with them than when arrayed against them.)

In a law-based social order, each person holds whatever powers she does by virtue of holding rights that match them. Such is Cohen's definition of the word "lawful" (KMTH, 232). One thus might infer that law assumes priority over the nonlegal relations of production. To infer that priority, however, one would be ending the analysis too soon. Legal rights will create access to corresponding powers, but they provide such access *because* they thereby entrench those powers more firmly. One must indeed comply with the legal system to obtain a place in the economic structure, but the legal system is as it is *because* it helps to sustain the economic structure that matches it. "Men do get their powers from their rights, but in a sense which is not only allowed but demanded by the way historical materialism explains rights by reference to powers."[36]

Part Two. Marxism and Textuality

Though the preceding Part contained more than a few critical observations, its basic purpose was to provide a reasonably fair outline of the approach to Marxism that Cohen champions. This Part will be more adventurously and more explicitly confrontational. Critical methods will be not so much brought to bear from a magisterial vantage point as they will be highlighted within the workings of Cohen's discourse. This process of highlighting will be imposed from the outside and revealed at the inside; that is to say, it will be both external and internal—and therefore neither one nor the other.[37] Disruptions and paradoxes in Cohen's work will extend to the discussion that brings them out. Nor is this a contingency that might be averted through greater caution.

Each of the two main sections in this Part will launch a critique of aspects of Cohen's arguments that have not been sufficiently thought out. Again, we are not now dealing with contingencies. If certain aporias have escaped Cohen's reflection, that is because "the whole of [his] philosophical conceptualization . . . is designed to leave in the domain of the unthinkable the very thing that makes this conceptualization possible [and therefore impossible]."[38] His blindness necessarily follows upon his insights, and puts them radically into question.

The first main section of this Part will interrogate Cohen's understanding of legal discourse. His conception of law will be at issue as we probe the apparent rigor of his theory of base/superstructure relationships. His approach will not be simply destroyed, but will be resituated in a network of queries that can highlight a certain fissure between his aspirations and his performance. The latter main section of this Part is more sweeping and deconstructive. Therein, we shall challenge Cohen's whole enterprise of singling out the productive forces as the prime mover of social life. His theses will come unraveled upon being articulated, because of their incompatibility with the chief assumptions from which they spring, and because of the dislocating uncanniness of articulation itself. As was mentioned earlier, different facets of Cohen's texts do not square well with one another. We shall plumb this disturbing heterogeneousness by emphasizing the textuality of Cohen's Marxism. Even more daringly than the first section, the latter half of Part Two will dislocate and resituate Cohen's work—rather than attempt to destroy it once and for all time.

Between the two principal critiques in this Part there are no obvious ties. Neither must depend on the other for its critical leverage. Nonetheless, the critiques eventually join forces, if only in a limited way. Our exploration of the disruptive power of law in Cohen's work can be put to some good use near the end of the subsequent critique of his so-called Primacy Thesis. In a brisk though not unimportant fashion, my neo-Realist critique of Cohen's jurisprudence will aid my deconstructive critique of his more general philosophy—in an approach whose task is not so much to demolish as to decenter.

A. The Facts of Law

Perhaps the most striking feature of Cohen's bold attempt to resolve the problem of legality is a certain absence that organizes and dominates the seeming presence of his solution. Nowhere at all does Cohen—who is hardly averse to multiple definitions—provide any explicit statement of what he means by "legality." *Évidemment*, the word is for him too simple to warrant a full-fledged definition. Like the category of "persons" (KMTH, 32), the word "law" amounts to one of his basic tools that must be plied without further grounding if he is to say anything at all. Such lacunae always involve danger, and we shall find that Cohen was unwise to evade the issue that has figured so prominently in jurisprudence: *viz.*, what is law? By tracing Cohen's scattered remarks on law and government, we shall see that he has addressed this query (by implication) along lines inimical to his efforts at shoring up a dichotomy between base and superstructure. Cohen has committed himself to a neo-Realist position that will render utterly problematic the deep structure of social life, the deep structure of law, and the purported difference between the two.

After staking out Cohen's vantage point—his unwitting vantage point—we shall look more closely at the attractions and shortcomings of neo-

Realism. While avoiding the most naive conceptions of language that accompany other jurisprudential standpoints, the neo-Realist perspective opens up an array of difficulties, some of which might be seized upon by Cohen as evidence that the view ascribed to him is not coherent or plausible enough to be entertained by anyone. He will not, however, escape quite so easily. We shall agree that neo-Realism cannot stand up to critical probing, but we shall scarcely conclude that Cohen profits thereby. Two responses present themselves to a neo-Realist under attack, and they are both devastating to the defense of Marxism that Cohen hopes to provide. If Cohen tries to salvage his argument by ruling out one possible reading of it, he will only bring to prominence the aporias that integrate and disintegrate his efforts.

1. *Law, Legitimacy, and State Action*

The aforementioned concern by Cohen to sever networks of law from economic structures is manifest in the phrasing with which he analyzes legality. For that purpose, his foremost analytical category is one often employed by social scientists to demarcate the public realm from the private sphere: "legitimacy."[39] It is the possession of "legitimate" powers that entails the possession of the rights matched by them (KMTH, 219). Likewise, a landowner can call upon the "legitimate authorities" to protect her holdings (KMTH, 223). Under Cohen's functionalist interpretation of Marxism, the role of law is to "legitimate" powers (KMTH, 231).

Now, the meaning of "legitimacy" is in no way self-evident. Left unadorned, the term might seem to push us into a circle—at the least, a circle of etymology—when put forward as a criterion for assessing law. (About this circle more will be said later.) Cohen thus recognizes the need to gloss his use of the word. At one point, he highlights certain affinities between legal discourses and ethics; in a passage quoted above, he points to what he calls a "logical feature" shared by moral and juridical propositions. Had he gone further and conflated those two genres of discourse, he would have posed no real problems for our critique, though he would have made it a few steps longer by forcing us to draw out a neo-pragmatist account of morality from his texts. In any case, Cohen usually does not make much of resemblances between law and ethics, perhaps partly because his socialist leanings have attuned him to the varied injustices of all hitherto existing legal arrangements, and perhaps because he is very much aware that all (or virtually all) actions—including the most brutal force—involve legitimating beliefs: "[H]uman beings are so constituted that they need to believe, at least from time to time, that what they are doing is morally right."[40]

Cohen's use of the concept of "legitimacy" therefore stems, by and large, not from a desire to collapse law into ethics but from a much more critical standpoint. His general analysis, like his specific language, takes its life from Weberian springs. Not only did Max Weber lay out a famed typology of "legitimate" domination,[41] but he employed the notion of "legitimacy" in order to express the two sides of *law-based* domination (in the form of the modern state). On the one hand, legal authority takes shape as "a consistent system of abstract rules" within which all legitimate commands "are given in the name of the impersonal norm rather than in the name of a personal authority."[42] On the other hand, the state is defined by Weber as an institution that has achieved "a monopoly of the legitimate use of physical force within a given territory."[43]

Legitimacy thus marks the two characteristic elements of legal authority (or state power): its abstract, rule-governed rationality and its ultimate reliance on brute coercion. In noting these two dimensions of state power, we need not pause—at this stage—to deconstruct Weber's formalistic conception of legality.[44] More relevant for now is the closeness of this Weberian analytical scheme to that put forward by Cohen. Like Weber, Cohen perceives law as a congeries of rules that are decreed and enforced by mechanisms of state authority. This becomes clearest in the many examples he provides to illustrate causal links between production relations and property relations (KMTH, 226–29). In every case, he shows that he has in mind statutory rules dealing with property and contract whenever he is writing about "law." Such statutes will generally be upheld (when necessary) by a coercive arm of the state, as Cohen realizes when mentioning the "legal owner of . . . land *whose tenure is protected by the legitimate authorities.*"[45]

A. LAW AND CONQUEST

Thus far, my account of Cohen's legal theory may seem unexceptionable and unexceptional. In a series of steps, however, we shall find just how much his theory has broken down. In the first place, we shall have to throw doubt on one of his important though brief examples of the law's ratification of ostensibly nonlegal production networks. He argues:

> Sometimes production relations are established without legal sanction, which they acquire at a later time. A conquering army might subject a defeated peasantry to new production relations, by enforcing a set of decisions which have no legislative or other legal backing. Once the relations have endured for a certain period, they will probably acquire the support of legal authority. The two stages in the aftermath of the conquest illustrate the distinction between production relations and the property relations which typically—but not necessarily—accompany them. [KMTH, 224–25.]

This description is more than slightly puzzling. If we call to mind the two aspects of domination-through-law, we can discover them in the foregoing scenario.

i. *Conquest as "Legitimate" Violence.* Presumably, the large element of brute force involved in successful military conquest is not a fact of which most people would need convincing. To the degree that conquest has been solidified, the invading army will enjoy a "monopoly of the legitimate use of physical force within a given territory." Legitimacy attaches to the outright force of the conqueror in at least two relevant ways. First, those perpetrating the violence will have acted on a presumed need for violence, even if their actions stem more from fear than from any feelings of ethical correctness or from any sense of official duty (though we have no reason to disallow the strength of these last two types of motives, as Cohen makes quite plain in his comment quoted above regarding the tendency of all people to rationalize their conduct). As Weber observed, those who put domination into effect are "bound by obedience to the power-holder [though] not alone by the concept of legitimacy. . . . The power-holder must be able to count on the obedience of the staff members, officials, or whoever else they may be."[46] Each subaltern obeys the power-holders *as if* she deems their power to be legitimate. Her real motives may consist in prudence or fear—in lieu of perceptions of legitimacy—but such a motivational pattern can prevail in *any* system of law. When soldiers behave *as if* they feel their superiors' commands are legitimate, then an underlying dearth of felt legitimateness will not *per se* have debarred the soldiers' actions from making up a regime of law. *No* legal system can ensure that its agents truly feel the sense of legitimacy that their official conduct will have bespoken. (This last point, stated more sweepingly in reference to non-officials, will be fleshed out in the next paragraph.)

A second way in which the violence of military conquest involves legitimacy will lie in the actions (or, what amounts to just the same thing, the *in*actions) of those upon whom the violence is inflicted. Their nonresistance or their futile resistance leaves the conqueror as the supreme wielder of force within the relevant territory. Indeed—as has been suggested above—if the mode of conquest has been brought to fruition, the invader will emerge as the *only* wielder of systematic force in the territory. This means that the populace submits to the conqueror's decisions as if those decisions have been deemed morally justifiable. To be sure, the decisions might not be morally acceptable in the least; they *might* be followed only because the sole alternative to obedience would be subjection to punishment too dire to be hazarded. But, as has been noted with regard to the agents of the law, a potential lack of felt legitimateness will overhang every possible legal system. As H. L. A. Hart concedes, an ordinary person may think of law "only as something demanding action . . . under threat of penalty; he may obey it out of fear of the consequences, or from inertia, without thinking of himself or others as having an obligation to do so and without being disposed to criticize either himself or others for deviations."[47] The reasons for the necessary persistence of a *potential* lack of legitimacy cannot be treated at length here—nor need they be, for I have discussed them at length already, in Chapter 1. Suffice it now to re-emphasize that the observed meaning and the true intention of any statement or any deed are perforce detachable. "[T]he intention which animates utterance will never be completely present in itself and its content. The iteration which structures it a priori introduces an essential dehiscence and demarcation."[48] As a result of the ineradicable potential for a noncoincidence between truth and meaning, Cohen will not discover in military conquest an absence of perceived legitimacy that might not also afflict legal systems generally regarded as legal systems (such as those now or recently in Czechoslovakia, South Africa, and China). In each case, people submit to rules as if those rules were morally justifiable; in each case, there may exist huge gaps between public order and private sentiment. *Pace* the Gospels, not everything that comes from the mouth is from the heart. Cohen has not proved that the mouths of conquered peasants are untrustworthy in ways that would not also be true of the mouths of other people. (Lest the argument in this paragraph seem too close to a positivist position,[49] the autocritique of neo-Realism that will be presented shortly is, among other things, a frontal challenge to all forms of empiricism.)

ii. *The Regularities of Conquest.* Let us look at the other aspect of legal domination: the exercise of power and the attendant structuring of society through general standards and rules. Had Cohen confronted us with examples of frenzied, indiscriminate depredation, we might have faced severe difficulties at this point. Even then, the difficulties would not have been insurmountable; chaotic transgression can establish itself as such exclusively through a process of differentiation (from law and order) that confirms what it exceeds in the very act of exceeding it.[50] As things stand, however, Cohen has made our present line of attack more easy. He tells us that the conquering army will "subject a defeated peasantry to new production relations" (KMTH, 224). Whatever may be the content of the new production relations, and whatever the exact methods used to bring them about, they never could have come into place without a system of rules and regularities, no matter how brutally enforced these are. Since economic structures by definition will comprise patterned duties, regularized roles, and carefully defined expectations, those who wish to transform prevailing structures cannot just set mischief afoot to take what course it will. The imposing of economic relations may be as harsh as club law, but—as Marx recognized—"club law is also law."[51] Codification, far from being a baptismal event, will have occurred already in the form of patterns imposed by conquest.

B. THE REALISM OF NEO-REALISM

For the second step in the challenge to Cohen's theory of law, we turn now to some of the most famous work in the rather loosely defined canon of American Legal Realism. To the Realists—particularly to Morris Cohen and Robert Hale—conventional views of public power and private right seemed naive and rigid.[52] In response, these scholars put radically into question the main grounds on which public/private distinctions had been built. They rejected the belief that the private sphere is unimplicated in the punitive violence that is normally associated with governmental authority. They argued, for example, that private actors possessed of property rights and contract rights are wielding state power as surely and as coercively as the executive agents who implement the commands of public lawmakers. In each case, someone has control over the disposition of certain assets, be they tangible or intangible. Both the private owner and the public official can expect to receive backing, if necessary, from the exertion of state power. Like an official of the state, an owner can forcibly exclude other people from having any say in the key choices that affect the use of whatever assets the owner lawfully holds. To be sure, neither public power nor private power is absolute; both the owner and the official face a variety of curtailments on the extent to which they can do whatever they please. Nonetheless, within the discretion granted, the commissar and the landowner reign supreme, owing to their ability to call on state force. Private rights of contract and property will amount, then, to public powers that have been delegated and given substance by the coercive authority of the state. Blood drips from free markets, which are best seen as elaborate structures of public violence and sovereignty. The private realm is always already public.

G. A. Cohen, it seems, would be quite receptive to the Realist position tersely summarized here. Indeed, in his lecture "Freedom, Justice and Capitalism," he advances arguments similar to those propounded by Hale and Morris Cohen. He criticizes defenders of the capitalist economic system who "see the freedom which is intrinsic to capitalism, but [who] do not give proper notice to the constraint which necessarily accompanies it" ("Freedom," 8). Defining the institution of private property as "a particular way of distributing freedom *and unfreedom*" ("Freedom," 9), Cohen makes clear that capitalist unfreedom derives from the enforcing of property and contract rights by public authorities.

> If the state prevents me from doing something I want to do, it evidently places a constraint on my freedom. Suppose, then, that I want to perform an action which involves a legally prohibited use of your property. . . . If I now try to do this thing I want to do, the chances are that the state will intervene on your behalf. If it does, I shall suffer a constraint on my freedom. The same goes for all unpermitted uses of a piece of private property by those who do not own it. ["Freedom," 9.]

Like the Realists, Cohen has descried public coercion—whether actual or latent—throughout the operations of "private" enterprise and "free" markets. He has no reason to cavil at the approach adopted by Hale and Morris Cohen, for (as sketched here) it is entirely compatible with his own theory. After all, G. A. Cohen splits the enforcement of production relations from the content thereof (KMTH, 223–24); he can thus preserve his two-tiered analysis of law by placing the *content* of production relations in his nonjuridical powers, and by assigning to legal claims the role of *enforcing* and consolidating those powers. Cohen's functionalism need not be gravely jeopardized by his view that law-based coercion is much more prominent—indeed, pervasive—than capitalist ideologues may think. If we define "law" expansively to include the ideological effects of legal relations,[53] Cohen should agree that law is the sole important device through which production relations are secured. Such a concession would apparently not be a concession at all, since it would seem to cause no damage to the coherence of his general approach. By portraying law as the sole *important* means of stability, the concession allows for the emergence of *un*important means outside law. As we are about to find, the Realists seem to have provided an opening that allows Cohen to fall back from their insights even as he embraces them. To bring about any real damage, we have to move from Realism to neo-Realism.

C. REALISM EXTENDED

Thus far, we have drawn from Cohen's texts a sophisticated argument that law has served as the lone important means of giving stability to the relations of production. We must now endeavor to do away with the word "important" (and make law the *lone* means, period), so that we can cast doubt on the dichotomy Cohen sees between content and enforcement. What has to be placed in question is yet another dichotomy, between that which the law does and that which the law does not do. If, as Clare Dalton writes, "law is present [even] in its statement[s] of non-intervention,"[54] then attempts to mark off a space for non-juridical powers will inevitably confirm their own failure.

Cohen's main feat is the delimitation of sets of economic relationships that are analytically independent of the structures of law that form their mantles. Though legal systems and economic relationships are interwoven too firmly to be studied in isolation, it may nevertheless seem that Cohen has "submitted a method of *conceiving* the economic structure which excludes from it the legal, moral, and political relationships of men" (KMTH, 235). How has he accomplished this remarkable feat? On what assumptions has he relied to find precincts of economic activity that, at least in principle, take shape beyond the assorted patterns of state-imposed coercion and ideology?

Implicitly aligning himself with the Legal Realists in their assault on public/private distinctions, Cohen must come up with a way to see outside the apparently omnipresent structuring mechanisms of public power.

This he purports to do through several examples in which legal relations and production relations either come into conflict or in other ways fail to coincide. Sometimes economic relationships burst through antiquated legal restrictions till the latter have been eventually transformed, so that harmony between the two is restored. In other cases, a legal system can manage to prevent the growth of illicit economic practices, but is "sooner or later changed, so that new production relations can be established." (Here, no gaps arise between legal evolution and economic developments, but Cohen's tracing of causal links—i.e., his use of the phrase "so that"—depends through and through on the *possibility* of such gaps.) At still other times, no law is flouted by new productive relations, but fresh laws are nevertheless enacted to give the new situation a legal blessing (KMTH, 225–29).

Common to the characterizations of these examples is a retreat from the Realist doctrine that private latitude is always already public force. To effect this backsliding from Realism—for which the dichotomy between content and enforcement has been a path—Cohen trades on a key disjuncture between actions and omissions, between what the law does and what it does not do. Each time there is a perceived discontinuity between legal relations and productive relations, it occurs because of the law's limited reach. Certain activities are beyond the law, either because the legal authorities do not effectively interdict them, or because the law has not spoken (or has not spoken clearly) on the precise matters involved. In either case, the law's failure to act is what makes room for the nonlegal.

Legal Realists did not fully address the problem of actions and omissions. Or, at least, they did not deal with all aspects of the problem that I am raising here. Hohfeld and his successors did indeed spurn the act/omission dichotomy when they classified privileges and no-rights as *legal* elements; nonetheless, they did not extend their critical outlook to examine unopposed violations, which figure so conspicuously in Cohen's Marxist approach to law.[55] In what follows, then, we shall be widening—not abandoning—the Realist critique of public/private distinctions.

Of primary interest is what Cohen himself has said about the dichotomy between actions and inactions. Let us first look, however, at the statements of a logician who is widely admired among the analytic philosophers. Writing in 1919, Gottlob Frege expressed his wariness in regard to the

> distinction between affirmative and negative thoughts. For logic at any rate such a distinction is wholly unnecessary; its ground must be sought outside logic. . . .
>
> What is more, it is by no means easy to state what is a negative judgment (thought). Consider the sentences 'Christ is immortal,' 'Christ

> lives forever,' 'Christ is not immortal,' 'Christ is mortal,' 'Christ does not live forever.' Now which of the thoughts we have here is affirmative, which negative?
>
> . . . Accordingly I am in favour of dropping the distinction between negative and affirmative judgments or thoughts until such time as we have a criterion enabling us to distinguish with certainty in any given case between a negative and an affirmative judgment. . . . For the present I still doubt whether this will be achieved.[56]

In light of my arguments in this section, Frege's view will cast doubt on Cohen's claim to have specified a "*logical* feature" of juridical propositions (i.e., the feature of potential discordance between *de jure* possibility and *de facto* possibility). Nonetheless, Cohen seems to uphold Frege's opinion—though without any specific reference—when he deals with the ostensible points of conflict between the Primacy Thesis and the observation by Marx that ruling classes in pre-capitalist societies frown on change, including changes in the productive forces (KMTH, 169–71). If such classes are so conservative, how can their rule possibly contribute to maximal development of the productive forces (as the Primacy Thesis says it should)? To defuse this apparent contradiction, Cohen resorts to an analogy. He asks that we focus on the claim that constitutional monarchies tend to further democratic ideals. He argues that someone who is taking this view will not have had to believe that "there is an activity, namely promoting democracy, in which constitutional monarchs engage" (KMTH, 170). Cohen's argument should be quoted at some length:

> [The person making the claim] could hold the subtle view that though . . . constitutional monarchs promote democracy, a constitutional monarch is likely to be an enemy of democracy; or the still subtler view which adds that it is because constitutional monarchs tend to be enemies of democracy that constitutional monarchs promote democracy. Again: someone who believes that a 'minimal state' promotes economic development does not believe that it engages in the activity of promoting economic development. His view is that its abstention from such activity is good for economic development.
>
> We say that the relations which obtain at a given time are the relations most suitable for the forces to develop at that time, given the level they have reached by that time. This entails that the relations, and the class they empower, promote the development of the forces, but, we may now add, in a sense which is compatible with what Marx says about pre-capitalist relations and classes. Having the relations in question, having that class in power, may be best for the development of the forces, even though the relations and the class pose many obstacles to their development. [KMTH, 170–71].

What Cohen has done here is to transcend the line between activity and inaction by looking at the main *effects* of behavior that a queen or king has adopted. A ruler can at times best promote democracy by doing her utmost to refrain from promoting it.

By the same line of thought, nonregulation is as much regulation as is regulation itself. Clare Dalton seems to have been right; the law can indeed be present by virtue of its absence. Just as democratic ideals can be promoted richly by governmental inaction, so a legal regime will be enforced through a policy of nonenforcement. By declining to intervene, the law will intervene *ipso facto*—for its policy of nonintervention will dictate certain effects that would not otherwise have obtained. There is no "outside" in which nonjuridical powers can take their shape, since everything that is not punished is authorized. All events lie within the sway of the law, which necessarily fosters everything it does not suppress. Once more, we see that codification will never serve as the baptismal event that Cohen's theory requires. Cohen has committed himself to holding that legal systems encompass all.

2. *Neo-Realism, Paradoxes, and Stories*

Perhaps at this point Cohen's best tack would be to assail the shortcomings of the position that has been highlighted in his texts. This could be a preliminary to refining his functionalist interpretation of Marxism. After all, if the neo-Realist standpoint—which, in the base/superstructure relationship, tolls the end of economistic functionalism—can be exposed as patently unacceptable, we might give credence more quickly to a later argument that would try to resurrect the seemingly dead functionalism. Hence, we should now look at one obvious line of criticism that might be raised by an analytic philosopher. As will be seen, neo-Realism does not ultimately survive intact, which is to say that it never was intact. Nevertheless, its disarticulation will scarcely warrant joy on the part of those in the analytic camp. Though survival intact is not to be hoped for, neo-Realism can still display a striking amount of life. The criticism advanced here will have pushed neo-Realist insights in two directions, neither of which can offer Cohen any assistance or reassurance. He will not be able to attack neo-Realism without highlighting the textuality of his own position.

An analytic philosopher might seize on uncurbed transgressions as an utterly unassimilated remainder in the neo-Realist account of law. Under the neo-Realist view, law governs *all* activities—not least those which it professes to brush aside. But if that is true, it would seem impossible to affirm that a given statute (say, a prohibition on jaywalking) is often violated though almost never enforced. If non-enforcement has been defined as authorization, then an unenforced law can never be violated. One would always have to conclude that a dormant ban on jaywalking, like the absence of a statute that deals with jaywalking, amounts indeed to official approbation of those who prance across streets with recklessness. At this point, the analytic philosopher will resort to his chief weapon: the first-person plural pronoun. He will say that "our" common intuitions demand the spurning of any claim that laws which are unenforced are consequently infrangible. He may even say, if he has read Wittgenstein or some Continental philosophy, that an indispensable precondition of the intelligibility of a given statute is its susceptibleness to being breached, quite apart from any measures of discipline that might be imposed on malefactors. It is sufficient that transgressions *can* be perceived and *are* perceived as transgressions. No punitive force is necessary; a gap always can still exist between law-in-writing and law-in-life.

To this critique proponents of neo-Realism may reply in at least two ways. The first is perhaps more sophisticated while the second is perhaps not as wooden, but the two are by no means incompatible. Be that as it may, one thing would appear certain: having unwittingly attached himself to the camp of the neo-Realists, Cohen cannot emerge without doing violence to his own theory.

A. THE DEFERRAL OF MEANING

For a first response, which can be worked out nicely in a structuralist or a Wittgensteinian argot, we must challenge Cohen's assumption that the wording of statutes is to some extent self-explanatory. Cohen has to rely on the existence of fairly definite statutory meanings that can then be compared with the realities of social and economic life. If such meanings did not prevail, it would make no sense—even on a theoretical plane—to try to sever legal relationships from nonjuridical powers, since the legal relationships would lack independent form. These meanings, moreover, have to be ascertainable wholly (or in large part) without regard to specific applications of rules and standards. If the language of legal rules will acquire meaning exclusively and essentially through particular applications, then the foregoing critique of neo-Realism was pointless: rifts will never open between law-in-writing and law-in-practice. (This is not necessarily to accuse Cohen of harboring a Platonic view of meaning. Even if Cohen were to become a hearty supporter of contextualist views, the present response would be entirely germane. For our current purpose, the perceived source and nature of linguistic determinacy will matter not.)

In response to the foregoing critique, a neo-Realist should fasten upon the naiveté of Cohen's implicit theory of language. Here we are returning to general arguments made in Chapter 1, in the remarks on frustrated closure and on structure/event antinomies. To a Wittgensteinian, it will seem that Cohen has endeavored to posit rules which can set bounds to the purview of their application. One of Wittgenstein's main concerns was to unsettle the commonsense idea that rules, if they are well drafted, will indeed dictate how and when they are to be applied. As Wittgenstein showed, a rule can never be carried far enough to stake out the sphere of its application.[57] This, as Chapter 1 stressed, is not because of the "ambiguity" of language, but because something will always be left out of a finite group of instructions: namely, guidance on how one should give effect to the instructions themselves. Each device for attaining closure can but bring forth new openness, because it will itself stand outside (as well as inside) the closure that it has brought about. Every additional instruction will have provoked a need for still more instructions, on how *it* is to be applied.[58]

Wittgenstein held that because rules are unavoidably indeterminate, they procure meaning only through application.[59] *Pace* Cohen, legal standards and rules gain content only as they become enforced or as they go unenforced. Without a process in which they can be given effect—and the "effect," of course, may be ineffectiveness—legal rules are as empty as Leibnizian concepts with no Lockean intuitions. Consequently, policemen who have failed to enforce a statute will have bestowed on it, thereby, a set of implicit qualifications that have authorized each instance of desuetude. In this way, no violation can go unpunished.

One might turn also to a structuralist vocabulary to achieve broadly similar conclusions, as was done in the first chapter. In this case, one would see legal rules as precisely formulated examples of the generative structures—the sundry generative structures—that shape the course of events. Such structures, and such rules, remain entirely abstract until they are concretized in the events that they govern. Until events of enforcement and nonenforcement rule out countless potential readings of the juridical structures from which they flow, those structures will always want definition and will always have yet to be determined. It is only in retrospect, for example, that the implicit qualifications needed to prescribe nonenforcement become accepted as a part of the statutory language. Structures exist, as such, only by becoming endowed with structure.

Most troublesome for the analytic philosopher are the paradoxes to which this neo-Realist response leads (and to which we devoted our attention in Chapter 1). A supporter of neo-Realism should not seek to resolve problems of meaning by upholding events as somehow more stable than the structures they constitute. Rather, the best course here is to highlight the never-ending seesaw between the structurality and the temporality of all meaning. Meaning is, as the existentialists have claimed, wholly a consequence of discrete acts (or, in Wittgensteinian terminology, discrete moves performed in language-games); but it resides *in toto* as well in rules and patterns that must precede those acts as the very source of their possibility. Events rely as completely on the structures they shape as do the structures rely on the events that give shape to them. Without structures, individual acts would be devoid of meaning, for there would be no patterns or regulated distinctions that allow meanings to be recognized. Intelligibility comes about through categories and systematical differentiations that provide the sole means by which events can receive their definition. The upshot of all this is that structures must antecede events, and events must forego structures. If language-games are indeed played, the "play" is paradoxical: each move has to have been performed already if its preconditions are to take shape. Cohen's view of meaning has proved to be not so much erroneous as both inescapable and impossible.

Cohen will thus compel the neo-Realist to highlight paradoxes that constitute and upheave all standpoints in regard to the location of meaning. Like the chains with which Aristaeus trapped Proteus, neo-Realism will more firmly entangle Cohen each time he endeavors to cast it off.

B. HERMENEUTIC CIRCLES

Though appropriate and persuasive at an abstract level, the first response of the neo-Realist may seem wooden. One may concede that paradoxes break loose when one looks squarely at some of Cohen's implicit starting points, yet one may nevertheless feel that the postulated critique of neo-Realism has not been fully answered thereby. It is of course true that widely shared interpretations of sundry texts (be they statutes, judicial holdings, or the general text of social and economic activity) cannot ever be grounded or strictly justified—that, in short, such interpretations always remain to be accounted for.[60] Notwithstanding that, there do appear to be regularized effects within the uncanny play of meaning-production. Specifically, it is pointless to deny that agreement often exists on the "plain meaning" of legal rules, and that the rules so interpreted can be held up against "real life" and can be tested for potency in bringing about expected patterns therein. Widespread agreement will be no less unstable, ultimately, than any other supposed bedrock of meaning; but to deny that such agreement ever exists would lead to an unintelligible and totally unconvincing narrative of social and economic life. A narrative that acknowledged no determinacy would always be its own first victim, as the most basic arguments against nihilistic versions of skepticism would apply with full force. Common sense, moreover, can be kept at bay for only so long, even when one concedes that "'everyday language' is not innocent or neutral. It is the language of Western metaphysics."[61] At least in some circumstances, it will be far more plausible to speak of unpunished violations than of implicit qualifications.

Does this mean, then, that we have revived Cohen's way of besting the problem of legality? The answer must be negative, for at least three reasons. First, even if Cohen could successfully throw doubt on the claims of neo-Realism, he would remain tethered to all those claims in the aspects of his theory that we have just considered. Second, as I have stressed, a position opposite to the neo-Realist position—quite as much as the neo-Realist standpoint itself—will hold plausibility just so long as it is kept at a mundane level, where the relationship between its assumptions and its conclusions is not carefully thought out. If neo-Realism can be successfully criticized, that is not because alternative theories can "resolve" the paradoxes discussed above. The matter is much more one of strategic impact than of "solutions."

Third—and here we must raise a point which was only touched on earlier and which will be studied at greater length in the next chapter—even if we disregard the preceding two reasons, Cohen still must provide a standard for determining what law is. Without an adequate definition of law, his theory of the base/superstructure relationship will founder sadly for want of any means to mark off bases from superstructures. Yet it is precisely this definition that eludes Cohen's valiant efforts. As we have seen, his resorting to "legitimacy" as an earmark of juristic phenomena will take us into a daunting circle, where the gods love piety because it is pious, and it is pious because they love it.[62] If Cohen tries to give substance to "legitimacy" by concentrating on state action, he will be no better off. Not only will he be heading forthwith toward neo-Realism, but he will have merely *displaced* rather than *dispelled* the problem of circularity. To separate publicly enforced rights from privately enjoyed powers, he will need to call on the very split between legal norms and nonlegal norms that the public/private duality was supposed to offer. Public enforcement, whether actual or potential, can be known as such (i.e., can be known as public) only when we have ascertained that it is being done by agents of legal institutions. Enforceable proscriptions and actual enforcement mechanisms are what they are, and do what they do, only in and with the seal of the law. Unless one already can differentiate legal norms and standards from nonlegal norms and standards, one cannot distinguish state action from private action, for the state is nothing else than the group of mechanisms by which the law is formulated, proclaimed, and given effect. A legal/nonlegal dyad is as much a presupposition as a product of public/private distinctions. More broadly, attempts to single out defining characteristics of any legal order must all get caught in frustrating circles. Consider Nigel Simmonds's critique of H. L. A. Hart, whose theory focuses on "official" behavior: "The central role that Hart gives to 'officials' in his theory is both striking and curious. Hart nowhere tells us just what an 'official' is or how we recognize one. Since we identify the *law* by reference to official behaviour (in the form of the rule of recognition) we cannot identify officials by reference to the law."[63] What Simmonds unearths here is one instance of the famous phenomenon dubbed the "hermeneutic circle": a whole (such as a whole legal system) can be known and described only through its parts, yet the parts in turn are dependent on the whole for their own identities. This aporia, which has figured prominently in many of the writings of Martin Heidegger and in the work of some of his greatest acolytes, will undo the rigor of Cohen's jurisprudence.[64] If a conception of "law" is to be brought into discourse, it cannot be left in a precomprehended or undifferentiated state; but it can be rescued from such a state, by being determined, only on pain of unrelenting and paradoxical circularity. (We shall return to this problem in the next chapter.) Even if one were to assume, absurdly, that a divine Being endowed the human mind with a latent concept of law, one still would meet the problem of circularity as one tried to account for any traffic between the latent precomprehension and the actual comprehension of human agents. Attaining self-presence is no less inconceivably problematic than arriving at other types of knowledge.[65]

In a certain sense, to be sure, Cohen is not really incapacitated by anything just said. He can continue to produce brilliant narratives of politico-economic life. Just as deconstruction leaves room for speech-act philosophy and structuralism,[66] an analysis that has highlighted circularity can leave room for a defense of Marxism and for a Marxist reading of history. That such projects will ultimately subvert their own claims, or beg their own questions, does not decrease their trenchancy in appropriate contexts—in particular, when they are competing against other persuasive versions of historical "truth," which will be subject to similar disruptions. What *does* seem out of the question now, however, is a return to the naiveté that permitted Cohen to denigrate the "readings" put forth by Hegel in comparison with the "theory" put forth by Marx. Though we cannot *simply* collapse theory into story-telling (since any such move would mean that "the difference in which [story-telling] took on its meaning breaks down"[67]), it is worthwhile, nonetheless, to reevaluate Cohen's project as one of artful narrative. Nor, it seems, would Cohen utterly disagree; in his accounts of functional explanation, he refers at least three times to the apparent need for heuristic "stories" whenever someone propounds a functionalist view (KMTH, 270, 286). Here, though not usually elsewhere, Cohen joins us in bringing into the foreground the status of his explanations as discourse. In so doing he has joined us, too, however reluctantly, in proposing that his account of law will beg all its questions yet still be able to yield powerful results.

B. Functionalist Marxism Deconstructed

Having scrutinized Cohen's theory of the base/superstructure relation, we turn now to his so-called Primacy Thesis, which encapsulates his view of the links between productive forces and the productive relations in which those forces abide. To an even greater degree than in the last section, the aim here is to plumb the textuality of the version of Marxism that Cohen advocates. By highlighting the unruliness of Cohen's discoursive medium, this section will place in doubt the fundaments of his texts, where discourse is regarded as a mere "medium." More properly than in the preceding section, our analytical strategies may here be called "deconstructive"—so long as we keep in mind that "properness" is one of the chief targets of deconstruction (even if, like the Hydra, "properness" regains strength through the very dislocation of being challenged).[68]

In the first subsection, we shall perceive a number of striking ways in which the discoursive texture of Cohen's work has made itself felt, sometimes in accordance with his intentions, sometimes strangely contrary thereto. A careful study of Cohen's language will set the mood for a general deconstruction of Marxist theory, at least as that theory is understood by Cohen. In the deconstructive critique set forth in the latter half of this section, Cohen's Marxism will be overturned and displaced and reinscribed into a vertiginous oscillation between pragmatism (or a view of knowledge as a matter of highly variable conventions) and philosophical realism (or a view of knowledge as the sensing and understanding of brute facts in the pre-existent natural and social worlds). Neither pole of this oscillation can triumph, for—as in any true paradox—each will have dismantled itself and have *become* the other by virtue of *excluding* and *disavowing* it.

Before we begin, however, three potential points of confusion should be cleared up, or at least warned against. First, language assumes a starring role in every part of this section, but the intended meaning of "language" will not hold still; it sometimes has a restricted and conventional scope but has at other times an unconventional, broader scope. Within its broader ambit, "language" refers to every system of categorization by which acts and phenomena are invested with their identities. Like the use of "interpretation" in Chapters 1 and 5, this expansive usage will comprise structures that are usually regarded as nonlinguistic—such as relations of production—as well as classificatory systems that are deemed "languages" in everyday parlance. It is mainly in the latter half of the section that this broad usage will have come into play. At any rate, one should generally have few problems in knowing where to distinguish the expansive meaning from the restricted meaning. Where statements would otherwise lie too far open to unproductive misreadings, the wide purview of "language" has been signaled prominently.

A second possible source of arid misinterpretations is the contingency and tenuousness of links between the two major subsections that follow. The first subsection ("Reality as Metaphor") does *not* undergird the second ("From Pragmatism to Deconstruction"); someone can reject arguments of the former while accepting the argument of the latter. Nevertheless, the former subsection will have helped to induce a mood appropriate for reading the latter subsection. By observing that Cohen intermittently underlines the importance of language in its narrow sense, the initial half of this section will have begun to show that texts must always be already submerged in forces that exceed them and overwhelm them. Having argued that Cohen's works quite frequently highlight the determining force of language, and having at least implied that *ainsi* they cut against their own principles of economic determinism, the first subsection below will have thus started to strip those principles of an air of reassuring self-mastery. In such a way, the analysis arguing that language *conventionally* understood has *now and then* been prioritized will fruitfully set the stage for the analysis showing that language *broadly* understood has been *systematically* (and unwittingly) privileged. But it is only in creating an atmosphere of hermeneutic suspicion that the former analysis connects with the later one. Nothing in the survey of Cohen's neo-pragmatist leanings will indispensably or directly shore up what follows: namely, the wholesale toppling and displacement of his materialism.

A third point that should be emphasized here is the uncanniness of the deconstructive critique in the latter half of this section. Because that critique highlights the self-subverting power of Cohen's Marxism, a defender of Cohen or of Marx will perhaps assume that deconstruction takes life from an idealist philosophy. Such a reading, like the equating of deconstruction with skepticism, grows from a desire to quash the truly vertiginous and discomforting movement of a deconstructive interrogation. Neither pragmatism nor any other mode of idealism, deconstructive philosophy will have comprehended idealism *and* materialism, and will always have already undone and reinscribed those positions. To be sure, the current section will emphasize the *idealist* grounding of *materialism* and will not have commensurately highlighted the *materialist* grounding of *idealism;* but that is a matter of strategic focus for an encounter with Marxist theory. Although this section will be posing a challenge to materialism, one could just as cogently marshal deconstructive techniques for a full-scale challenge to idealism. As was noted above, neither pole of an antinomical pendulation can ultimately emerge triumphant, for each pole has always lost by virtue of having always won.

1. Reality as Metaphor

A. COHEN'S APPARENT PRAGMATISM

Cohen's texts highlight the supreme importance of language in providing structure to that which we call "reality." They do this in a variety of ways, not least in some quite explicit statements. For example, near the end of his introductory chapter on the "images of history" in Hegelianism and Marxism, Cohen writes that "the entire national community sustains the independence at work in economic life but complements it by providing collective identity and culture, without which an economy is impossible, for at the very least a common language is required in which contractual agreements are expressed" (KMTH, 21). To be sure, this sentence is by no means univocally supportive of the interpretation advanced here; it can readily be construed as cutting against a pragmatist position. Cohen does, after all, seem to be implying that we need language only for the "expression" of economic activities, which presumably take place in a manner sharply divergent from the manner in which discourse unfolds. More strikingly tied to pragmatist assumptions is Cohen's stand on the nature of explanatory accounts. Noting, in a slightly different discussion, that "the only symbols and thought-forms available are those which come from the past,"[69] Cohen proceeds to offer some pragmatist remarks on the "symbols" and the "thought-forms" that necessarily structure explanations:

> All phenomena may be described more or less specifically, and an explanation of a phenomenon succeeds or fails relative to some finitely specific description of it, not irrespective of how it is described. . . .
>
> All explanation operates against a background of theoretical presupposition to which candidate explanations which satisfy structural and confirmational criteria must conform. [KMTH, 163, 264.]

These remarks fit in both with Cohen's aforementioned proclivity to characterize explaining as story-telling—stories being the most widely conceded (though not otherwise unique) case of words read within conventions[70]—and with his general method of formulating a Marxist theory of history. At every stage of his theorizing, Cohen introduces his key dyads by reference to *descriptions* of socioeconomic activities and forms rather than by reference to the activities and forms themselves. Of the many examples that could be given, only a few need be adduced here. In one of his early essays, Cohen defines "social role" as follows: "A description under which a person falls allocates him to a social role or position in the measure that the attribution to him of some rights and/or duties is inseparable from the application of the description" ("Roles," 93). A like approach can be found throughout *Karl Marx's Theory of History*. For instance, when addressing the problem of superstructure/base entanglements (which we examined in the preceding section), Cohen states that his first move is "to formulate a non-legal interpretation of the legal terms in Marx's characterizations of production relations" (KMTH, 219). As he observes, his definition of the nonjuridical powers that are matched with rights is "purely syntactical," in that "we . . . transform any phrase of the form 'the right to ϕ' into a phrase which denotes a power by dropping the word 'right' and replacing it by the word 'power'" (KMTH, 221, 219).

A similar focus on descriptions is to be found, even more significantly, when Cohen draws his distinction between social and material aspects of human life: "How may we demarcate the material from the social situation? Let us try this criterion: a description is social if and only if it entails an ascription to persons—specified or unspecified—of rights or powers *vis-à-vis* other men" (KMTH, 94). What this suggests is that the split between sociality and materiality does not antecede discourse, but instead emanates from it (i.e., from germane contrasts between opposing types of descriptions). Cohen's reliance on descriptions may serve to emphasize that we are empowered *and* entrapped by language; if Cohen appears fixated on discourse to the exclusion of "real life," that is perhaps because real life always is already deferred.[71] Cohen's methodology and his express statements align his version of Marxism with Nelson Goodman's pragmatist insight that approaching the world without some controvertible frame of reference is inconceivable.[72] Under this view, what we classify as "real life" becomes such only by being under description. One cannot ever attain to a realm of pure facticity uncontaminated by language and free from all particular points of view. Utterly problematic, then, is the line between description and explanation, or interpretations and theories.

All this can plausibly be inferred from some of Cohen's explicit claims and central procedures. Nonetheless, before we go too far toward portraying Cohen as a self-conscious adherent to the pragmatist cause, we should acknowledge powerful countervailing strains in his work. Like most other analytic philosophers, he displays a strong tendency to uphold signified meanings over signifying linguistic elements. As Richard Rorty has commented, most philosophers think that "[w]riting is an unfortunate necessity; what is really wanted is to show, to demonstrate, to point out, to exhibit, to make one's interlocutor stand at gaze before the world."[73] Perhaps the most frequent channel for Cohen's tendency to depreciate signifiers is his rephrasing of Marx's principles and conclusions in the hope of "clarifying" their sense. Thus, for example, Cohen sets out to "criticize [Marx's] formulations [of the social/material dichotomy] in order to clarify his idea" (KMTH, 89). A comparable move occurs when Cohen elects to scrutinize some statements from Marx's "Preface" to *A Contribution to the Critique of Political Economy.* Those statements are recast and brought "into terminological conformity with one another . . . [f]or subsequent ease of handling." Cohen advises that "we allow ourselves a little syntactical leeway" (KMTH, 172). Likewise, when looking at one of Marx's dicta on the essential harmony between capital accumulation and free labor, Cohen maintains that "[t]he sentence is syntactically complex, and what it says is easier to survey in [a] semantically equivalent rewrite [*sic*]" (KMTH, 185). Yet again, that is, Cohen follows one of the classic gestures of Occidental philosophy, as described by Barbara Johnson:

> Presiding over classical notions of philosophy and translation are thus the separability of style and thought and the priority of the signified over the signifier, whose only legitimate role is to create order and sequence. Faithfulness to the text has meant faithfulness to the semantic tenor with as little interference as possible from the constraints of the vehicle. Translation, in other words, has always been the translation of *meaning*.[74]

B. COHEN'S UNWITTING PRAGMATISM

Cohen's contempt toward signifiers, for which we had been prepared by his denigration of "reading," ought to discourage analysts from too neatly assimilating his views to those of writers in the neo-pragmatist camp. At the level of his explicit claims—the level of what is *said*, as determined by our hermeneutic assumptions, which remain to be analyzed—Cohen's texts waver between pragmatism and realism. To educe from his work a pragmatist position, we shall have to proceed more subtly. We must look beyond that which his texts *say*, to ferret out also some of the ways they *work*; very much at odds with Cohen's intentions, his writings highlight their own status as writing. We shall now look at two devices, metaphoricity and abstraction, through which this highlighting comes about.

i. *The Perils of Abstraction*. Abstraction and generality were, as is well known, the categories employed by Marx to analyze the peculiar economic structure imposed by capitalism on the material processes of production. The accumulating of capital, and the processes of exchange that are both its cause and its effect, can take place only if concrete goods have been made commensurable through abstraction. Participants in a capitalist economy must be able to exchange each good for varying quantities of other goods, and the substitution of one good for another good demands commensurability. Commensurability, by definition, entails some abstract standard that will allow products to be measured against each other.[75] This standard, which Marx labeled "exchange-value," involves abstraction from all the concrete characteristics of individual goods and from all particular modes of working that engender those goods. "Exchange, in other words, knows only impropriety in figuring the physical as the metaphysical, the concrete as the abstract; blindly enabling commodities to 'take one another's place,' exchange thus proceeds in total ignorance of 'the specific character of the needs [these commodities] satisfy as use-values.'"[76] In a capitalist economy, "abstraction is made from every concrete form and useful property of actual work," and each "particularized concrete kind of labour has to pass for abstract human labour."[77]

Now, our aim will be not so much to assail Marx's approach as to trace its functioning in Cohen's theory.[78] Specifically, what merits attention here is Cohen's subsuming of the use-value/exchange-value relationship under the materiality/sociality distinction. Like Marx, who held that "exchange-value is produced by . . . abstract universal labour, and this belongs to a social framework,"[79] Cohen sees the abstraction that forms exchange-value as contingent rather than elemental, as socially determined rather than ineluctable. Use-value is concrete and material, whereas exchange-value is abstract and social. Abstraction is a social phenomenon through and through.

> Labour productive of use-value is concrete, or qualitatively differentiated: it is tailoring, weaving, mining, etc. Labour productive of exchange-value is abstract, just a featureless proportion of the total labour of society. The sum total of use-values is the concrete or material wealth of society, whereas the ensemble of exchange-values—the same totality socially viewed—is its abstract or social wealth. [KMTH, 101.]

Once again, our aim is not to dislodge the mode of analysis just outlined. *Arguendo,* we shall agree with Cohen that abstract value "is a 'purely social' and hence 'non-natural' property of the product" (KMTH, 100). We can agree, in short, that the abstraction intrinsic to exchange-value plays a role like the one played by discoursive structures as understood within neo-pragmatism. Each discoursive structure (in any field) is a historically fashioned set of conventions through which problems are formulated and tackled. Just so is capitalist abstraction, which frames economic dealings in "'purely social' and hence 'non-natural'" terms. Like any discoursive networks, the languages of abstraction—"languages" being used in a broad sense here—pose and develop problems that, *ipso facto,* are socially defined.

What makes this so noteworthy is that abstraction plays yet another part in Cohen's version of Marxism. Not only is it one of the *objects* of his analysis, but it is a *structuring principle* as well. Time and again, Cohen informs us that abstraction is necessary for an illuminating critique of capitalist life. In the last chapter of his book, for example, he proclaims: "The capitalist essence is at issue here, not the accidents of geography and history. . . . [T]he consequences of principles animating the society are explored *in abstracto,* but the results bear on reality, since the animating principles are really there" (KMTH, 298). Even more revealing are caveats he offers when peddling his distinction between sociality and materiality. This distinction, which—as we have observed—includes the abstract/concrete distinction, does not occupy a commanding perch outside the array of contrasts that it delimits. Quite the contrary; if the social/material diremption is to exist, a feat of abstracting must have occurred already.

> [W]e may always abstract from the social form and display the current state of the relation between man and nature, and the material relations between men underlying their social relations. . . .
>
> The relationship between man and nature is 'mediated' by the social form: it does not occur outside it. The development of nature, described in socio-neutral terms, is therefore an abstraction. But it is a theoretically important abstraction. . . .
>
> . . . Production in its asocial aspect is '*material* production,' this being the *content* of capitalist or any other form of production. And that content may be described in illuminating abstraction from the form with which it is integrated. . . .
>
> Material production does not occur in history except enveloped in a social form, for 'non-social man,' if he ever existed, disappeared when history began. Hence the purely material process is an 'abstract conception which does not define any of the actual historical stages of production.' [KMTH, 97–99; emphasis in original.]

Cohen's foremost dyad is thus an outcome of processes that have been described as generative of "'purely social' and hence 'non-natural'" qualities. Just as capitalists tend to disregard the specific *content* of every good to focus exclusively on exchange-value, so Cohen strips away the specific *form* of each economic system to focus solely on the productive agencies. In each case, an operation is carried out that imposes an artificial arrangement on the rich details of reality, and in each case an arrangement has come to be what it is through the analytical device of abstraction. Yet abstraction is not only the means whereby materiality is discerned, but is itself the capitalist version of sociality (which, as Cohen notes, is the lone version to which he and Marx devote much analysis [KMTH, 102]). This suggests that "materiality" is always already social, in the sense that it can come into view only as a result of the procedure (that is, abstraction) which resides at the social end of the sociality/materiality split. Cohen's texts thus establish the inescapable sway of language—in a broad sense—by acting out the social delimitation and definition of material life.

That Cohen's texts have borne out pragmatist theses may already appear unsettling, quite apart from any critique of pragmatism that one might offer. After all, Cohen can no longer enjoy the steady and clear-cut oppositions (between, say, "physical necessities" and "social arrangements" [KMTH, 107]) that his theory needs. Nonetheless, the most severe difficulties have yet to be drawn out; this is but the beginning of the sufferings. Before we turn to those deeper problems, let us explore one additional respect in which Cohen's writings support pragmatism.

ii. *Metaphor in the Text of Marxism.* Early in his chief text, Cohen acknowledges that he makes "free use of . . . spatial metaphor" in setting up his tripartite analytical framework of the productive forces, the production relations, and the superstructure (KMTH, 30). Hardly is this a cause for astonishment, since the metaphoricity of Marxist explanations has long been recognized—not least by those who are sharply hostile to the specific metaphors chosen (and who articulate their hostility through more sobering metaphors): "It [i.e., the base/superstructure distinction] is . . . a dead, static, architectural metaphor, whose potential for illumination was never very great and which has for too long cast nothing but shadows over Marxist theory and Marxist practice."[80] However that may be, Cohen certainly does indulge in the classic Marxist metaphors quite profusely. His rhetorical skills, however, are not invariably self-conscious and self-controlled, and indeed they sometimes patently clash with the intentions that he expresses.

Some of Cohen's favorite metaphors cluster round the themes of illumination and visibility. Insouciantly disregardful of the strong challenges to these notions that have increasingly been mounted in recent decades,[81] Cohen avers that in a society with club law, powers remain "openly visible," whereas in a more advanced legal system, "rights screen powers" (KMTH, 225). Broadly similar tropes appear when capitalism is contrasted with socialism: "Capitalism is obscure. Only science can illuminate it. But in the bright light of socialism the torch of the specialized investigator is invisible" (KMTH, 338).

In the above examples, Cohen's ocular metaphors may seem stimulating and harmless, at least to someone who enjoys readings as much as theories (or who is unsure about the difference between the two). At other times, however, his rhetorical strategies become much more dubious. For instance, Cohen defines the general meaning of "explanation" as follows: "Probably to explain is, quite simply, to make clear" (KMTH, 252 note 1). Here, if anywhere, one might have expected Cohen to strive for literality, as the difference that he perceives between interpretation and theorizing lies exactly in the presumed power of theoretical discourse to *explain* (rather than just to *tell*). What he has done, however, is to resort to one of the most tried figures of speech in Western metaphysics, made perhaps most famous in Descartes's "clear and distinct" ideas—which were guaranteed by the "natural light"—but going back much further, as one can see in Jacques Derrida's investigation of Aristotle's metaphorology: "The appeal [by Aristotle] to the criteria of clarity and obscurity would suffice to confirm what we stated above: this entire philosophical delimitation of metaphor already lends itself to being constructed and worked by 'metaphors.' How could a piece of knowledge or a language be properly clear or obscure?"[82] Cohen's account of explanation thus takes its place in a long history of quests for "the assured legibility of the proper."[83] Far from standing outside metaphoricity, explanations of explanation must lodge in what they try to exclude.

More troublesome still for Cohen are two passages where his jaundiced outlook on metaphor becomes explicit, with a reliance on tropes. The first such occasion figures in his account of legal systems. After vividly describing the superstructure-and-base as a roof resting on four struts, Cohen tries to depict the same configuration "[n]on-metaphorically: the property relations are as they are because their being so is conducive to the initiation or maintenance of the production relations (demanded by the productive forces)" (KMTH, 232). Two comments seem appropriate here. First, anyone who has read Nietzsche (or even Hume) should be less willing to regard causal language as a transparent window on brute reality. One need not concur blindly with the subjectivist tone of Nietzsche's ridiculing of causal discourse, to understand—as indeed Cohen sometimes does—that causal links take place only in stories.[84] Second, and more important, the image of production relations as "demanded by the productive forces" is an anthropomorphic trope *par excellence*. Productive forces are cast as an imperious sovereign that "demands" fulfillment of its main needs by the ever-dutiful production relations;[85] it is the forces that amount to the chief actor in history, as Cohen *makes clear* in the first chapter of his book:

> The growth of human power is the central process of history. The need for that growth explains why there *is* history. . . .
>
> . . . Marx's conception of history preserves the structure of Hegel's but endows it with fresh content. For Hegel, as we have seen, history shows an expansion of consciousness giving itself form in cultures, which subvert themselves through their success in advancing consciousness. . . . For Marx, as we shall see in the rest of this book, the important forms are not cultures but economic structures, and the role of consciousness is assumed by expanding productive power. [KMTH, 23, 26.]

Unfortunately, Cohen seems later to forget that his first chapter is titled "Images of History in Hegel and Marx." Those "images" haunt Cohen's attempts at literality, like a specter that stalks Europe.

Cohen further reveals his marked impatience with metaphors, as well as his inability to escape them, near the end of his book. There he dwells upon a distinction between essences and appearances. He discusses phenomena (such as the geocentric universe and the unitary composition of air) which *prima facie* appear true but which turn out to be false when they are more carefully examined. He writes:

> The appearances just reviewed are, like mirages, part of the world around us. They comprise the outer form of things, which enjoys an objective status, and which science alone can strip away. To express

> the thought with less imagery, let us say that *there is a gulf between appearance and reality when and only when the explanation of a state of affairs falsifies the description it is natural to give of it if one lacks the explanation*. Gulfs are due to the way reality itself appears, and only when they exist is science required for a state of affairs to be intelligible. [KMTH, 329; emphasis in original.]

Suffice it to say that there exists a wide gulf between the underscored sentence and the promised diminution of (spatial) imagery. As Barbara Johnson has noted, spatial figures of speech tend only to en-gulf those who try to dispense with them: "[S]ome measure of the difficulties involved [in 'attempts to break out of spatial logic'] may be derived from the fact that *to break out of* is still a spatial metaphor."[86] (One need scarcely add here that "explanation"—whose referent Cohen distinguishes from description in the above passage—is derived from *explanare*, which means "to spread out.")

Nor is Cohen on any firmer ground with his reference to "the description it is *natural* to give." Here he trades on one of the most unstable metaphors in the whole Western tradition.[87] Because, as Cohen tells us, "nature is of course a product of history, changing within and as a result of social forms," and because "nature, described in socio-neutral terms is therefore an abstraction" (KMTH, 96, 98), his use of the word "natural" as applied to certain descriptions must be seen as a metaphorical evocation of some pristine state (with an Adamic language outside social conditioning) that could never exist.[88]

In the Book of Numbers, the diviner Balaam is called upon by Balak to curse the people of Israel. Each time Balaam opens his mouth, however, he can but laud those whom he has been commanded to execrate. Cohen's struggle against pragmatism seems as ill-fated as Balak's wicked request. Each time Cohen seeks to discount language, he can but prove that in the beginning was the word.

2. *From Pragmatism to Deconstruction*

Having traced the outlines of a pragmatist stance in Cohen's theory (both in its substance and in its structure), and having consequently offered a glimpse of the uneasy role of language within that theory, we now shall find that language does not submit to being accommodated and mastered. Rather, what at present may seem to be a slight annoyance will soon turn out to be a fundamental disruption that has overturned the values inscribed in Cohen's Marxism. His system divides against itself along lines whose general shape—though not their specific course—could have readily been foretold. We shall not be lifted, however, to a secure vantage from which we "rectify" Cohen's faults. His missteps are irremediable, and we shall therefore be implicated in everything we denounce. Deconstruction leads not to a sublime posture of unequivocal triumph, but to an unstoppable pendulation between standpoints both incoherent and necessary.

Let us call to mind Cohen's theory that the development of productive forces will underlie the development of the economic structures that enfold a given society. According to his Primacy Thesis, the relationships of production assume whatever contours are most appropriate for advancing the further evolution of the productive forces. This will imply, as we have noted, that the relations of production affect the paths of development of productive forces; precisely *because* relations can affect that development, a specific array of forces will cause a certain set of relations to win out. The great virtue of this line of analysis—from Cohen's point of view—is that it anticipates and defuses the most salient objections to its own claims. Every time a critic points to what seems a devastating example of the enormous influence exercised by the production relations on the productive forces, Cohen can make a much more devastating riposte: not only does the enormous impact *not* belie the Primacy Thesis, but it actually helps to strengthen that Thesis, for it helps to explain why given productive forces opt for a particular network of relations. Relations get singled out precisely owing to their stimulative capacity, their capacity to enhance the growth of productive power.

In his brilliantly ingenious argument, Cohen has had to take many things for granted. Most notably, he has had to presuppose that the meaning of "productivity" can be fixed without any danger to the substance of his analysis. If we look back to his early definitions, we find remarkably little guidance. However meticulous and subtle those definitions may be, they prove less than helpful in the matter at hand—that is, in attempting to delimit "production." We are told, for example, that the productive forces are used "by producing agents to make products" (KMTH, 32). Happily, we fare somewhat better when we move to the definitional appendix in Cohen's book. There Cohen informs us that the term "use-value" applies to things with "power to satisfy, directly or indirectly, a human desire," and he also remarks that use-value is a necessary condition of exchange-value (KMTH, 345, 348). Now, since he elsewhere divides all forms of production into production purely for use-value and production for exchange-value (KMTH, 80–81), we may infer that all production—properly so called—aims at the creation of goods and services that can "satisfy, directly or indirectly, a human desire."

Production, then, involves the output of desirable things. Cohen has succeeded in specifying, albeit vaguely, his presupposed definition of what counts as "productive." By so doing, however, he has provided us the wedge needed for overturning his whole analysis. In a passage quoted earlier, Cohen recognizes the vital role of discourse in the conducting of economic life, and throughout my last subsection we observed the pragmatist moments of his philosophy—moments that lay stress on the importance of languages in giving shape to conceptions of what is real. It now becomes clear that language, understood both broadly and narrowly, is not just a crucial factor in socioeconomic life but is also the antecedent condition of its possibility. Only through the categorizing power of the languages that make up social life can there ever emerge a demarcation between what is desirable and what is undesirable in a given culture. Without the categories and systematic distinctions that form the stuff of a language, no activity like production ever could have come into being, for no difference could obtain between "productivity" and "counterproductivity." Only language provides the space within which goods and productive forces are classed as such. Without categorizing schemes, production would be reduced to nonsense—to non-sense in the strictest *sense* of the term. Production acquires sense (and therefore its status as production) only through the classificatory arrangements that mark off undesirability from desirability. Aversions and preferences define what counts as productive, and they are defined in turn by socially current schemes of differentiation.

Cohen cannot respond successfully to the argument just made by asserting that "desirableness" and "undesirableness" enjoy universal applicability as concepts that will have to appear in all conceivable forms of life. Such a response, though scarcely disputable, would nevertheless be unavailing since, as Cohen notes elsewhere, "the universal can exist only in a determinate embodiment: there is no way of being human which is not *a* way of being human."[89] That all social units will distinguish desirability from undesirability does not mean that the demarcational line will take exactly the same shape (or even roughly the same shape) everywhere. As Cohen tells us: "It is false that all human beings desire the same things, or that, when they do, they want the same services from them" (KMTH, 345). *Particular* medleys of discriminative judgments will antecede the "productiveness" of productive forces, for those judgments delimit what is to be deemed "good" and hence what is to be deemed "productive."

Nor can Cohen fall back on the remarkably clever argument that he has hitherto used. It is no good for him to retort as follows: "A particular kind of discourse has come along *precisely as a result* of its stimulating impact on the productive forces." Such a reply will necessarily run aground, for discourse—that is, categorizing networks—cannot take shape (at least as a whole) in service of the demands of productive power, since it is discourse that allots boundaries to what is acceptable or desirable and hence to what is or is not productive. Productive power gains its identity *as such* only through the categorizing reach of language. Outside that reach, the concept of "productivity" loses any meaning; there thus cannot be any *productive* forces until languages have already given shape to the productivity/disutility distinction. Languages thus take form as analytically prior, and not just chronologically antecedent, to the developing of productive forces.[90] The set of possible pathways of such developing is marked out by the classificatory frameworks that have defined "productivity." Those pathways can never predecide any overall constellation of such frameworks, for the pathways become defined as such only after the frameworks are in place. To retain primacy, the forces will have had to emerge as a conceivable option before they can emerge as a conceivable option.

To see how far Cohen's theory has broken down, we may take a cue from the critique of his jurisprudence. There it was argued that the structures of legal language gain definition, if they can indeed do so at all, only by application to the specifics of "real life" (which in turn can bestow meaning only within structures that have always already gained definition). What that suggested (or assumed) was, among other things, that legal relationships which pattern "real life" can usefully be treated as constituting a language. Such relationships will hence function and misfunction like any other language, for, like all other languages, they elaborate themselves through structure/event antinomies.

We should expect, therefore, that the distribution of wealth will antecede the productivity of productive forces as much as will the classificatory structures that are more typically regarded as languages. Distribution's priority will be structural or logical in addition to being temporal. That is, legal relations, even when conventionally rather than expansively understood,[91] should play an important role in *defining* "goods" and thus in *defining* "productivity."

Our expectations are indeed realized when we look at the work of scholars who have explored this issue. Duncan Kennedy, for example, has observed that "[i]t is a commonplace that there will be different allocations of resources in the same economy according to how income is distributed," and he details (with admirable sophistication) the many ways in which this "commonplace" holds.[92] It need only be added here that a distribution of wealth affects not simply the *allocation* of resources but also their very *definition*. Along with the other languages in which human beings come to describe themselves, the law provides categories and applications that shape the meanings of "desirableness" and "undesirableness." In addition to forming one's ability to indulge preferences, any distribution of assets will have a hand in shaping the preferences themselves through and through. This it will have, because "preferences evolve with the consumption pattern one chooses,"[93] and because a "consumption pattern" will be determined importantly by distributional outcomes. Thus, in combination with many other important languages, the legal "language" will have determined the cast and will have written the script for the performance and indeed the very emerging of the productive forces; language can never be reduced to a handservant or puppet, for the alleged puppet master could then never exist. The letter gives life and makes the spirit (of productivity) possible.

Part Three. Conclusion

Thanks to Cohen's pragmatist inclinations, we were alerted to the supreme importance of language in his analyses. This led us to highlight the disruptive effects of language when it has been seemingly relegated to a subordinate position. Language can never be contained within the analytical hierarchies that Cohen sets up. We have thus upended the systematic priorities in which Cohen's Marxism consists; the base and the superstructure have taken precedence *vis-à-vis* the productive forces, which had been viewed thus far as causally antecedent. Language holds sway indeed as a mighty specter that torments Communism.

To be sure, this reversal will enjoy no greater stability than the theoretical framework that it puts into question. A suitable analysis could make clear that this reversal depends on the anterior status and development of productive forces. And the new overturning of the new priorities would itself have supplied the grounds for its own undoing, *ad infinitum*. As has been noted, deconstruction can never halt its own impetus; every critique always already undermines itself. But none of this affords Cohen any comfort. Certain is it that deconstructive critiques "inhabit philosophical opposition, resisting and disorganizing it, *without ever* constituting a third term, without ever leaving room for a solution."[94] Just as certain, however, is that Cohen's standpoint is comprehended and situated by deconstruction. His Marxism will dislocate itself in paradoxical overturnings that both demand and forbid the constitution of a "third term."

CHAPTER 3

THE RULE OF MISRECOGNITION IN THE HART OF JURISPRUDENCE

The hallmark of liberalism is a secularized earnestness. Having drowned the heavenly ecstasies of religious fervor, of chivalrous enthusiasm—and even of philistine sentimentalism—in the icy waters of analytical scrutiny, the liberal philosophers had to introduce a new tone of public discourse to match their substantive outlook. Just as liberalism had overall been a salutary response to what had preceded it, so its characteristic tone would improve upon the tenor of discourse that had prevailed under the *ancien régime*. Christianity had been pessimistic, murderously intolerant, fanatical, and dogmatic; liberalism would hence be optimistic, generously open-minded, cool-headed, and responsive to rational persuasion. Truth would be tied no longer to sacred writings and divine revelations, but would be seen henceforward as the product of close analysis and wide-ranging debate. If the old order, with its pious sublimity and its monstrous vindictiveness, had received its highest expression in the work of Dante,[1] the new order would be captured most gracefully in the tolerance, reasonableness, and eloquence of John Stuart Mill. Earnestness, in short, would carry the day.

Liberalism's passion for truth—which Nietzsche mocked as a sign of lingering religiousness, no matter how strikingly metamorphosed[2]—had to find its expression in a balanced and conciliatory form. Science and philosophy might indeed be the new religions chasing ever so ardently after truth, but the verities that they could produce would not grow from bloody endings of irreconcilable disagreements. Not to a liberal's taste were the unyielding antagonisms of the Christian era that had delivered countless souls early to the next life. Liberals had found a manner of swallowing up death in victory that Christians had far too seldom deigned to employ: compromise. Compromise would dislodge schisms as the most trustworthy road to truth. Mill maintained, with characteristic elegance, that most frequently "conflicting doctrines, instead of being one true and the other false, share the truth between them, and the nonconforming opinion is needed to supply the remainder of the truth of which the received doctrine embodies only a part."[3] To be sure, Mill conceded that "in the human mind, one-sidedness has always been the rule, and many-sidedness the exception," and he acknowledged that "[t]ruth . . . is so much a question of the reconciling and combining of opposites that very few have minds sufficiently capacious and impartial to make the adjustment with an approach to correctness, and it has to be made by the rough process of a struggle between combatants fighting under hostile banners" (OL, 56, 58). Nonetheless, however imperfect compromise tends to be, Mill's conviction that truth is many-sided—a conviction also expressed by myriad other thinkers[4]—hurled intransigence into disrepute. As Mill himself stated: "[I]t is not on the impassioned partisan, it is on the calmer and more disinterested bystander, that [a] collision of opinions works its salutary effect. . . . [T]here is always hope when people are forced to listen to both sides" (OL, 63). Christianity's Via Dolorosa had been replaced by the earnest *via media* of the new age.

H. L. A. Hart's writings, perhaps more clearly than those of any other present-day jurisprude, display the qualities of high liberalism that have just been remarked upon. Hart's generosity and his open-mindedness need scarcely be proved,[5] and his optimism, analytical keenness, and cool-headedness are equally patent. Above all is Hart's fierce dedication to liberals' search for truth, with the help of subtle clarification of conceptual puzzles. Hart leaves little doubt that it is truth he desires. For example, in his most famous book, *The Concept of Law*—on whose arguments, by and large, the present chapter will focus[6]—Hart explains that he will consider some nineteenth-century legal theories because they serve as a "pointer to the truth." Their function of pointing to the truth derives from the fact that they "contain, in a blurred and misleading form, certain truths about certain important aspects of law" (*Concept*, 16, 97). Even more striking than this preoccupation with truth is the technique Hart advocates for building on what his predecessors accomplished. Taking Mill's themes in just the direction that was proposed in my last paragraph, Hart declares that earlier theories "are *both* illuminating and puzzling: they are more like great exaggerations of some truths about law unduly neglected, than cool definitions. They throw a light which makes us see much in law that lay hidden; but the light is so bright that it blinds us to the remainder and so leaves us still without a clear view of the whole" (*Concept*, 2; emphasis in original). A championing of the middle road emerges most clearly when Hart weighs the competing claims of formalism and Legal Realism (or rule-skepticism): "Formalism and rule-skepticism are the Scylla and Charybdis of juristic theory; they are great exaggerations, salutary where they correct each other, and the truth lies between them."[7] Here, as elsewhere, Hart pronounces his loyalty to an ancient ideal that liberalism revived: moderation in all things.[8]

Hart evinces yet a further peculiarity of the liberal temperament in his striving to give birth to himself. His confident assertion that he has made a "fresh start" in positivist jurisprudence (*Concept*, 77), his denigration of "the belief that a book on legal theory is primarily a book from which one learns what other books contain"[9] (despite his acknowledgment that he is "heavily and obviously indebted to other writers" [*Concept*, v]), his admiration of Bentham's brilliant originality,[10] and his somewhat derogatory reference to Austin's "later and obviously derivative work" (*Bentham*, 108) combine to give the impression of a man who feels that individual subjectivity can and should go beyond the contexts in which it has developed its shape. In making and articulating such an assumption, Hart of course demonstrates his immersion in his own context of liberal thought, for which the primacy of the individual subject—both in a metaphysical sense and in a political sense—has been seen as a nearly irrefragable starting point.

To be sure, as Nicodemus discovered, Christians had long placed central importance on the need to be "born anew"; but the Christian rebirth was an otherworldly ideal to be fulfilled only by those who *lost* rather than *gained* their individuality. A person who was truly born anew (by being baptized into the Spirit) had to die to the mundane world and enter the blessedness of eternal life by being restored to union with God through Jesus. Liberalism, one may observe with thanks, was focused too healthily on the here and now to be much attracted to life-denying ideals. For liberals, being born anew would come henceforth to consist in activating one's individuality, in a process of self-engendering, whereby one aims not at some ethereal banquet but at terrestrial bank notes (or at other, less banausic sources of earthly bliss). A liberal may endeavor to turn his back on history, but he does not cease trying to make new history. It is this secularized ideal of originality that Hart has affirmed.

Hart, then, stands as a worthy representative of the liberal tradition. A happy coincidence is that, for some thorny problems concerning representation will here preoccupy us. Specifically, we shall probe Hart's representation of the elusive concept of law, a concept that is supposed to be fully realized in what Hart calls the "clear standard cases constituted by the legal systems of modern states" (*Concept*, 3). Should Hart's representation prove to be incoherent, and should it do so in ways that are irremediable, one may then be led to throw gravely into doubt the founding ambition of mainstream jurisprudence—the aim of representing law accurately. It may turn out that law is nothing other than that which stymies representation: law as the law of unrepresentability.

Be that as it may, this chapter will probe the difficulties and paradoxes in Hart's effort to represent the major components of a legal system. Part One provides a critical overview of Hart's general theory in *The Concept of Law.*[11] Though other works by Hart are occasionally referred to, his classic text will receive the bulk of my attention, and even the arguments of *that* text are not scrutinized comprehensively. Such issues as the relationship between law and morals or the debate between formalists and Legal Realists are mentioned only in passing, even though Hart treats them at great length in *The Concept of Law* and elsewhere. Those issues are scarcely unimportant—though my approach to them would be very different from that of Hart—but they bear less crucially on the second Part of this chapter than do some of Hart's other arguments. In that Part, which will advance a more thoroughgoing critique than any of the critical comments made in Part One, two points of uncanniness in Hart's theory are highlighted and plotted. Suffice it here to say that the route taken by the first of these points is circular; by the second, infinitely regressing. Hart's theory establishes itself only at the cost of losing itself.

Part One. Hart's Concept of Law

Hart begins by trying to figure out why legal scholars have spent so much time arguing over what law is. He maintains that three fundamental questions have impelled most of the debate (*Concept*, 6–13). First, writers have pondered the resemblances and the differences between law-based obligation and the sort of compulsion that is brought about by an order backed with threats. How close is the similarity between a lawmaker and an armed culprit who threatens victims with death if they refuse to follow his bidding? A second problem consists in pinning down the exact relationship, if any, between legal obligation and ethical obligation. What should one infer from the prevalence of deontic language in both legal discourse and moral discourse? Third, while most jurisprudes would accept that legal systems are built of rules, the seemingly elemental notion of "rules" will have become curiouser and curiouser when examined more closely. How are widely obeyed rules distinguishable from patterns of convergent behavior that derive their existence not from generally heeded duties but from generally shared habits? And if that question is answered, one must face yet another problem: does the openness of every rule to a multiplicity of interpretations make nonsense of the idea that decisions by judges (and by other officials) are prescribed by rules in any meaningful sense?

A. Austin's Model of Law

To address these persistent underlying issues, Hart undertakes a lengthy investigation of the shortcomings in the theory of legal rules *qua* coercive orders that was evolved in the nineteenth century by John Austin. Austin's theory takes as its fundament the situation of an armed robber who demands that people relinquish to him their money if they want to avoid a hail of bullets. By amplifying this situation of stark force, Austin hoped to construct a fully adequate legal theory.[12]

Hart praises Austin's point of departure on the ground that "whatever its defects, . . . the elements of the gunman situation are . . . not themselves obscure" (*Concept*, 20). This is but one instance of a myriad of vision-related metaphors that pervade and brighten Hart's text. Indeed, Hart's ultimate rejection of the Austinian model likewise springs from his marked desire to eschew obscurity: "[T]he model of orders backed by threats obscures more of law than it reveals" (*Concept*, 48). Established at the outset, and running through his analysis, the interplay of darkness and light may prove to be more glaring than illuminating. We should keep an eye on these ocularcentric tropes as we proceed through Hart's arguments.

In any case, to the transparently clear relation between the armed robber and the victims, Austin appended several qualifications that were meant to embrace the full complexity, or opacity, of a legal system. Unlike demands issued by a gunman, statutes and other legal rules are general in form, in two important senses (*Concept*, 21): they bear upon categories or general types of conduct (which may be specified in great detail) rather than on individualized actions; and they apply to a general class of people rather than to a specified person, at least in the huge majority of cases—though, of course, a generally defined group may chance to consist of only one member. Aside from being general in form in these two ways, legal rules contrast with the dictates of an armed robber in the duration of their applicability. Whereas the gunman's orders are normally *ad hoc*, laws have an enduring or standing force. Within the terms of the Austinian model, this means that "there is a general belief on the part of those to whom the [laws] apply that disobedience is likely to be followed by the execution of the threat not only on the first promulgation of the [law], but continuously until the [law] is withdrawn or cancelled" (*Concept*, 23).

Apart from bringing out the characteristics of legal rules that distinguish them from a gunman's orders, Austin described how legal norms produce their effects. He explained that, if laws and a legal framework exist as such, then most people are complying with most of the commands issued by a supreme authority. (Acts of compliance can involve different degrees of willingness, and the promulgation of orders can be direct or indirect.) The supreme rulemaker is called a "sovereign" and can be either a person or a body of persons. A sovereign enjoys habitual obedience on a wide scale when issuing directives; further, a sovereign owes no obedience to any person or any body of persons. As Hart summarizes:

> On this simple account of the matter, which we shall later have to examine critically, there must, wherever there is a legal system, be some persons or body of persons issuing general orders backed by threats which are generally obeyed, and it must be generally believed that these threats are likely to be implemented in the event of disobedience. This person or body must be internally supreme and externally independent. [*Concept*, 25.]

B. Hart's Criticism of Austin

Hart devotes two important chapters in the first half of his *magnum opus* to criticism of Austin (*Concept*, 26–76). Such criticism, Hart feels, will clear the path for his vaunted "fresh start" in jurisprudence. His critique of Austin will here be studied in some depth, for much of what Hart maintains is directly pertinent to my deconstructive analysis in Part Two. Though he has—in my view—sometimes misinterpreted Austin, his approach will not be contested here on grounds of unfaithfulness. Problems of interpretive faithfulness are suspended, as we examine Hart's critique aside from such problems on its own merits.

1. *Law without Interdiction*

Hart grants that there is a strong analogy between certain species of laws—namely, criminal laws and tort laws—and the commands of an Austinian sovereign. But, he holds, the analogy breaks down when one looks at many other classes of laws. Laws that confer public or private powers cannot readily be assimilated to Austin's model. In private law, power-conferring rules are those that prescribe conditions for such legal desiderata as valid contracts and valid wills and valid transfers of property; in public law, power-conferring rules specify the organization and procedures of government. In neither their public forms nor their private forms do such rules impose direct obligations of the type imposed by sovereign commands (*Concept*, 27–41).

At times, Hart elucidates the function of power-conferring rules in terms that would please any Hohfeldian. He writes, for example, that such rules "provide individuals with . . . legal powers . . . to create, by certain specified procedures and subject to certain conditions, structures of rights and duties within the coercive framework of the law" (*Concept*, 27). This language comes very close indeed to Hohfeld's conception of a legal power as the ability to "effect [a] particular change of legal relations."[13] Such a conception would by no means be unassailable—though exploring its difficulties would lead much too far afield[14]—but it would be less glaringly objectionable than some of Hart's other formulations, on which we now have to turn our scrutiny.

One way in which Hart tries to illuminate the unique function of power-conferring rules is his observation that such rules "do not require persons to act in certain ways whether they wish to or not" (*Concept*, 27). Anyone familiar with contract law or property law must find this assertion rather puzzling; after all, the main purpose of those bodies of law is to compel people to structure their transactions in certain forms, to the exclusion of other forms. One must concede, of course, that the compulsory shepherding by the rules that govern contracts and transfers will be felt only by those wishing to engage in valid transactions that can be enforced. But such a concession holds no greater significance than does the like fact that laws which adjure motorists to stop at red lights will have an impact only on those people who wish to drive along public streets. In each case, people desiring to pursue a certain objective must comply with all conditions attached to the pursuing of that objective. They must comply, "whether they wish to or not." Empowerment and coercion cannot be sundered in the way Hart wants them to be; laws regulating contracts and transfers will give rise to desiderata of legal enforceability and attendant security, but will *ipso facto* create new forms of coercion. People who seek enforceability can be empowered by the pertinent laws, but such people will *gain* enforceability—and thereby gain the powers held out to them—only if they submit to all the requirements laid down. Every road to empowerment involves coercion of those who wish to travel on it successfully. Power-conferring rules do indeed "require persons to act in certain ways," and they do so through the very procedures of endowing persons with new capacities.

A second dubious distinction between power-conferring rules and duty-imposing rules is that power-conferring rules, and *only* power-conferring rules, "provide individuals with facilities for realizing their wishes" without which every citizen "would be a mere duty-bearer" (*Concept*, 27, 40). Aside from being vulnerable to the objection noted in the last paragraph above, Hart's disjuncture between facilitation and imposition holds up only if one reverses one's standpoint when proceeding from either side of the dualism to the other side. When Hart analyzes duty-imposing norms, he takes the view of people whose conduct has been constrained, rather than of people whose conduct or whose enjoyment of goods is authorized and protected as a result of the obligations that are imposed on other people. As Hohfeld taught us, there are no duties without rights; the duty-imposing rules could hence equally be dubbed "right-conferring."[15] When Hart examines power-conferring rules, *par contre*, he takes the view of people whose actions have been authorized and protected, rather than of people whose legal standing becomes subject to alteration as a result of the powers that are vested in other people. As Hohfeld taught us, every power entails a liability; power-conferring rules expose some people to the bidding of others, and can therefore be classified with full warrant as "liability-imposing." Hart concedes this last point when he adverts to power-conferring rules as "recipes for creating duties" (*Concept*, 33), but in general he does not take sufficient notice of the relationality or reciprocality of law. Because rights correspond to duties, and liabilities correspond to powers, Hart's contrast between facilitation and imposition will fade into a contrast between powers and rights (or liabilities and duties). As has already been noted, this latter contrast (or latter pair of contrasts) will not be challenged directly here.

Yet another way in which Hart tries to single out the unique status of the power-conferring rules is his argument that the general "relationship between the conforming action and the [power-conferring] rule is ill-conveyed by the words 'obey' and 'disobey,' which are more apposite in the case of the criminal law where the rules are analogous to orders" (*Concept*, 30). To flesh this out a bit, he goes on to say:

> In some cases it would be grotesque to assimilate these two broad types of rule. If a measure before a legislative body obtains the required majority of votes and is thus duly passed, the voters in favour of the measure have not 'obeyed' the law requiring a majority decision nor have those who voted against it either obeyed or disobeyed it: the same is of course true if the measure fails to obtain the required majority and so no law is passed.[16]

Hart is himself legislating on the permissible terminology to be used if one henceforth wants to treat of power-conferring legislation. By proscribing the word "obey," he is defining the conditions for valid theories about power-conferring rules. (Or is he imposing on us a duty to forgo all use of the word "obey" in this context? In that case, any breach of the duty would be punished by condemnation of one's work as a "grotesque" slighting of what Hart sees as a "radical difference" between power-conferring rules and duty-imposing rules.[17])

Fortunately, no rule of recognition requires us to accede to Hart's legislating as an authoritative guide to juristic parlance. Let us look critically at his example of the lawmaking institution that does not "obey" anything throughout its normal procedures. For someone not wedded to the idea of a sharp distinction between rules that create powers and rules that impose duties, it should be clear that a legislative body *does* obey the exact laws which hold that a majority is needed for the enactment of any bill. Such laws are obeyed, precisely in that the legislative leaders and other members do not try to enact bills that have failed to win the necessary support. Not only can legislators' restraint quite justly be called "obedience," but any efforts to gain unauthorized enactment can fittingly be termed "disobedience." A focus by Hart on legislative voting, to the disregard of processes of enactment, leads him astray. Even so, the members who vote for or against a bill are strictly obeying laws that govern enactment, in the sense that no one—presumably—is seeking to get bills fraudulently enacted. This may be a rather strained sense of "obey," but no more so than in the statement that someone is obeying laws against homicide while peacefully reading a book of verse at home.

A related difficulty arises in a fourth attempt by Hart to stake off power-conferring rules. He denies that they involve sanctions like those associated with duty-imposing rules. This denial emerges while Hart is analyzing the view, held most notably by Austin and his disciples, that sanctions *do* attach to power-conferring norms; these sanctions lie in the voidness that ensues when a necessary condition for the exercise of a power is not met. For Hart, equating voidness with sanctions can amount only to "a source (and a sign) of confusion" (*Concept*, 33). He explains:

> In the case of a rule of criminal law we can identify and distinguish two things: a certain type of conduct which the rule prohibits, and a sanction intended to discourage it. But how could we consider in this light such desirable social activities as men making each other promises which do not satisfy legal requirements as to form? This is not like the conduct discouraged by the criminal law, something which the legal rules stipulating legal forms for contracts are designed to suppress. The rules merely withhold legal recognition from them. [*Concept*, 34.]

These remarks unfortunately resemble Actaeon's dogs, which turned their shuddersome wrath upon the hart that had wielded them against others. Perhaps the "confusion" generated by Hart's forerunners has through osmosis affected the response thereto. By focusing once again on an irrelevant stretch of conduct, Hart misstates what his opponents have been contending (or what they should be contending). Even if one grants the belief that contract law is not meant to disincline people from "making each other promises which do not satisfy legal requirements as to form" (*Concept*, 34)—a belief not nearly so obvious as Hart would have us presume—one can still point out that specific modes of behavior are indeed discouraged by laws that regulate contractual form. Attempts by a promisee to win state enforcement of a pact will result in nothing except squandered funds and wasted time when prescribed forms have not been followed. Such attempts will not be prohibited, of course, just as a wide array of tortious actions are not strictly prohibited, but they will be an unpalatable and futile option for anyone who does not "satisfy legal requirements as to form." Contract law deals with the *enforcement* of contracts, and it will have imposed its penalties (consisting in bootless effort, time, and expense) when someone makes unenforceable agreements *and* attempts to enforce them.

Determined to confute the assimilation of nullity to sanctions, Hart presses forward with yet another argument. He insists that, whereas rules of criminal law can clearly be disjoined from the threats of punitive measures that deter infractions, power-conferring rules permit no such separation. A duty-imposing rule not carrying any sanctions could still exist as an intelligible (though nonjuridical) standard of behavior, but a power-conferring rule that does not provide for legal nullity when its key conditions have gone unmet "could not be intelligibly said to exist . . . even as a non-legal rule" (*Concept*, 34). This seems a curiously weak argument. It does not strain plausibility, much less intelligibility, to imagine rules that favor some ways of exercising powers (and that oppose alternative ways) without a sanction of nullity to inhibit noncompliance. Perfectly conceivable is it that a social grouping reserves its praise for a certain method of exercising a power, even while—through its legal system—it grudgingly tolerates the exercise of the power in less favored ways. In such a case, a community will harbor a moral standard prescribing certain conditions for the exercise of a power, but legal nullity will not loom as a necessary concomitant of actions that breach the moral standard.

Hart might try to rejoin that moral rules like the one just sketched are duty-imposing, and that they hence do not contradict his view of power-conferring rules. But such a maneuver would imperil his whole project of making sharp distinctions between duty-imposing rules and power-conferring rules. If the rule just sketched is duty-imposing, then should not the same be said about *all* rules that authorize certain means (and thus prescribe certain conditions) for the exercise of a power? Hart might reply that when a narrow power-conferring rule in the moral sphere consorts with a generous power-conferring rule in the legal sphere, the former rule becomes duty-imposing. Such a retort seems highly questionable, from Hart's own viewpoint; if coexistence can have such an effect, should we presume that a stringent power-conferring *law* is duty-imposing when coincident with a liberal power-conferring rule of ethics? Even if the dubious retort be accepted as a plausible reading of coexistence, Hart will scarcely have shown that other readings are "unintelligible" (or even implausible).

In his final effort to distinguish power-conferring rules from duty-imposing rules, Hart adds naught but a recapitulatory flourish: "[P]ower-conferring rules are thought of, spoken of, and used in social life differently from rules which impose duties, and they are valued for different reasons. What other tests for difference in character could there be?" (*Concept*, 41). There are two glaring difficulties in Hart's appeal to our common practices. First, as Jonathan Cohen has suggested, the terms of this final "argument" would imply that numerous distinctions will have yet to be made among different types of rules; there will be, Cohen maintains, "no neat dichotomy of [power-conferring rules and duty-imposing rules] but as many different kinds of rules as the complexity of our legal system allows. . . . [O]ne can draw many distinctions and construct . . . many different schemes of classification."[18] This first problem may not, however, be insuperable. Hart does recognize that a modern legal system contains far more diversity than one might conclude from his analytical scheme. He concedes that "a full detailed taxonomy of the varieties of law comprised in a modern legal system . . . remains to be accomplished. In distinguishing certain laws under the very rough head of laws that confer powers from those that impose duties. . . . we have made only a beginning" (*Concept*, 32). In the meantime, Hart would argue, his "rough heads" can serve powerfully as heuristic aids for a fresh start (but only a start) in jurisprudence.

A second difficulty in Hart's last try at demarcating his two broad classes of legal norms will prove more intractable. To proclaim that power-conferring rules are "thought of, spoken of, and used in social life differently from rules which impose duties" is to beg the question. The question is, precisely, whether power-conferring rules *are* thought of, spoken of, and used differently. One cannot persuasively answer such a question by simply molding it into an assertive dogma. A question-begging structure of repetition is unavoidable, but the assertoric form of the original query—if it is to count as an explanation—must be considerably more elaborate than Hart's rehearsing of his own view of social usages. Such a bare reassertion will add no more to his other arguments than would the assurances that Daniel appended to the decipherment of Nebuchadnezzar's dream: "The dream is certain, and its interpretation sure" (Daniel 2:45).

2. *Lawgivers Bound*

Unlike orders backed up with threats, most laws apply to all the people who issue them. In general, the legislators of modern governments are included in the ambit of the directives that they produce. To this extent, each law resembles a joint promise (though without any specific promisees); as a promisor is bound by the undertaking she gives, so—in general—a legislator is bound by the directives she helps to formulate. An especially close analogy, in Hart's view, is the self-imposed obligation that one incurs by becoming a trustee of assets for someone else. Perhaps inducing some readers to recall the canny philosophers who had sought to glimpse the Creator through meticulous study of His handiwork,[19] Hart declares that the "making of law by enactment is something we shall understand best by considering such private ways of creating particular legal obligations" (*Concept*, 43).

3. *From Custom to Law*

Austin's theory of law must presuppose that all legal norms derive from a central locus of sovereignty and that they do so through intentional law-creating acts. Hart objects that the Austinians overlook the formative role of custom in a regime of law (*Concept*, 43–48). To this objection Austinians can object *à tour*. Customs become law only because agents of the sovereign—judicial agents—treat certain types of customs as legal rules. Such agents must have at least the tacit approval of the sovereign, for they exert their power without any interference (except in truly extraordinary cases). The sovereign's noninterference should be construed as an implicit command.

Hart rejoins by bringing in an example of a top officer in the military who, through noninterference, lends his unspoken imprimatur to a sergeant's directives that the enlisted men perform certain fatigues. Hart notes that "it is not a necessary inference from the fact that the general did not interfere with the sergeant's orders that he wished them to be obeyed. He may merely have wished to placate a valued subordinate and hoped that the men would find some way of evading the fatigues" (*Concept*, 47). At this point, Hart compares his depiction of the general's tacit approval to the Austinian theory of the sovereign's tacit commands:

> No doubt we might in some cases draw the inference that he wished the fatigues to be done, but if we did this, a material part of our evidence would be the fact that the general knew that the orders had been given, had time to consider them, and decided to do nothing. The main objection to the use of the idea of tacit expressions of the sovereign's will to explain the legal status of custom is that, in any modern state, it is rarely possible to ascribe such knowledge, consideration and decision not to interfere to the 'sovereign', whether we identify the sovereign with the supreme legislature or the electorate. Only very rarely is the attention of a legislature, and still more rarely that of the electorate, turned to the customary rules applied by courts. Their non-interference can therefore not be compared to the general's non-interference with his sergeant; even if, in his case, we are prepared to infer from it a wish that his subordinates's orders be obeyed. [*Concept*, 47.]

The main problem with this argument is that it proves too much. A desire for obedience cannot ever be deduced with certainty from the passage of *any* legislation, even if the explicit countenance of the sovereign has been clearly bestowed. Ulterior motives can inspire approval as well as acquiescence. Similarly, one's plain endorsement of an underling's edicts can be a mere rubber stamp involving little or no knowledge of what has been upheld; indeed, one may presume quite safely that ignorant approval was very much the norm for President Reagan. What Hart has written, in other words, will in no way distinguish approbation from acquiescence. If there are verificative difficulties peculiar to the idea of a tacit dictate, Hart has failed to adduce them.

4. *The Continuity of Law*

Hart avers that the Austinian model of habitual obedience to a sovereign cannot account for the normal uninterruptedness of lawmaking authority in many (perhaps most) legal systems. When one lawmaker succeeds another, no hiatus goes by in which the orders of the new legislator eventually become "legal" as obedience to them grows habitual. Instead, there obtains a continuity of lawmaking regarded as such; throughout a series of legislators, the authority to create laws does not usually ebb and flow. From the outset, each new lawgiver is recognized as duly possessed of the legitimate power to make laws. And, Hart argues, this continuity of power does not square with the bald notions of "habit" and "obedience." Because each new legislator is held to be empowered to issue laws, legal theory must take into account the background norms that give rise to this unbroken entitlement. Such norms will have laid the ground for any habitual obedience that develops (*Concept*, 50–60).

Oddly, Hart does not give any consideration to a potential alternative. Under some credible conditions, Austin's theory could at least arguably account for the continuousness of law-creating prerogatives. To discover these conditions, we may turn to the Bible. When Solomon's title to the throne of Israel fell into grave jeopardy, his kingship was finally won through the express commands of his dying father. One could refer to an abundance of like examples, such as the presentation of Joshua to Israel by the elderly Moses. There would seem to be no conclusive reason that an Austinian monarch could not establish lines of successors in a roughly similar way. Every sovereign might adjure citizens to obey the precepts of the next sovereign. Indeed, one might even aim to generalize this approach by introducing the model of an implicitly ensconced line of succession; when explicit commands are lacking, a new lawmaker who peacefully succeeds the old lawmaker can be regarded as moving into the sovereign status by dint of the preceding sovereign's tacit commands, commands calling for obedience to the new lawmaker.

Aside from any problems associated with relying on tacit orders, the foregoing attempt to salvage Austin's position lies quite obviously open to an important challenge, which will be debated more generally in the next subsection: can commands retain any force when the lawmaker who issued them does not hold sway any longer? In this particular case, the challenge can of course be debated endlessly without definitive resolution; the defense of Austin made in this subsection can thus hardly purport to be decisive. That the defense is at least arguable, however, means that Hart ought to have addressed it.

Hart's view of continuity can be criticized from a slightly different direction. Hart does not explain why habituated obedience must be individualized in its focus. That is, he takes for granted that people will direct their obedience to an individual sovereign (whether it be a person or a body of persons), rather than to *anyone* lodged in the position of sovereign power *vis-à-vis* the general populace. He does not see that habitual obedience can have a certain relationship as its focus, transcending the specific people who occupy the dominating position(s). Hart would rejoin that if the focus of obedience has become transindividual, a full-fledged secondary rule must be operating to confer rights on each person (or on each group of persons) holding the sovereign status. However, if we return to the situation of the armed culprit, we can perceive that this postulated reply moves much too fast. Suppose that Gunman *G* relieves Gunman *F* and is in turn succeeded by Gunman *H* in the task of brandishing a weapon to cow a specific person or group of persons into obedience. It seems fully plausible that the victims will continuously defer to the gunmen as they succeed one another, and that the victims will submit thus because they feel obliged to do so—obliged, that is, to submit to anyone who can bring to bear deadly force against them. Likewise, the general public may feel continuously obliged to bow before sovereign dictates, no matter who is issuing them at a given time. People would not be yielding to a particular sovereign *qua* particular sovereign, but to a particular sovereign *qua* incumbent of a position that involves the ability to overpower dissent. Unbroken obedience would amount to unbroken efforts at avoiding punishment, and would not orient itself toward an individual sovereign as such. Nobody need feel that any one of a succession of sovereigns has a "right" to enjoy the dominant position; there need be only a presumed lack of alternatives to obeying someone, *someone or other*, who can punish contumacy with violence. Habits of submission would therefore stem from the threat of punitive force, and they would not be determined by the identities of the people who wield that threat at a given time.

5. *The Persistence of Law*

How, Hart wonders, can laws passed decades or centuries ago still carry binding force in the present? (*Concept*, 60–64). (As a "picturesque" example of this phenomenon, he adverts to the prosecution and subsequent conviction in 1944 of an English woman under the Witchcraft Act of 1735 [*Concept*, 60]. Why he holds this to be a "picturesque" example is not explained.) Hart argues that we will understand how ancient laws can persist (as laws) only if we acknowledge that the power to legislate is conferred by rules, rules that make possible a certain degree of timelessness. If, with Austin, one regards legislative authority as a function of mere habitual obedience, one will not have accounted for the durably binding character of laws passed by defunct sovereigns.

Hart raises and then dismisses a potential objection to his argument (*Concept*, 62–64). It might be maintained, he ventures, that hoary laws continue to bind because of tacit approval by the existing sovereign. Such laws could be modified or repealed if the present sovereign so wished; the fact that they go unchanged is hence a tacit expression of the sovereign will that they should continue to be observed. Once again, noninterference could be construed as authorization. Each time a judge enforces an ancient statute, the sovereign's acquiescence has turned the statute into current policy.

Hart's dismissal of this objection proceeds too hastily. To take the objection seriously, Hart writes, one has to believe that ancient laws do not secure their status as laws until they are now enforced by judges (or other agents). As Hart contends, such an assumption seems ludicrously implausible:

> Victorian statutes and those passed by the Queen in Parliament today surely have precisely the same legal status in present-day England. Both are law even before cases to which they are applied arise in the courts and, when such cases do arise, the courts apply both Victorian and modern statutes because they are already law. In neither case are these law only after they are applied by the courts; and in both cases alike their status as law is due to the fact that they were enacted by persons whose enactments are now authoritative under presently accepted rules, irrespective of the fact that these persons are alive or dead. [*Concept*, 63].

What Hart says is persuasive, but he has given only one conceivable reading of the criticism that he rebuts (and only one conceivable reading of the judiciary's enforcement of old statutes). Enforcement of laws created long ago might readily be perceived not as *constituting* but as *acknowledging* the current validity of such laws. A judge who enforced such laws would be thereby recognizing their status as pre-existent legal rules, which were given their life by the implicit refusal of the lawmaker to modify or repeal whatever laws have been handed down. Under this view, a sovereign has wordlessly approved statutes not only by allowing them to be implemented in certain cases, but also—and more importantly— by declining to alter them as the background law against which cases must be decided.

This form of the objection eliminates the ludicrousness that Hart points out, but it seems to run afoul of a new problem. That is, it seems to require—contrary to Austin's premises—that a secondary rule be involved, to the effect that statutes created long ago will continue to be valid till they are explicitly changed. To postulate such a rule would be to embellish the spartan furnishings of Austin's command theory, and would therefore seem to prove Hart's contention: an Austinian theory cannot explain the persistent force of law. But positing such a rule may not be an inevitable consequence or an integral aspect of this second form of the underlying objection. On the one hand, it would seem that we can infer acceptance from a lack of repealment only if there obtains some rule that prescribes repealment as the exclusive means to negate continued applicability. On the other hand, to presume automatically that a rule obtains is to overestimate the divergence between *norms* governing repealment and tacit *orders* relating thereto. To be sure, one reading of judicial decisions which enforce old statutes is that all such decisions manifest a rule that prescribes continued enforceability; but this is not the only possible reading. Those judgments can be regarded also as manifesting submission to a tacit command, where the submission will have sprouted from shared beliefs about the ways to interpret silence.

In imitation of Hart, let us take a game of some type as an illuminating analogy. Suppose the head scorer of the game has been entitled to fashion all or some of the rules, which serve as guides for the other scorers. Suppose further that a Head Scorer *B* replaces Head Scorer *A* and subsequently forbears repealing at least some rules that Scorer *A* had put forth. When confronted with situations that could be settled by an unrenounced rule, all the assistant scorers will probably invoke that rule in arriving at their decisions, and their reason for doing so need not be the existence of a recognized norm (i.e., a norm requiring continued applicability in the absence of repealment). Instead, they might simply share a hermeneutic assumption about the most appropriate way of explicating the silence of the head scorer. If the new head scorer has proposed nothing in conflict with the rules promulgated by the old head scorer, then each of the present scorers may feel it thoroughly natural to surmise that Head Scorer *B* wishes to retain the old scheme of things. And this assumption can be made safely even if the scorers do not derive it from an explicitly formulated norm (or from a direct order by their chief).

Let us return to the legal setting. Even in Austin's jurisprudence, room can be made for some amount of interpretation by each one of the sovereign's deputies. If each of them operates on an assumption like that attributed to the scorers in our example, then laws can be endowed with persistent force even if there prevail no secondary rules that have been acknowledged as such. In that case, we have to re-evaluate criticisms by judges aimed at their fellow judges who have declined to give an old statute its proper force. Such criticisms are aimed not at departures from an explicit rule of recognition, but at perceived failures to implement the will of the present sovereign. A devout Austinian, moreover, would try to generalize this point. From Austin's point of view, the criteria of recognition are but interpretative assumptions focused on realizing the tacit will or explicit will of the sovereign legislator (who is established as sovereign through the criteria themselves); thus, an Austinian would say, whenever a judge is censured for failing to enforce an old statute, he or she is "really" being upbraided for neglecting the tacit will of the sovereign, even if the terms of the criticism are rule-focused. At a deep level, or at what Austinians would see as a deep level, the judiciary's chastising of itself—oriented toward standards of recognition—will have reduced to no more than the exchanging of hermeneutic assumptions.

Someone loyal to Hart might counter that the foregoing argument will sustain its message only if one elides the difference between jointly accepted rules and individually harbored interpretations that chance to coincide. But that is precisely the point which is at stake here; the distinction between rules and shared interpretations is not nearly as clear-cut as Hart would like it to be. One need hardly be enamored of Austin to decide that the norms/interpretations split is chiefly a matter of emphasis and mood. Indeed, if we were to pursue this further—which, in a sense, is exactly what will be done throughout the second half of Part Two—we would find that rules and interpretations paradoxically intertwine through the very process of being differentiated.

6. *In Search of Sovereignty*

Some of Hart's most convincing arguments appear in his challenge to the Austinian portrait of a supreme lawmaker who does not habitually obey anyone and who is habitually obeyed by all or most persons to whom the dictates of the lawmaker reach. Hart rightly points out that Austin's definition of sovereignty, with its focus on substantive or factual patterns of obedience, cannot do justice to the potential fissure between those substantive patterns and the formally structured hierarchies that constitute any legal system (*Concept*, 68–69). (Hart's argument of course rests on an assumption that legal discourse and "real life" both bear sufficiently settled meanings to permit a comparison between them. Queried in Chapter 2, that assumption remains doubtful but will not once more be controverted at length.) Hart is equally persuasive when he contends that a society's populace as a whole cannot be enlisted by a fervent Austinian to play the role of the supreme legislator. Decisions would be made either by informal consensus-building (which, aside from being prodigiously far-fetched, would expose the silliness of a model based on "commands") or through recourse to secondary norms (which would introduce a new element into Austin's theory, at least if one assents to Hart's view of what "obeying" a law means [*Concept*, 74–75]). Hart admirably succeeds also in demonstrating that the existence of a legal system does not depend on the presence of a sovereign with unlimited powers (*Concept*, 66–69).

With this last-mentioned argument, however, there would seem to be one main problem: it is not at all clear that Austin's theory inevitably imputes unrestricted powers to sovereign legislators. Hart takes it as obvious that, in the account which Austin provides, "[t]here are, and can be, no legal limits on [a sovereign's] law-creating power . . . [,] by definition" (*Concept*, 64–65). Hart disregards the possibility of some self-imposed limitations. One might concede that such limitations could not stem from a secondary rule defining the legislative capacity of the sovereign; such a rule, handed down of course by the sovereign, might be thought to lack the characteristics of "commands." Even so, a sovereign could effect limitations through the use of duty-imposing orders. Specifically, all judges could be threatened with punishment for acting to enforce legislation touching on certain areas, and they could be threatened further if they pay any heed to dictates that purport to revoke the limit-setting order. This type of self-imposed limitation would naturally give rise to fiendishly tortuous (and also quite torturous) debates over the effect of later commands that override it—debates parallel to those that were once waged over the ability of the British Parliament to restrict its future legislative capacity. As Hart is fully aware, the British resolution of those debates is far from logically necessary (*Concept*, 145–46; *Jurisprudence*, 177). Given that that is so, however, one cannot rightly claim that an Austinian sovereign *has* to have unlimited powers.

C. Legal Theory's Fresh Start

1. *Rules and Obligations*

Having exposed the many weak spots in the command theory of law, Hart moves on to make an earnest "fresh start" in jurisprudence. As a preliminary, he offers a quite detailed analysis of the chief earmarks of rules and obligations. He presents three ways in which rules (of any sort) differ from shared habits (*Concept*, 54–56). First, when a rule holds sway, deviations from the standard form of behavior will, as such, usually arouse criticism and pressure for conformity. When mere habits are involved, aberrations do not generally provoke censure. Second, where certain rules have become established, most people will regard criticism of infractions as justifiable; that an infraction has occurred is a good reason for criticism. Third, people who live by norms must view them from an "internal" perspective. In essence, this third point is a systematized version of the other two points.

> What is necessary is that there should be a critical reflective attitude to certain patterns of behaviour as a common standard, and that this

> should display itself in criticism (including self-criticism), demands for conformity, and in acknowledgements that such criticism and demands are justified, all of which find their characteristic expression in the normative terminology of 'ought', 'must', and 'should', 'right', and 'wrong' (*Concept*, 56).

People who live by rules do not simply engage in regularized patterns of behavior that can be adequately expressed in terms stripped of normativity. On the contrary, they see their patterns as desirable norms that ought to be upheld.

Not all rules impose obligations. Hart declares that obligations arise when the demand by most people for compliance with rules is serious and insistent and when the punishment or the moral suasion brought to bear on transgressors is strong (*Concept*, 84). (In the case of a legal system, not every rule that can be said to impose an obligation need be treated too seriously, so long as the general system enjoys significant backing.) Hart is concerned to draw a sharp dichotomy between "being obliged" and "having an obligation" (*Concept*, 80–81). To have an obligation consists in being under a rule, seriously regarded, which commands or forbids a certain act. To be obliged, on the other hand, is to be compelled to do (or forbear doing) a certain action, owing to fear of punishment or other unpleasant consequences. Being obliged and having an obligation will frequently conjoin, but will also frequently be dissevered. A jaywalker has an obligation to cross the street at specified points, but she will not be obliged to do so; a gunman's victim is obliged to relinquish money, but does not have an obligation to do so.

If obligations arise from norms that are backed by serious social pressure, can "obligation" be defined in terms of the probability that someone having an obligation will incur punishment or severe disapproval in the wake of noncompliance? Hart's answer is an emphatic "no" (*Concept*, 81–88). Apart from the fact that being under an obligation does not always consort with being obliged, a "predictive theory" of obligation overlooks the so-called internal aspect of rules. Violations of rules are seen, by those people who accept the rules, not merely as grounds for postulating that disciplinary measures will very likely ensue, but as good grounds for positing that disciplinary measures *should* be taken. For those who embrace a rule, the specific rule in question does not amount to a mere cause of convergences; rather, it holds as an authoritative guideline, and any breach of it ergo justifies the imposing of sanctions (in the form of physical or financial punishments or of general disapprobation). Hart elaborates this point by distinguishing between "signs" and "signals."[20] An outside observer who does not adopt a hermeneutic approach for understanding a social system will regard a breach of the system's rules as a *sign* that punitive measures (or a hostile reaction) will in all probability take place. From the internal viewpoint, breaches are not just signs but are also *signals* that punishment (or hostility) *should* occur.

2. *Primary and Secondary Rules*

Hart asks us to picture a society without courts, legislators, or governmental officials of any kind. He identifies three principal shortcomings that such a society will exhibit (*Concept,* 89–91). First, there will prevail great uncertainty regarding the scope and composition of the duty-imposing rules under which the members of the society coexist. No one can authoritatively ascertain the exact boundaries of accepted rules concerning the allocation of resources and the protection of personal integrity. Second, the society's fundamental rules will be largely static; the rules cannot be altered deliberately, for they develop and evanesce in accordance with the imperceptible evolution of shared moral assumptions. Third, without an authoritative agency to determine whether rules have or have not been breached, a social order will suffer unrest and inefficiency stemming from the interminable disputes that will almost certainly rankle. A closely related cause of inefficiency is the lack of a formal punitive mechanism to oblige wrongdoers to pay for misdeeds.

To remedy these three defects, a social grouping requires a "supplement" to its primary rules of obligation.[21] This supplement Hart characterizes as a regime of "secondary rules" that can both perfect and extend the arsenal of duty-imposing rules. As most critics of Hart have seen, he often appears befuddled in his attempts to capture just what he is referring to as the "secondary" norms. Here is his first attempt:

> Rules of the other type are in a sense parasitic upon or secondary to the first; for they provide that human beings may by doing or saying certain things introduce new rules of the primary type, extinguish or modify old ones, or in various ways determine their incidence or control their operations. Rules of the first type impose duties; rules of the second type confer powers, public or private. Rules of the first type concern actions involving physical movement or changes; rules of the second type provide for operations which lead not merely to physical movement or change, but to the creation or variation of duties or obligations. [*Concept,* 79.]

Corresponding to the three major imperfections of a pre-legal society, secondary rules are divided into three types. The first of these "parasitic" rules is what Hart calls the "rule of recognition."[22] In every legal system, officials have to resort to some criterion or set of criteria for conclusively ascertaining what the rules of the system are. Through the existence of authoritative criteria, the aforementioned problem of uncertainty can in large part be defused. A rule of recognition, even if it has never formally been enacted—through processes of enactment that can be recognized as such only within the rule—imposes on every member of the judiciary (and on other officials) a duty to abide by the determinations it warrants. Thus, even if one accepts Hart's duty-imposing/power-conferring framework, one should discount his implication (in the long passage above) that all secondary rules are power-conferring.[23] (More will be said shortly about the rule of recognition.)

Next among the chief types of secondary rules are what Hart calls the "rules of change," which are designed to address the problem of stagnancy (*Concept*, 93), and which are a large subset of the entire class of power-conferring rules. Included in this subset are all the rules conferring private powers and all the rules conferring the public power of legislation. Whether all the rules of inheritance would here be comprised is not apparent, but Hart presumably would include only those varieties of inheritance (such as bequests through wills) that have obviously involved some deliberation on the part of the legator.

"Rules of adjudication" alleviate the problems of inefficiency that result when a social unit lacks an authorized body to decide whether its basic rules of obligation have been infringed (*Concept*, 94–95). Secondary rules of adjudication empower certain individuals to make binding judgments when presented with allegations that accepted rules have been breached. In every advanced legal system, this adjudicatory power is combined with the power to impose sanctions against malefactors.

A regime that has supplemented its primary rules with secondary rules (of recognition, change, and adjudication) will, in Hart's view, merit being categorized as a full-fledged system of law. Indeed, for Hart the importance of this supplementary union of primary rules and secondary rules can hardly be overestimated. He refers to the combination of the two classes of rules as "the heart of a legal system," "the centre of a legal system," "the 'essence' of law," and "'the key to the science of jurisprudence'" (*Concept*, 95, 96, 151, 79). A theory that accords the primary/secondary conjunction its rightful prominence will reject the sadly "blurred" vision of other theories, which have left the truth about law veiled in the dark mists of "obscurity."[24] To acknowledge the central site of law is to regain one's own sight.

3. *Recognizing the Rule of Recognition*

If we now perceive the combination of primary and secondary rules as the "heart of a legal system," then the rule of recognition turns out to be nothing less than the true "foundation" of a regime of law (*Concept*, 97). This "foundation" operates like a rule, but its existence is a pure matter of fact; the rule of recognition is "*shown* in the way in which particular rules are identified . . . by courts or other officials" (*Concept*, 98; emphasis in original). Officials employ the rule of recognition to ascertain all the other laws, even though they seldom articulate the rule fully. It serves them as an often implicit guide that enables them to make judgments—from an "internal" point of view—concerning the validity of the other rules in their legal system. For Hart, statements that a particular law is valid can only mean that it satisfies the criteria which make up the rule of recognition. Such statements "most frequently though not always" stem from the engaged viewpoint of judges or attendant officials (*Concept,* 100), and they should not be confused with statements (usually issuing from an external viewpoint) that a particular rule of recognition is followed in a particular society.

Hart emphasizes that an internal statement pronouncing the validity of a rule does not have to take as given the general efficaciousness of the legal order within which it is advanced, though "the normal use of internal statements is in such a context of general efficacy" (*Concept,* 101). Hart denounces, as even more mistaken than seeing general efficaciousness as an unavoidable presupposition of validity statements, the belief that such statements are tantamount to predictions that particular rules will be enforced. Applicable, in Hart's view, are the objections that were raised earlier to predictive analyses of obligation. A predictive analysis excludes understanding of the internal point of view—whence validity statements furnish *reasons* for judgments rather than serve exclusively to *foretell* them—and hence it obscures the characteristic function of the claims that it analyzes.

In an important sense, rules of recognition perform a role similar to that played by the God of Thomas Aquinas as the *prima causa efficiens.* All valid rules in any legal regime derive their status from the operative rule of recognition, but the validity-conferring rule can itself never be validated. As has been argued in Chapters 1 and 2, a norm can never embrace itself without leaving an irreducible remainder. Thus, a rule of recognition is "ultimate" in the sense that, within the legal order it shapes, no question of its own validity can be answered.

> We only need the word 'validity', and commonly only use it, to answer questions which arise *within* a system of rules where the status of a rule as a member of the system depends on its satisfying certain criteria provided by the rule of recognition. No such question can arise as to the validity of the very rule of recognition which provides the criteria; it can neither be valid nor invalid but is simply accepted as appropriate for use in this way. [*Concept,* 105–106.]

Hart exudes confidence that a focus on rules of recognition will lead jurisprudential thought out of the "shadow" cast by Austinian command theories—theories that cannot but "obscure the facts."[25] He assures us that "when we take off the spectacles constituted by [the standard] terminology and look at the facts," we shall see the truth, and the truth will make us free (*Concept,* 109). As the vision-related tropes multiply, Hart returns to one of his previous contentions—the claim that public officials do not "obey" the laws that empower them to discharge their official roles. At first, his argument sounds quite similar to the one that has already been criticized. He proceeds, however, to draw a more interesting diremption between "obedience" and "acceptance" (*Concept*, 112–13). To "obey" a law, under Hart's new definition, is to conform one's behavior to it without manifesting a commitment to it as a desirable norm. A person who obeys particular laws may be committed to them as well, of course, but obeying "*need* involve no thought on the part of the person obeying that what he does is the right thing both for himself and for others to do. . . . He need not think of his conforming behaviour as 'right', 'correct', or 'obligatory'" (*Concept*, 112). *Accepting* a rule is quite a different matter, for, in Hart's definition, somebody who "accepts" a rule must show a commitment to it. This entails adopting the attitude that was described earlier by Hart when he differentiated between rules and habits: namely, the "critical reflective attitude," which impels criticism of violations, demands for renewed compliance, and "acknowledgement that such criticism and demands are justified" (*Concept*, 56).

Ordinary citizens, Hart claims, need only *obey* laws (though of course a legal regime will be much more hearty if most citizens support most of its enactments as worthwhile standards of behavior) (*Concept*, 112). Officials cannot afford to be so detached, particularly concerning the rule of recognition. If judges declined to reprehend deviations from the perceived criteria of validity, and if they spurned reprimands from other judges, they would destroy the harmony of objectives which Hart presumes to be "a necessary condition of our ability to speak of the existence of a single legal system," and without which "the characteristic unity and continuity of a legal system would have disappeared" (*Concept*, 112–13). In a long sentence, Hart summarizes the two bedrock conditions for the abiding efficacy of a legal system: "On the one hand those rules of behaviour which are valid according to the system's ultimate criteria of validity must be generally obeyed, and, on the other hand, its rules of recognition specifying the criteria of legal validity and its rules of change and adjudication must be effectively accepted as common public standards of official behaviour by its officials" (*Concept*, 113).

Part Two. Circularity, Paradox, and Blindness

In the preceding Part, the theory articulated in *The Concept of Law* (or, rather, the portion of the theory developed in the first half of that book) was met on clearly hostile terrain: the terrain of concepts and terminology which are highlighted in Hart's text and which serve as the precondition of its persuasive force. Most of the discussion proceeded in a vocabulary of which Hart could approve with ease, and the critical observations were rather sparse though at times lengthy. Even the critical remarks accepted the basic contours of Hart's discussion. In the second half of this chapter, my approach will take a markedly different route. This does not mean that we must fall back from Hart's discourse to a radically new selection of key terms. Attempts to retreat would always fail, and would take for granted—as Hart probably does—that the meanings of *The Concept of Law* are stable and univocal (or nearly univocal). Only if one infers univocality and stability does one feel entitled and compelled to look for a safe exterior, because only then will one have rashly supposed that the *interior* of Hart's discourse is sufficiently well defined and coherent to be regarded as self-same. In question here will be inside/outside diremptions, both as they have been thematized by Hart and as they have implicitly operated in assumptions (made by him and by his interpreters) relating to the integrity of his discourse. Through analyses that can best be situated as neither internal nor external, I shall endeavor to jolt Hart's theory against itself. As Jacques Derrida observes:

> Each proposition, which is already interpretive in nature, can be interpreted by another proposition. Therefore, if we proceed prudently. . . , we can detach an interpretation from its reinterpretation and submit it to another interpretation bound to other propositions of the system. Which, without interrupting general systematicity, amounts to recognizing the strong and weak moments in the interpretation of a body of thought by itself, these differences of force keeping to the strategic necessity of finite discourse.[26]

No new concepts or terms will be required, for Hart's own concepts and terms will take on functions—of self-unraveling—very different from those that are highlighted in his text. In the process, the distinction between "new" vantage points and "old" vantage points will not have emerged intact (even though it cannot be simply erased); but this suggests that it may never have been intact. Moreover, the "strategic necessity of finite discourse" will disseminate its effects throughout procedures that highlight those effects. Whether the dynamic of my analyses has always yet to take place (as an imposition) or has always already taken place (before revelation) is a vexed puzzle that demands and postpones an answer.

This Part is divided into two sections. In the first of these, circular repetition in Hart's theory will conflict with the aspirations thereof. Some aspects of this initial challenge have been touched on by other critics,[27] but the treatment here will be more wide-ranging and will give greater emphasis to the details of Hart's text. In the second half of Part Two, the dichotomies that lend structure to Hart's discourse—dichotomies between rules and habits, norms and facts, internal positions and external positions—will be deconstructed. This, it should be urged, does not mean that those conceptual pairings will be simply obliterated; they have to be retained, that they may undo themselves. Hart's dyads will ensure their continuation by virtue of dismantling themselves. My analysis should therefore never pretend to be the "last word" on any issue. On the contrary, it serves as a mere step (and thus a misstep) in the unceasing play of paradoxical dislocation.

A. Presupposed Conclusions as Disqualifications

1. *The Problem in Hart's Theory*

For Hart, the foundation of any legal regime is an observable rule of recognition that guides official behavior in the ascertainment of laws. An analyst who wants to identify the ground of a given legal system will thus have to provide responses to two main queries: *Whose* behavior is structured by the operative rule of recognition? *Which* behavior is structured by the operative rule of recognition?

Hart's answer to the first problem is in general quite clear, though sometimes a bit muddled. In several places, Hart writes that a rule of recognition can be distilled from the relevant behavior of private persons as well as of officials. He maintains, for example, that "the rule of recognition exists only as a complex, but normally concordant, practice of the courts, officials, and private persons in identifying the law by reference to certain criteria."[28] As P. M. S. Hacker notes, however, from Hart's point of view private persons are more like spectators than like participants.[29] They *may* keep themselves apprised of the chief criteria of recognition, but they *need* not do so. Sufficient and necessary for the immanence of a rule of recognition in a society is *officials'* upholding of the criteria embraced in such a rule. As was pointed out near the end of the first Part, the distinction posed in *The Concept of Law* between obedience and acceptance is aimed at showing that private citizens do not have to accept any of the rules in a legal system. Much less need they affirm the usually unspoken and complex rule that grounds the validation of all other directives. One may thus conclude that a hopeful theorist seeking to ferret out the foundation of a legal regime should concentrate her attention on the behavior of officials.

Hart's response to the second query—about *which* behavior will be demonstrative of the rule of recognition—is more uniform. He states repeatedly that the rule of recognition enables judges (and certain other officials) to determine the exact set of rules, both secondary and primary,[30] that belong to a particular legal system. By far the most frequent term that Hart wields in his discussions of this activity is "identification" (along with cognate terms, such as "identify" and "identifying"). He declares, for instance, that "a secondary rule of recognition is accepted and used for the identification of primary [and secondary] rules" (*Concept*, 97). Identification, to which Hart also refers as "determination" and "ascertain[ment]" (*Concept*, 95, 92), is effected in each case through a minute search for some feature (an "authoritative mark" [*Concept*, 93]), or group of features, which officials employ to separate all rules of a specific regime of law from all other rules. Any rule bearing a germane feature, such as legislative enactment or judicial pronouncement, will assume its niche in the panoply of rules that officials recognize. As surely as a mark on the forehead from Ezekiel's God could winnow the faithful from the wicked, the "marks" addressed by the rule of recognition will separate the legal from the nonlegal. By pointing explicitly or implicitly to an established earmark of law, officials can gird themselves with authoritative groundings for their decisions. Unlike the determinations of private people, the ascertainment of laws by governmental agents has to be seen (at least over the long run) as coherently defining the sundry characteristics that—separately or in combination—qualify rules as laws.

As was noted briefly in Chapter 2, a rather obvious difficulty arises here: what Hart deems to be the foundation of any legal system turns out to presuppose that a legal regime exists beforehand. In describing whose behavior is given shape by the rule of recognition, Hart claims that the foundational rule is immanent in *official* practices. But "officials" can be identified as such only when a framework of laws has come into existence already. As Ian Duncanson has observed: "[W]ho *is* an official, and how is he constituted as such? He can only be a person, natural or corporate, whose 'officiality' has been conferred by a rule or norm, justified by reference to a rule or rules."[31] The actors whose decisions supposedly amount to a juridical fundament would now appear to be wholly epiphenomenal.

Much the same can be said about *identification*, the activity with which Hart so often tries to flesh out the category of "recognition." If certain acts are to count as having "identified" the rules of a particular legal system authoritatively, they can do so only within a context of legal baselines that specify the acts which are sufficient and necessary thereto. Officials who identify legal rules are supposed to watch sedulously for "marks" that confer on rules their status as laws; inevitably omitted from the account, however, are the marks that denote identification as such. The specifying or authorizing of certain agents and certain acts will require a background of legal systematicity from which authorization comes. Hart here faces a problem similar to that highlighted in Jacques Derrida's critique of the Declaration of Independence, where the feat of validating that noble document turns out to have rested all along on the power that it supposedly generated:

> Thus, there is the "good people" that engages itself and engages itself only in signing itself, in signing its own declaration. The "we" of the declaration speaks "in the name of the people."
>
> But this people does not exist. It does not exist *before* this declaration, not *as such*. If it gives birth to itself as a free and independent subject, as a possible signatory, that can hold only in (or with) the act of this signature [. . . *cela ne peut tenir qu'à l'acte de cette signature*]. The signature invents the signatory. This signatory can authorize itself to sign only once it has reached the end of its signature, if one can say this, in a sort of fabulous retroactivity. Its first signature authorizes it to sign. This happens every day, but it is fabulous.[32]

When we turn to look more closely at Hart's text, the distressing problem of circularity emerges time and again. Through a persistent focus on the "identifying" of legal traits when Hart discusses the rule of recognition, he offers nothing more than a group of question-begging restatements of his theory's ungroundedness. Quite obvious is it that he does not employ "identification" as a term reaching to all conjectures about the content of a society's laws. Such usage would do away with the whole idea of a *rule* of recognition, and would elide the difference that Hart tries to affirm between a legal system and a pre-legal system. (Such usage would furthermore introduce the problem of specifying what counts as a "conjecture," along with the equally forbidding problem of saying what counts as a "society.") For Hart, identification must proceed through authorized acts performed by official agents. But this means that the basic arguments of *The Concept of Law* will endlessly chase after themselves in circles, for legal systematicity will be presupposed by the origin of legal systematicity. One can discover such a plight at many key junctures in Hart's text, but—to avert tedium—only two examples will here be marshaled.

While arguing that the general public does not have to accept laws but only has to obey them, Hart alludes revealingly to what he regards as the foundational norm of every legal order: "So long as the laws which are valid by *the system's* tests of validity are obeyed by the bulk of the population this surely is all the evidence we need in order to establish that a given legal system exists" (*Concept*, 111; emphasis added). Another reversal of foundations occurs while Hart is acknowledging that most lawyers who identify rules as valid do not expressly invoke the rule of recognition. If lawyers are somehow challenged, Hart contends, "what is thus presupposed but left unstated could be established by appeal to the facts, i.e. to the actual practice of the courts and officials *of the system* when identifying the law which they are to apply" (*Concept*, 245; emphasis added). In each of these instances, and in many others, the supposed ground of a legal system turns out to be derived from systematicity. Legal regimes must always have already come forward into being if they are ever to gain existence. In legal thought, systematicity will always sneak in before it can be permitted entry.

At this point, one might object that the standard of explanation which Hart is being asked to meet here is based on antiquated conceptions of what "explaining" something entails. If we cleave pertinaciously to models of philosophical inquiring as logically precise deduction, then Hart will have indeed trapped himself in a perpetual game of mirrors. He cannot seize on the rule of recognition as a ground for deductive argument, since he will inevitably presuppose what he imagines himself to be explaining. But, it might be argued, there exist other models of explanation and other ways in which Hart might classify rules of recognition as "fundaments" of their legal systems. One might follow the lead of Richard Rorty in shifting from a philosophy of argumentation to a philosophy of narrative.[33] Hart, it might be claimed, aspires merely to furnish us a convincing if abstract story (or narrative portrayal) of what we can expect to encounter when we study the workings of a legal regime. Having renounced chimerical quests for rigor, he would then be seeking to paint evocative portraits of the dynamics and the structure of law. He would be attempting to see "how things . . . hang together" in legal discourse and legal practices.[34] Those who might favor such a pragmatist version of his thought can seize happily on his statement that *The Concept of Law* "may . . . be regarded as an essay in descriptive sociology" (*Concept*, v). Under this view, the rule of recognition will shoulder its "foundational" task in a distinctly limited sense. It will not serve as a *Grund* or fountainhead from which everything must flow—including that which it presupposes—but will instead function as the hallmark of the discrete existence of a legal regime. Just as uniform attitudes toward some problem (such as the self/other distinction) might be viewed as an index of a particular literary genre, so uniform behavior in regard to the ascertainment of laws might function as the characteristic mark of a particular legal system. Hart would still be begging all the important questions, of course; he would still have to presuppose the systematical context of certain actions if he is to decide *whose* actions and *which* actions are to count as manifesting a rule of recognition. But that might no longer seem so troubling if his aim is to tell a story rather than to construct a theory (or, better, if his aim in articulating a theory is to relate a story). Once we make Hart into a storyteller, we may be less disturbed by his having to presuppose what are ostensibly his conclusions, his dénouement, in order to start his narrative. We may be less worried, too, over the fact that his conclusions cannot emerge unless his theoretical story has begun independently. Disquiet might wane once we recall that Zeno could deftly fashion tales of Achilles chasing a tortoise even while Zeno showed such narratives to be incoherent.

Difficulties raised by the foregoing attempt to salvage Hart's theory would be legion, far too numerous and extensive to be explored adequately here. A pragmatist interpretation of Hart professes to transcend or forswear the dualisms that have structured Western philosophy, but it remains firmly in thrall to them—especially to the literature/philosophy distinction—precisely insofar as it tries to leave them behind. Suffice it to say that one's upholding narrative discourse as in some way free of antinomical turbulence would occasion great surprise on the part of critics who have found deconstruction to be a penetrating set of approaches in the reading of literary texts. Consider, for example, Paul de Man's claim that "[c]ontrary to common belief, literature is not the place where the unstable epistemology of metaphor is suspended by aesthetic pleasure, although this attempt is a constitutive moment of its system. It is rather the place where the possible convergence of rigor and pleasure is shown to be a delusion."[35] At any rate, no full-scale critique of pragmatism is at all necessary yet; any pragmatist reading of *The Concept of Law* will run afoul of a peculiarly unsettling obstacle. Hart himself has disqualified such a reading in remarkably strong terms. In the first chapter of his book, he considers the possibility of responding to the question "What is law?" by presenting a "skeleton account of the salient features of a municipal legal system." Such an account, he notes, would involve "a series of reminders of what is already familiar" (*Concept*, 4–5). Having sketched such an account, he quickly decides against it, for reasons that deserve to be quoted at some length:

> Such a way with the question would be agreeably short. But it would have nothing else to recommend it. . . . [I]f we consider the terms of our skeleton account of a legal system, it is plain that it does little more than assert that in the standard, normal case laws of various sorts go together. This is so because both a court and a legislature, which appear in this short account as typical elements of a standard legal system, are themselves creatures of law. Only when there are certain types of laws giving men jurisdiction to try cases and authority to make laws do they constitute a court or a legislature.
>
> This short way with the question, which does little more than remind the questioner of the existing conventions governing the use of the words 'law' and 'legal system', is therefore useless [*Concept*, 5.]

For a man who thinks so highly of Bentham's work, the epithet "useless" may amount to the gravest charge that can be leveled against anything. Hart declines to have any truck with circularity, be it the vicious circularity that afflicts question-begging deductive arguments or the so-called virtuous circularity of stories that "remind the questioner of . . . existing conventions." One could say that Hart has now brought us back *full circle* from our pragmatist divagation. In so doing, however, he appears to have blocked his theory from ever being "useful" for anything.

2. *MacCormick to the Rescue*

A. CIRCULARITY UNDONE?

With Scottish élan, Neil MacCormick has come gallantly to the rescue of his erstwhile colleague from Oxford. In *Legal Reasoning and Legal Theory* and in *H. L. A. Hart*, MacCormick endeavors to allay any fears of circularity. In the former book he tackles the problem twice, once frontally and once in passing. Let us first examine his passing shot: "We know the rules of law because we have 'criteria of recognition' or something like that. . . . If we could not and did not have rules of law, law examinations would be even more pointless than those who sit and those who mark them are in their gloomiest moments inclined to think them" (*Reasoning*, 232–33). These remarks can be read in at least two ways. First, and most apparently, they amount to a light-hearted dismissal of the whole problem, a dismissal whose very jauntiness purports to be the sole refutation needed. Construed in this manner, the remarks enjoy a distinguished pedigree: the "disproof" of Zeno's paradoxes of motion by the miffed person in his audience who proceeded to walk away; the abrupt move by Descartes to throw away the hypothesis that he was mad, on the ground that he would have to be mad to entertain such a proposition seriously; Locke's defense of the dream/reality distinction, with his advice to skeptics that they place their hands in "the glowing heat of a glass furnace" so that they "may perhaps be wakened into a certainty greater than [they] could wish that it is something more than bare imagination"; Johnson's vigorous kicks against a stone to "refute" Berkeley's idealism.[36]

A second reading of MacCormick's rebuffs would treat them as more serious (or as less serious, depending on how one views such matters). They could be interpreted as a pragmatist reminder that "recognition" of laws, like all other social practices, can proceed only within the shared assumptions and understandings of a hermeneutic community. As Stanley Fish declares: "[C]ommunication occurs only *within* . . . a system (or context, or situation, or interpretive community) and . . . the understanding achieved by two or more persons is specific to that system and determinate only within its confines."[37]

Now, whether one accepts the first reading or the second reading of the passage in question, one will have to conclude that Hart's position has not been bolstered. Each interpretation will leave Hart with a "useless" theory, either because (in the first interpretation) the problem of circularity is allowed and left willfully unresolved, or because (in the second reading) pragmatism has once more raised its head to "remind the questioner of the existing conventions." A theorist who professes to have uncovered the "foundation" of every legal system cannot endorse MacCormick's jocundity. Suitors of truth have scant time for frolicking.[38]

Indeed, MacCormick seems not to take his own banter very seriously, for he elsewhere views the problem of presupposed conclusions with as much earnestness as one could reasonably expect. In an early chapter of *Legal Reasoning and Legal Theory,* he acknowledges that Hart's theory can be attacked as "viciously circular" (*Reasoning,* 55), and he goes on not to dismiss and jeer such attacks but to explain why they are ill-founded. He begins by turning the problem of circularity into a problem of institutional bodies (and the fitness thereof): "Courts are not self-sustaining institutions endowed with legitimacy by their own say so, clothed with might by their own bodily vigour. They are institutions established (however informally or formally) by a wider community from which they derive their legitimacy and authority as determiners of controversies" (*Reasoning,* 55). Hart, of course, had never maintained that judges pull themselves up entirely by their own bootstraps. He had always taken account of the full range of officials whose behavior collectively decides the exact lineaments of the rule of recognition, though (like most jurisprudes, especially in the United States[39]) he had assigned judges the central role in deciding what should be recognized. MacCormick wants to take this point further—far enough, indeed, to eliminate the problem of circularity. In the following sentences, he elaborates his conception of the "wider community" from which derives the authoritative stature of judges:

> That wider community which accords to the Courts their legitimacy and authority is not necessarily the whole 'community of the realm' to use an attractive old phrase. It may perhaps be no wider than that of the power group or ruling class which can by one means or another muster force and fear enough to sustain order within what *they* define as the whole community of the realm. . . .
>
> To have 'judges' at all, at the very simplest and most informal analytical level, we must therefore postulate the existence of some group of people who ascribe to some individual or individuals of their number the function of determining controversies. [*Reasoning,* 55.]

Judges do not have to rely *seulement* on their own bodily vigor, since the rule of recognition that they have followed "is not a norm whose existence depends solely and sufficiently on the will of the judges; it is accepted, and its continued observance is willed, by the substantial majority of at least the most powerful and influential groupings in our society" (*Reasoning,* 56).

MacCormick presumes thus that he has banished the fearsome specter of circularity. He appears, however, to have become quickly entangled in the flow of what he is analyzing, for he has carried us (in a circle) to the questions that unbridled the specter in the first place. That is, we shall have to specify just *whose* behavior and also *which* behavior go toward establishing the rule of recognition, and we shall have to make these specifications on independent grounds, grounds not presupposing a particular rule of recognition. We cannot know, in other words, that instances of behavior amount to what we are searching for, before we decide that they amount to what we are searching for. To be sure, the problem has been slightly displaced. No longer are we looking for acts of recognition; now we are looking for the tacit or explicit approval of such acts. But on all other counts, the problem has not abated. A "useful" legal theory has to define such entities as "the power group or ruling class," "the whole community of the realm," and "the most powerful and influential groupings," without simply designating them as groups that adhere to a particular rule of recognition. If we are to ferret out the criteria of recognition by looking at the behavior of certain groups—i.e., the group of officials who perform acts of recognition, and the other groups that support those acts—then we cannot identify the relevant groups by presupposing the rule of recognition. Likewise, a "useful" theory will have to state exactly which actions "accord to the Courts their legitimacy and authority" and "ascribe to some individual or individuals . . . the function of determining controversies," without deriving the needed specifications from an already identified rule of recognition. If a mode of behavior is to be classified as supporting a rule of recognition, then such a rule will have to be known already; but that rule is precisely what has yet to be ascertained. In short, MacCormick has not escaped the problem of circularity but has merely tied on another level to it. Behavior supporting recognition, like recognition itself, cannot be defined unless the criteria of recognition are discovered beforehand. One cannot identify the support of X without knowing what X is—but that means that definitions of the support of X cannot serve to ground our knowledge of X. Ian Duncanson is hence justified in asserting that "the 'powerful and influential groupings' are identified from within legal theory, as those who accept the highest norm. They are not independently theorized."[40]

Perhaps stung by the obvious inadequacy of his foregoing attempt, MacCormick has tried again—four years later—to overcome the problem of circular repetition (*H. L. A. Hart*, 109–20). His approach, in line with some suggestive remarks by Rolf Sartorius,[41] differs from his earlier strategy in being more diachronic (or historical) than synchronic (or structural). By plumbing the obscure roots of modern systems of law, MacCormick hopes to make clear that the judicial implementation and identification of specific laws need not rest on power-conferring rules of adjudication—that, in other words, the judicial functions (which are supposed to be foundational, in the world according to Hart) need not rest on a precursory legal framework. MacCormick would thus seem to evade the endlessly question-begging structure of repetition to which Hart's writings had appeared to condemn us.

MacCormick aims to show that "an apparent logical absurdity [can] be a working actuality" (*H. L. A. Hart*, 111). He begins in a fairly puzzling manner, by hypothesizing a primitive society in which all rules stem from tradition rather than from deliberate legislation. Not all the difficulties in this part of MacCormick's argument can be dredged up here, but a few key points must be noted. In his primitive society there exists a standard, a customary standard, prohibiting the use of violence except when the perpetrator of violent acts is "enforcing compensation or retribution against one who is *adjudged* to be a wrongdoer" (*H. L. A. Hart*, 112). Allegations of wrongdoing must be passed upon and confirmed by the village elders before violence can legitimately be used. MacCormick argues that "our theoretical concept of 'normative power' is inapplicable" to the adjudicative role of the village elders (*H. L. A. Hart*, 112). In his view, the elders have a *duty* to hand down judgments, but they do not exercise a *power* in doing so.

Most of the brief argument that MacCormick offers in support of this view does nothing more than reiterate his premise that the "concept of 'normative power' is inapplicable," but he concludes with an interesting analogy that deserves some comment. Dispute-resolution by the village elders "[n]o more . . . involve[s] an exercise of normative power than does this case: boys playing football in a park have a dispute whether something one of them did was a foul, so they ask a spectator to give his opinion, and he gives it and they accept it" (*H. L. A. Hart*, 112). MacCormick has here demonstrated too little *and* too much. He proves too much, because his analogy involves obligations not one whit more than it involves powers. He proves too little, because his football example lacks the most important feature of his imaginary primitive social setting. When the boys receive an opinion from the spectator, their choice of him to judge their dispute is *ad hoc* and arbitrary, whereas one will find no such randomness in the choice of the village elders to resolve a given dispute; a customary standard allots to them the exclusive power of reaching judgment on allegations of wrongdoing. Of course, why someone should be considered a village elder is an open choice *at the outset*, just as criteria for the occupation of any judgeship in any system are an open choice *at the outset*. But once the criteria are shaped, as they are shaped in the primitive society that MacCormick pictures, assignment of disputes to the exact people who qualify as elders will have become regularized, by definition. In the case of the spectator and the football players, there exist no such regularities; the spectator's "judgeship" is *ad hoc* and informal.

It is precisely the lack of randomness in the referral of conflicts for settlement by the elders that makes MacCormick's entire line of argument so implausible. Within his postulated society the elders inhabit a unique position, conferred by the customary rule: they, and they only, can legitimate a resort to violence—or authoritatively check such a resort—through their prerogative to decide between claims and counterclaims. In handing down decisions, they expressly or tacitly invoke the norm that endows them with their adjudicative role, just as much as does any judicial officer in an advanced legal system. It would seem, in fact, that the sole reason for withholding the label "powers" from what the primitive elders do is an unexplained assumption that duties necessarily exclude powers. MacCormick, however, would deride that very assumption even more caustically than would Hart;[42] that the elders have an obligation to patch up rents in the social fabric will scarcely have forbidden their holding powers to do so. Indeed, their *duty* to render judgments will make little or no sense, at least in practical terms, unless accompanied by the *power* to render judgments.

B. A Germane Excursus

This point can be extended, well past anything Hart says (though also within his discourse). One can say of MacCormick's primitive social structure, or of any primitive social structure, that it displays a rule of recognition; the distinguishing feature or "authoritative mark" of rules will consist merely in their having been followed for a long period of time. Recognition is carried out by all members of the society, for in a primitive social framework the split between officials and private citizens is largely effaced. Some citizen-officials, such as the elders, will of course occupy a stratum higher than that of other citizen-officials, but everyone will take on roughly the role that Hart ascribes to "officials" in advanced legal regimes: i.e., the role of shaping criteria of recognition. There eventually may emerge a marked differentiation between officials and other citizens—a differentiation approaching that in modern systems of law[43]—but this possible outcome hardly entails that in the meantime no one will exercise the "official" power of giving shape to a rule of recognition. Under this view, Hart errs in saying that primitive societies lack criteria of recognition. What they lack, if they lack anything at all in this particular matter, is a rule of recognition that lends itself to easily verifiable and foreknowable applications. A rule preoccupied with hoary traditions will perhaps engender too much uncertainty.

To the argument just made, Hart would respond with earnest laughter:

> There is indeed something comic in the efforts made to fashion a basic rule for the most simple forms of social structure which exist

> without one. It is as if we were to insist that a naked savage *must* really be dressed in some invisible variety of modern dress. Unfortunately, there is also here a standing possibility of confusion. We may be persuaded to treat as a basic rule, something which is an empty repetition of the mere fact that the society concerned (whether of individuals or states) observes certain standards of conduct as obligatory rules. . . . For it says nothing more than that those who accept certain rules must also observe a rule that the rules ought to be observed. This is a mere useless reduplication. [*Concept*, 230; emphasis in original.]

Perhaps Hart's mirth is not the last laugh. This indictment of "empty repetition" does not carry as much force as Hart might think. In the first place, one is left to doubt whether Hart's own statements about rules of recognition avoid his indictment. Even if we have made the doubtful conjecture that a custom-based rule of recognition will be less often articulated than an advanced counterpart, we shall have done nothing to detract from the status of a tradition-hallowing rule as a rule of recognition. As Hart stresses repeatedly, the content of the criteria of recognition is a matter of facts externally perceivable, not a matter of self-conscious reflection:

> In the day-to-day life of a legal system its rule of recognition is very seldom expressly formulated as a rule. . . . For the most part the rule of recognition is not stated, but its existence is *shown* in the way in which particular rules are identified. . . .
>
> The use of unstated rules of recognition, by courts and others, in identifying particular rules of the system is characteristic of the internal point of view.[44]

Given that Hart conceives of the rule of recognition this way, any account of such a rule constitutes "empty repetition" and "useless reduplication" which "says nothing more than that those [in this case, officials] who accept certain rules must also observe a rule that the rules ought to be observed."

Hart would try to distinguish the advanced rule of recognition from the custom-based variant, on the ground that the latter type of rule has no independent substance; each shared norm in a primitive society ought to be observed simply because it ought to be observed, whereas an advanced rule of recognition provides independent grounds for observance (such as the overarching criterion that legislative enactments ought to be observed). But, at least for present purposes, one should differentiate between (1) saying that norm *X* ought to be observed because norm *X* has traditionally been observed and (2) saying that norm *X* ought to be observed because norms that have traditionally been observed should continue to be observed. If the former rule—instantiated by each norm in a primitive social structure—were the only inference that one could glean from primitive norms, then Hart's complaints about "empty repetition" might appear to withstand scrutiny. The latter rule, however, is an equally justifiable inference, and it does more than state tautologically that each social norm ought to be observed simply because it ought to be observed. To see this, one only has to note that the second rule is not entailed by the first (which can itself be perceived as tautological only if we ignore the arguments set forth in the latter half of this Part). No more and no less than the advanced rules of recognition that Hart *recognizes* as such, does the second primitive rule constitute "empty repetition." It offers a general "mark" that transcends the particularity of compliance with any single norm (or subset of norms). Moreover, and more important, my argument in this whole section is leading up to—or perhaps circling around—the proposition that Hart's jurisprudence (dis)locates itself endlessly in a flow of circular repetition. Hart should thus be a bit more hesitant in denouncing repetition, for he *repeats* what he castigates. He proves to be a jurisprudential antitype of Narcissus, who sought to flee from the Echo of his language only to find himself forlornly echoing his own love.[45]

In the primitive society that MacCormick posits, the village elders will have a special part in maintaining and amplifying the rule of recognition. This should occasion very little surprise, since judges in almost any legal order will be the chief exponents of the criteria of recognition (even if they rarely advert to them directly). Like other rules of recognition, moreover, the convention-hallowing rule does not arise solely as a consequence of judicial actions. MacCormick frequently overstates the importance of the judiciary when he is discussing the rule of recognition:

> [Hart's] theory of a 'rule of recognition' is a theory concerning a rule about the standards which it is obligatory for *judges* to observe. . . .
>
> If we say that the rule of recognition settles what is 'binding law', and if we say, as Hart says, that it is a rule determining judges' duties, then we can *only* mean that it settles what rules are *binding upon judges* as bases of justified decisions on questions of right and wrong. Equally, if we wanted to say that custom is a source of valid law, we could only mean that custom is a source of rules valid as legal grounds for decisions by judges. [*H. L. A. Hart*, 114, 115; emphasis in original.]

Hart gives much greater prominence to the role of other officials than MacCormick suggests here. Generally MacCormick himself realizes, not least in the passages that were quoted earlier about "powerful and influential groupings," that judges do not carry the whole burden nor enjoy the whole privilege of creating a rule of recognition.[46] In his primitive society, all or most residents (or all or most heads of families) influence the course of the rule of recognition—much as officials would in a modern legal setting. (The major difference would be the lack of a mechanism for the deliberate change of rules in MacCormick's primitive social structure.) Citizen-officials will be producing and manifesting the rule of recognition in many ways, most saliently by continuing their adherence to long-established norms and by bringing their disputes to the village elders, who are in turn devoted to safeguarding tradition. What is true of modern legal regimes is true of MacCormick's primitive social structures: judges can have established a foundational rule only with the assistance and acquiescence of their fellow officials—even if those officials are citizen-officials. It is this process of support and collaboration, with regularized expectations, that empowers a judge of any type to carry out her judicial role.

C. THE WHITE KNIGHT VANQUISHED

MacCormick, then, cannot find the space (outside the systematicity of law) that he requires in order to "avoid the view that judges *cannot* pre-exist a power-conferring rule of adjudication" (*H. L. A. Hart*, 119). In primitive social frameworks, a community-wide rule of recognition prevails. This rule will impose duties, as MacCormick rightly contends (*H. L. A. Hart*, 120), but it will impose them on *all* the citizen-officials and not on judges alone. In the development of criteria of recognition, the village elders play a unique and vital role. Their role, though *governed* by the prevailing norms of recognition, and though *supportive* or *constitutive* of them, is not *authorized* by them. Instead, the role of the elders exists by virtue of a power-conferring norm of adjudication, which resides in the practice of submitting unresolved conflicts to them for their consideration and judgment. In their judicial role, the elders decisively affirm the criteria of recognition that bind (and are constituted by) everyone in their social structure, but they can do this only because they are vested with the power to do so—vested, that is, by a traditional norm of adjudication immanent in everyone's practice of turning all disputes over to them. If the elders did not enjoy the power to judge disputes, and if no one else possessed such a power, then adjudication would not proceed at all.

After making his argument about primitive societies, MacCormick goes on to give a pithy account of British legal history (*H. L. A. Hart*, 115–19). Here he aims to produce a narrative, the sheer possibility of which would belie the notion that daunting circles must incapacitate legal theory and legal discourse. At one with Lukàcs, who maintained that "in the case of almost every insoluble problem we perceive that the search for a solution leads us to history,"[47] MacCormick believes that stepping outside the present to construct *un grand récit historique* is the most effective way to counter the circularity that may seem to threaten Hart's project: "The discussion . . . shows that rules of recognition, changes and adjudication are indeed necessarily interlocking and interacting, so that change in or redefinition of one must be mirrored by change in or redefinition of another. But since the process of development and redefinition is an historical one, it does not involve a vicious circularity after all" (*H. L. A. Hart*, 119).

Crucial to the flow of MacCormick's narrative is his presumed starting point outside a system that creates powers of adjudication. In a feudal order, so we are to believe, the king's judicial agents bear duties without powers. Only later, as feudalism evolved toward the modern state, did power-conferring rules of adjudication come gradually into being. By tracking the slow formation of modern power-conferring rules, MacCormick will demonstrate that "it is possible to see how a legal system can 'get off the ground' and develop" (*H. L. A. Hart*, 119–20).

If one examines the account that MacCormick gives, however, his purported escape from circularity appears far less sure. What he wants to show is the path from (1) a royal agent who will discharge the king's judicial duties (and who will therefore be operating under a rule of recognition) without having been empowered by any rules of adjudication, to (2) full-fledged judges who exercise their authority on the basis of rules of adjudication. Alas, the point of departure for this journey trades on the very fragile assumptions that impelled MacCormick's account of primitive societies. Within the feudal order, the king owes duties of protection and judgment to each one of his vassals. He delegates the fulfillment of these duties to a justiciar because "[b]y custom it came to be accepted that he could" (*H. L. A. Hart*, 115). Now, what MacCormick must take as given is that the feudal structure which imposes the duties of protection and judgment does not yield any attendant powers. Only thus can he argue that the justiciar does not hold powers from the beginning. But this view will call to life the objections that were earlier trained upon MacCormick's account of primitive societies. Without judicial powers, a person obligated to serve in a judicial capacity would experience the considerable frustration of being wholly unable to get started. Furthermore, the customary acceptance of judicial authority—a custom presumably involving the king's chief vassals—is as much indicative (or productive) of a power-conferring rule as the similar acceptance of the authority of the village elders. When the chief vassals acknowledge the judicial standing of the king's delegate, they perform at least three functions. First, and most abstractly, as the regime's top "officials" they manifest and continue a rule of recognition, oriented toward custom, that will hereafter be most importantly determined by the king's delegate. Second, and more specifically, they have established a legal power on the part of the king to delegate the task of fulfilling his obligation to settle conflicts involving his chief vassals. Third, and most important for our purposes, they endow the monarch's justiciar with adjudicatory powers; the patterning of the vassals' acceptance will work, in its effect, as a power-conferring rule of adjudication. When the vassals accede to the fulfillment of royal duties by the justiciar, the understandings and expectations that impel their assent will function as a power-conferring rule, even if that rule is not clearly or explicitly understood as such.

MacCormick concedes readily that a power-conferring rule exists "[o]nce instructions to a justiciar how he is to proceed become conceived as standing instructions or standing rules of a court comprising several regular judges" (*H. L. A. Hart*, 116). Why he chooses this as the magic moment is inexplicable. Perhaps he is arguing that a rule of adjudication cannot emerge till it has been formally written down. In that case, however, he would impugn the status of all traditional rules as rules. Alternatively, MacCormick may be suggesting that a rule of adjudication comes onto the scene only when the monarch "impose[s] on the justiciar procedural requirements as to how he is to go about judging" (*H. L. A. Hart*, 116). But such requirements, albeit possibly in a roughcast form, will already have been imposed—probably by the king and certainly by the vassals, who cannot bespeak their endorsement of delegated functions until they know (more or less precisely) which functions they are dealing with. To say that a customary norm allows the monarch to delegate his role as adjudicator is to imply that the chief vassals share at least a minimal understanding of what that role consists in. If the vassals could not agree at all on what counts as the fulfillment of royal duties, it would make no sense to claim that they together approve of the vicarious fulfillment of those duties. They might agree on the abstract principle that royal duties may be discharged by a delegate, but they could not ever join hands in sanctioning a specific instance of delegation. Because of that, there would never exist a rule of delegation like the one that MacCormick outlines; royal functions would in those circumstances not have been delegated, but would instead have disintegrated. As long as a rule of delegation prevails, there will be at least a modicum of agreement on whether given processes count as adjudication. Procedural requirements that are later imposed will differ only in the degree of elaborateness.

MacCormick's attempted rescue of Hart's theory, however powerful, must hence be adjudged a failure, for two reasons. First, as my foregoing arguments have endeavored to show, MacCormick's narratives have been unable to root themselves in a secure origin—in a point outside the systematicity that those narratives purport to explain and master. As an explanation of legal concepts and legal practices, his historical account can but yield a series of presupposed conclusions, an assortment of "useless" ways of begging the question. MacCormick has not explained and cannot possibly explain, *in a noncircular manner,* why he has singled out certain actions and certain functionaries for his account of the rise of legal powers. What he views as pre-legal forerunners of advanced legal systems turn out always to be enmeshed in legal systematicity.

A second reason that MacCormick's analysis should be deemed a failure relates to its conclusion. Even if, against the insurmountable odds, MacCormick had been successful in unearthing the pre-systemic roots of systematicity, he would have had to presuppose the exact nature of the plant whose roots he had brought to light. His historical narratives take on their significance, from his perspective, only in the light of the terminus or *telos* to which they lead. MacCormick tells his story of the development of the British legal system because the story culminates in the advent and solidification of a full-fledged regime of law; but this entails that he knows what qualifies as a full-fledged regime of law. If he tried to justify his selection of particular narratives, he would confront all the problems that the narratives supposedly had eliminated. Just as Hart had to specify which agents and which behavior were relevant, so MacCormick now has to vindicate his own choice of narratives and narrative endpoints. And just as Hart ultimately repeated his assumptions when he was seemingly enunciating conclusions, so MacCormick will end up justifying his choice of narrative termini by reiterating what he ought to be showing—that those termini do indeed amount to full-fledged legal regimes. His narratives, which profess to give his theory a grounding, will themselves need to be grounded by his theory.

Does all this mean, then, that Hart cannot engage in his discourse? Is G. P. Baker correct to hold that the possibility of a noncircular jurisprudence must "be defended on the ground that meaning is not ineffable"?[48] Such a position rests upon a hasty nonsequitur. The Declaration of Independence has not been without a certain degree of import, and neither has *The Concept of Law* (though its influence has not been quite as profound as that of the Declaration, at least outside Oxford). That these major works cannot have succeeded finally, save by taking as given what they aim to establish—that in an important sense they therefore cannot succeed at all—does not seem to have prevented them from producing significant displacements in their respective fields of discoursive movement. One should not assume too dogmatically that circular discourses cannot develop themselves as discourses. This cautionary note must apply as well to the following several pages, where Hart's theory is assessed in a more explicitly deconstructive fashion. A deconstructive analysis, quite as much as the critique in this section, will produce effects too equivocal and uncanny to be disabling *tout court.* As one might conclude from the proliferation of discourse among Hart's votaries,[49] words such as "ineffable" along with such words as "useless" should not have been so lightly bandied about. Discourse may indeed structure itself as an abyssal echo, but in any case it structures itself persistently.

B. Deconstructing the Rule of Recognition

Henceforth, the clarity of Hart's vision will come under sustained challenge. His rule of recognition will have become a rule of misrecognition organized around a disruptive blindness. What Hart needs in order to build his theory will unremittingly work against his theory; his positivist ambitions will run afoul of their own requirements. His analytical framework will unweave itself through the very process of being sewn together. To see how Hart's jurisprudence subverts itself by constituting itself, we shall first examine parts of his separate criticisms of two thinkers—John Austin and Hans Kelsen—and we shall then have to look at how these criticisms always already intertwine paradoxically.

1. *Two Lines of Criticism*

A. HABITUDE CONTRA NORMATIVITY

Here it is necessary to review Hart's critique of the Austinian doctrine that habitual obedience to the dictates of a supreme commander is the essence of law. As has been discussed, Hart refers to several phenomena that he views as probative of the shortcomings in Austin's jurisprudence: the uninterruptedness of legislative authority, the persistent enforceability of old laws, the limits on legislative power, the role of custom in law, and so forth. Through his invocation of these sundry examples, Hart hopes to draw a sharp dichotomy between habits and norms, for each example is intended to show that Austin fails—of necessity—to forge an explanational link between the regularized conduct depicted in his texts and the normativity of actual legal systems. Hart insists that all rules involve a "critical reflective attitude to certain patterns of behavior as a common standard" (*Concept*, 56), whereas mere habits involve no such reflective attitude. Those who accept a rule must do so from an internal standpoint that entails criticism of violations, but those who share a habit do not reproach conduct that departs from whatever habit they share (unless, of course, their habitual behavior itself stems from their accepting a rule). They may consider aberrant conduct to be unwise for the person who is engaging in it, but they would not deem it a *méfait*, and they would not consider themselves entitled to demand that it be forsworn.

What one must stress here is the tenacity with which Hart seals off the positive repetition of habits from the normative internality of accepted rules. He emphasizes time and again that rule-based normativity cannot be derived from habit-based regularity; there exists no passage from statements that something *is* or *was* to statements that something *ought* to be or *ought* to have been. Hart always stands ready to remind us that "habits are not 'normative'; they cannot confer rights or authority on anyone" (*Concept*, 58). In his discussion of legislative continuity, for example, he maintains that "habits of obedience to each of a succession of . . . legislators are not enough to account for the *right* of a successor to succeed." On the same issue, he writes that "mere habits of obedience to orders given by one legislator cannot confer on the *new* legislator any *right* to succeed the old" (*Concept*, 58, 53–54; emphasis in original). Repeatedly Hart points out, as the prime failing of Austin's theory, the impossibility of deriving norms from mere habits. He sums up his diagnosis of Austin's shortcomings by getting to the root of the matter: "The root cause of [Austin's] failure is that the elements out of which the theory was constructed, viz. the ideas of orders, obedience, habits, and threats, do not include, and cannot by their combination yield, the idea of a rule, without which we cannot hope to elucidate even the most elementary forms of law."[50] Hart adopts a closely similar line of disapproval when he examines Bentham's theory of law. Normativity, in Hart's view, is the "feature of statements of legal obligation which cannot be characterized by the aid of Bentham's conceptual resources of command and habit of obedience" (*Bentham*, 144).

Not by chance does Hart take such pains to distinguish sharply between habits and rules; the importance of this disjunction for his entire theory cannot be overstated. It impels most of his criticisms of Austin, and it underlies, or is related directly to, an array of key distinctions: internal viewpoints versus external viewpoints, statements of validity versus statements of future patterns, acceptance versus obedience. In connection with the last of these dualisms (i.e., acceptance versus obedience), the habit/rule dichotomy interacts with the division between primary rules and secondary rules, since only the latter set of rules need be accepted by all or most of the people to whom those rules apply. Given that the habit/rule opposition figures in so many of the principal strands of argument throughout *The Concept of Law*, one hardly can feel surprised at the importance that Hart attaches to it:

> We have found it necessary, in order to elucidate features distinctive of law as a means of social control, to introduce elements which cannot be constructed out of the ideas of an order, a threat, obedience, habits, and generality. Too much that is characteristic of law is distorted by the effort to explain it in these simple terms. Thus we found it necessary to distinguish from the idea of a general habit that of a social rule, and to emphasize the internal aspect of rules manifested in their use as guiding and critical standards of conduct. [*Concept*, 151.]

B. THE BASIC NORM AND ULTIMACY

At first glance, Hart's critique of Kelsen's idea of the "basic norm" may strike one as bearing very little relation to the attack on command theories and to the concomitant embrace of the rule/habit distinction that we have just been exploring. In my next subsection, the interplay between Hart's two lines of criticism will become more apparent. First, however, Hart's disapproval of the Kelsenian "basic norm" must here be elaborated. Hart engages Kelsen over the knotted issue of the validity and ultimacy of the criteria of recognition within a structure of law. Kelsen had argued that the unity of a legal system grows from the fact that every one of its laws can be attributed to a basic norm, which structures the whole system; rules belong to a system if and only if they derive ultimately from its basic norm.[51] In every system of law, the validity of each rule depends on the presupposed validity of the basic norm of the whole system. This basic tier is formally though not substantively the same in every legal order: it posits, as an underlying assumption, that one ought to comply with the initial constitution (or set of principles) whence arose the legal order. "That the first constitution is a binding legal norm is presupposed, and the formulation of the presupposition is the basic norm of this legal order" (*General Theory,* 115). And just as the validity of the constitution is presupposed by way of the basic norm, so the validity of the basic norm is presupposed in its own right, "because without this presupposition no human act could be interpreted as a legal . . . act" (*General Theory,* 116). (This reading of Kelsen, which piles one presupposition onto another, will presumably disconcert those who look askance even at just the first of Kelsen's presupposed norms.[52] Nonetheless, although my reading finds very little support in Kelsen's *Pure Theory of Law,* it seems the most plausible interpretation of references in his *General Theory of Law and State* to the presupposed validity of the basic norm.[53] At any rate, the general argument of this section turns not at all on winning over adherents to a particular construal of Kelsen's work. That is not to say, however, that the reading proposed here has been highlighted fortuitously; it has been given salience because it points the way toward the general problem—of infinite regression—that will soon occupy center stage, where in a sense it has always been.)

Hart differs with Kelsen on a number of counts, though only one main point need concern us here. In getting at this point of contention, Hart occasionally appears confused. For example, when faced with Kelsen's remarks on presupposing the validity of the basic norm, Hart declares that "no question concerning the validity or invalidity of the generally accepted rule of recognition as distinct from the factual question of its existence can arise" (*Concept*, 245). Hart's development of this theme will be studied shortly, but first we should *en passant* notice two ways in which his argument falters as a reply to the exact issues raised by Kelsen. First, since Kelsen defines validity with a much more expansive scope than does Hart, the two great positivists seem to some extent to be talking past each other. Whereas Hart specifies that a rule is valid if it "satisfies all the criteria provided by the rule of recognition" (*Concept*, 100), Kelsen defines "validity" with a much more sweeping ambit, as "binding force" (*General Theory*, 30). If this latter definition is kept in mind, Hart's critique may seem less warranted (if indeed it is warranted at all—a question to be explored presently). Second, Hart misdescribes the target of his critique. He is contesting not the validity of the basic norm, but the validity conferred *by* the basic norm on the first constitution of a legal regime. To be sure, the tenor of Hart's objection would strike *a fortiori* at the validity of the basic norm, but his attention is focused here on the validity bestowed *by* rather than *on* that norm.

Hart comes much closer to a direct engagement with Kelsen when he complains that the Kelsenian basic norm is a "needless reduplication" (*Concept*, 246). To some extent, this complaint reduplicates the position Hart espouses when arguing that no rules of recognition prevail in customary societies; that position has already been criticized. But Hart is touching upon a more profound theme as well. His main thesis is that criteria of recognition in any legal regime are ultimate, in the sense that they identify all the valid rules within a particular regime but are themselves "neither valid nor invalid [and are] simply accepted as appropriate for use" (*Concept*, 105). Ultimacy of this sort, which was described briefly in Part One of this chapter, obviates and excludes the presuppositions that Kelsen deemed to be necessary. Even if "validity" be defined as Kelsen defined it, Hart still would press the view that—within a legal order—the rule of recognition has no ground but its own emergence. One ought never to speak of some extra layer of guidance through which one presupposes the normativity of the rule of recognition, for every such rule that has materialized is *ipso facto* endowed with binding force. Rules of recognition, like other rules that exist only by becoming accepted, must be binding to be in place at all. Such rules come forth and continue only insofar as they govern conduct; thus, to perceive rules of recognition at all is to perceive them as binding in their respective spheres. Their obligatory purview is manifested in certain forms of behavior on the part of those who accept such rules—criticism of deviations, demands for renewed conformity, and acknowledgment that such criticism and such demands are appropriate. (These, of course, are the general forms of behavior that were singled out to demarcate rules from habits.)

To attach a presupposed validity to these patterns of conduct is, in Hart's view, "useless reduplication"; anything that could possibly be gained from such a presupposition will already be present.

While classifying the rule of recognition as "ultimate," Hart does not commit the blunder of postulating that such a rule will be accepted and used as *bonne-en-soi*. Indeed, he lists some considerations that may have weight in inducing acceptance—foresighted self-interest, respect for time-honored practices, disinterested concern for others, and so on.[54] In his discussion of the "minimum content of natural law," Hart ascribes a singular force to the pursuit of survival as determinative of the most basic functions and categories of legal systems (*Concept*, 187–95); and since equable norms of recognition may foster general orderliness, the aim of survival also may contribute (in some cases) to stabilizing such norms.[55] But the pursuit of survival and the other considerations that Hart invokes are extrasystemic. That is, they furnish reasons for operating within a given legal order, but they do not amount to an official criterion with which every authoritative rule must comply. They function outside the system, though their importance is felt inside. Rules of recognition, *par contre*, function inside their legal frameworks and supply the conclusive tests for intrasystemic normativity. It is in the production of this intrasystemic flow of normativity—a flow that consists precisely in validation, in both Hart's sense and Kelsen's sense—that criteria of recognition are ultimate. Nothing can take intrasystemic precedence over such criteria, since it is those criteria that decide which things qualify as the parts of the system (and, ergo, which things qualify as enforceable precepts).

2. *Hartian Normativity Deconstructed*

One of the three fundamental questions with which Hart orients his whole inquiry is the following source of bafflement: What are rules, and to what extent is law an affair of rules? (*Concept*, 13). For those who cavil that not all normative guides are rules,[56] Hart's question can be made more sweeping if we interpret "rules" as a synonym for "normative guides or standards." Suitably generalized, Hart's query activates the paradoxical reading of *The Concept of Law* to be proposed in this subsection. Quite natural is it that a critique of Hart should focus on his conception of normativity; after all, that conception permeates every aspect of his theoretical enterprise, from his criticism of Austin to his laying bare the "essence of law" (which is composed of *rules*, both "primary" and "secondary") to his subsequent chapters on some points of articulation between morality and law. To derange Hart's understanding of normativity is thus to solicit his entire approach, "in the sense that *sollicitare*, in old Latin, means to shake as a whole, to make tremble in entirety."[57] As the edifice of Hart's thought is shaken, the inside/outside dualism that his edifice needs will come inescapably and radically into doubt, almost like the sides of an edifice in a lithograph by Escher.

One of the chief directions in which Hart steers his writing about rules is toward debates between the formalists and the Legal Realists over the "open texture of law" (*Concept*, 121–50). Those debates, however, will not be highlighted here. Of prime interest, rather, is the way in which normativity works—or, more specifically, the precise way in which it works to upheave itself. What gives rules their stature as rules also undoes that stature, as we shall see by according prominence to a certain disruptive temporality in Hart's text (and in the internal view of rules). This temporality dislocates all reassuring answers that Hart provides, throughout his theory, to the question of what rules are.

The argument that follows is an effect of the interweaving of Hart's critical remarks on Austin and his remarks on the Kelsenian basic norm. However, it is not the aim of this subsection to splice the two lines of criticism *in toto*, whatever that might involve. Instead, some crucial strands of each line will have become entangled in a paradoxical knot with strands of the other line. It is to that knot, which can untie itself only by again gnarling itself, that we must now turn.

Hart's thesis that rules of recognition are ultimately authoritative brings out the most pressing need of normative systems and of theories of normativity: a stopping place in which binding force can take hold. Without self-sustaining soil for the roots of normativity, a legal theorist will plummet through an infinite regress of failed attempts to place law on a distinct footing from that of coercive orders. This becomes clear when Hart discusses the chain of reasoning by which rules are validated. He asserts that "[i]f the question is raised whether some suggested rule is legally valid, we must, in order to answer the question, use a criterion of validity provided by some other rule," and he traces validity from a humble by-law (passed by the Oxfordshire County Council, of course) to the ultimate rule of recognition that "what the Queen in Parliament enacts is law" (*Concept*, 103–104). That ultimate rule brings the inquiry to a halt, since a self-enveloping rule of validation is completely impossible: "[T]here is no rule providing criteria for the assessment of its own legal validity" (*Concept*, 104). A rule of recognition decides the normative standing of all rules in a legal order except itself. It acts as an organizing principle that cannot be subject to any tests for validity, though its binding power can be evaluated in the light of extrasystemic factors. Within a system, the organizing rule must be taken for granted as a bench mark; even when the rule changes, the events by which it is changed must pass the tests that the rule has authorized. As a prime mover, the rule of recognition shuts off the infinitely regressing flow of normativity, for the rule functions as its own ground. It cannot be treated as either valid or invalid, because questions of validity can arise only within a legal matrix upheld by a rule of recognition, and it possesses binding force simply as a matter of fact—i.e., because it is a norm that relevant persons have accepted. Hart claims thus to have put to rout the vortex that haunts his legal theory: the vortex of infinitely proliferating explanations that explain nothing.[58]

Kelsen would agree with Hart that procedures of validation must have a stopping place, and he would further agree that such procedures involve moving from lesser rules to more basic rules: "The reason for the validity [i.e., binding force] of a norm can only be the validity of another norm" (*Pure Theory*, 193). Unlike Hart, however, Kelsen would not see the rule of recognition (or the first constitution) as an appropriate terminus. Nor would he accept that validity derives only from the fulfillment of tests laid down by the rule of recognition. As has already been remarked, Kelsen defined validity as general normative force. He located the bedrock of this force in the basic norm or perhaps in the presupposed validity of the basic norm. Whichever be the case, Kelsen transferred the origin of intrasystemic normativity from behavior evincing certain attitudes—the manifestations of a "critical reflective attitude" that make up the rule of recognition—to the outlook that impels such behavior (that is, to the critical reflective attitude itself, or to the presumption that it is valid). Thus, despite their differences, Hart and Kelsen are very clearly at one in trying to avert the infinite regress that imperils normativity; what Hart accomplishes with the ultimate rule of recognition is accomplished by Kelsen with the presupposed basic norm.

At this point, let us look once again at Hart's critique of Austin. What that critique does, among other things, is to supply an extensive definition of norms and normativity. Without such a definition, subsequent chapters of *The Concept of Law* could not proceed, for they depend crucially on an understanding of what norms are. In particular, the whole theory of validation—which involves using certain norms to support other norms—would be set adrift if Hart had not specified exactly what he has presumed norms to be. What, then, does Hart say about norms in his critique of Austin? His main concern, nicely in keeping with the etymology of "define," is to define norms by differentiating them from what they are not, from habits. As we have seen, Hart points repeatedly to the "critical reflective attitude" as the characteristic that distinguishes a norm from a habit. Over and over, he affirms strongly that mere routines can never yield norm-based attitudes and conceptions. This demarcation between the bare factuality of habits and the internal bindingness of norms would have met with the full approval of Kelsen, who was inclined to be even more emphatic (and more Kantian): "From the circumstance that something *is* cannot follow that something *ought* to be."[59]

Through his conception of what norms are, Hart has deconstructed his theory of how norms work. He and Kelsen insist that normativity cannot be educed from naked habits and regularities. This contention—which of course is a defining contention (perhaps indeed *the* defining contention) of legal positivism, as of other positivist theories—will have thoroughly overturned Hart's whole account of normative concepts, in an endless to-and-fro of unraveling. Here it is necessary to highlight the dimension of time. At any moment within a legal system, one is faced with diverse imperatives. To explain why imperatives have force, to explain why they ought to be upheld, one must join in the validative process that Hart describes: an appeal from lesser norms to more basic norms. One soon reaches a stopping point, be it the rule of recognition or the Kelsenian basic norm. Having gone thus far, one will have explained nothing unless the basic norm or the rule of recognition can vest itself with normative power. (Extrasystemic reasons for embracing rules will be *temporarily* disregarded here, because introducing them would deprive the intrasystemic stopping point of its character as a stopping point.) Ungrounded groundedness, Hart declares, is precisely what we unearth in rules of recognition, which are ultimate rules that can exist as such only if they have been accepted as binding. But if one considers the rule of recognition at any moment, one must confine oneself to austerely factual declarations. One can affirm merely that such and such a rule has hitherto been accepted (by oneself or only by other people) as binding. That is, one can perceive foregoing acceptance, even one's own foregoing acceptance, only in terms of factual regularities—the sorts of patterns and regularities that Hart bears in mind when arguing, apropos of the rule of recognition, that "[i]ts existence is a matter of fact" (*Concept*, 107). (This is not a charge of behaviorism: the unnerving effects of temporality will disrupt any nonbehaviorist version of Hart's theory.) All that one can say is that a particular rule has heretofore been accepted, and that acceptance has been instantiated in patterns of norm-referring discourse, attitudes, and behavior. One can observe and describe such patterns in great detail, through introspection and through empirical study, but one cannot extract from them any normative inferences. In relation to the present and future, past acceptance of norms can only have the status of a collective or individual habit, a habit of respecting those norms. Given Hart's assumptions regarding normativity, "*X* ought to be obeyed at time *T*" cannot entail "*X* ought to be obeyed at time *T* + 1." When one apprehends that a rule has been accepted by oneself or by other people, one distills in thought all the patterned facts of behavior and attitudes that have constituted acceptance; but, as Hart has insisted, one cannot draw normative messages from mere factual regularities. That the regularized facts in question have amounted to the acceptance of a rule cannot make the least difference, for the relevant point in time is the moment at which the facts are apprehended, not the immediately preceding point during which they happened. At the moment of apprehension, the regularities of foregoing acceptance can be grasped only as such (i.e., as factual regularities), and can therefore provide no reason whatsoever for *continued* acceptance, at least under Hart's theory. If one is to draw normative conclusions from the patterns of bygone acts and outlooks, one will need independent reasons for doing so, since the normativity of those acts and outlooks will have abided no longer than the acts and outlooks themselves, and will therefore lie in the past.[60] Normative standards as they exist in time—which is to say, at all times—will thus fail, ineluctably, to afford grounds for their own continuation. Once the diachronic dimension comes to the fore, we can observe that factuality always already permeates normativity and prevents its functioning.

What has been said here generally about norms will bear quite obviously on the rule of recognition. At every moment, the officials who ascertain the rules belonging to a particular legal system will take cognizance of the patterns of identification that have thitherto been accepted. But those patterns can only testify that specific criteria have *been* accepted, not that they should *continue* to be accepted. Under the Hartian definition of normativity, the latter inference (of a continued application) cannot derive from the former inference (of a past application), because the latter inference is a normative statement whereas the former inference is purely factual. To move from the former inference to the latter inference, one would require independent reasons for ascribing normative strength to patterns of rule-governed behavior and rule-governed convictions that have prevailed heretofore; the rule of recognition as it holds sway through time can never in itself provide grounds for its continued normativeness. Yet any external anchor will come apart through just the type of displacement that has unraveled the rule of recognition. If, say, one sets one's hopes on the Kelsenian basic norm, one will be hoist with the petard of temporality that disrupted the rule of recognition. A presupposition of binding force will prove utterly unable to endow *itself* with normative force from one moment to the next. That X ought to be presupposed at time T does not entail that X ought to be presupposed at time $T+1$. We would thus need an infinitely long chain of presuppositions to produce diachronic normativity. Problems of a similar kind will thwart appeals to extrasystemic sources of normativity. That certain goals have been normatively prized can never *per se* warrant the continuation of their esteem. Once again an infinite regress looms, as each goal reproduces the lack it was supposed to eliminate.

Two aspects or corollaries of this critique of Hart's conception of norms are most unsettling. First, it should be clear that if the ultimate rule of recognition cannot justify the continued force of its own requirements throughout time, then all the lesser rules of a system will be completely unmoored. Those lesser rules can furnish no reason that they ought to command acceptance, since their obligatory strength rests on a purportedly firm foundation that has always already founded itself by disarticulating itself. Each law will depend throughout on the rule of recognition as the ultimate source of normativity, but each will hurtle down an abyss as the dimension of time itself precludes the continuation of the ultimate rule.

Second, the critique can be generalized not only across norms but also throughout time. All the moments in the duration of a rule will have forbidden themselves, as factuality engulfs normativity from one moment to the next; no moment can escape the uncanny regress that has been highlighted here. Normative acceptance in moment M can appear and function in moment $M+1$ only as the *fact* of acceptance that has prevailed thus far, a fact from which normativity cannot grow (at least in the absence of extrinsic reasons, which will themselves be liable to the same process). This pushes the critique back to any rule's point of origin, which should perhaps be called a nonorigin. At no time would a rule of any sort be able to get started, for the moment of origin would stand in relation to the next moment as pure facticity, from which Hartians cannot draw obligatory directives. Hart's theory will thus have led to problems of genesis just as much as to problems of continuity. No matter where one locates the founding instant, it will necessarily prove unable to transmit normativity to succeeding instants, which means it will necessarily prove unable to serve as a founding instant. Moreover, that founding moment could never have arisen in the first place—which is where founding moments *should* arise—since whatever might cause it to emerge would stand in relation to it over time as pure facticity, whence normative consequences cannot spring.

Hart's theory of legal systems, with its sharply defined split between factuality and normativity, would thus seem to do away with any such split by overwhelming all normativity with factuality—a most precarious enterprise, through which "the very idea of [factuality] is menaced and the difference in which it took on its meaning breaks down."[61] With the sequentialist portrayal of temporality in the work of both Hart and Kelsen,[62] Hart's portrayal of normativity becomes a relentless counterstatement to its own views and ambitions. This counterstatement will forever pursue itself, ceaselessly tearing down what it always has already rebuilt. Hart can present his theory only by having blinded himself to its aporias. His clarity of vision has based itself through and through on his profound inability to observe that his starting points dislocate themselves. It is perforce a rule of misrecognition that one recognizes in Hart's text.

CHAPTER 4

NOTHING IN PARTICULAR

A Critique of the Legal and Moral Theory of David Hume

Conservatism looms as the ideology of particulars. With rage and often with eloquence, conservative thinkers have derided the grand schemes of visionaries who seek to turn politics into an arena of experimentation. Making all things new may be an essential part of God's grisly Final Assize, but it is not an aim that sublunary beings should endorse; God in the *Revelation to John* bears far too appalling a resemblance to Joseph Stalin. In the eyes of the conservative theorists, far-reaching novelty and abstraction go hand in hand, because overenthusiastic innovators tend (of necessity) to disparage or overlook the homely concreteness and observances of everyday life. Such innovators look upon the particularities of experience as ephemeral resting points or obstructions to be transcended as rapidly as possible. They substitute their leaps of imagination for the quotidian specificities that guide most people through life. Conservatives have resoundingly taken up the gauntlet and have heaped scorn on the rarefied dogmata to which radicals pin their hopes. From Edmund Burke's scathing reminder that "[t]he science of constructing a commonwealth, or renovating it, or reforming it, is . . . not to be taught *a priori*," and his strictures against "those extravagant and presumptuous speculations which have taught [radicals] to despise all their predecessors,"[1] to Michael Oakeshott's denunciation of "rigid systems of abstract ideas,"[2] conservatives have inveighed repeatedly against those who employ abstract visions and broad ideals to delegitimate the arrangements and regularities that make up social life. As one writer has recently observed: "Conservatives have believed, following Burke, that general principles always must be tempered, in any particular circumstances, by what Burke called expedience, or prudence; for particular circumstances vary infinitely, and every nation must observe its own traditions and historical experience—which should take precedence over universal notions drawn up in some quiet study."[3]

David Hume fits comfortably into the British conservative tradition as an older contemporary of Burke. Writing before the French Revolution gave a sharp urgency to the rearguard cause, Hume expressed many of the themes that were later wielded by Burke and others against apologists for the Jacobins. Hume was indeed the philosopher of particularities *par excellence*. In his overhauling of contractarian analyses of political and social order, for example, he upheld the particulars of evolution against the abstract thinking required for a social compact:

> No compact or agreement, it is evident, was expressly formed for general submission, an idea far beyond the comprehension of savages. Each exertion of authority in the chieftain must have been particular, and called forth by the present exigencies of the case. The sensible utility resulting from his interposition made these exertions become daily more frequent; and their frequency gradually produced an habitual and, if you please to call it so, a voluntary and therefore precarious acquiescence in the people.[4]

This development of political hierarchy is one effect of the principle that "the imagination is more affected by what is particular than by what is general."[5] Such a principle, furthermore, can be quite readily put to use as an underpinning of conservative ideology; it can incline people to demand, for instance, that legal doctrines be very closely attuned to whatever concrete circumstances they regulate: "[L]aws have, or ought to have, a constant reference to the constitution of government, the manners, the climate, the religion, the commerce, the situation of each society."[6] From here one can slide with ease into a thoroughgoing disdain toward calls for abrupt and massive departures from the particularities of the status quo:

> [A]s human society is in perpetual flux, one man every hour going out of the world, another coming into it, it is necessary in order to preserve stability in government that the new brood should conform themselves to the established constitution, and nearly follow the path which their fathers, treading in the footsteps of theirs, had marked out to them. Some innovations must necessarily have place in every human institution; and it is happy where the enlightened genius of the age give these a direction to the side of reason, liberty, and justice. But violent innovations no individual is entitled to make.[7]

As may be evident from the first two quotations in the preceding paragraph, Hume's conception of politics—with his embrace of established specificities—is tied to a theory of the human mind. His privileging of particularity extends into the very foundation of his science of human consciousness. All awareness, from a Humean point of view, can ultimately be analyzed into simple units of feeling and sensation. These units, along with the diverse connections among them, are the building blocks (and the mortar) from which even the most intricate thoughts grow.

> [The] creative power of the mind amounts to no more than the faculty of compounding, transposing, augmenting, or diminishing the materials afforded us by the senses and experience. . . .
>
> . . . [W]hen we analyze our thoughts or ideas, however compounded or sublime, we always find that they resolve themselves into such simple ideas as were copied from a precedent feeling or sentiment. [*Enquiries*, 19.]

One of the most lively issues in the debates over Hume's work is whether a noncontingent link can be traced between his epistemology (or psychology) and his political views. Important though that question may be, it will not affect the critique of Hume that will be developed in this chapter; moreover, the general issue of links between metaphysics and politics (in relation to deconstructionist discourses) is touched upon several times in the next chapter.[8] Nonetheless, it would seem advisable to begin taking a stand on one form of that general issue in this chapter's preliminary section. Consider, then, the following three reasons for denying that Hume's politics flow perforce from his metaphysics. ("Metaphysics" is used here expansively to cover Hume's psychological-epistemological investigations.) All of these reasons may indeed turn out to be question-begging—but the same would be true of reasons for favoring an opposed perspective.

First, many thinkers have championed metaphysical precepts correspondent to those of Hume while embracing leftist or liberal views on matters of politics. The most renowned example in recent times is, of course, Bertrand Russell, but an even more pertinent example is the critical legal studies movement. Many of the critical legal scholars adhere to a still more skeptical version of philosophy than the one defended by Hume himself, yet they can scarcely be counted as his political allies.[9] Presumably, one main reason for such divergences is the ineliminable potential for an array of motives whenever someone announces a perceived fact of human psychology. One can point to a limitation of human knowledge—such as people's propensity to continue in their longstanding beliefs even when those cherished beliefs are *hors de propos*—either to embrace the limit in question (and thus, naturally, to counsel against resisting it) or to push back the limit as much as possible. One can submit to general limitations wholeheartedly or resignedly, or one can struggle to minimize their effects on institutions and practices. (One of course can also adopt some intermediate standpoint.) For example, one can affirm that racial prejudice dies hard, yet be fully able to choose between the following pair of inferences: (1) "folkways" ought to be "stateways" to avert widespread civil unrest;[10] or (2) the state must be especially active in its roles of guiding and prodding public opinion away from prejudice, *because* the task is so formidable. One's starting point in epistemology or psychology does not lead one with *inexorable* force to either political conclusion. Moreover, one could choose among any number of conceivable inferences not specified here.

Second, a denial of necessary relations joining metaphysical postulates and political standpoints need not involve any denial that there are common themes and structural elements throughout Hume's philosophy. His account of human judgment pervades all parts of his work, as major studies have succeeded in demonstrating,[11] but one can admit this happily without fear of portraying Hume's conservatism as ineluctably tied to his empiricism and skepticism. That Hume employed largely similar methods for examining many aspects of human thought and behavior does not mean that his quietistic evaluations of what he had uncovered were equally the product of a concern for uniformity. It is decidedly not true that someone who exposes ungrounded habitude and inertia in varied human activities *must* contend that such features should be accommodated meekly or gaily rather than be resisted. That homologous methods yield homologous findings will not determine what we ought to *do* with those findings.

Third, and most important, to think that Hume was committed to a complacent politics by virtue of his skeptical metaphysics is to presume that his politics and his metaphysics enjoy stability and coherent order. Absent such stability and coherence, the links between these dimensions of his thought will always remain fluid and indefinable. It makes no sense to find an inherent bond between two positions, if each of them is a radically unstable process of undermining itself. Because each doctrine of every kind will not have an untroubled identity, it cannot serve as an element in a necessary relation; for its endless toppling of its own hierarchies and principles will likewise topple its putative entailment of certain other positions. An ineluctable correlation would demand a quietus to the unthinkable movement of paradoxes that generate and undo every outlook. Unless that enabling and disabling movement has inconceivably been arrested, every standpoint will lay itself open to a multiplicity of relations with other standpoints, since every doctrine will have always already been upheaving the ground on which its valences with all other doctrines are established. Yet, as has been argued throughout this book, all positions—be they metaphysical or political—will perforce dismantle themselves as the condition of their being elaborated. No position, then, can lay claim to the determinacy and coherence needed to play the part of an element in a necessary relation. And, one should add, this will be true of deconstructive critiques as much as of discourse that has less explicitly thematized its undoing. A critique of Hume's privileging of particulars will not automatically impair the effectiveness of his theorizing, for any such critique will powerfully reconfirm particular units in the very process of undermining them; but if the intraphilosophical effects are so dizzyingly incalculable, then one should hesitate before making predictions about politics.

One caveat should be entered, before we move to the first Part of this chapter. The foregoing considerations may seem to resurrect a positivist division between facts and values, and may thus seem vulnerable to the critique of jurisprudential positivism advanced in Chapter 3. That critique certainly does apply with full force here, but such applicability need not mean that one has been trying to enroll in the camp of positivism *sans réserve*. Unlike positivism, the foregoing considerations in no way privilege one set of inquiries as "objective" or "hard" while denigrating all or most other sorts of inquiries as "subjective" or "soft." As this book has maintained throughout, *all* inquiries will have become ensnared in aporias; hence, the positivist criteria for discriminating among sets of inquiries cannot possibly be sustained. Moreover, the above reasons for a gap between metaphysics and politics do not compel one to side with an approach that regards experiential particulars as singularly reliable points of knowledge. Indeed, it is precisely a focus on particularized sense data that is radically questioned in this chapter's third Part.

More widely, it is the project of this fourth chapter to examine some of the points of self-subversion in Hume's texts. The chapter will concentrate on Hume's *Treatise* and on his two *Enquiries*, and—in line with Ben-Sira's advice that one should not winnow with every wind nor follow down every path—no more than a few topics will be treated in depth. Unlike the preceding two chapters, the critique in this chapter does not begin with a compendious overview of the texts that are being scrutinized. A summation of the relevant strands of Hume's philosophy would have to encompass far too much, even if few critical remarks were added; hence, the task of synopsizing has been broken up and deferred to the last two Parts, where it can proceed with the utmost brevity. In lieu of an overall conspectus, the first Part will trace Hume's understanding of rhetorical and linguistic phenomena, both through his remarks pertaining specifically thereto and through other strands of his writing that can be reinterpreted with the aid of modern linguistic theory. Because questions of language figure prominently in the last two Parts, the first Part is an important though rather indirect means of orientation for what follows. My critique of Hume begins more engagedly in Part Two, the longest of the three Parts. Therein, Hume's theory of justice will be shown to necessitate and to presuppose what it has disabled itself from using, and the attendant rupture within his theory will turn out to include grave consequences for his broader conception of morality.

Part Three is a still more fundamental critique of Hume's metaphysics and moral theory, a critique that interrogates the whole structure of Hume's thought. As has been argued, nothing in Hume's metaphysics can decide the exact shape of his politics; still, as has been noted, his epistemology and his ideology are shot through with common structures and themes—most notably with the theme of particularized perceptions as the component bases of sentiment and knowledge. By subjecting Hume's underlying dogma to a sustained challenge, Part Three attempts to show that his metaphysical speculations ultimately have found nothing in particular.

Part One. Hume and Language

Perhaps the most striking feature of Hume's conception of language is the dearth of his express comments on the subject. Not a single section in the *Enquiries* or the *Treatise* is devoted specifically to exploring how words and other signifiers can function—surely a quite remarkable omission for a science of human nature! One of the appendices to the *Enquiry concerning the Principles of Morals* is titled "Of some verbal Disputes," but even that short section acts mainly to warn readers against becoming bogged down in "disputes of words." As Hume concluded: "[I]t is of greater consequence to attend to things than to verbal appellations" (*Enquiries*, 322). To be sure, this breezy conclusion is indicative of a whole congeries of assumptions about linguistic matters, several of which will presently be explored; yet it more glaringly demonstrates Hume's puzzling lack of interest in all such matters. Thus, to tease out from Hume's work a valuable store of insights concerning language, we frequently shall have to read through the lines and brush against the grain of *Hume's* language.

A. The Depreciation of Language

1. *Disputes Over Words*

In the *Second Letter to Timothy*, the author (writing under the name of Paul) insists that one should "avoid disputing about words, which does no good, but only ruins the hearers."[12] Totally in accord with this admonition are the majority of Hume's statements on the functioning of words in philosophy. His disdain for inquiries that involve nothing but disputes over language can be found with almost monotonous repetition in all of his chief texts. In his view, such inquiries would inevitably amount to nothing but puerile games. Thus, Hume cautioned repeatedly against "merely verbal" points of contention, which "are to be regarded rather as grammatical than as philosophical difficulties."[13] A dispute over wording hence "belongs to *Grammarians*" and is "influenced by verbal distinctions [rather] than by real differences" (*Treatise*, 610; *Enquiries*, 281). Withering contempt for those who make much ado about words is very much on display in the rhetorical question that Hume asked when confronted with "a dispute, which is chiefly verbal": "[I]s there any reason for being so extremely scrupulous about a *word*. . . ?" (*Enquiries*, 319 note 1, 316). As Hume summarized, "a question, being merely verbal, cannot possibly be of any importance." Philosophers who become embroiled in quibbles over semantics may "imagine that they are handling controversies of the deepest importance and concern," but are in fact mired in "altercations, so frivolous and endless" (*Enquiries*, 314, 312). They substitute ersatz problems of terminology for genuine conflicts of ideas, and they therefore "talk instead of thinking in their reasonings" (*Treatise*, 62). They have fallen prey to "the caprice of language, which ought not to be regarded in reasoning" (*Enquiries*, 213 note 1).

All in all, then, Hume's animadversions on linguistic debates import a markedly hostile attitude toward language. His ambition was to raise disputes over words in quite a different sense; rather than disputes over *words*, wherein words displace ideas, one should hope to see disputes *over* words—wherein substantive issues have been elevated to their appropriate level, over mere signifiers. It may well be, as one commentator has argued, that (in Hume's view) "to call attention to the fact that a dispute is a dispute of words (is verbal/is not real) is the province of philosophers,"[14] but it apparently is further the province of philosophers (in the view of Hume) to equate "is verbal" with "is not real."

What might account for such extreme antipathy toward verbal disputes? At least three factors seem worthy of consideration. First, Hume's contempt for semantic quibbles clearly instantiates his far-reaching contempt for language, which in turn amounts to an instance of the devaluation of mundane signifiers that has imbued so much of Occidental philosophy.[15] Second, as has been noted by Michael Morrisroe, Hume's blithe dismissals of debates over words obviously comport with his general aim to "produce a dispassionate frame of mind in the reader. . . . Verbal disputes are not worth the energy spent in their pursuit."[16] Hume felt that philosophical wrangling could too easily spill over into political animosities, and thus viewed philosophical peace as a condition for peace in general; he could not allow reason to degenerate into "nothing but a [potentially rancorous] play of words" (*Treatise*, 32). Third, and closely related to the last point, Hume's enmity toward religion caused him to look askance at discourses that resembled the maunderings of theologians. Interminable gabbling in philosophy, like the sterile controversies among Christians, could not but stem from poorly defined terms. In the *Dialogues Concerning Natural Religion*, Hume launched this complaint forcefully: "All men of sound reason are disgusted with verbal disputes, which abound so much in philosophical and theological inquiries; and it is found that the only remedy for this abuse must arise from clear definitions, from the precision of those ideas which enter into any argument, and from the strict and uniform use of those terms which are employed."[17]

2. *The Perils of Rhetoric*

Less often remarked upon than Hume's disparaging of verbal debates, but at times equally condescending toward language, is his treatment of rhetoric and figurality. Observations by Hume on rhetoric are not infrequent—though often made *en passant* or *malgré lui*—and a later subsection of this Part will attempt to show that a systematic account of tropes can be educed from his major texts. To be noted here are his comments that display open antagonism toward figurative language.

Hume's basic complaints were twofold: rhetoric is untrue and deceitful, *and* it is immensely alluring. Near the very beginning of the *Treatise of Human Nature*, we encounter a fusillade of splendid metaphors aimed (ironically enough) at stripping themselves of their authority by contesting the use of tropes in philosophical discourse.

> Amidst all this bustle 'tis not reason, which carries the prize, but eloquence; and no man needs ever despair of gaining proselytes to the most extravagant hypothesis, who has art enough to represent it in any favourable colours. The victory is not gained by the men at arms, who manage the pike and the sword; but by the trumpeters, drummers, and musicians of the army. [*Treatise*, xiv.]

As Paul de Man has said of a cognate passage from Locke: "Nothing could be more eloquent than this denunciation of eloquence."[18] Similarly bizarre discoursive movement occurred when Hume decided against the introduction of "the flowers of rhetoric" into metaphysical speculation (*Enquiries*, 79). His distrust of the wiles of figurality traded here on one of the classic figures of speech, a florid trope from which an entire theory of rhetoric could derive.[19]

Less flowery, but as hostile toward rhetoric, are Hume's attempts to equate figurative discourse with impropriety. At least twice, Hume described figurality as improper—once by criticizing a particular way of speaking as "figurative and improper" (as well as "odd" and "abusive"), and again by drawing a distinction between speaking "in a figurative sense" and "[p]roperly speaking" (*Treatise*, 459, 461, 505 note 1). (Once more, we might observe, Hume had to resort to figurality for a means of assailing figurality; to invoke "propriety" is to invoke a timeworn figure of speech from the tradition of Western metaphysics, wherein moral uprightness and the establishment of self-presence converge.[20])

In a like vein are some of Hume's remarks on the metaphoric and metonymic propensities of the imagination, whose pathways Hume regarded as "the more frivolous properties of our thought" (*Treatise*, 504). His associationist theory of the mind will be studied in some depth presently; for now, it will serve us as a point of entry into his often mordant view of poetic language. Claiming that the figurative tendencies (particularly the metaphoric tendencies) of the mind "cause . . . many mistakes and sophisms in philosophy," Hume maintained that "there are few mistakes in reasoning, which do not borrow largely from that origin." He went on: "We might produce the figures of poets and orators, as sufficient proof of this, were it as usual, as it is reasonable, in metaphysical subjects to draw our arguments from that quarter" (*Treatise*, 61). In a sense, to be sure, Hume was according poets a certain dignity by suggesting that they are worthy of notice by philosophers. *But* they are worthy of such notice on the exact ground that their creations are so replete with mistakes.

Hume's attitude toward poets was (on the whole) decidedly less than generous, as one might gather from his two-edged defense of them. Poets, Hume wrote, are "liars by profession" who employ tropes to gird their output with an air of veracity.[21] Even more wounding are some passages in which he associated poetic undertakings with childishness and madness. While mounting a brief attack on introjection or personification, Hume flung his impish mockery at poets as well as at some ancient metaphysicians:

> There is a very remarkable inclination in human nature, to bestow on external objects the same emotions, which it observes in itself; and to find every where those ideas, which are most present to it. This inclination, 'tis true, is suppress'd by a little reflection, and only takes place in children, poets, and the antient philosophers. It appears in children, by their desire of beating the stones, which hurt them: In poets, by their readiness to personify every thing: And in the antient philosophers, by these fictions of sympathy and antipathy. We must pardon children, because of their age; poets, because they profess to follow implicitly the suggestions of their fancy: But what excuse shall we find to justify our philosophers in so signal a weakness? [*Treatise*, 224–25.]

Yet even to accuse poets of behaving like children is to ascribe to them some measure of rationality; Hume's animus could hence not have been satiated had not a more resounding charge already been leveled. Earlier in his *Treatise*, Hume had compared poetry to mad raving and had found very little difference between the two, for reasons that are directly pertinent here:

> 'Tis difficult for us to withold our assent from what is painted out to us in all the colours of eloquence; and the vivacity produc'd by

> the fancy is in many cases greater than that which arises from custom and experience. We are hurried away by the lively imagination of our author or companion; and even he himself is often a victim to his own fire and genius.
>
> Nor will it be amiss to remark, that as a lively imagination very often degenerates into madness or folly and bears it a great resemblance in its operations; so they influence the judgment after the same manner, and produce belief from the very same principles. When the imagination, from any extraordinary ferment of the blood and spirits, acquires such a vivacity as disorders all its powers and faculties, there is not means of distinguishing betwixt truth and falsehood. . . .
>
> We may observe the same effect of poetry in a lesser degree; only with this difference, that the least reflection dissipates the illusions of poetry, and places the objects in their proper light. 'Tis however certain, that in the warmth of a poetical enthusiasm, a poet has a counterfeit belief, and even a kind of vision of his objects: And if there be any shadow of argument to support this belief, nothing contributes more to his full conviction than a blaze of poetical figures and images, which have their effect upon the poet himself, as well as upon his readers. [*Treatise*, 123.]

A blaze of poetic figures will temporarily lead a writer into the grip of madness, or so Hume thought. Of course, tracing affinities between madness and poetical writing need not be a reproach; establishing a relation between these two phenomena can be a first step toward situating them within philosophy and against philosophy.[22] However, it would take a truly prodigious feat of interpretation for someone to perceive Hume's remarks as favorably disposed toward the cause of poetry. Once more, we have encountered philosophy's disdain for linguistic usage not tethered closely enough to truth. Such disdain, directed against another target, is patent even in the most laudatory remark on poetic writing in the whole *Treatise:* "[H]owever philosophers may have been bewilder'd in [certain] speculations, poets have been guided more infallibly, by a certain taste or common instinct, which in most kinds of reasoning goes farther than any of that art and philosophy, with which we have been yet acquainted" (*Treatise*, 494). Hume was less concerned here to praise poetry than to denounce pre-Humean philosophy (and theology).[23] Even poetic "taste" was more palatable for him than drivel conceived by nonempiricist speculation.

3. *Language as Representation*

A third way in which Hume tended to devalue the operations of language is his focus on the *representative* role of signifiers. In his view, a medium of discussion is always secondary to the ideas that it represents and articulates. Truthful discourse is most obviously derivative of the content that it conveys, but even fallacious discourse must represent some pre-existing ideas in order to transmit meaning (though the ideas need not be entertained at present, or, if they are currently entertained, they need not derive from complex impressions that would match their precise lineaments). Just as ideas represent impressions—at least if analyzed fully into their elemental constituents—so words represent ideas. Ideas, Hume contended, are (at least in their simple form) "exact representations of . . . impressions" and "nothing but copies of our impressions"; likewise, words are "signs of certain ideas," and conversation is but "a transcript of the mind" (*Treatise*, 3, 83, 611; *Enquiries*, 62). In the same way that "ideas are preceded by other more lively perceptions [i.e., impressions], from which they are derived, and which they represent," so discourse has "an intimate connexion with certain ideas . . . and is to be consider'd as an image as well as an effect" (*Treatise*, 7, 113).

The secondary (or, rather, tertiary) status of discourse is affirmed in several examples. At one point, for instance, Hume described how language reflects an antecedent division between moral sentiments and the sentiments of self-love. He maintained: "The distinction, therefore, between these species of sentiment being so great and evident, language must soon be moulded upon it, and must invent a peculiar set of terms, in order to express those universal sentiments" (*Enquiries*, 274). This prioritizing of inner sentiment over outward expression transforms language into a mirror and a servant that dutifully adapts its functioning to the changing shape of reality. Closely similar moves turn up in Hume's treatment of verbal quibbling. In the appendix relating to this topic in the *Enquiry concerning the Principles of Morals*, Hume argued that we should not aspire to resolve every debate over linguistic classification: "[I]t is no wonder that languages should not be very precise in marking the boundaries between virtues and talents, vices and defects; since there is so little distinction made in our internal estimation of them" (*Enquiries*, 314). A privileging of extradiscoursive facts is also in evidence in Hume's account of abstract ideas: "When we have found a resemblance among several objects, that often occur to us, we apply the same name to all of them, whatever differences we may observe in the degrees of their quantity and quality, and whatever other differences may appear among them" (*Treatise*, 20). Once again, language plays the role of a humble servant. When it forsakes that role, as it does most often in theological discourse, it enkindles the wrath of *le bon David*: "[A]s [theology] admits of no terms of composition, but bends every branch of knowledge to its own purpose, without much regard to the phenomena of nature, or to the unbiased sentiments of the mind, hence reasoning, and even language, have been warped from their natural course, and distinctions have been endeavoured to be established where the difference of the objects was, in a manner, imperceptible" (*Enquiries*, 322).

Hume's representational account of language condemns all signifiers to a derivative, fallen status. A conception of signifiers as mere representations is, of course, not uniquely Humean; as Alice Jardine has written, in every field the "process of representation, the sorting out of identity and difference, is . . . [a] process so seemingly natural to us as to be beyond question."[24] Moreover, representation (and accounts of representation) should not be seen as a transitory cloud that will eventually dissipate to reveal the glow of unmediated presence. There is no alternative to seeing through a glass darkly, as Jacques Derrida has pointed out: "[T]o determine language as representation is not the effect of an accidental prejudice, a theoretical fault or a manner of thinking, a limit or a closure among others, a form of representation, precisely, which came about one day and of which we could rid ourselves by a decision when the time comes."[25] While avoiding *some* paradoxes, however, an embrace of representation will give rise to equally intractable and mind-bending problems. Though such problems cannot now be explored,[26] we should at least note the devaluation of language that is intrinsic to Hume's approach. Hume granted temporal and epistemological priority to ideas *vis-à-vis* linguistic units (and to impressions over ideas). To argue that language does and should re-present ideas is to characterize and denigrate signifiers as mere substitutes. Of primary concern in any representational account is the presence that a signifier seeks to regain. It is only because the content has to be regained that a signifier is necessary at all. When all goes well, in the view of representationalists, the signifier will have become transparent and will thus have abased itself in order to give a properly unobstructed channel to whatever it signifies; an obtrusive medium of expression arouses as much discomfort as smog in air. (Air, after all, is the medium of respiration and visibility.) In restoring its signified idea to presence, a signifier should not divert attention to an extraneous matter such as its own performance and needs, except in special cases like poetry. In fact, a signifier does its best work when it goes virtually unseen, for only then can it draw notice exclusively to that which is being signified. If the re-presentative role of signifiers is ever to be fulfilled, then the flow of representation should not be blocked at the outset by an attention-stilling opacity. This general point is implied in Hume's analysis of signification as a species of causal interaction, at least if we keep in mind that Hume thought signifiers and signified ideas to be not just causally linked but also representationally connected—i.e., connected as image and original:

> [B]ecause such a particular idea is commonly annex'd to such a particular word, nothing is requir'd but the hearing of that word to produce the correspondent idea; and 'twill scarce be possible for the mind, by its utmost efforts, to prevent that transition. In this case it is not absolutely

> necessary, that upon hearing such a particular sound, we shou'd reflect on any past experience, and consider what idea has been usually connected with the sound. The imagination of itself supplies the place of this reflection, and is so accustom'd to pass from the word to the idea, that it interposes not a moment's delay betwixt the hearing of the one, and the conception of the other. [*Treatise*, 93.]

In short, the Humean view of language reduces signifiers to derivative surrogates that best carry out their functions when they come closest to disappearing. A representative signifier presents an absent idea by becoming nearly absent itself. Hume's representationalism thus amounts to a key ingredient of his devaluation of language.

4. *Against Dissemination*

Partly in conflict with some of his own insights (which will be explored shortly), Hume set his face against interpretive multiplicity. He wanted words and their signified ideas to be clearly bounded and free of sterile contention; this we have seen already in his remarks on the foolishness of verbal disputes. His aversion toward such disputes led him to resolve to "fix, if possible, the precise meaning of . . . terms, and thereby remove some part of that obscurity, which is so much complained of in this species of philosophy" (*Enquiries*, 62). But occasionally Hume went further. He felt that not only *should* terms be used precisely, but in fact language *is* a peculiarly dependable institution. Although connections between observed facts and people's ideas may be tenuous more often than not, connections between ideas and words are much more reliable: "The words or discourses of others have an intimate connexion with certain ideas in their mind. . . . Other effects only point out their causes in an oblique manner; but the testimony of men does it directly" (*Treatise*, 113). In the world according to Hume, connections between ideas and language are more trustworthy than connections between ideas and conduct, and this difference can affect everyday attitudes: "*[T]he world . . . more easily excuses a person in acting than in talking contrary to the decorum of his profession and character.* A fault in words is commonly more open and distinct than one in actions, which admit of many palliating excuses, and decide not so clearly concerning the intention and views of the actor" (*Treatise*, 153; emphasis in original).

At first sight, Hume may appear to have accorded language a rather noble position; semantic functioning is here depicted as singularly reliable. Even so, Hume's paeans to the dependableness of language try to denude language of one of its essential properties. By fusing words and intentionality, Hume sought to repress what was described in my first chapter as the iterability of all signs. His vision of a felicitous harmony between purpose and meaning would entail robbing linguistic units of their capacity for infinite recontextualization. Unlike the taste of manna, the definitions of words could not adjust to their particular circumstances. Admittedly, Hume's pronouncements on these questions were not unduly rigid or smug—as is borne out by the quotations in the preceding paragraph—and other strands of his texts contain accounts of iterability, however inchoate. Nonetheless, Hume's often tacit assumption that linguistic signs are uniquely trustworthy impelled his overreactions to his discovering of semantic equivocality. Given his premise of reliability, we can understand his revulsion at the fact that "[t]he word *natural* is commonly taken in so many senses and is of so loose a signification," as well as his observation that "nothing [is] more contrary to true philosophy, than . . . that the word, imagination, is commonly us'd in two different senses" (*Enquiries*, 307; *Treatise*, 117 note 1). Hume was frequently unable to reconcile himself to the multifariousness of meaning, which is to say that he was frequently unable to reconcile himself to what makes signification possible. And this devaluation of discourse flowed quite naturally from his attempts to grant discourse a uniquely favored position.

B. Insights into Signification

Hume's linguistic asides are far from uniformly disparaging; even the observations discussed so far have not been unalloyedly negative. In this section, we shall be examining some of his remarks on language that are by no means derogatory, but are profound insights into the processes and prerequisites of signification. These insights were not developed by Hume at length, and so he never appreciated their powerfully subversive ramifications throughout his writings. In the second and third Parts of this chapter, some of Hume's insights (in a much more elaborate form) will enter prominently into the deconstruction of his main texts. For now, however, those insights will be recounted summarily. We shall begin with a theme directly contrary to the last topic of the preceding section.

1. *Iterability*

Despite his yearning for semantic univocality, Hume admitted on more than one occasion that we can never achieve full confidence in educing a specific intent from any combination of signifiers. His ideal may have been the full uniting of inner purpose and outer manifestation, but he sagely did not contend that his harmonizing ideal is actualized in every case. He took only the more sophisticated position that his ideal *can* be realized in every case. This viewpoint emerges, for example, near the very beginning of the *Treatise*'s reflections on justice. Therein, Hume argued that "when we praise any actions, we regard only the motives that produced them, and consider the actions as signs or indications of certain principles in the mind and temper." He noted that we cannot "look within to find the moral quality . . . directly; and therefore [we] fix our attention on actions, as on external signs" (*Treatise*, 477). Hume then considered whether acts usually performed from virtuous motives will arouse esteem even when the typical motives are not present; his answer was affirmative. In explaining why such actions are still regarded as virtuous, Hume gave a remarkable account of the iterability of signs:

> A man that really feels no gratitude in his temper, is still pleas'd to perform grateful actions, and thinks he has, by that means, fulfill'd his duty. Actions are at first only consider'd as signs of motives: But 'tis usual, in this case, as in all others, to fix our attention on the signs, and neglect, in some measure, the thing signify'd. But tho', on some occasions, a person may perform an action merely out of regard to its moral obligation, yet still this supposes in human nature some distinct principles, which are capable of producing the action. [*Treatise*, 479.]

Here Hume recognized that virtuous motives are merely *capable* of lying behind acts normally considered to merit praise. He conceded that they are likewise capable of *not* lying behind such acts; other motives, sinister or benign, may take their place.

An equally forceful statement on the elusiveness of signs is to be found in Hume's discussion of promises. Focusing on linguistic signs, Hume remarked that a particular form of words is invented "by which we bind ourselves to the performance of any action. . . . After these signs are instituted, whoever uses them is immediately bound by his interest to execute his engagements" (*Treatise*, 522). Through the authorized form of signs, a person can indicate her will to become legally or morally bound in such and such a matter. But what should happen if somebody has invoked the form of words without harboring a will to become bound? The twists and turns of Hume's answer to this problem ought to be quoted at some length, for therein resides another splendid account of signifiers' iterability:

> 'Tis evident, that the will alone is never suppos'd to cause the obligation, but must be express'd by words or signs, in order to impose a tye upon any man. The expression being once brought in as subservient to the will, soon becomes the principal part of the promise; nor will a man be less bound by his word, tho' he secretly give a different direction to his intention, and with-hold himself both from a resolution, and from willing an obligation. But tho' the expression makes on most occasions the whole of the promise, yet it does not always so; and one, who shou'd make use of any expression, of which he knows not the meaning, and which he uses without any intention of binding himself,

> wou'd not *certainly* be bound by it. Nay, tho' he knows its meaning, yet if he uses it in jest only, and with such signs as shew evidently he has no serious intention of binding himself, he wou'd not lie under any obligation of performance; but 'tis necessary, that the words be a perfect expression of the will, without any contrary signs. Nay, even this we must not carry so far as to imagine, that one, whom, by our quickness of understanding, we conjecture, from certain signs, to have an intention of deceiving us, is not bound by his expression or verbal promise, if we accept of it; but must limit this conclusion to those cases, where the signs are of a different kind from those of deceit.[27]

Once again Hume gave voice to what he had expressed earlier in a much more simple form when he had maintained that, although everybody is "free to use his terms in what sense he pleases" in the face of the "common signification of words," the "common signification" may inflict penalties—such as misunderstandings and sheer bewilderment—on those who avail themselves of their freedom (*Treatise*, 124). All we must add is that the slipperiness of intentionality and the orderliness of common signification are inextricably intertwined.

2. *Meaning and Difference*

Despite his repeated emphasis on particularized data, Hume relied sometimes on a portrayal of meaning as an effect of difference. This portrayal becomes conspicuous on two borders: the border between sanity and madness, and the borderline between nature and culture. In a passage that we have already scrutinized, Hume compared the rhapsodies of poets to madness. Of interest here is Hume's contention that madness, like exuberant rhetoric, involves the elimination of difference. For someone gone mad, "there is no means of distinguishing betwixt truth and falsehood" (*Treatise*, 123). A mad person can never tell the truth, save by coincidence—in the same way that a totally illiterate person might compose *Hamlet* while pressing keys on a typewriter—and the precise reason he cannot tell the truth is that he cannot discriminate between truth and falsehood. Knowing what counts as true entails knowing what counts as false, for one cannot know what counts as true unless one knows what counts as not false. Truth receives its identity as a result of its being separated from falsehood; a mad person, who cannot separate truth and falsity, *ipso facto* cannot grasp what would count as true. (This straightforward analysis of difference will of course deconstruct itself into the paradoxical play of *différance*, as we have discovered in the first chapter and as we presently shall behold again in the current chapter's last Part. But we are here interested only in the crucial first step of demonstrating that presence is as much an effect of difference as difference is an effect of presence.)

Hume turned to a more directly language-focused example in his etiology of the moral sentiments that uphold the institution of justice. He considered the allegation that moral standards derive from social conditioning. He rejected the view that stratagems of political leaders can account *entirely* for the distinction made by almost everyone between vice and virtue:

> Any artifice of politicians may assist nature in the producing of those sentiments, which she suggests to us, and may even on some occasions, produce alone an approbation or esteem for any particular action; but 'tis impossible it should be the sole cause of the distinction we make betwixt vice and virtue. For if nature did not aid us in this particular, 'twoud be in vain for politicians to talk of *honourable* or *dishonourable*, *praiseworthy* or *blameable*. These words wou'd be perfectly unintelligible, and wou'd no more have any idea annex'd to them, than if they were of a tongue perfectly unknown to us. The utmost politicians can perform, is, to extend the natural sentiments beyond their original bounds; but still nature must furnish the materials, and give us some notion of moral distinctions. [*Treatise*, 500.]

This passage, the gist of which will presently be examined in greater depth, was echoed in the *Enquiry concerning the Principles of Morals*:

> Had nature made no [moral] distinction[s], founded on the original constitution of the mind, the words, *honourable* and *shameful*, *lovely* and *odious*, *noble* and *despicable*, had never had place in any language; nor could politicians, had they invented these terms, ever have been able to render them intelligible, or make them convey any idea to the audience.[28]

While obviously giving credence to a representational conception of discourse—with the mirroring by linguistic contrasts of antecedent contrasts within our minds—these passages also point to a conception of meaning as a product of difference. Words become intelligible only by being differentiated; until each word has been subsumed into a network of oppositions and contrasts, in ways that systematically mark it off from the other elements in the network, it will remain unrealized as a meaningless nullity in an amorphous nonstructure. A word like "honorable" could never function if it were left to its own devices, and indeed it would not have any such devices at all. It acquires meaning once it has been located within a broader system of contrasts (which, according to Hume, is grounded and galvanized by a set of pre-existing ideational contrasts). Once again we see Hume taking an indispensable first step, though only a first step, toward discovering that identity and relationality are caught in a ceaseless interchange that will constitute both of them by having disqualified them from being constituted.

3. *Generality*

A. GENERALITY OF PERSPECTIVE

Hume recognized, however inadequately, that language displays a generalized structure in two senses: a generality of perspective and a generality of inclusion. The former sense was invoked by Hume while he was attempting to establish why one's approval of benevolent deeds will have retained its general character as approval even though the intensity of one's feelings (i.e., the measure of satisfaction that one enjoys) will vary in a direct relation to the proximity of the deeds. His explanation, which he propounded in both the *Treatise* and the second *Enquiry*, entailed (to some extent) a reversal of privilege and subordination between discourse and ideas; here the flow of perceptions must submit sooner or later to the demands of linguistic intercourse. Each person begins with feelings of sympathy and self-love unique to his or her standpoint, but

> we every day meet with persons who are in a situation different from us, and who could never converse with us were we to remain constantly in that position and point of view, which is peculiar to ourselves. The intercourse of sentiments, therefore, in society and conversation, makes us form some general unalterable standard, by which we may approve or disapprove of characters and manners.[29]

Even though our feelings will not fall into step with generalized moral language, the latter will be "sufficient, at least, for discourse, [and] serve all our purposes in company, in the pulpit, on the theatre, and in the schools."[30] An obliging servant no longer, discourse must have its way. As Hume stated:

> The more we converse with mankind, and the greater social intercourse we maintain, the more shall we be familiarized to these general preferences and distinctions, without which our conversation and discourse could scarcely be rendered intelligible to each other. Every man's interest is peculiar to himself, and the aversions and desires, which result from it, cannot be supposed to affect others in a like degree. General language, therefore, being formed for general use, must be moulded on some more general views.[31]

Hume made clear that the foregoing analysis would apply to our observations of physical phenomena just as much as to moral feelings (*Enquiries*, 227–28). What he never realized sufficiently, however, was that he had descried an essential aspect of signification and communication. That he did not see this is most apparent in his dichotomy between certain words: (1) words such as "adversary" and "enemy," which are applied to an individual or a group from the particular standpoint of another person or group, and (2) words such as "odious" or "immoral," which should properly stem from an impartial perspective (*Enquiries*, 272). Even if we were to acknowledge such a distinction, it would bedim a much more interesting point to which the generality of perspective in moral discourse could have been made to lead. Such generality will structure *all* modes of discourse, even discourse that would seem tied to one or another viewpoint. Let us consider Hume's first assemblage of words ("enemy," "adversary," and so forth). To call someone "my foe" in a manner that will be comprehended by other people, one must comply with the established conventions for employing the words "my foe." One must abide by all the discoursive rules concerning what counts as hostile or "adversarial" relations. That is, one has to adopt a general or disinterested viewpoint in regard to the range of circumstances that would provide grounds for calling someone "my foe." An excessively idiosyncratic use of the term "foe" will have rendered one's statements unintelligibly obscure, just as idiosyncratic uses of moral terms will lead to "perpetual contradictions" (*Treatise*, 602). Of course, idiosyncratic usage may transform settled conventions, but that can happen in moral dialogue as much or as little as in other genres of discourse.

It is the generality of perspective within *all* discourse that Hume perceived far too gropingly. Had he better followed up his own insights, he could have proceeded to evolve a structure/event aporia, setting to work the themes of "uniqueness" and "generality." Such a move would have both undone and confirmed the generality described here, with no hope of a dialectical resolution (though the unresolved paradox would of course be changing its forms constantly). Alas, Hume's attention lay elsewhere.

B. GENERALITY OF INCLUSION

While discussing "abstract ideas," Hume ferreted out a second important type of generality that all languages must exhibit. He explained that processes of abstraction emerge together with a process of naming: "When we have found a resemblance among several objects, that often occur to us, we apply the same name to all of them, whatever differences we may observe in the degrees of their quantity and quality, and whatever other differences may appear among them." This process of naming is inherently inexact, but it suffices for "all . . . purposes of reflexion and conversation." It consists in a relation of customary conjunction: "[A] general term . . . from a customary conjunction has a relation to many . . . particular ideas, and readily recalls them in the imagination" (*Treatise*, 20, 18, 22). With the word "pleasure," for example, "we comprehend sensations, which are very different from each other, and which have only such a distant resemblance, as is requisite to make them be express'd by the same abstract term" (*Treatise*, 472). How we manage to comprise heterogeneity within unity is "inexplicable by the utmost efforts of human understanding," and can only be ascribed to "a kind of magical faculty in the soul, which [is] always most perfect in the greatest geniuses, and is properly what we call a genius" (*Treatise*, 24). Given that abstract terms are based on resemblances, Hume's tribute to such terms as the progeny of a special genius may bring to mind a comment by Aristotle: "[I]n philosophy also an acute mind will perceive resemblances even in things far apart."[32] Indeed, Hume's theory of naming-and-abstraction resonates with more than a few echoes, both antecedent and subsequent, within Western philosophy. From Condillac to Rousseau to Nietzsche to Wittgenstein (whose doctrine of imbricated "family resemblances" can be seen as a sophisticated rewriting of Hume's stance), major theorists have advocated broadly similar views of names as heterogeneities-within-unities.[33] Moreover, Hume's theory of naming implicitly harks back to the foremost ancient theory of metaphor. Looming over his text is Aristotle's pronouncement that "[m]etaphor is the application of the name of a thing to something else." (In the terminology of the master of those who know, Hume's doctrine of general terms could be construed as involving either a metaphor that works from "species to genus" or a metaphor that works from "species to species."[34]) Hume's account of naming and classifying is through and through an account of metaphor, albeit a fumbling account.

Furthermore, we can *generalize* Hume's doctrine of generality. His account furnishes yet another reason—in addition to paradoxes of differentiation and the iterability of signifiers—to think that proper names are always already *im*proper. In this case, they are improper because they function as the belated metaphors of an irretrievable oneness. They denote unity, but they can only arise in circumstances of fragmentation. To confirm this, we must look *brièvement* at Hume's conception of identity. Our best starting point is a long quotation:

> When we have been accustom'd to observe a constancy in certain impressions, and have found, that the perception of the sun or ocean, for instance, returns upon us after an absence or annihilation with like parts and in a like order, as at its first appearance, we are not apt to regard these interrupted perceptions as different, (which they really are) but on the contrary consider them as individually the same, upon account of their resemblance. But as this interruption of their existence is contrary to their perfect identity, and makes us regard the first impression as annihilated, and the second as newly created, we find ourselves somewhat at a loss, and are involv'd in a kind of contradiction. In order to free ourselves from this difficulty, we disguise, as much as possible, the interruption, or rather remove it entirely, by supposing

> that these interrupted perceptions are connected by a real existence, of which we are insensible. . . .
>
> . . . The imagination is seduc'd into such an opinion only by means of the resemblance of certain perceptions; since we find they are only our resembling perceptions, which we have a propension to suppose the same. This propension to bestow an identity on our resembling perceptions, produces the fiction of a continu'd existence; since that fiction, as well as the identity, is really false, as is acknowledg'd by all philosophers, and has no other effect than to remedy the interruption of our perceptions, which is the only circumstance that is contrary to their identity. [*Treatise*, 199, 209.]

Once the pure unity of an object enters the flow of time, it can never be reunited except by way of a "gross illusion" (*Treatise*, 217). (*Mutatis mutandis*, everything that I am about to say here would apply in full to perceptions that are not interrupted, for even when perceived without gaps an object can retain its unity over time solely through a "fiction of the imagination" [*Treatise*, 200–201]. However, because Hume wrote far more on interrupted perceptions than on their uninterrupted counterparts, it is on interrupted dealings with objects that we shall train our attention.) The mind unifies its perceptions that exactly resemble one another, but in reality "our perceptions are broken, and interrupted, and however like, are still different from each other" (*Treatise*, 213). What this means is that the identity of a given object, denoted by a specific label, corresponds in every pertinent way to an assortment of things conjoined by an abstract term. In each case, naming will unify distinct perceptions as a result of the similarities among them; in each case, then, a metaphorical process will hold sway. Perceptions that exactly resemble one another may seem totally undivided, but "a very little reflection and philosophy is sufficient to make us perceive the fallacy of that opinion" (*Treatise*, 210). Specific objects and abstract groups are therefore homologous, since every identity must comprise discrete units. Proper names, as much as their abstract counterparts, establish themselves through metaphorization.

4. *Metaphor and Metonymy*

Hume advanced his greatest linguistic insights while he was not discussing language. In his associationist account of human psychology, he anticipated some of the leading work in modern linguistics. Structures that he deemed to be fundamental in human thought and emotion have been charted more recently by scholars in studies of the rhetorical patterns that shape discourse. Hume contended that all or most ideas in a person's mind are associated in one or more of three ways: resemblance, contiguity, and causation. These principles of connection amount to central themes in the *Treatise* and in both the *Enquiries*. Hume thought them to be of paramount importance across the gamut of human institutions and practices, from the acquisition of property by accession, to the weaving of historical narratives, to the conferring of moral praiseworthiness on someone whose good intentions do not succeed in giving rise to good acts.[35] Now, if (like Hume) we suppose causation to be merely a special type of contiguity, we shall see that Hume's associationist picture of the mind has paralleled the account of language offered by Roman Jakobson and others. In a classic essay, which drew upon the analyses of Saussure, Jakobson put forward the theory that "[t]he development of a discourse may take place along two different . . . lines: one topic may lead to another either through their similarity or their contiguity." To the similarity-based flow of discourse Jakobson fixed the label "metaphoric"; to the contiguity-based flow he fastened the label "metonymic."[36] He thus apportioned symbolic sequences between the two great generic tropes, which correspond to Hume's principles of connection. Just as Hume had averred that the associationist principles of contiguity and resemblance will "in the mental world . . . be found to have as extraordinary effects as [gravitational force has been found to have] in the natural, and to shew [themselves] in as many and as various forms" (*Treatise*, 12–13), so Jakobson could maintain that "competition between both devices, metonymic and metaphoric, is manifest in any symbolic process, be it intrapersonal or social."[37]

In short, Hume's psychology now seems to have been a veritable tropology, and his connections between ideas have turned out to be syntactical and semantic. His discourse on human nature has doubled back on itself and has become a discourse on human discourse. But this need not incline one automatically to contend that Hume was in fact analyzing language when he professed to be studying pure thought. That is, one should not posit (in any simple way) that language governs perception. After all, one could take a roughly opposite stand; one could argue that the discoveries of modern linguists confirm that language *follows* perception. In favoring either standpoint, we would presume to have a good grasp of what thought and language are, for only then could we confidently divide the one from the other to the extent required for privileging the one in relation to the other. Yet it may well be that thought and language are utterly unthinkable, in the way that every paradox is. Close resemblances that connect thought and discourse will bespeak not so much a unidirectional causation as a conjoint array of incoherences and deferrals. Nor will the relation between thinking and discourse stand outside that array. On the contrary, any such relation can but subvert itself in the act of situating itself, as thought and language presuppose and preclude each other.[38]

Part Two. The Deferral of Nature

A. Just in the Transition from Nature to Culture

In the first chief section of this Part, we must position ourselves in an obscure passage, a passage from the hostilities of nature to the serenity of civilized life. It is precisely here, at the dawn of social existence, that Hume located the beginnings of law. His search for origins would eventuate in a narrative describing the spread of public peace by way of the greatest obstacle to such peace: unslacking self-interest. (That is what some refer to as an economy of means.) Along the route, language entered into his story with such prominence that it cannot safely be disregarded. We have to read Hume's narrative as a narrative—that is, as a textual framing—if we hope to do justice to its arguments (about justice). To cross the gap between nature and society, we shall have to remind ourselves that the gap does not lie simply *between* them, but also lies *within* each of them. More specifically, we shall find that nature is perforce hollowed out by culture.

1. *Hume's Story of Justice*

Believing that any moral judgment has reference only to the intention that ordinarily lies behind a specific type of deed, Hume inquired whether there exists any primal motive for engaging in acts of justice. Because a form of behavior can be esteemed only if it is prompted generally by a virtuous motivation, and because just acts tend to elicit high esteem, there must be some commendable motive that impels the performance of such acts. Yet, Hume argued, nothing in human nature can prod people at all times to carry out just deeds in the absence of conventionalized rules. (The phrase "just deeds" here refers to actions consistent with the most basic rules of property, even if such rules have not yet come into being.) Neither self-interest nor any type of concern for others can regularly produce just conduct, and therefore no naturally occurring motive can ever account *per se* for the lofty moral standing of justice. Only when rules of property are established, does any justice-oriented motive come into play. Only then, that is, does justice become a moral standard.[39]

Conventions of justice plant no *new* motive within people but redirect an existing motive. Egoistic drives will remain too potent to be overcome by anything but themselves. "'Tis certain, that no affection of the human mind has both a sufficient force, and a proper direction to counter-balance the love of gain, and render men fit members of society. . . . There is no passion, therefore, capable of controlling the interested affection, but the very affection itself" (*Treatise*, 492). Possessive individualism restrains itself by enlightening itself—that is, by taking a longer-term perspective for procuring its aims. Five facts of *la condition humaine* together make self-control both possible and overwhelmingly probable: (1) every person has countless wants (including such basics as the need for bodily nourishment), combined with meager abilities for satisfying those wants; (2) when people join to create a full-fledged social order, their strengths and secureness and productive power are synergistically augmented; (3) the natural inclination of people is to favor themselves, along with their relatives and friends, at the expense of all other people (and thus at the expense of social cohesion); (4) material goods are scarce and can be seized and conveyed readily; (5) if a system of restraints is devised to limit myopic selfishness for the sake of broader cohesion, then the gains to everybody or almost everybody (from the growth in productiveness and secureness) will far outweigh the lost opportunities for immediate grasping (*Treatise*, 484–89). Given these five assumptions, the key remaining prerequisite of a social order–*viz.*, agreement on forms and mechanisms of self-control—will have become virtually inevitable, for it is only through this agreement that selfish passions can be optimally indulged. As Hume emphasized, an appropriate structure of controls will advance rather than stymie the pursuit of one's own well-being.

> [B]y a convention enter'd into by all the members of the society. . . , every one knows what he may safely possess; and the passions are restrain'd in their partial and contradictory motions. Nor is such a restraint contrary to these passions; for if so, it cou'd never be enter'd into, nor maintain'd; but it is only contrary to their heedless and impetuous movement. Instead of departing from our own interest, or from that of our nearest friends, by abstaining from the possessions of others, we cannot better consult both these interests, than by such a convention; because it is by that means we maintain society, which is so necessary to their well-being and subsistence, as well as to our own. [*Treatise*, 489.]

Hume's tack was to explore not only *why* people adopt conventions that originate justice but likewise *how* they go about doing so. It is here that his philosophical anthropology takes its most directly narrative form. Hume knew that "in order to form society, 'tis requisite not only that it be advantageous, but also that men be sensible of its advantages" (*Treatise*, 486), and he felt that he should offer a story to recount how people came to sense those advantages in due time. His narrative begins curiously, with an abortive reference to family life as the "first and original principle of human society." After giving some cause for hope by adverting to the emollient influence of families, which prepare children for society by "rubbing off those rough corners and untoward affections, which prevent their coalition," Hume then declared that the generosity and affection which pervade family life are "almost as contrary to [fitting men for large societies] as the most narrow selfishness" (*Treatise*, 486, 487). Close ties among family members tend to exclude all other people as much as individual egoism does; the war of each against all has therefore turned out to be a war of each *family* against all, and Hume's depiction of family life will have moved us not one bit nearer to explaining the growth of "large societies." Jerome Christensen nicely captures this dead end in Hume's story: "Society will always stand slightly beyond the family group, the very naturalness of which is its flaw: there is too intimate a connection between the family unit and the individual; society depends on remote connections having the force of close ones."[40]

At this point, Hume's narrative displays some striking lacunae. We are told that people must enter and do enter into some type of arrangement that will provide for the stability of their holdings, but we are left to wonder how this can possibly come about. On the one hand, Hume had announced that people "in their wild uncultivated state" could never glimpse the advantages of society "by study and reflexion alone," and he had further written that justice "as it is now understood, wou'd never have been dream'd of among rude and savage men" (*Treatise*, 486, 488). On the other hand, he proceeded shortly to urge that "nothing can be more simple and obvious" than the establishment of restraints on unrefined egoism, and that such curbs therefore "necessarily take place upon the least reflection" (*Treatise*, 493, 492). Odd, too, is some proleptic invoking of experience. Hume wrote, for example, that a structure of checks on short-term gratification will arise "[w]hen . . . men have had experience enough to observe, that . . . the whole system . . . is infinitely advantageous," and "[a]fter men have found by experience . . . that society is necessary to the satisfaction of [selfish] passions" (*Treatise*, 497–99). Experience and reflection thus appear to take on dual roles; they *occasion* the founding of society (by making its benefits apparent), but they also *preclude* the founding of society (because they cannot take place until people have already emerged from the state of nature).

Some assistance in resolving these difficulties—if indeed they can be resolved—may be summoned from the following passage, which might at first seem equally doubtful:

> [W]hen men, from their early education in society, have become sensible of the infinite advantages that result from it, and have besides acquir'd a new affection to company and conversation; and when they have observ'd, that the principal disturbance in society arises from those goods, which we call external, and from their looseness and easy transition from one person to another; they must seek for a remedy . . . by a convention enter'd into by all the members of the society. [*Treatise*, 489.]

In this passage, the first use of the word "society" must be different from the succeeding two uses. Unless Hume was flagrantly contradicting himself, he must have used "society" near the passage's outset to refer to the cohesive structure of a typical family, rather than to the broad social framework that comprises all families. But if that was his meaning here, he presumably adopted a like usage on some other occasions. Consequently, we can eliminate the most glaring double bind in his text; neither crude reflection nor the experience of family life will *alone* manage to prepare the way and make straight the paths that lead toward social tranquility, but reflection and family life *together* will prove quite adequate to the task.[41] Under this reading, where reflection and family life combine to achieve what neither can separately accomplish, Hume can be rescued from the grosser absurdities that beset his myth of legal and social origins. Whether he could escape *all* absurdities, however, is quite a different question. In the next subsection of this chapter, we shall confront other paradoxes in Hume's story. These narrative antinomies are more subtle than those produced thus far, and at least one of them will prove inevasible.

2. *The Disarticulation of Hume's Narrative*

The preceding subsection reviewed only the bare outlines of Hume's model of the transition leading from natural enmities to civilized harmony. Nevertheless, we may proceed to examine three attractive lines of critique to which one might essay to have recourse against Hume. Two of these approaches, so I shall be maintaining, do not finally succeed. By contrast, the third approach will effect an irredeemable dislocation in Hume's quest for origins. In the course of the analyses in this subsection, many details of the Humean quest will be filled in.

At the beginning, it is perhaps advisable to make clear that this subsection is not attacking a straw man. Theorists of very different persuasions have adverted to Hume's pronouncement that the state of nature is "a mere philosophical fiction, which never had, and never cou'd have, any reality" (*Treatise*, 493). Jerome Christensen, for example, has proclaimed: "[F]or Hume, we can understand the passage from nature to society historically only if we understand nature as a 'philosophical fiction.' We can understand the origin of society, its history, only if we rid ourselves of the idea that there was any time before society, that society has any history except for that which is going on right now."[42] He concludes: "Bold Hume, to assail so openly the premise that seems to underwrite his historical procedure" (PE, 32). Now, from this it may seem to follow that a critique of Hume's historical narrative will necessarily prove redundant. Why should one seek to challenge the recountal of a transition from nature to collective life, when Hume himself gainsaid the veracity of any such tale?

To this query two replies seem appropriate. In the first place, Hume's confession that people never existed in a state of nature was not as utterly unequivocal as some scholars allege. On the one hand, to be sure, Hume depicted the state of nature primarily for analytical rather than historical purposes (i.e., to explain why justice constantly merits our devotion, rather than to account for the emergence of such devotion at some point in the obscure past), and he affirmed that people's "very first state and situation may justly be esteem'd social."[43] On the other hand, he came close a few times to classifying the state of nature as an ephemeral but true stage in the development of humanity. Thus, he wrote in the *Treatise* that " 'tis utterly impossible for men to remain any considerable time in that savage condition, which precedes society" (*Treatise*, 493). Likewise, in the second *Enquiry* his impugning of a presocial state was rather less than unqualified: "Whether such a condition of human nature could ever exist, or if it did, could continue so long as to merit the appellation of a *state*, may justly be doubted. . . . But this must be admitted, that, if such a state of mutual war and violence was ever real, the suspension of all laws of justice, from their absolute inutility, is a necessary and infallible consequence" (*Enquiries*, 190).

Second, and considerably more important, this subsection will highlight paradoxes that go unnoticed in the skeptical view of the state of nature. Those who reject notions of an original state of nature do not think that Hume's narrative is by any means incoherent; rather, they follow Hume in holding the state of nature (and the transition to social life) to be obviously fictitious and entirely implausible but nonetheless coherent. That is why they continue to laud his story as a "useful analytical tool."[44] For them, the fictitiousness of the narrative's state of nature derives from its unrealistic slighting of human impulses toward sociality, and not from any deep aporia in the transition that Hume recounted. This subsection will opt for a much more venturesome tack, by arguing that Hume's story disrupts itself when it narrates certain events that cannot possibly materialize until they have already occurred.

A. TWO ULTIMATELY UNSUCCESSFUL CRITIQUES

i. *Obligation Before the Fact.* One might hope to attack Hume along lines laid down by critics of social contract theories. In the debates surrounding such theories, a repeated source of complaint has been that the social contract must have already gained its force if it is ever to come into existence. This type of complaint can be articulated in several forms. Thus, one can observe—as Louis Althusser has done in his critique of Rousseau[45]—that an essential party to the originating contract cannot ever exist until the contract has been effectuated. People as individuals will predate their contract, but as "the people" (*"le peuple"*) they make their entrance exclusively through their consummated agreement. Abstractly identified as "the people," a collectivity can begin and develop *as such* only as a result of an original compact; but this means that the compact will not ever emerge, since "the people" must always antecede it as one of its indispensable parties. When individuals alienate some or all of their powers in return for security and collective organization, there has to be a contractual party to whom the powers can be assigned (and from whom security is delivered). But that party cannot make its appearance until such transfers have already been made. A covenantal theory of sociopolitical institutions will hence drive us toward an unnerving "logic" similar to what Derrida has marked in the Declaration of Independence.[46]

Another way of firing this shot is described well by Robert Derathé in his study of Rousseau: "[Critics of contractarian theories] will say that a contract has meaning only if an authority exists which can guarantee its execution, and that consequently one cannot explain the origin of political societies by appealing to an institution that supposes them to have been constituted already."[47] Whereas the earlier formulation discovered transfers without a transferee, this second version of the aporia has revealed obligations without obligatoriness. Nor would the power of this argument be diminished by Hume's belief that social structures can perfectly well exist (though in a primitive fashion) before any mechanisms of government arise;[48] the "authority" referred to by Derathé can as easily be moral as governmental. Problems of pre-existing obligatoriness are thoroughly generalizable, and will cut as sharply into tales of a social structure whose only means of enforcement is remonstration as into tales of a more centralized regime that depends on systematic coercion.

Now, however one chooses between these formulations, Hume's theory of justice will emerge unscathed. Indeed, Hume himself savaged contractarianism in ways closely connected to the latter version of the critique just sketched. He mocked those who held that duties of political loyalty are traceable in the end to tacit promises of allegiance by the persons who have to shoulder the duties. Any such explanation, besides being implausible, will answer one question by proceeding to raise another. John Stuart Mill learned from his father that we cannot convincingly postulate a God to explain how the universe's apparent order could first have come into being; after all, we then have to ask how *God* first came into being.[49] Similarly, in Hume's view, someone who attempts to explain duties of allegiance by referring to duties of integrity will have wasted his or her breath: "We are bound to obey our sovereign, it is said, because we have given a tacit promise to that purpose. But why are we bound to observe our promise? The obligation to allegiance being of like force and authority with the obligation to fidelity, we gain nothing by resolving the one into the other."[50]

Hume's theory escapes both versions of the critique set forth here, because Hume shunned contractarianism. Far from positing an abrupt transition from a feral state of avidity to a cultured world of restraint, Hume was at pains to underscore that the "convention" of justice which he described "is not of the nature of a *promise*" (*Treatise*, 490; emphasis in original). Such a convention will arise gradually, in a long sequence involving neither a promise nor a distinct transfer. People with a shared view of their common interest will have made known to one another that they intend to act (or refrain from acting) in certain ways, on condition of reciprocity. They will accordingly adjust their behavior; yet no one will have exchanged a promise or have accepted a strictly binding obligation. The whole process is more diffused, gradual, and free-floating than the contractarian model would suggest. Within Hume's myth, people who come together to form society do not exchange statements that amount to real undertakings—the obligatory power of which could not be activated unless it pre-existed itself and had already been activated. Rather, their statements collectively construct an emergent plan for setting up the roles to be played by each of them in an institutional framework that will be beneficial for all of them. As Hume wrote:

> I observe, that it will be for my interest to leave another in the possession of his goods, *provided* he will act in the same manner with regard to me. He is sensible of a like interest in the regulation of his conduct. When this common sense of interest is mutually express'd, and is known to both, it produces a suitable resolution and behaviour. And this may properly enough be call'd a convention or agreement betwixt us, tho' without the interposition of a promise; since the actions of each of us have a reference to those of the other, and are perform'd upon the supposition, that something is to be perform'd on the other part. Two men, who pull the oars of a boat, do it by an agreement or convention, tho' they have never given promises to each other. [*Treatise*, 490.]

People who violate the rules of contract and property will be penalized or upbraided not for having reneged on an original promise but for impeding the current operation of a superbly useful scheme of restraints (as well as for breaching the *particular* rules and promises that have come to be accepted).

ii. *Recognizing the Unseen.* A second line of assault on Hume's conception of justice bears on the aforementioned difficulties that at first seemed to ravage his attempts to portray a justice-based system as a product of reason and reflection. Jerome Christensen has powerfully built on the surmisal by Hume that primitive reflection would not suffice to move people to restrain their avidity (PE, 26–34). Christensen describes the role of avid self-interest in Hume's theory of natural drives: "Avidity is not one passion among others. It is identical with and constitutive of the original existence of man himself. Man alone is no more capable of getting perspective on his avidity than he is of independent reflection. Indeed, he is incapable of reflection because he is possessed by avidity" (PE, 28–29). Hardly surprising will it be, in light of this quoted passage, that Christensen so strongly objects to Hume's claim that people will create a system of justice "upon the least reflection" (*Treatise*, 492). Christensen retorts: "But whose reflection? It cannot be the savage's. I would suggest that it is Hume's (and by extension his companionable reader's) 'least reflection' which governs or produces the necessity for an alteration of direction in avidity" (PE, 29). According to Christensen, the main stumbling block is that Hume's empiricist principles would rule out the sort of innovation required at the alleged founding of society; one cannot "view something that is not yet existent and of which one can therefore form no impression (*re*cognize what one has never cognized)" (PE, 28 note 9).

Christensen's reading, however subtle, will prove at best to be inconclusive. As has been remarked, Hume's disparagement of the efficacy of primitive reason can be best viewed as applying only to someone without any experience of family life. When one takes account of the "natural appetite betwixt the sexes" (*Treatise*, 486), one can harbor new hope that primitive reflection will combine with the sociability of family life to move groups of people toward a full-fledged system of justice, even though reflection and partial domestication would each be powerless *alone* to cause such an effect. *En tout cas*, Hume nowhere maintained what Christensen takes for granted—namely, that the obsessive greed of primitive human beings will utterly disenable them from pondering fruitfully on their plight. Hume's only contention was that crude reasoning *in itself*, detached from any acquaintance with the advantages of cooperative intercourse (in the family), would not lift people out of unrefined avarice.

Nor does Christensen fare much better in his appeal to Hume's empiricist principles. True it is that Hume's philosophical assumptions will impose severe limits on the extent to which any person can innovate, but his theory of the imagination was not quite as restrictive as it would have to be to suit Christensen's argument. Though Hume insisted that a person's imagination can employ only those ideas that have been derived from the person's antecedent impressions, he declared also that the imagination "is not restrain'd to the same order and form with the original impressions. . . . [A]ll simple ideas may be separated by the imagination, and may be united again in what form it pleases" (*Treatise*, 9, 10). At issue, then, when we examine Christensen's argument, is whether appropriate impressions *in some form* have preceded the rise of justice and self-restraint. Christensen assumes flatly that one will perforce answer in the negative, but he offers no grounds for thinking that the matter can be resolved with such ease. Hume could have at least plausibly argued that familial life provides the appropriate impressions. After all, he avouched that "every parent, in order to preserve peace among his children, must establish [rules for the stability of possession]" (*Treatise*, 493), and he could have asserted that the imagination can generalize this pattern of rule-governed stability (i.e., by picturing the rule-governed stability as obtaining throughout a broad group of people rather than seeing it as confined to autarkic families). Indeed, Hume described just such a progress of the imagination in the following lines from the second of his *Enquiries:*

> But suppose the conjunction of the sexes to be established in nature, a family immediately arises; and particular rules being found requisite for its subsistence, these are immediately embraced; though without comprehending the rest of mankind within their prescriptions. Suppose that several families unite together into one society, which is totally disjoined from all others, the rules, which preserve peace and order, enlarge themselves to the utmost extent of that society; but becoming then entirely useless, lose their force when carried one step farther. But again suppose, that several distinct societies maintain a kind of intercourse for mutual convenience and advantage, the boundaries of justice still grow larger, in proportion to the largeness of men's views, and the force of their mutual connexions. History, experience, reason sufficiently instruct us in this natural progress of our regards to justice, in proportion as we become acquainted with the extensive utility of that virtue. [*Enquiries*, 192.]

Christensen could reply that Hume's theory of the imagination will lead to endless disputes over how much we can disjoin things: can we, in an inversion of Yeats's line, tell the dance from the dancer? Such a reply would carry substantial force on its own merits, but it would scarcely resolve the present point of contention unequivocally. In fact, it would seem to indicate that the present problem cannot be settled very convincingly one way or the other.

Christensen might also point out that Hume averred "that married people . . . mutually lose their property, and are unacquainted with the *mine* and *thine*, which are so necessary, and yet cause such disturbance in human society" (*Treatise*, 495). Thus, a primitive forerunner of wedlock would appear to be rather barren as soil for the impressions needed to prepare human beings for society (where the rules governing ownership have to counterbalance the dearth of comradeliness). Two problems, however, would afflict this hypothetical parry. First, it is far from beyond all doubt that Hume gave full credence to the view of matrimony expressed in the quotation above. Christensen himself points out Hume's awareness of male dominance in the family,[51] yet such awareness would militate against the belief that "married people . . . *mutually* lose their property." In the second *Enquiry,* Hume's reference to the elimination of rights of ownership between married persons contained a final clause that made his endorsement of patriarchal fictions considerably less than vehement: "Between married persons, the cement of friendship is by the laws supposed so strong as to abolish all division of possessions; and has often, in reality, the force ascribed to it" (*Enquiries,* 185).

Second, even if Hume had given wholehearted approval to the classic fictions of patriarchy, he would not have afforded Christensen any solace, for Hume never implied that *families* (as opposed to mere couples) will have no need of proprietary restrictions. As we have seen already, he emphasized that children will give their parents little or no peace unless restraints are applied; hence, all offspring are "trained up by their parents to some rule of conduct and behaviour" (*Enquiries,* 190).

B. A PROPOSAL FOR A NEW CRITIQUE

> The Lord will bring a nation against you from afar, from the end of the earth, as swift as the eagle flies, a nation whose language you do not understand.
>
> —*Deuteronomy* 28:49

When directed against Hume, all of the foregoing critiques ultimately founder because they pay too little attention to the discoursive elements in his theory. More precisely, they will not have remarked that his account of justice and property is (among other things) a discourse on discourse. All of the foregoing approaches will have failed to ponder on what Hume said about communicational needs, and they will accordingly have allowed him to take a certain linguistic framework for granted. Without knowing it, they will have collaborated with Hume in glossing over the indispensable moment of discoursive forgetfulness that both animates and disrupts his theory.

Let us briefly review the process by which natural avidity becomes sublimated—rationally sublimated—into conformity with a system of justice. As a result of crude reflection and the restraints of family life, most people come to realize that a persistent demand for goods can be better filled within society than without it. However, that each person has attained such a realization will not *per se* induce anyone to submit to the necessary controls; individual self-restraint will ensue only when each person is confident that all or most other persons will join him or her in following an enlightened course of behavior. But confidence in the future actions of other people does not materialize out of thin air, especially when complicated and mutually referential behavior is involved. An intent to forbear seizing the possessions of other people (on condition of reciprocity) is not something that can be readily inferred, or even inferred at all, from a single action or set of actions. A well-founded expectance of unbroken restraint by others can arise only through the explicit communication of an intent shared by all. As Hume acknowledged repeatedly, the forming of a social convention that establishes justice will unavoidably presuppose an array of dialogues in which people exchange their views on the desirability of reciprocal temperance. Without such dialogues, people can have no basis for presuming that their own willingness to form a society has become widespread. Yet until they know that the willingness has become widespread, they will never make the transition from stark rapacity to a refined pursuit of self-interest through self-control.

Communication is thus an integral feature in Hume's narrative of the early development of justice. In passage after passage, we spy the unforgoable work of discourses in laying the very fundaments of society. For example, while declaring that the originary social arrangement cannot be founded on a promise, Hume made strikingly clear that *communication* is nevertheless involved:

> This convention is not of the nature of a *promise:* For even promises themselves, as we shall see afterwards, arise from human conventions. It is only a general sense of common interest; which sense all the members of the society *express* to one another, and which induces them to regulate their conduct by certain rules. I observe, that it will be for my interest to leave another in the possession of his goods, *provided* he will act in the same manner with regard to me. He is sensible of a like interest in the regulation of his conduct. When this common sense of interest is *mutually express'd*, and is known to both, it produces a suitable resolution and behaviour.[52]

Hume advanced a similar view several pages later, in the course of insisting that the rules which determine ownership are rightly evaluated as an overall structure:

> When therefore men have had experience enough to observe, that whatever may be the consequence of any single act of justice, perform'd by a single person, yet the whole system of actions, concurr'd in by the whole society, is infinitely advantageous to the whole and to every part; it is not long before justice and property take place. Every member of society is sensible of this interest: Every one *expresses* this sense to his fellows, along with the resolution he has taken of squaring his actions by it, on condition that others will do the same. No more is requisite to induce any one of them to perform an act of justice, who has the first opportunity. [*Treatise*, 497–98; emphasis added.]

In Hume's account of the instituting of norms that govern promises, we once again see the overriding importance of communication: "[N]or is there any thing requisite to form this concert or convention [governing promises], but that every one have a sense of interest in the faithful fulfilling of engagements, *and express that sense to other members of the society.* This immediately causes that interest to operate upon them" (*Treatise*, 522–23; emphasis added).

Quite properly, Hume left little doubt that intentions based on an enlightened self-seeking must be communicated if they are ever to coalesce into the shared confidence needed for the formation of society. No promises will be made, but there must emerge some common awareness that enlightened self-seeking has become widespread; and the sole means to such awareness is the exchanging of plans through discourse. An enlightened sense of concern for public order will have to be *expressed* by all those who share it and who hope to live by it. In short, Hume's narrative portrayal of the originary convention that has brought about justice will necessarily presuppose a discoursive framework which has enabled human beings to formulate the generalities and the specificities of that founding convention.

But it is precisely such a framework that Hume could not call upon. If language must be in place already when transfamilial ties are founded, then all such ties will never come into being, for they would have to precede themselves. Sophisticated concepts and modes of discourse, such as the ones that are employed in suggestions for reciprocal self-restraint, are hardly built in a day; rather, they stem from a lengthy chain of usages in the past. As Hume himself pointed out, language is "gradually establish'd by human conventions" (*Treatise*, 490). Hume regarded signification as a standard causal activity,[53] which is to say that he perceived meanings in normal signification as the products of manifold past conjunctures between words and signified ideas. A multiplicity of conjunctions will be most patently crucial when the ideas being expressed are highly subtle and involuted, like the concepts that will be needed for laying out a pattern of mutual controls stretching far off into the future. Such concepts may be entirely *thinkable*—because of experiences in family life—before the growth of society, but they could not be *expressed* throughout a transfamilial group (in ways that could constitute a shared understanding), unless the relevant words had been infused with meaning through past usages.

What all this suggests, then, is that the founding of a societal unit can take place only if such a unit has already been founded. It is, after all, *within society* that discoursive usages carry meaning into the words required for the formation of social ties. One may infer this point from Hume's observation that "[w]ere all society and intercourse cut off between man and man, . . . so solitary a being would be . . . incapable of . . . social discourse and conversation" (*Enquiries*, 191). Signifiers come to be vested with their functions inside complexes of discourse and behavior, where the routines of everyday life can provide people with indispensable backgrounds for the elaboration of ideas and the consequent impregnation of words with meaning. A collection of people in which the families war constantly against one another would not give rise to the iterated usages and extensive patterns of intercourse that can foster a shared and stabilized set of meanings. Ergo, stories of a transition from a completely atomized grouping (of familial units) to a society based on some extensive degree of cooperation will have disabled themselves from starting. A shared discoursive structure is vital for the transition, but an atomized grouping will inevitably preclude the growth of such a discoursive network. If there had ever been a primeval state of humanity, then the passage out of it to a new state would have had to postpone itself forever.

In this analysis, we have gone a crucial step further than Hume's own argument that discourse will exhibit a generality of perspective. Hume made an important contribution by realizing that "every particular person's pleasure and interest being different, 'tis impossible men cou'd ever agree in their sentiments and judgments, unless they chose some common point of view, from which they might survey their object, and which might cause it to appear the same to all of them," and that "we every day meet with persons, who are in a different situation from ourselves, and who cou'd never converse with us on any reasonable terms, were we to remain constantly in that situation and point of view, which is peculiar to us" (*Treatise*, 591, 603). Note that, in these last two quotations, society has been posited as the civilizing milieu in which the normalization of discoursive usage proceeds. The growth of a societal unit presupposes a generality of perspective in its inaugural discourses, but a generalized perspective can only have come about *within* a society:

> [W]e every day meet with persons who are in a situation different from us, and who could never converse with us were we to remain constantly in that position and point of view, which is peculiar to ourselves. The intercourse of sentiments, therefore, *in society and conversation*, makes us form some general unalterable standard by which we may approve or disapprove of characters and manners. [*Enquiries*, 229; emphasis added.]

This point had been made just as emphatically in the *Treatise*: "We are quickly oblig'd to forget our own interest in our judgments . . . by reason of the perpetual contradictions, we meet with *in society and conversation*, from persons that are not plac'd in the same situation, and have not the same interest with ourselves."[54] What Hume did not adequately bring out, however, is that the argument comprised in these four quotations will extend with full verve not merely to the level of finished judgments, but also—and more importantly—to every part of the medium of expression with which the judgments are formulated. One cannot know if one's judgments clash with the views of other people unless a common discoursive medium is at hand to enable judgments to be communicated. And such a discoursive framework, as we have seen, will emerge as the product of an extensive and multifaceted commerce in ideas. That is, it will emerge as the product of society. Signifiers become signifiers, *with subtle meanings*, through the regularized employment of them as such; and this regularized use occurs in the webbings of interaction that distinguish society from a feral state of unenlightened self-interest. Such interaction will be the locus not merely of the normalizing of judgments, but also of the birth and development of any complex communication. That the networks of interacting must be founded in turn on complex and large-scale communication is a source of no slight embarrassment for Hume's theory of justice.

B. More Thoughts on the Deferral of Nature

This section will explore two further lacunae in Hume's account of the division between naturalness and social arrangements. Herein also will be set forth a general predicament to which the lacunae might give rise. Our focus now will be less on Hume's description of justice than on his broader theory of morals, though inevitably the former is implicated through the latter. Neither as systematically organized as the first section nor related to it directly, the arguments here propounded are a bridge joining the deconstruction of Hume's legal theory in this Part and the deconstruction of Hume's general theory in the following Part. This section will continue my theme of the deferral of any "natural" presence, but it will not so much build on the approach of the first section as guide us—however strangely and indirectly—toward the approach of the next Part.

1. *The Natural Kingdom*

A. REVERSALS WITHOUT EXPLANATION

In a fine essay published in 1976,[55] James King tries to salvage a place for human nature in the moral philosophy of Hume. King maintains that a sharp reversal took place between the *Treatise* and the second *Enquiry*. In the *Treatise*, Hume had relied on certain postulates about human nature and had professed to draw from them various conclusions and explanations regarding moral practices; in the second *Enquiry* he turned his argumentative scheme around, as King has related: "In the *Enquiry* human nature is no longer the *explanans*—it has become the *explanandum;* moral language indeed is not that about which conclusions are drawn, but the starting point which provides the source and impetus for the explanatory endeavor culminating in conclusions about something else, something non-normative" (PLM, 347). This shift by Hume was a significant breakthrough, in King's opinion, because the argument in the *Treatise* had run aground when it failed to offer any convincing links between its *explanandum* and its *explanans.* King quite persuasively contends that Hume's cleavage between passions (on the one hand) and faculties of imagination and reason (on the other hand) will have left us unable to educe our generalized moral judgments from our innate moral sentiments.

> Hume recognizes that he must explain how the natural sentiments are, as he puts it, *corrected* so as properly to inform a moral judgment—that is, a judgment which is general and capable of entering into a common language establishing norms. . . .
>
> . . . Correction of the sentiments . . . is problematical because there seems to be no element available among the "springs and motives" inventoried in Hume's Science of Man to cause the correction in question. [PLM, 351.]

In King's view, Hume transcended this problem in his later work by realizing that the judgments contained in everyday discourse, rather than abstract "springs and motives," should be the primary data of his philosophizing about morals. Common judgments as expressed in our quotidian language were henceforward to be treated as given, while the abstract principles that had formerly been seen as the *starting* point of any analysis were hereafter to be *derived* from the common judgments. Thus, according to King, Hume finally gave the world a tenably naturalistic account of morals. Connections that had been sadly missing in the *Treatise*'s speculation were clearly present in the more sober analysis that informed the second *Enquiry:*

> Hume began the *Enquiry* . . . by adducing a revamped experimental method which starts from the public, social fact of men sharing a language of morals, and promises to arrive at the general principles of morals; once these are established, Hume can offer broad statements about human nature which occupy in his theory the position of conclusions governed by facts, rather than that of principles determining the causal conditions of morality. [PLM, 354.]

> By reasoning from patterns in our approvals and disapprovals to their principles in pleasure and utility, Hume was able to arrive at well-grounded philosophical conclusions about human nature. [PLM 357.]

Our concern here is not with King's complacent assumption that the language of morals is "readily accessible for examination,"[56] nor with his overstated view of the shift between the *Treatise* and the *Enquiries.* (In regard to the latter view, one might note—*inter alia*—King's cavalier dismissal of the importance of Hume's Appendixes to the *Enquiry concerning the Principles of Morals* [PLM, 355]. Therein, Hume championed a speculative approach quite like the one that King discerns in the *Treatise*.) Our concern, rather, is with a central thread of King's argument: namely, the presumption that Hume could "use the moral order to confirm the attribution of certain properties to human nature" (PLM, 349). King assumes that inferences can be drawn from observations of moral discourse to natural traits of the human species, despite the fact that inferences will not work when made in the opposite direction. Yet he provides no reason to think that a reversed inferential line will enjoy any advantages *vis-à-vis* the old line. When Hume sought to derive the judgments of common discourse from supposedly natural principles, his attempt foundered for want of causal interaction between the principles and the judgments. Exactly the same problem will stymie a reversed flow of reasoning. If there is no causal linkage between the promptings of human nature and the pronouncements of human discourse, then—irrespective of how much the latter may be in evidence—one has no reason to postulate the former. When one uses one's observations of moral judgments to reach certain findings about human nature, one will have had to presuppose a stream of causality. This becomes clear in King's enumeration of alleged facts that are uncovered in the second *Enquiry:*

> The conclusions about human nature which this new method permits are of the highest moment. First, the selfish hypothesis is vanquished, since the view that benevolence is not a natural human characteristic would render simply incomprehensible how men could participate in a system of approving what pleases or benefits others. . . . Third, men must be capable of correcting the momentary appearances of things, not only the easy corrections which relate to visual perception, but particularly the much more demanding corrections which relate to the passions and interests of the individual; were this not the case, there would be no such thing as a common moral language. [PLM, 348.]

It makes no sense to infer natural principles from concrete evaluations unless one can presume soundly that there exist causal ties between them—or, at the very most, it makes no more sense than reasoning in the opposite direction. Until one can introduce a causal relationship between utterances and instincts, one cannot justify a move from the observed utterances to the hypothetical instincts. Yet it was precisely the lack of such a causal relation that impelled us to switch our *explanandum* and *explanans* in the first place. In short, King's view amounts to saying that one can characterize *and* disqualify certain traits as the natural causes of moral judgments. Without any causal ties between traits and judgments, the extolled outcome of the second *Enquiry* will partake of just as much arbitrariness as the disfavored conclusions of the *Treatise*. King has not succeeded in gaining access for Hume's theory to the brute facts of nature.

B. KING'S DEFERRAL OF NATURE

Quite unwittingly, King has thrown intense doubt on Hume's endeavor to ground his moral doctrines in the firm soil of "nature." Suppose, at this stage, one makes the *natural* judgment that further efforts to moor Hume's theory to a "natural" base of assuredness will prove unavailing. Where will that leave his project? Cut off from the alluring solidity of a natural ground, Hume's conception of morals would be thrust squarely into language, which would become the object of his philosophy as well as the medium thereof. As King has suggested, Hume undoubtedly would have had to reorganize his approach to the human psyche, by using as his point of departure the psyche's public manifestations in discourse. Having to shed the baggage of his theory of instincts, Hume would have then become an analyst of the language of morals *par excellence*—as he did, to some extent, in the second of his *Enquiries*. This would, of course, imply an overturning of antecedence: far from serving to individuate the contexts in which specific evaluations are reached appropriately, feelings would now be viewed as by-products of contextualization. Because language can operate as a signifying fabric (and hence be suffused with meaning) only through its employment in particular circumstances and contexts, and because the prelinguistic realities such as instincts have been exposed as powerless (within Hume's philosophy) to determine judgments and usages, Hume's theory must end up privileging circumstances and contexts as the founts of subjective meaning. Despite Hume's contention that the judgments we make on moral issues will hinge ultimately on "some internal sense or feeling" (*Enquiries*, 173), his texts must situate the internal feelings as epiphenomena, for moral sentiments and reactions can never have been experienced as such until contexts of shared usage have defined when and how the sentiments can emerge. Once a Humean can no longer appeal to instincts as the generators of moral meanings, she will have to renounce subjectivism and give full weight to the common structures of discourse. Without the rules that those structures fix for the application and articulation of moral concepts, no sentiment could ever be categorized or experienced as moral; such a categorization would be utterly meaningless. King makes this point in his discussion of the advantages enjoyed by the line of argument that Hume followed in the second *Enquiry*:

> If one asks, "How is it that we know what 'moral' means?"—is it by reference to sentiments or by reference to approvals as given in the moral language?—the epistemic superiority of an approach which presupposes ordinary usage immediately emerges. Clearly, if one starts from the common language of morals, one has at hand the information

> necessary for identifying the "pleasing sentiment of approval" (for one is in a position to know that a judgment is a moral approval independently of knowing what sentiments are concomitant to it): but it is not at all clear, I submit, that one could identify an impression, an instance of sympathy, a sentiment, and so forth, as *moral* independently of participating in the common language of morals. . . . If moral language is not acknowledged as a presupposition—or if we imagine that we can stand outside it and account for its very constitution *ab ovo*—then it is thoroughly problematic by what license we may subsequently introduce the adjective "moral" into our theory at all. [PLM, 356.]

What is so troubling about this standpoint for Humeans is that a prioritizing of contexts will sharply clash with a precondition of moral discourse laid down by Hume. As we have seen in Part One, Hume argued that moral judgments would be impossible had not nature girded us with a precomprehension of such matters. "[H]ad not men a natural sentiment of approbation and blame, it cou'd never be excited by politicians; nor wou'd the words *laudable* and *praise-worthy, blameable* and *odious*, be any more intelligible, than if they were a language perfectly unknown to us" (*Treatise*, 579). Hume would thus seem to have created a hopeless quandary for himself. On the one hand, he affirmed several times that we cannot grasp moral distinctions, even at a crude level, unless nature has "aid[ed] us in this particular" (*Treatise*, 500). On the other hand, he was unable to show how natural instincts could furnish the requisite support. Hume's discourse will have been going round the whirlpool of the structure/event paradox. Hume was justified in thinking that his account of moral experience demanded the postulating of a thoroughly self-reliant subjective core in each person, which would antedate social life as a set of primal impulses; without radically autonomous subjectivities, the structures of moral discourse (which is to say, the structures of moral judgment) could never have arisen, and moral feelings could never have been experienced. Yet in elaborating the qualities and conditions of a naturally self-determining consciousness, Hume could not help cutting it off unbridgeably from that which it was supposed to shape, i.e., the structures of moral discourse. With this irreparable disjunction, Hume's theory has led to a completely uncompromising structuralism that must classify subjectivity as a myth or as a structural offshoot. As we should have expected, Hume's phenomenological focus, privileging subjectivity, is an anti-subjectivist position. And, as Hume cogently observed, that position is completely untenable—even if it is also inescapable.

2. *Unnatural Multiplicity*

Hume himself provided still further grounds for doubting his purported success at making contact with presocial reality. Throughout the *Treatise* and the *Enquiries*, Hume professed to write about instincts that compose human nature. But in some remarkable pages of the second *Enquiry*, he undermined his own tenets. To support his view that justice arises out of utilitarian reflection, he found it necessary to argue that a regime of justice cannot possibly have derived from "a simple original instinct in the human breast, which nature has implanted" (*Enquiries*, 201). If such an instinct had been the originator of justice, then the rules of property would be known to a level of awareness unshaped by any social conventions, and would "not [be] ascertained by any argument or reflection." This, Hume felt, is clearly ridiculous; the institution of property involves far too many variables to make a naturalistic theory convincing: "[T]hough it seems a very simple proposition to say, that nature, by an instinctive sentiment, distinguishes property, yet in reality we shall find, that there are required for that purpose ten thousand different instincts, and these employed about objects of the greatest intricacy and nicest discernment" (*Enquiries*, 201). Attributing our knowledge of property to instinct would take for granted the scarcely credible view that each of us is intimately familiar *ab ovo* with a complex proliferation of legal concepts. Every child born alive would be not only a little liberal or a little conservative, but a lawyer as well. "Can we think that nature, by an original instinct, instructs us in all these methods of acquisition? . . . Does nature, whose instincts in men are all simple, embrace such complicated and artificial objects, and create a rational creature, without trusting anything to the operation of his reason?" (*Enquiries*, 202). As opposed to true instincts, a respect for justice stems from an institution whose specific embodiments diverge strikingly (in matters of detail, though not in their broad outlines): "All birds of the same species in every age and country, build their nests alike: In this we see the force of instinct. Men, in different times and places, frame their houses differently: Here we perceive the influence of reason and custom. A like inference may be drawn from comparing the instinct of generation and the institution of property" (*Enquiries*, 202). Moral codes may likewise exhibit prominent variations, but natural virtues do not gain force exclusively through such codes; natural virtues would inform human behavior irrespective of any codes.

That systems of ownership display uniform general patterns amid the diversity of their details is not at all inconsistent with the diversity. Rather, it simply demonstrates that those systems have all been founded in order to achieve social stability—which requires in turn that "questions of property [be] subordinate to the authority of civil laws, . . . *according to the particular convenience of each community*. . . . Here we must have recourse to statutes, customs, precedents, analogies, and a hundred other circumstances" (*Enquiries*, 196–97; emphasis added). Why, then, would any theorists assume that notions of property are instinctive?

Hume had a ready answer: they mistake the time-honored for the timeless. "The views the most familiar to us are apt, for that very reason, to escape us; and what we have very frequently performed from certain motives, we are apt likewise to continue mechanically, without recalling, on every occasion, the reflections, which first determined us" (*Enquiries*, 203).

At this stage, we should take note of an ambiguity in Hume's argument—a pronounced ambiguity that has not been fully brought out in the quotations above. More than once, Hume stressed the marked dissimilarity of legal regimes, in order to emphasize that we cannot hold up any single package of laws as the unique expression of fancied instincts; this vein of Hume's argument has been highlighted above. Most of the time, however, Hume apparently had in view not the multiplicity *of* legal regimes, but the multiplicity *within* each regime. That is, the reason for his denying the innateness of legal categories was not that systems of law diverge from one another so strikingly (though they may indeed do so), but that each regime of law is so multifarious in itself. Complex ramifications within each system of law, rather than the diversity of the systems, belie the notion that instincts are what cause people to approve of just acts. Fortunately, it will not matter—for present purposes—which of these two constructions of Hume's argument is to be given pride of place; the thesis put forward at the start of my next paragraph will apply in full to either of the two variants.

The main point advanced herein can be stated bluntly: Hume's argument, in either of its two lines of attack, will forcefully rebut his own premise that the natural virtues proceed from natural motives or instincts. Hume had written:

> [T]he first virtuous motive, which bestows a merit on any action, can never be a regard to the virtue of that action, but must be some other *natural* motive or principle. . . . [*Treatise*, 478; emphasis added.]
>
> [T]ho', on some occasions, a person may perform an action merely out of regard to its moral obligation, yet still this supposes in human *nature* some distinct principles, which are capable of producing the action. [*Treatise*, 479; emphasis added.]

Yet Hume's analysis of legal regimes should warn against a hearty endorsement of this appeal to "natural" impulses. Under the first reading of that analysis, which laid stress on the multiplicity *of* regimes, this appeal to nature is highly suspect. Hume never insisted that the overall uniformity of the sets of motives in people would entail that those sets of motives culminate in exactly the same deeds from one person to the next. Though a passage in the *Enquiry concerning Human Understanding* admittedly seems to offer such a contention (*Enquiries*, 83), it is straightaway followed by an important disclaimer:

> We must not, however, expect that this uniformity of human actions should be carried to such a length as that all men, in the same circumstances, will always act precisely in the same manner, without making any allowance for the diversity of characters, prejudices, and opinions. Such a uniformity in every particular, is found in no part of nature. On the contrary, from observing the variety of conduct in different men, we are enabled to form a greater variety of maxims, which still suppose a degree of uniformity and regularity.
>
> Are the manners of men different in different ages and countries? We learn thence the great force of custom and education, which mould the human mind from its infancy and form it into a fixed and established character. [*Enquiries*, 85–86.]

Elsewhere, Hume conceded that natural drives can express themselves in remarkably diverse forms. Fathers in ancient Greece, he observed, might be prompted by their paternal affection to resort to infanticide, if that seemed the only way to rescue their children from a life of poverty; modern sensibilities are quite different.[57] Though Hume felt that natural virtues will be the same *in general* across societies[58]—as will the norms of justice—he accepted that room remains for dramatic variations of detail. Therefore, if one approves of the first construction of Hume's argument about legal knowledge, then moral systems and legal systems will correspond exactly: across societies, institutions of each type will exhibit common fundaments while diverging in their specifics. Hence, an argument opposing the view that instincts underpin legal knowledge will cut as well against the idea that instincts underpin "natural" virtues.

Under the second version of Hume's anti-instinctivism—which laid stress on the multiplicity *within* legal structures—the extended applicability of his critique may be much less evident, for what appears to distinguish natural virtues from artificial virtues like justice is that the latter must always be systemic. That is, particular rules and acts of justice, *qua rules and acts of justice,* will have a claim on our moral favor solely through their location in a scheme that earns our approval as a result of its usefulness (which in turn wins our approval naturally). As Hume freely avowed, just actions may frequently collide with one's moral sense when considered in themselves (*Enquiries*, 304–306), and rules of justice (such as minutiae of contract law) may in themselves be of no moral significance; but when they are seen as parts of a mechanism that ensures general peace, they win our active approval. All of this is decidedly in contrast to the unmediated attention that we bestow on circumstances involving the natural virtues. Such circumstances are evaluated entirely on their own merits, without any need for recourse to a broader framework of acts and judgments. When one opts in these circumstances for a particular course of action, one does not take into account the broader frameworks, because one is here dealing with facts that tug on one's innate principles immediately. There is no question of insignificant details that secure a place in our feelings and our judgment exclusively through our need to uphold a system.

For reasons that can be drawn *in toto* from Hume's work, the naturalistic theory of morals will not escape as readily as my last paragraph has implied. Judgments founded on natural virtues are not sharply distinct from judgments founded on artificial virtues; indeed, for our present line of analysis, these two sorts of judgments have exactly the same form. Hume was able to separate the two types only by disregarding his empiricist predilection for particulars. He had to overlook the particularity of each judgment that would proceed from one or more of the abstract motives which he had postulated. It is one thing to argue for the existence of primal urges, but it is quite another thing to decide or predict how someone's urges will manifest themselves in specific settings. Particular judgments will be made in light of their roles in an overarching "system" of such judgments, impelled by a given urge. Hume himself had drawn due attention to this point earlier, when he wrote about the need to correct moral evaluations in the interest of maximizing public utility (which thus amounts to a goal that serves as the fundamental dynamic in a "system" of moral judgments). He submitted four highly relevant examples, of which only the first is quoted here: "Giving alms to common beggars is naturally praised; because it seems to carry relief to the distressed and indigent: but when we observe the encouragement thence arising to idleness and debauchery, we regard that species of charity rather as a weakness than a virtue" (*Enquiries*, 180). Hume's other examples touched on the waste of public money by dynasts whose generous spirit leads them to confer bounty on parasitic courtiers, the tendency of untrammeled opulence to promote civilized life, and the fact that tyrannicide can increase the jealousy and cruelty of princes (*Enquiries*, 180–81). Though Hume considered these revealing examples from the perspective of an outside evaluator, his general point can be carried into our present discussion, which concentrates on the actual performance of the deeds that have been evaluated. All four examples demonstrate, at a crude level, what occurs in a much more nuanced fashion in other settings: the adjustment of particular actions and particular choices to make them fit correctly into a broader sweep of decisions.

Let us consider one of the primal instincts which Hume referred to, that of parental love. Parents may be happy to know that the affection and tenderness they shower upon their offspring are based on natural impulses, but they will not have been freed thereby from the often harrowing process of making judgments in pursuit of their children's welfare. Each decision will have to be adapted to this principal aim (i.e., the furtherance of the children's well-being), and therefore some decisions—especially those regarding discipline—will, *when examined in them-*

selves, seem grossly at variance with a putative instinct for affection. (I am not suggesting, of course, that every punitive measure will appear unwarranted on its own, but some such measures *will* appear this way even though they are not reproachful from a systemic point of view. One example would be the punishment of a young child who cannot fully distinguish right from wrong; the punishment is imposed in order that he or she will begin to grow acquainted with moral differences. Unless one properly keeps in mind the long-term objective of implanting good moral judgment into the child, one will condemn the discipline as draconian or bizarre, and will refuse to engage in it oneself.) Aside from the fact that many parents will sometimes have to express their love through actions that in themselves are quite harsh, they also may think it prudent to insist on certain minutiae of behavior (e.g., salutational gestures) which are trifling in themselves but which play an important role in a wider framework of discipline. Just as legal decisions may be individually irksome or may pertain to requirements that are of negligible importance when considered alone, so also may parental decisions. With each type of decision, one has to take a systemic view of individual judgments if one is ever to understand how they can further a goal from which they seem to depart. In principle, a parent's decisions can involve as many complexities, countervailing considerations, and systemically oriented adjustments as can any legal decision. What Hume overlooked, despite his general philosophy, is that each natural judgment is a particular. As a particular, each judgment will both stand on its own *and* involve a weighing of factors that will adjust its particularity to the needs of a framework of decisions. For natural judgments, quite as much as for legal judgments, there perforce exists the potential for a discontinuity between the most laudable decision viewed on its own and the most laudable decision against a background of many other decisions. Natural feelings do not eliminate this potential rift—or the consequent adaptation and sacrifice of short-term objectives for the sake of long-term objectives—any more than conventions do.

Hume's talk of "simple original instinct[s] in the human breast" led him at times to overlook the particularity of each judgment arising from those putative instincts (*Enquiries,* 201). Each judgment may involve the consideration of sundry factors, as Hume had earlier noted with regard to moral assessments: "[I]n order to pave the way for . . . a [moral] sentiment, and give a proper discernment of its object, it is often necessary, we find, that much reasoning should precede, that nice distinctions be made, just conclusions drawn, distant comparisons formed, complicated relations examined, and general facts fixed and ascertained" (*Enquiries,* 173). Crucial to our present discussion is a factor implicit in this remark by Hume: i.e., the need for conforming each decision to the objectives immanent in a general flow of related judgments. Like conventions, instincts cannot preclude the possibility of realizing themselves in ways that do not manage to harmonize the general and the particular. Precisely because our natural decisions are as much particulars as legal decisions, there is as much potential in the former as in the latter for a conflict between the general impulse behind a judgment (such as parental love) and the specific outcome considered alone. Humean instincts may be simple, original, and undivided, but the decisions to which they lead are frequently snarled and compromised. Perhaps it was a dim realization of this point which led Hume into his otherwise baffling insistence that moral judgments relate only to the principles that inspire given acts:

> If any *action* be either virtuous or vicious, 'tis only as a sign of some quality or character. It must depend upon durable principles of the mind, which extend over the whole conduct, and enter into the personal character. Actions themselves, not proceeding from any constant principle, have no influence on love or hatred, pride or humility; and consequently are never consider'd in morality.[59]

In all relevant respects, then, natural decisions will resemble law-based decisions, and Hume's sardonic rejection of the naturalness of the latter will apply equally to the former. Natural decisions can embrace as many complexities as legal decisions, and they can be as systemic in their orientation. The homology between these types of decisions will extend the scope of the argument (by Hume) that was outlined at the beginning of this subsection. We should thus amend the verdict to which the subsection on King led us: not only do moral instincts have no way whatsoever of forming causal ties with specific moral evaluations, but the instincts themselves have now apparently dissipated. Because of the very intricateness and systematized character of the judgments that are part of good deeds, we must view the underlying instincts as spurious—or, at best, as empty non-explanations like the "dormitive faculty" of opium or the "phlogiston" that impels combustion. Neither moral evaluations nor the objects of those evaluations (i.e., the motives that inspire virtuous acts) can ever take root in "nature."

Part Three. Nothing in Particular

> The scepticism of Hume . . . should be clearly marked off from Greek scepticism. Hume assumes the truth of the empirical element, feeling and sensation, and proceeds to challenge universal principles and laws, because they have no warranty from sense-perception.
>
> —G. W. F. Hegel[60]

> From Parmenides to Husserl, the privilege of the present has never been put into question. It could not have been. It is what is self-evident itself, and no thought seems possible outside its element.
>
> —J. Derrida[61]

In this third Part, we look once more at Hume's efforts to commend particularized data as reality's unique mode of present-ation. Perhaps Hume differed from many of the ancient Greek skeptics in his reliance on sensation and feeling, but in his hankering for presence he was at one with a tradition that stretches back beyond Plato. Hume in no way forbore seizing on a foundation for his philosophy; doing battle with the absurd theological abstractions that had enthralled so many of the thinkers who came before him, he cherished the particulars of sensation and feeling as a substitute ground of certainty. Anchored in the secure flow of experience, his project could do away with "[p]rinciples taken upon trust [and] consequences lamely deduced from them." Like other valid forms of inquiry, a so-called science of human nature must not "go beyond experience, or establish any principles which are not founded on that authority" (*Treatise*, xiii, xviii). Experience can enjoy its authoritative standing because particulars that compose it are thoroughly and uniquely *present* (to the observer's mind). Hume's references to experiential data as fully and intrinsically present units are abundant indeed, though only a few examples can be adduced here. (A few more examples will be adduced later.) One of Hume's most frequent refrains was the assertion that "nothing is ever really *present* with the mind but its perceptions or impressions and ideas."[62] This article of faith, which united empiricism and Cartesianism, was stated with equal bluntness in a positive form: "The only existences, of which we are certain, are perceptions, which being *immediately present* to us by consciousness, command our strongest assent, and are the first foundation of all our conclusions" (*Treatise*, 212). Hume reformulated this point, and hence made clear that for his idealism there ultimately is no disjuncture—no disjuncture that makes a difference—between objects and percepts, when he announced that things with spatial dimensions are "capable of being . . . *present* to the sight or feeling" (*Treatise*, 429; emphasis added). This confirmed what he had already maintained when he described sensory perception as "a mere passive admission of . . . impressions . . . when . . . objects are *present* to the senses" (*Treatise*, 73; emphasis added).

Making up the rest of this chapter is a critique of Hume's appeal to particularities as the grounding presences of his thought. In effect, his moral theory (and thus, by indirections, his legal theory) will be hurled into doubt through a critique of his metaphysics. As has already been discussed in this chapter, Hume's metaphysical positions do not lead automatically to his somewhat complacent politics; but the critiques set forth in this Part do not make bold to revise or censure his political leanings in the process of challenging his metaphysics. Rather, this Part will focus on certain themes in his metaphysical work that also structure his moral theory (and legal theory). Albeit those themes can never finally settle his views on politics and society, they nevertheless play an indispensable part in shaping the general philosophical system that has informed those views. That is, although Hume could have been much further to the left (politically) than he was—and, in this sense, his political hue did not flow perforce from his epistemological theses—he would in any event have clung to the basic doctrines of his empiricism, just as the left Hegelians and the right Hegelians alike set store by the dialectical method.

Even the most cursory examination of Hume's moral philosophizing will disclose structural affinities with his general outlook. Specifically, Hume had to rely on notions of self-presence, wherein consciousness is immediately aware of its own sentiments and sensations. Each person must always be in the most intimate contact with any feelings (of approval or disapproval) that she may have as a result of beholding certain actions: "[T]he distinguishing impressions, by which moral good or evil is known are nothing but *particular* pains or pleasures. . . . [I]n our judgments concerning all kinds of beauty, and tastes, and sensations . . . [our] approbation is imply'd in the *immediate* pleasure they convey to us" (*Treatise*, 471; second emphasis added). Apart from feelings of approbation and disapproval, the sense data that elicit those feelings will be grasped in their immediate fullness by the mind: "[A] complication of circumstances, . . . being *presented* to the spectator, excites the *sentiment* of blame [or approval]. . . . [I]n moral deliberations we must be acquainted beforehand with all the objects, and all their relations to each other. . . . All the circumstances of the case are supposed to be laid before us" (*Enquiries*, 287–88, 290; first emphasis added). Particular facts, and the "complications of circumstances" that they make up, will come to be known and classified by having left themselves open to the unmediated gaze of the moral spectator.

Given the prominence of empiricist attitudes—concerning the presence of particularized data—within Hume's ethical thought, critiques of his empiricism will also serve to interrogate his account of morals; as has been mentioned, it is just such critiques that will be undertaken throughout the rest of this Part. Along the way, we shall give special notice to the Humean account of present-ation, which may turn out to provide leverage for deconstructing its fundaments. Section A of this Part will emphasize the discord between Hume's zealous nominalism and his proclivity for invoking abstractions to explain the presumed flow of our experience. Section B moves from discord to paradoxes, as Hume's empiricist arguments undo their own theses. As we shall find, the arch-empiricist Hume could not help putting observed particulars unrelentingly into question. *Malgré lui*, Hume was very much aware of the problems that can be exploited to shake his thought to its roots. To the potential for exploitation of his work he of course had to remain blind—even if the process of exploitation may have always already come about.

A. Nominalism Forsaken

Hume's most devastating maneuver in his assault on moral rationalism lay in his appeal for a careful study of all data with regard to which moral judgments are made. When we consider all the relevant facts, he claimed, we shall be forced to posit an inside/outside distinction: morality is a matter of inward sentiments evoked by external facts, and the facts do not themselves contain vice or virtue.

> Take any action allow'd to be vicious: Wilful murder, for instance. Examine it in all lights, and see if you can find that matter of fact, or real existence, which you call *vice*. In which-ever way you take it, you find only certain passions, motives, volitions and thoughts. There is no other matter of fact in the case. The vice entirely escapes you, as long as you consider the object. You never can find it, till you turn your reflexion into your own breast, and find a sentiment of disapprobation, which arises in you, towards this action. [*Treatise*, 468–69.]

If we temporarily grant the soundness of Hume's approach, we can read some of his own theorizing with a healthy degree of skepticism.

1. *General Rules*

If one supposes Hume's nominalism to be sound, one will be hard put to endorse the exposition of "general rules" that receives a prominent place in both the second *Enquiry* and the *Treatise*. With a deceptively bland rubric, Hume was referring to an important tendency of the mind to apply principles beyond the specific cases in which they have thitherto been employed. As Thomas Hearn has maintained, a Humean general rule stems from "a propensity of the imagination to generalize."[63] Let us look at one of Hume's many statements of this phenomenon: "*General rules* are often extended beyond the principle whence they first arise; and this in all matters of taste and sentiment. . . . The imagination is influenced by associations of ideas; which, though they arise at first from the judgment, are not easily altered by every particular exception that occurs to us" (*Enquiries*, 207; emphasis in original). By what right can Hume discover these leanings of the imagination and classify them as "rules"? If one examines the particular groups of facts that together constitute all the workings of the imagination, one can see nothing (from a Humean point of view) except "passions, motives, volitions, and thoughts" and the connections among them. Heeding Hume's desire to probe the assembled facts "in all lights," one can unearth only specific judgments (on moral issues or factual issues) that are presumed to be parallel in whatever respects have been deemed pertinent. (For now, we may presuppose—as did Hume—that the category of "pertinence" can be applied without endless paradoxes. This presupposition is by no means beyond serious challenge.[64]) No matter how closely one has studied the discrete choices that one perceives as relevant, one will not be able to find in them any rules that are separate from the choices themselves and the relations among those choices. By reifying such rules, Hume would appear as guilty of aiming to bestow life on abstract phrases as were any of the ethical rationalists. (Here the term "reifying" is employed in a way that will be frowned on in Chapter 5; but the present usage derives from our temporary acceptance of Hume's nominalism, which hereafter will be shown to undo itself.)

Supporters of Hume could parry in at least two ways. First, they might respond that Humean "general rules" consist merely in structured similarities that can be revealed with hindsight, either by outside analysts or by those who have made the judgments that are being perused. Alternatively, they might declare that a "general rule" is simply a state of mind that accompanies every judgment concerning some or another issue. This state of mind can amount to either an expectation that future choices will be made to accord with a present choice, or a feeling that a current choice should be made to square with past choices. Either one of these attitudes could form part of the ensemble of "passions, motives, volitions, and thoughts" that any Humean would acknowledge when looking over a judgment "in all lights."

Unfortunately, neither of these responses will harmonize with what Hume wrote about general rules. He did not deem such rules to be nothing more than patterns that can be retrospectively known; rather, he saw them as fulfilling an active part in the formation of judgments. Nor did he regard general rules as the states of consciousness that attach to some or all judgments. Instead, he pictured them as deep forces of human thought which are not simply *identical* with states of awareness in the psyche but are *causative* of them. The following quotation, which summarizes Hume's theory of general rules, makes clear the shortcomings of the two suggested responses:

> Shou'd it be demanded why men form general rules, and allow them to influence their judgment, even contrary to present observation and experience, I shou'd reply, that in my opinion it proceeds from those very principles, on which all judgments concerning causes and effects depend. Our judgments concerning cause and effect are deriv'd from

> habit and experience; and when we have been accustom'd to see one object united to another, our imagination passes from the first to the second, by a natural transition, *which precedes reflection, and which cannot be prevented by it.* [*Treatise*, 147; emphasis added.]

General rules, which spring from proclivities to establish such rules, are themselves proclivities that determine consciousness: "*General rules* create a species of probability, which sometimes influences the judgment, and always the imagination" (*Treatise*, 585). Yet, as has here been argued, it is precisely this character of the Humean general rules—their status as glibly reified tendencies—that puts them so sharply into conflict with Hume's privileging of particulars.

A modern empiricist might endeavor to intercede on behalf of Hume by suggesting that we should classify general rules as predictive instruments. That is, we might be able to predict judgments accurately if we assume that general guides will have channeled judgments into specific paths. We should postulate that the mind acts *as if* it were driven by some general rules, even if we cannot account for such rules.[65] Such an intercession would prove too much, however, for it would give free rein to the moral rationalists; why should rationalists not strive for good predictions of moral judgments by postulating objective moral facts, even if they can never single out such facts among the particularities of experience? Perhaps some theorists would blithely sanction the conjectures of Hume's most unremitting opponents, but a strong sentiment of disapproval would surely have arisen in Hume's breast.

2. *Custom*

In Hume's texts, the word "custom" appears even more often than the phrase "general rules" as a device for capturing the inertia of human minds. Like the phrase, the word has an unsettling tendency to perform as an active subject within Hume's prose. If we explore judgments "in all lights," we shall find no "custom" that overarches the concrete facts—the "passions, motives, volitions, and thoughts"—of the specific judgments involved (along with any relations among them); nonetheless, Hume often portrayed "custom" as a vital force that somehow exceeds its consequences. Neither conscious reflection nor mere patterns, custom emerges in Hume's texts as a structuring principle of the mind. Consider, as an example, his description of causal inferences: "[C]ustom . . . determines the imagination to make a transition from the idea of one object to that of its usual attendant. . . . [U]pon the appearance of one of the objects, the mind is *determin'd* by custom to consider its usual attendant" (*Treatise*, 170, 156; emphasis in original). For a more sweeping statement of the vast power of custom, we may consult the *Enquiry concerning Human Understanding*:

> [W]herever the repetition of any particular act or operation produces a propensity to renew the same act or operation, without being impelled by any reasoning or process of the understanding, we always say, that this propensity is the effect of *Custom*. By employing that word, we pretend not to have given the ultimate reason of such a propensity. We only point out a principle of human nature, which is universally acknowledged, and which is well known by its effects. Perhaps we can push our enquiries no farther, or pretend to give the cause of this cause; but must rest contented with it as the ultimate principle, which we can assign, of all our conclusions from experience. . . . [A]fter the constant conjunction of two objects—heat and flame, for instance, weight and solidity—we are determined by custom alone to expect the one from the appearance of the other. . . .
>
> Custom, then, is the great guide of human life. It is that principle alone which renders our experience useful to us, and makes us expect, for the future, a similar train of events with those which have appeared in the past. [*Enquiries*, 43–44.]

Once more, then, it appears that Hume could not furnish a convincing narrative of the dogged activity of judgment except by peopling it with ghostlike abstractions that supposedly animate the mind. Going against his nominalism, Hume succeeded only in shifting unobservable constructs from the affairs that have been perceived to the general flow of perceiving them.

3. *Sympathy and Benevolence*

Two more of Hume's reified abstractions deserve brief comment. First, the mechanism of sympathy, to which the *Treatise* so frequently adverts, is as much an empty abstraction (for a thoroughgoing empiricist) as are custom and general rules. If one accepts Hume's nominalism, one will see only individual instances of the transfer or communication of feelings from one person to another (which Hume described quite brilliantly). One might even conjoin those like events under an abstract word such as "sympathy"; that would be allowable under Humean standards. But what one should never do is to populate one's account of those instances with a gross hypostatization of the abstract term. If one wants to be a faithful Humean, one ought to eschew pointing to mysterious agencies that bring about circumstances with which *ipso facto* they are not simply identical. One therefore ought to be puzzled by the master's pronouncements in regard to "sympathy."

> Thus it appears, *that* sympathy is a very powerful principle in human nature, *that* it has a great influence on our taste of beauty, and *that* it produces our sentiment of morals in all the artificial virtues. From thence we may presume, that it also gives rise to many of the other virtues. . . . [*Treatise*, 577–78.]

> We are certain, that sympathy is a very powerful principle in human nature. We are also certain, that it has a great influence on our sense of beauty, when we regard external objects, as well as when we judge of morals. We find, that it has force sufficient to give us the strongest sentiments of approbation. [*Treatise*, 618.]

Hume adopted nearly the same conclusions when he was treating of benevolence, which performed functions in the second *Enquiry* that resembled some of the functions that had belonged to sympathy in the *Treatise:*

> [I]n whatever light we take this subject, the merit, ascribed to the social virtues, appears still uniform, and arises chiefly from that regard, which the natural sentiment of benevolence engages us to pay to the interests of mankind and society. . . . [*Enquiries*, 230.]

> [T]hese principles of humanity and sympathy enter so deeply into all our sentiments, and have so powerful an influence, as may enable them to excite the strongest censure and applause. [*Enquiries*, 231.]

For someone attempting to remain loyal to Hume's nominalism, these remarks on sympathy and benevolence must give cause for dismay. Hume's work abounds with indiscernible forces, of exactly the type that it condemns. Believing that transparticular abstractions are the causes of particular judgments is as much at odds with Hume's staunch empiricism as is proclaiming objective moral facts to be the determinants of our inner feelings; each of these inferences would require that one transcend the perceivable specificities that Hume had wanted to privilege. Nor could Hume have salvaged his words-made-flesh by resorting to the claim that our moral judgments proceed *as if* they were driven by abstract principles. As has been noted, such a claim would rescue the moral rationalists as well.

What, then, should one conclude about these apparent inconsistencies in Hume's texts? First, there may be a deeper contradiction between Hume as epistemologist and Hume as psychologist than has generally been perceived. The exigencies of writing his mini-narratives—narratives based either on introspection or on a keen perusal of outward life in society—appear to have forced Hume to relinquish some of his philosophical starting points. In Robert Paul Wolff's terms, we may tentatively infer that Hume's adoption of a "theory of mental activity" in his major writings must carry into limbo some key critical thrusts which stemmed from the content-based explanation of human thought that was advanced in those writings simultaneously.[66]

A second conclusion that one should draw is more straightforward and more germane for what follows. If fairly obvious conflicts jar some important strands of Hume's theory, one should start to question the soundness of each strand. That is, the conflicts have very likely been symptomatic of a much more profound disruption that constitutes and disables each of the strands. It is high time that Hume's privileging of particularities received careful and suspicious attention.

B. Presence Differentiated (from Itself)

Throughout the last section, we took an indulgent view of Hume's empiricist dogmas; such a view was indeed essential for underlining the discord between some crucial parts of his texts. To be sure, the emphasizing of conflicts has itself tended to raise some queries concerning Hume's ability to uphold a stalwart empiricism, but it has also implied that his philosophy will by and large prove coherent (though admittedly not incontrovertible or univocal). The last section, in other words, has perhaps left one to think that a thoroughly empiricist doctrine (which escapes the antinomies of discoursive movement) is at least possible. This section, by contrast, will overturn the whole empiricist project in a forceful interrogation. In spite of its narrow base of leverage, my critique will turn empiricism against itself by showing the disarticulation of the undoubted backbone of Hume's philosophy: particularized experience. *Somme toute,* this section's argument will closely resemble the first chapter's account of paradoxes of differentiation, but now the points of departure will be supplied by a careful study of Hume's texts.

As has already been observed, Hume's empiricism has relied through and through on his appeals to the *presence* of particular feelings and sense data. One could verify this claim of dependence in almost any part of Hume's work, but—to keep this study manageable—we shall look at merely a few of his remarks, on causation. Causal beliefs are central to our existence, wrote Hume, because without them no one could "be assured of anything beyond what was immediately present to his memory and senses" (*Enquiries,* 42). This does not mean, of course, that immediately present data have here been stripped of their fundamental importance. On the contrary, such data are a *sine qua non* of any well-founded causal inferences: "[T]hough our conclusions from experience carry us beyond our memory and senses, . . . yet some fact must always be *present* to the senses or memory, from which we may first proceed in drawing these conclusions." Without solidly present data, causal inferences would be nothing but castles in the air: "[I]f we proceed not upon some fact, *present* to the memory or senses, our reasonings would be merely hypothetical; and however the particular links might be connected with each other, the whole chain of inferences would have nothing to support it" (*Enquiries,* 45, 46; emphasis added). Presence creates a stable and reassuring foundation for the anticipatory move from one object to another: "When we infer the existence of an object from that of others, some object must always be present either to the memory or senses, in order to be the foundation of our reasoning" (*Treatise*, 97). Sound causal beliefs, stemming from a constant conjunction between particular things, will have to take root in presence:

> [F]rom the constant conjunction the objects acquire an union in the imagination. When the impression of one becomes present to us, we immediately form an idea of its usual attendant; and consequently we may establish this as one part of the definition of an opinion or belief, that 'tis *an idea related to or associated with a present impression*. . . . [*Treatise*, 93; emphasis in original.]

> [T]hat object, which is present to my senses, . . . is to be consider'd as the true and real cause of the idea, and of the belief which attends it. [*Treatise*, 102.]

Hume's thirst for presence, as the above passages may bear out, was not merely an incidental factor in his philosophizing. But no matter how fiercely Hume might have endeavored to slake that thirst, he could not help bringing forth thereby an utterly intractable problem, which we may call the problem of individuation. Grounding one's thought in the perceived presence of individual mental units will come to nothing unless one can individuate those units. Not only will the simple impressions each have to be marked off from other simple impressions, but each complex impression will likewise have to be capable of being duly distinguished or set apart from other impressions. Presences have to be *defined*, in that verb's strictest etymological sense; they have to be given borders that will establish each unit's mode of present existence by disjoining it from all other units. If perceptions cannot be individuated, if no borders can be discerned to mark off one presence from another, there will be no present data or perceptions at all. One will be left with an undifferentiated night in which all cows are black.

Hume could not escape recognizing the need for the individuation of perceptual contents. Indeed, as will now be stressed, the problem of individuation occupied center stage in his theorizing. His basic tack was to argue or presuppose that the elements of thought must be *separable* from one another. "[T]here are not any two impressions which are perfectly inseparable" (*Treatise*, 10). This way of proceeding flowed quite naturally from his insight that presence will have always required borders: "[N]o object can appear to the senses; or in other words, . . . no impression can become present to the mind, without being determin'd in its degrees both of quantity and quality. . . . [T]here must be something, which terminates the idea of every finite quantity" (*Treatise*, 19, 44). Borders must entail severability, and so Hume often observed that present thoughts can always be separated from one another. Let us again look at his account of causation. While criticizing the maxim that everything must have had some cause, Hume expressly invoked the sunderability of causes and their results:

> [A]s all distinct ideas are separable from each other, and as the ideas of cause and effect are evidently distinct, 'twill be easy for us to conceive any object to be non-existent this moment, and existent the next, without conjoining to it the distinct idea of a cause or productive principle. The separation, therefore, of the idea of a cause from that of a beginning of existence, is plainly possible for the imagination; and consequently the actual separation of these objects is so far possible, that it implies no contradiction nor absurdity; and is therefore incapable of being refuted by any reasoning from mere ideas; without which 'tis impossible to demonstrate the necessity of a cause. [*Treatise*, 79, 80.]

His approach to specific causal linkages took essentially the same route, as he tirelessly underscored our ability to uncouple a given cause and a given outcome:

> There is no object, which implies the existence of any other if we consider these objects in themselves, and never look beyond the ideas which we form of them. Such an inference wou'd amount to knowledge, and wou'd imply the absolute contradiction and impossibility of conceiving any thing different. But as all distinct ideas are separable, 'tis evident there can be no impossibility of that kind. When we pass from a present impression to the idea of any object, we might possibly have separated the idea from the impression, and have substituted any other idea in its room. [*Treatise*, 86–87.]

These quotations from Hume's critique of causality are still more significant than they might first seem. For one thing, they begin to make clear how much his empiricism had to rely on taking separability for granted. Once the separability of data is not viewed as a given that can be unproblematically presupposed—in an argument that needs to *establish* separability—Hume's account of causation will have become notoriously circular.[67] Hume reviled his opponents for having begged the question (*Treatise*, 80–82), but, like King David responding to Nathan's parable, he did not take notice of his own culpability. Besides this first point (about presupposed conclusions), the quoted passages also raise a more straightforward point about Hume's dependence on the sunderability of the mind's data. His associationist theory would make no sense if perceptions could not be individuated, for there would not be any units among which principles of association (such as causality) could prevail. Modes of association are, intrinsically, modes of separateness.

Perhaps, however, the most significant aspect of the quotations above is their aligning of separateness with distinctness; it is because ideas are distinct from one another that they can be at least vaguely separated.

This equating of distinctness and separation becomes still more revealing when we consider a passage from the account of causal sequences in Hume's first *Enquiry:* "The mind can never possibly find the effect in the supposed cause, by the most accurate scrutiny and examination. For the effect is totally different from the cause, and consequently can never be discovered in it. Motion in the second Billiard-ball is a quite distinct event from motion in the first" (*Enquiries,* 29). Here one comes upon an alignment of distinctness and difference, which should prod one to ask whether it is indeed *difference* that we have all along been referring to in this section. This suspicion can easily be confirmed if we attend carefully to Hume's repeated pronouncements that separateness entails difference and that difference entails separateness.

> In order to know [whether] any objects, which are join'd in impression, be separable in idea, we need only consider, if they be different from each other; in which case, 'tis plain they may be conceiv'd apart. Every thing, that is different, is distinguishable; and every thing, that is distinguishable, may be separated. . . . If on the contrary they be not different, they are not distinguishable; and if they be not distinguishable, they cannot be separated. [*Treatise,* 36.]

This passage sets forth a biconditional relationship of equivalence between separation and differentiation, which had been announced even more directly in an earlier passage:

> We have observ'd, that whatever objects are different are distinguishable, and that whatever objects are distinguishable are separable by the thought and imagination. And we may here add, that the propositions are equally true in the *inverse,* and that whatever objects are separable are also distinguishable, and that whatever objects are distinguishable are also different. For how is it possible we can separate what is not distinguishable, or distinguish what is not different? [*Treatise,* 18; see also *id.* at 10, 40.]

Difference, then, has turned up as the leading actor in Hume's texts. Problems of individuation are problems of differentiation. Because separability has emerged as the criterion by which presences can be individuated, and because separability has been equated with difference, we may now see that difference acts as an underpinning of Hume's philosophy. At first, any such view may strike the reader as baffling, since Hume appeared to contemn difference near the end of the *Treatise*'s recountal of the relationships among thoughts. He sneered that he construed difference "rather as a negation of relation, than as any thing real or positive" (*Treatise,* 15). But, as has been pointed out, it is precisely by negating pure unity that difference clears the indispensable gaps within which the relations (including the relation of identity) can take hold. (Even pure unity will have to *differ* from its negation—and thus be *impure*.) Without difference, in other words, there would be no particularities, perceptions, presences, or associations. Little wonder is it, therefore, that Hume was inclined to highlight difference—denominated as such—in central parts of his theory. While oppugning the notion of a continuous self, for instance, he proclaimed that each mind is "nothing but a bundle or collection of *different* perceptions," and he insisted that "the true idea of the human mind, is to consider it as a system of *different* perceptions or *different* existences, which are link'd together by the relation of cause and effect" (*Treatise*, 252, 261; emphasis added). Here Hume realized that difference, far from working as any *simple* negation of the mind's coupling principles, is equally that on which the principles rest.

In other passages, Hume's need to rely on difference became even more marked. Early in both the *Treatise* and the first of the two *Enquiries*, Hume recognized that difference is what makes possible not only particularity in general (if one will allow this oxymoron), but also particularity in particular (if one will allow this pleonasm). Difference, in other words, is not only what enables particulars to come forth as presences, but also what makes them into presences with specific qualities.

> I believe it will readily be allow'd, that the several distinct ideas of colours, which enter by the eyes, or those of sounds, which are convey'd by the hearing, are really different from each other, tho' at the same time resembling. Now if this be true of different colours, it must be no less so of the different shades of the same colour, that each of them produces a distinct idea, independent of the rest. For if this shou'd be deny'd, 'tis possible, by the continual gradation of shades, to run a colour insensibly into what is most remote from it; and if you will not allow any of the means to be different, you cannot without absurdity deny the extremes to be the same.[68]

Without differences among simple perceptions, everything would perforce be everything else, and therefore nothing could possibly be anything. Until definition enters the world, there *is* no world.

Having tied the present particularity and substantive content of perceptions to the shaping power of difference—in moves and gestures that could not simply have been eschewed—Hume's work has thrown us into a paradox of differentiation. Each perception must depend wholly on differences for the general fact of its (particular) presentation, and each must likewise depend on differences for the qualities that characterize it as a *specific* unit. If there were no differences, there would be no borders and thus no particularity. Difference must always operate as more than a secondary or derivative factor in Hume's system, because it has to serve as the very structuring principle that allows everything comprised in his system to *be* something. As Hume well saw, he had to devise a way to individuate presences if they were to be at all presentable. Yet he could achieve this only by putting the individuated units alarmingly into doubt. Hume's insight into the structuring role of difference will bear in full upon *every* datum (whether a given datum be a simple impression or a complex impression), and will hence have characterized each datum as a sheer product of contrasts. A perceptual unit can emerge exclusively and precisely insofar as it differs from other units; but since this will always have to be true of *every* unit, Hume's system cannot ever begin. That is, each unit will have proved to be the conjunction of its differences from each of the other units, and thus no unit can serve as a grounding point of reference from which all the other units can demarcate themselves. Any move toward grounding will be endlessly shuffled from one unit to another, as each unit relies for its own presence on the presence of other units (from which it is differentiated), which in turn depend for their presence on the presence of *that* unit or on the presence of other units, and so forth. Since *every* datum becomes caught up in this movement, there is no stopping point or keystone; whenever units seek to attain presence, it has always already fled. The condition for the emergence of present data is their inability to arise. Furthermore, without any baseline units, differences can never exist at all nor arise at all—because no present units can be in place to differ even slightly from one another. Accordingly, this will mean that no present units can exist or arise, since they could do so only by way of differences among them (which would confer the identities of the units). Hume's system demands what it must render impossible. One will have to pendulate hopelessly between viewing every unit as a completely self-defined presence and viewing every unit as a mere junction of differences from what is not it. Each of these radically opposed positions will have to tear itself from itself by having always had to confirm the other.

Suppose that consciousness is made up of two units or groups of units, *X* and *Y*. Now, *X* is wholly determined by its difference from *Y*, and *Y* in turn amounts to a trace of *X* (i.e., to a product of its difference from *X*). Thus, the endowment of each with form and substance must presuppose that the content of the other has been established. But if this is true of both units (or both groups of units), then their respective identities cannot become stable or coherent. Only if one of them could serve as a baseline would the other become fixed. However, since all perceptions are differentially constituted, none can act as a baseline—and we therefore shall attain no quietus to the unthinkable oscillation between *X* and *Y*. Differences (and thus presences) need bench marks in order to establish themselves, but nothing can serve here as a bench mark; every toehold will have always already crumbled. Precisely because *everything* remains undetermined (in relationships of complete mutual dependency), we are not dealing with simultaneous equations that can be jointly solved. Such equations provide at least a few data that can be parlayed into suitable answers, but we here do not have such starting points.

In short, Hume's thoroughgoing empiricism has placed very much in doubt the whole empiricist project. Individuation (or definition) is absolutely essential for the advent and presentation of presences, but it is also relentlessly incapacitating, since it creates presences through differences and thereby subverts presences before they can be established (because nothing can operate as a bench mark that would allow presences to become established). Moreover, because no presences can emerge, no differences can emerge, either. Perhaps Hume had gained an inkling of the most uncanny effects of difference when he sought to disparage difference as neither "real [n]or positive." At any rate, he was soon forced repeatedly to rely on difference in order to construct his theory of presences. But when difference has been unleashed—as it always already has—its paradoxical workings will not subside. Let us end with a felicitous passage from Derrida's critique of Claude Lévi-Strauss:

> If totalization no longer has any meaning, it is not because the infiniteness of a field cannot be covered by a finite glance or a finite discourse, but because the nature of the field . . . excludes totalization. This field is in effect that of *play*, that is to say, a field of infinite substitutions only because it is finite, that is to say, because instead of being an inexhaustible field, as in the classical hypothesis, instead of being too large, there is something missing from it: a center which arrests and grounds the play of the substitutions.[69]

CHAPTER 5

NOTES ON REIFICATION AND CRITICAL LEGAL STUDIES

In the growing output of books and articles that fall under the controversial and open-ended rubric of "critical legal studies," the theme of reification plays an important role. Drawing upon Marxist and existentialist thought, critical legal writers have been analyzing the multilayered institution of law as both a consequence and a source of mystified social interaction. This chapter is both a contribution to the critical legal movement and a first step in transvaluing the use of "reification" as a poorly defined but central term in the movement's discourse. Part One provides brief overviews of the writings (by Marx, Lukács, and Sartre) that are mentioned most frequently by critical legal scholars in their attacks on reification. In addition, I have summarized Peter Gabel's "Reification in Legal Reasoning,"[1] the most extensive look at this problem heretofore by a member of the critical legal movement. My overviews make no special claims to objectivity or neutrality; as Jorge Luis Borges has remarked, "every writer *creates* his own precursors."[2] Nonetheless, the aim of Part One is chiefly expositive. The summaries in that Part will afford a context in conjunction with which—and likewise in opposition to which—the detailed arguments in Part Two can be understood. Part Two endeavors to rearticulate current diagnoses of routinized social patterns. It may perhaps best be viewed as an encounter between the matted "concept" of reification and some piquant strands of French, Anglo-American, and German thought. Since, as Derrida has observed, "there is no nucleus of meaning, no conceptual atom, but . . . the concept is produced within the tissue of differences," Part Two should be seen as a "regulated transformation of one language by another."[3] Within this scheme, the transforming language—which will itself, of course, be transformed—is a congeries of discourses that are just beginning to make themselves resoundingly felt in work by critical legal scholars.

As Chapter 1 has suggested, the prime purpose of this critique and rewriting of some major discourses on reification is to explore how jurisprudence might be continued and enhanced through the highlighting of deconstructionist themes. This chapter will not be arguing anew for the tactics and motifs developed thus far, but will presuppose them and will draw out their programmatic vitality. By and large, the chapter fulfills this purpose by advocating programs that are unprogrammatic; for there exists no clear division between strategies and objectives. While laying stress on the crucial and creative role of strategic thinking, the chapter will decline to posit an ultimate destination that would allow the conclusive judging of tactics. Every approach will be examined for its power to highlight paradoxes and to overturn the priorities of discoursive movement in which it has intervened, but these ambitions do not themselves constitute a program with defined aims in politics. To be sure, the themes and problems to which this chapter will be addressing itself are of great concern to radical theorists, and the chapter generally favors leftist positions. Nonetheless, conservative theorists should encounter few difficulties in taking over and suitably reorienting the basic style of analysis that will be developed here. Deconstruction, that is, does not entail or require leftism—or any other assortment of prescriptions and goals concerning matters political. But things appear rather different when the question of linkages between politics and deconstruction is approached from the other end. As this chapter will maintain, and indeed as this whole book has maintained, the deconstructive method cannot so easily be ignored by anyone for whose politics it will have no need. One can endeavor to stay unmindful of deconstructionist insights as they have been articulated herein, but the penalty for such ostrich-like neglect is a flabby and undiscerning totteriness.

Part One

A. Karl Marx and the Fetishism of Commodities

A scathing critique of fetishism—including the fetishism of commodities—appears more than once in Marx's work, most notably in the famous last section of the first chapter of *Capital*. Marx quite often wrote in a cryptic style, and he frequently was determined to connect his model of fetishism to an ill-advised labor theory of value. Nevertheless, the gist of his assault can be readily understood, and it is germane and powerful beyond the dubious context in which he placed it.[4] (It is also highly problematic in certain ways, as we shall see presently.)

What Marx meant by the word "fetishism" is rather different from the word's principal meaning since the time of Freud. Marx did not wield the term as a means of objurgating the crassness and acquisitiveness of bourgeois life; he was not focusing on what C. B. Macpherson has called "possessive individualism."[5] Rather, the fetishism of commodities, as Marx described it, is a collective delusion "in which the process of production has the mastery over man, instead of being controlled by him" (*Capital*, I, 81). People are controlled by productive forces not—or, at any rate, not only—because they are preoccupied with amassing wealth, but because they have ascribed a phantasmal subjectivity to their own products. What has occurred, in sum, is a metalepsis—an inversion of an effect and a cause. Most people's interpretations of their everyday practices are obscured by a "mist through which the social character of labour appears to us to be an objective character of the products themselves." As a result, we live in "an enchanted, perverted, topsy-turvy world in which Monsieur Le Capital and Madame la Terre do their ghost-walking as social characters."[6]

This type of bizarre mystification, Marx avouched, is endemic to societies in which the distribution and the production of needful things are controlled by the commodity form. Commodities, as Marx analyzed them, are first and foremost the incarnations of human toil. This of course does not mean that people make their goods out of thin air. Marx was at pains to emphasize that human activity interacts with "materials furnished by Nature."[7] From his standpoint, however, there were two reasons for highlighting the role of labor in the production process. First, the "natural" world exists largely as the outcome of past labor. "Animals and plants, which we are accustomed to consider as products of Nature, are in their present form, not only products of, say last year's labour, but the result of a gradual transformation, continued through many generations, under man's superintendence, and by means of his labour" (*Capital*, I, 181). Second, even in areas of the world that have been untouched by human hands, the bounty of Nature would remain useless if it were not eventually "adapted . . . to the wants of man" through toil (*Capital*, I, 180). (Toil that brings about adaptation can of course be extremely crude—the picking of fruit off trees, for example.) Physical or mental work is therefore a necessary, though not sufficient, factor in the production of useful things.[8] And just as human activity is a crucial element of *production*, so too it is the *sine qua non* of any framework of *distribution*.[9] For the purpose of Marx's theory, the distribution of goods produced by labor consists in but a free-floating constellation of acts and judgments taken by human beings. The overall distributive scheme may be conflict-ridden and uncoordinated or wildly inegalitarian, but in any case it must flow from the intentions of human subjects, and ergo can be transformed when enough people decide (jointly or severally) to modify their behavior. Hence, at every point of the economic process, we find support for William James's remark—propounded as a metaphysical tenet, but adaptable to suit more specific practices of creation—that "the trail of the human serpent is over all."[10]

But when useful items become *commodities*—that is, when they become objects of *exchange* in a market—the key role of human agents and their volition will be submerged. As a commodity is exchanged, it acquires a fluctuating value in its relation to all other commodities. A market is thus a general system of values; and, as Marx pointed out, those values tend to exhibit a bizarre life of their own.

> The character of having value, when once impressed upon products, obtains fixity only by reason of their acting and re-acting upon each other as quantities of value. These quantities vary continually, independently of the will, foresight and action of the producers. To them, their own social action takes the form of the action of objects, which rule the producers instead of being ruled by them. . . .
>
> A commodity is therefore a mysterious thing, simply because in it the social character of men's labour appears to them as an objective character stamped upon the product of that labour; because the relation of the producers to the sum total of their own labour is presented to them as a social relation, existing not between themselves, but between the products of their labour. . . . [I]t is a definite social relation between men, that assumes, in their eyes, the fantastic form of a relation between things. [*Capital*, I, 75, 72.]

The producers of commodities suffer from a collective blindness that prevents them from recognizing the full contingency of their markets. Seeing values as the intrinsic properties of exchanged goods, they submit to the demands of the marketplace as if to an unrelenting Moloch:

> Circulation is the movement in which the general alienation appears as general appropriation and general appropriation as general alienation. As much, then, as the whole of this movement appears [to the analyst] as a social process, and as much as the individual moments of this movement arise from the conscious will and particular purposes of individuals, so much does the totality of the process appear [to the producers of commodities] as an objective interrelation, which arises spontaneously from nature; arising, it is true, from the mutual influence of conscious individuals on one another, but neither located in their consciousness, nor subsumed under them as a whole. Their own collisions with one another produce an *alien* social power standing above them, produce their mutual interaction as a process and power independent of them. [*Grundrisse*, 196–97; emphasis in original.]

Only in a communist world will fetishism have been transcended, and only then will people reclaim the social powers from which at present they have alienated themselves. No longer will people have to construe their acts through the mediating web of a market; instead, all social relations and all social pursuits will have become immediately and fully plain to everyone's consciousness.

> Let us now picture to ourselves, by way of change, a community of free individuals, carrying on their work with the means of production in common, in which the labour-power of all the different individuals is consciously applied as the combined labour-power of the community. . . . The social relations of the individual producers, with regard both to their labour and to its products, are in this case perfectly simple and intelligible, and that with regard not only to production but also to distribution. . . .
>
> The life-process of society, which is based on the process of material production, does not strip off its mystical veil until it is treated as production by freely associated men, and is consciously regulated by them in accordance with a settled plan.[11]

Brilliant as this analysis may be, it is liable to a number of telling criticisms. Though much of Part Two will be a critical rewriting of Marx, some salient points should be noted briefly here. First, despite a few countervailing passages—the necessity of which would have to be underlined in a deconstructive reading—Marx's critique of fetishism trades on a humanistic conception of subjectivity.[12] In general, Marx portrayed fetishism as a lapsing or deviation from an authentic control by subjects over their products; he was thus forced to appeal to notions of self-mastery and self-presence that have come under withering attack in more recent years. Despite some passages to the contrary, Marx discounted or suppressed what Neil Hertz has called "[a] troublesome interior difference—the . . . self-division implicit in all . . . activity."[13] Marx had to disregard—or, rather, to treat as a mistake—the expropriation that a self undergoes as the essential condition of its possibility. This is not exactly to say that the critique of fetishism is *wrong* (for we should then have to presuppose that the critique is univocal, and that it can somehow be made "correct"). It *is* to say, however, that Marx's yearning to bind the human subject and its creations can readily be deconstructed as an unstable moment in a paradoxical interplay between subject and object.[14]

Second, and very closely related to the first point, Marx seized Hegel's "absolute knowledge" and ingeniously brought it down to earth as the communist future. By looking forward to a time when "the practical relations of every-day life offer to man none but perfectly intelligible and reasonable relations with regard to his fellowmen and to Nature" (*Capital*, I, 79), Marx joined the menacing and deeply religious quest for an end to subject/object disjunctures through some grand synthesis or harmonization. As Shlomo Avineri observes:

> Turning the possibility of human redemption into an historical phenomenon about to be realized here and now secularizes the Hegelian synthesis that saw the dialectical tensions resolving themselves in the present generation and finding their *Aufhebung* in an apotheosis through which the historical process would achieve its ultimate height. It is immaterial that whereas Hegel called this act the culmination of history, Marx sees it as the beginning of true history; the implications are the same. From a systematic point of view the difference between Marx and Hegel in this respect can be reduced to Marx's rejection of the Hegelian postulate about the existence of a super-historical essence, Absolute Spirit, and to his contention that the process of the *Aufhebung* of the antagonisms has yet to occur, while Hegel thought that it had already occurred. Endowing the present generation with such an eschatological significance was common to Marx and Hegel—despite the conservative, quietistic implications of Hegel's philosophy and the revolutionary and activist implications of Marx's.[15]

To be sure, Marx used largely hypothetical (rather than predictive) language when outlining the mode of human association in which fetishism will have ceased to prevail. This may have been a rather oblique way of acknowledging that transparent social intercourse is no more achievable within time than is the descent of New Jerusalem, where God's glorious light renders the sun unnecessary. There may be a much more striking resemblance between Marxism and Augustinianism than at first meets the eye.[16] On the whole, however, the dominant impression gained from *Capital* and the other works is that Marx viewed full collective self-consciousness as a reachable (if remote) aim.[17] Like so much of the rest of Marx's writing, the critique of fetishism has pointed us toward a future too dazzling for the eye and too inconceivable for the mind.

Third, in his discussion of the "mystical character of commodities" (*Capital*, I, 71), Marx evinced a dearth of self-criticism and self-reflection. His frequently resorting to phrases such as "mystical veil," "illusions of the monetary system," and "mist-enveloped regions" (as synonyms for the life and thought of bourgeois society) was indicative of a general failure to reflect on his own assumptions. Likewise, Marx's brazen attempts to garb his diagnosis of fetishism with the mantle of "science" were indicative of a bootless search for an Archimedean point from which to analyze and censure the rank injustices of capitalism. For all his skill at uncovering the particularity of pretensions to universal truth, Marx often neglected to extend his critical insights to his own theorizing. As Barbara Johnson has noted: "Every theory starts somewhere. . . . [T]he starting point is . . . usually blind to itself."[18] Marx could give credence to the ideal of objectivity—and to the rather audacious claim that his own standpoint partook of such an ideal—only by pretermitting the relativistic overtones of his challenge to bourgeois thought. By clinging fast to "truth" as a touchstone for the critique of fetishism, Marx helped to bolster the conventional lines of discourse that he despised.

Admittedly, Marx could not have managed to break with "truth" altogether; an ambition to do so would have been its own first casualty, as my first chapter made clear in its curt rejection of nihilism. This point has been made in a slightly different fashion by Derrida in an essay on structuralist anthropology:

> If one calls *bricolage* the necessity of borrowing one's concepts from the text of a heritage which is more or less coherent or ruined, it must be said that every discourse is *bricoleur*. . . . The notion of the engineer who supposedly breaks with all forms of *bricolage* is therefore a theological idea; and since Lévi-Strauss tells us elsewhere that *bricolage* is mythopoetic, the odds are that the engineer is a myth produced by the *bricoleur*. As soon as we cease to believe in such an engineer and in a discourse which breaks with the received historical discourse, and as soon as we admit that every finite discourse is bound by a certain *bricolage* and that the engineer and the scientist are also species of *bricoleurs*, then the very idea of *bricolage* is menaced and the difference in which it took on its meaning breaks down.[19]

Moreover, self-reflection cannot be pure or immune to further displacement. As Paul de Man wrote convincingly, the language of critics has been able to "grope toward a certain degree of insight only because their method remained oblivious to the perception of this insight. The insight exists only for a reader in the privileged position of being able to observe the blindness as a phenomenon in its own right—*the question of his own blindness being one which he is by definition incompetent to ask.*"[20]

Nevertheless, even if we cannot abandon "truth" for all time, we can come up with "figures not dominated by the value of truth, which then becomes only an included, inscribed, circumscribed function" (MP, 18). Likewise, though we can never meet the ancient command to "know thyself," we should not take comfort in intellectual slovenliness. Once more, let us turn to Derrida's essay on structuralism and anthropology:

> Now, ethnology—like any science—comes about within the element of discourse. And it is primarily a European science employing traditional concepts, however much it may struggle against them. Consequently, whether he wants to or not—and this does not depend on a decision on his part—the ethnologist accepts into his discourse the premises of ethnocentrism at the very moment when he denounces them. This necessity is irreducible; it is not a historical contingency. We ought to consider all its implications very carefully. But if no one can escape this necessity, and if no one is therefore responsible for giving in to it, however little he may do so, this does not mean that all the ways of giving in to it are of equal pertinence. The quality and fecundity

> of a discourse are perhaps measured by the critical rigor with which this relation to the history of metaphysics and to inherited concepts is thought. Here it is a question both of a critical relation to the language of the social sciences and a critical responsibility of the discourse itself. It is a question of explicitly and systematically posing the problem of the status of a discourse which borrows from a heritage the resources necessary for the deconstruction of that heritage itself. A problem of *economy* and *strategy*.[21]

On this strategic question—the question of impugning (without renouncing) one's methods and assertions by having pitted one's own critique against itself—Marx can be found too smug. A self-critical theory that would build upon his ideas must take this into account.

B. Reification and Class Consciousness: Georg Lukács

In the early 1920s—several years *before* much of the early Marxian corpus had been discovered—Georg Lukács produced a fresh and powerful interpretation of Marx that blew like a cold wind through the fog and drabness of earlier exegeses. As a leading figure in a broad resurgence of interest in Hegelianism, Lukács arrived at doctrines that were strikingly close in many ways to the views advanced by Marx in his (then unpublished) "Economic and Philosophic Manuscripts."

Lukács's most remarkable essay—and the one most directly relevant to this chapter—is "Reification and the Consciousness of the Proletariat," which forms the core of *History and Class Consciousness*.[22] I shall be concentrating here on the first half of the essay, which explains the reified subjective and objective forms of bourgeois society. The second half of the essay, which attempts to show how the proletariat can "function as the identical subject-object of the social and historical processes of evolution" (*HCC*, 149), has not found a very warm reception among critical legal scholars, for two main reasons. First, its basic dogma—the view that the proletariat can act as the saintly fighters in a secular Armageddon—is risibly far-fetched and incoherent, no matter how brilliantly it is formulated. Attempts to single out a messiah (even a collective messiah) do not fare well against the blistering sarcasm of scholars like Duncan Kennedy and Mark Kelman.[23] Indeed, Lukács himself in later years had notably jaundiced feelings about his erstwhile hopes for an "identical subject-object of history," which he now correctly perceived as incoherent:

> But is the identical subject-object here anything more in truth than a purely metaphysical construct? Can a genuinely identical subject-object be created by self-knowledge, however adequate, and however truly based on an adequate knowledge of society, i.e. however perfect that self-knowledge is? We need only formulate the question precisely to

> see that it must be answered in the negative. For even when the content of knowledge is referred back to the knowing subject, this does not mean that the act of cognition is thereby freed of its alienated nature. . . . Thus the proletariat seen as the identical subject-object of the real history of mankind is no materialistic consummation that overcomes the constructions of idealism. It is rather an attempt to out-Hegel Hegel, it is an edifice boldly erected above every possible reality and thus attempts objectively to surpass the Master himself. [HCC, xxiii.]

Second, Lukács's purported answer to dialectical paradoxes fit comfortably with his Leninist belief that a vanguard movement should arouse workers to play their vital part in world history. To cherish hope for a negation of all negations has all too frequently been to create a pretext for barbarism with a human face.[24]

Thus, since the main purpose in Part One of this chapter is to summarize the critiques of reification that have been most important for the critical legal scholars, Lukács's heroic claims regarding the "standpoint of the proletariat" will hardly be touched on here. This chapter is not propounding a full-scale exegesis or a rigorous deconstructive critique of Lukács's essay. A breezily dismissive view of the second half of his essay will have struck a suitable balance, for my defined aims, between relevancy and fairness.

Lukács's great success lay in bringing to the fore the paradoxes that had been glimpsed but not fleshed out or highlighted by Marx in the first volume of *Capital*. Lukács began his argument by defining the "essence of commodity-structure" in terms similar to those of Marx: "Its basis is that a relation between people takes on the character of a thing and thus acquires a 'phantom objectivity,' an autonomy that seems so strictly rational and all-embracing as to conceal every trace of its fundamental nature: the relation between people" (HCC, 83). The humanist tenor of this preliminary definition seeped through at some other places in Lukács's text—for example, in the argument that "the personal nature of economic relations was still understood clearly on occasion at the start of capitalist development, but . . . as the process advanced and forms became more complex and less direct, it became increasingly difficult and rare to find anyone penetrating the veil of reification."[25] From the outset, however, Lukács made clear that he was not interested in merely rehearsing the critiques of fetishism that graced some of the finest pages of *Capital*. Rather, his objective was to explore the antinomies of bourgeois institutions and bourgeois thought which Marx had so fleetingly but suggestively uncovered: "Our intention here is to *base* ourselves on Marx's economic analyses and to proceed from there to a discussion of the problems growing out of the fetish character of commodities, both as an objective form and also as a subjective stance corresponding to it" (HCC, 84). Here we see the concepts of "subjectivity" and "objectivity" emerging as the chief elements of Lukács's approach. For Lukács, as for Hegel, the dialectical interplay between these dimensions served as an Ariadne's thread that could take a suitably informed analyst through an entire complex of problems. The problems that mattered most to Lukács, of course, were those produced by Marxian efforts to "portray capitalist society in its totality and to lay bare its fundamental nature" (HCC, 83). In taking up some key problems from Marx's legacy, Lukács generated a series of profound insights into the paradoxical dynamics of social and material life.

At many points in "Reification and the Consciousness of the Proletariat," we encounter various formulations that try to capture both the complete falsity and the stark necessity of reified social patterns. À la Marx, Lukács described reification as a state of affairs in which "a man's own activity, his own labour becomes something objective and independent of him, something that controls him by virtue of an autonomy alien to man," but he immediately went on to observe that "[t]here is both an objective and a subjective side to this phenomenon" (HCC, 87). Reified social networks were seen not as the conquest of subjectivity by objectivity, nor as the transformation of the subjective into the objective, but as a particular mode of interaction and interpenetration between these categories of our experience. The processes of reification will hence not prove strictly verifiable or conceptually masterable. They are processes which must drive themselves through their own incapacitation, which can get under way only through an inability to get started, and which nevertheless yield certain consequences and structures (which will have yielded the processes that yield *them*), for reasons that remain to be analyzed.[26] Thus, we are told that abstract labor exists "both as the presupposition and [as] the product of capitalist production" (HCC, 87). Similarly, an "environment where time is transformed into abstract, exactly measurable, physical space . . . [is] at once the cause and effect of the scientifically and mechanically fragmented and specialized production of the object of labour" (HCC, 90). With a deft touch, Lukács wielded parentheses for his most explicit statement of the aporia that engulfs even the most adroit inquiry into the genesis of reification: "Thus the universality of the commodity form is responsible both objectively and subjectively for the abstraction of the human labour incorporated in commodities. (On the other hand, this universality becomes historically possible because this process of abstraction has been completed.)"[27] In short, a reified commodity system will have to presuppose itself; it can finally become established only on the condition that it has already become established.

Notwithstanding this paradox, it was to outlining the *results* of reification—for which, most strictly speaking, we can provide no account[28]—that Lukács skillfully devoted the major part of his essay. Among his various descriptions of these results, two themes figured most pointedly. First, he saw that reification may be characterized in terms of subjectivity as a massive failure of visionary thought; that is, in a reified socioeconomic structure most people confuse what is familiar with what is necessary. This makes it difficult and uncommon for people even to think seriously about a world that departs much from the one they meet in their everyday lives. Lukács referred to capitalist society as a "second nature" with laws as seemingly resistant to change as laws turned up by Einstein and Mendel.[29] In such a society, "the *contemplative* nature of man . . . makes its appearance. . . . The contemplative stance [is] adopted towards a process mechanically conforming to fixed laws and enacted independently of man's consciousness and impervious to human intervention" (HCC, 97, 89; emphasis in original). Widespread adoption of this debilitatingly passive outlook means that human activity "does not go beyond the correct calculation of the possible outcome of the sequence of events (the 'laws' of which [are found] 'ready-made'), and beyond the adroit evasion of disruptive 'accidents' by means of protective devices and preventive measures (which are based in their turn on the recognition and application of similar laws)" (HCC, 98). Nor is it only at the practical level of quotidian labor that this sense of necessity is evoked. In intellectual life, too, paralyzing constraints on the imagination appear at every turn. Thus, for example, the economists who study "primitive capitalism" see the object of their perusal not as one mode of interaction among others, but as the prototype of all cultured existence:

> The commodity character of the commodity, the abstract, quantitative mode of calculability shows itself [in primitive capitalism] in its purest form: the reified mind necessarily sees it as the form in which its own authentic immediacy becomes manifest and—as reified consciousness—does not even attempt to transcend it. On the contrary, it is concerned to make it permanent by 'scientifically deepening' the laws at work. Just as the capitalist system continuously produces and reproduces itself economically on higher and higher levels, the structure of reification progressively sinks more deeply, more fatefully and more definitively into the consciousness of man. [HCC, 93.]

Reification will consist therefore in a narrowing of horizons, a closing of the mind to transformative possibilities. Social life (broadly understood) comes to appear frozen and as far beyond human governance as the daunting shears of Atropos.

> The reified world appears henceforth quite definitively—and in philosophy, under the spotlight of 'criticism' it is potentiated still further—as the only possible world, the only conceptually accessible, comprehensible world vouchsafed to us humans. . . . [HCC, 110.]

> [T]he unexplained and inexplicable facticity of bourgeois existence as it is here and now acquires the patina of an eternal law of nature or a cultural value enduring for all time. [HCC, 157.]

It may not be amiss to recall here Coleridge's disdain for "the lethargy of custom. . . . [which blinds us to] the loveliness and the wonders of the world before us; an inexhaustible treasure, but for which, in consequence of the film of familiarity and selfish solicitude we have eyes, yet see not, ears that hear not, and hearts that neither feel nor understand."[30]

The second main way in which the results of reification were described was in terms of objectivity. Time and time again, Lukács insisted that it is not exclusively the structure of people's consciousness, but also the structure of their society, that impedes the forces of social transformation. Context and consciousness, as perceived by Lukács (and in a similar way by Marx), are fully interlaced though distinct: each wholly determines, and is determined by, the other. If reification can quite properly be deemed an illusion, "it is a necessary one,"[31] for capitalist society is organized in ways that almost inevitably squash efforts at fundamental revision. In fact, the reified outlooks displayed by workers and intellectuals will fit perfectly with a system "in which for the individual the commodity structure of all 'things' and their obedience to 'natural laws' is found to exist already in a finished form, as something immutably given" (HCC, 92). Social arrangements have become ossified not just in everyone's imagination, but in the political institutions and socioeconomic structures within which people must live and move and have their being.

> *Objectively* a world of objects and relations between things springs into being (the world of commodities and their movements on the market). The laws governing these objects are indeed gradually discovered by man, but even so they confront him as invisible forces that generate their own power. The individual can use his knowledge of these laws to his own advantage, but he is not able to modify the process by his own activity. . . . [HCC, 87.]

> Neither objectively nor in his relation to his work does man appear as the authentic master of the process; on the contrary, he is a mechanical part incorporated into a mechanical system. He finds it already pre-existing and self-sufficient, it functions independently of him and he has to conform to its laws whether he likes it or not. . . . [HCC, 89.]

> [M]en . . . erect around themselves in the reality they have created . . . a kind of second nature which evolves with . . . inexorable necessity. [HCC, 128.]

The "second nature" produced by capitalism will avert meaningful change not simply as a result of the narrow visions of possibility that rule people's minds, but also because of countless ways in which bourgeois institutions—like other institutions—nullify the attempts at transformation that are indeed made. One example mentioned by Lukács is the pronounced tendency of a legal system to cleave cautiously to its past. Borrowing from Weber, Lukács maintained that the inertia of the law can be traced to a

> need [by capitalists] for exact calculation . . . [which] requires that the legal system should confront the individual events of social existence as something permanently established and exactly defined, i.e. as a rigid system. Of course, this produces an uninterrupted series of conflicts between the unceasingly revolutionary forces of the capitalistic economy and the rigid legal system. But this only results in new codifications; and despite these the new system is forced to preserve the fixed, change-resistant structure of the old system.[32]

Another example, which was discussed at some length by Lukács, is the bafflingly uncoordinated and atomistic flavor of bourgeois life. Of special interest to Lukács was the breakdown of "organic" communities and "organic" work schemes by the division of labor under capitalism. A factory-based system will have divided organic groups of people into "isolated abstract atoms whose work no longer brings them together directly and organically" (HCC, 90), and will therefore prevent the working class from becoming a class-for-itself that could reshape (and realize some practical control over) the conditions of its day-to-day toil. Even the administrative ranks of society discover that extreme specialization "has the effect of making . . . partial functions autonomous and so they tend to develop through their own momentum and in accordance with their own special laws independently of the other partial functions of society (or that part of the society to which they belong)" (HCC, 103). A fractionated society of narrow fiefdoms involving a minute division of labor will have reared up against those who are brash enough to seek to transform it. Lukács, then, supplied a contemporary gloss on an old saying by Heraclitus: "To do the same thing over and over again is not only boredom: it is to be controlled by rather than to control what you do."[33]

As in the preceding section on Marx, I shall conclude this highly condensed summary with a few brief critical observations. These observations are in no way intended as a thorough critique of Lukács's theories. First, as Lukács himself avowed in 1967, *History and Class Consciousness* tended to collapse all forms of objectification *(Vergegenstandlichung)* into alienation *(Entfremdung)* and reification *(Verdinglichung)*, which were in turn treated as equivalents. It will be useful here to distinguish reification from objectification once more, though the distinction is construed somewhat differently from the way Lukács (in his later years) interpreted it.[34] Here, "objectification" will refer to the structured side of the antinomical seesawing between a structure and its events; that is, it will signify the decentering and constituting of human subjects (and other agents) by the material, cultural, and linguistic networks that are the presuppositions—quite as much as the outcomes—of subjectivity. "Reification," on the other hand, will be understood in a clearly narrower sense. It will denote a specific kind of objectifying process wherein people lose sight of the contingency of social arrangements with which they have become long familiar. When the two terms have been defined in this way, it should be clear that reification can perhaps be eschewed, whereas objectification never will be—except in the wildest visions of John of Patmos (or, for human beings, in the event of an all-out nuclear war).[35] As Lukács rather tartly observed in 1967:

> [I]t is in Hegel that we first encounter alienation as the fundamental problem of the place of man in the world and *vis-à-vis* the world. However, in the term alienation he includes every type of objectification. Thus "alienation" when taken to its logical conclusion is identical with objectification. Therefore, when the identical subject-object transcends alienation it must also transcend objectification at the same time. But as, according to Hegel, the object, the thing exists only as an alienation from self-consciousness, to take it back into the subject would mean the end of objective reality and thus of any reality at all. *History and Class Consciousness* follows Hegel in that it too equates alienation with objectification. [HCC, xxiii–xxiv.]

By following Hegel on this point, and by preserving a Marxist faith in the possibility of transcending alienation, Lukács upheld the most problematic tendencies of his own thought. The humanist leanings and the millenarianism of *History and Class Consciousness* are tied closely to Lukács's failure to carve out reification from objectification. It is not purely coincidental that Lukács sought to disclose a unified "subject-object of history"; nor is Part III of "Reification and the Consciousness of the Proletariat"—titled "The Standpoint of the Proletariat"—a fortuitous excrescence that can be neatly severed from the main body of his critique. "[T]he identical subject-object," James Schmidt has remarked, "is the point toward which all of the other moments [of Lukács's critique] lead."[36] Particularly revealing in this respect is Lukács's stance toward the paradoxes that were discussed near the beginning of this section. Lukács declared that those and like paradoxes are specific to bourgeois thought, and that the momentous standpoint of the proletariat "makes possible the solution of problems which the greatest thinkers of the bourgeois era have vainly struggled to find" (HCC, 164). The following lengthy paragraph, which concluded a provocative and sometimes obscure review of German philosophy, manifests the hostile attitude Lukács harbored toward the "antinomies of bourgeois thought":

> Classical philosophy did, it is true, take all the antinomies of its life-basis to the furthest extreme it was capable of in thought; it conferred on them the highest possible intellectual expression. But even for this philosophy they remain unsolved and insoluble. Thus classical philosophy finds itself historically in the paradoxical position that it was concerned to find a philosophy that would mean the end of bourgeois society, and to resurrect in thought a humanity destroyed in that society and by it. In the upshot, however, it did not manage to do more than provide a complete intellectual copy and the *a priori* deduction of bourgeois society. It is only the *manner* of this deduction, namely the dialectical method that points beyond bourgeois society. And even in classical philosophy this is only expressed in the form of an unsolved and insoluble antimony. This antimony is admittedly the most profound and the most magnificent intellectual expression of those antinomies which lie at the roots of bourgeois society and which are unceasingly produced and reproduced by it—albeit in confused and inferior forms. Hence classical philosophy had nothing but these unresolved antinomies to bequeath to succeeding (bourgeois) generations. The continuation of that course which at least in method started to point the way beyond these limits, namely the dialectical method as the true historical method was reserved for the class which was able to discover within itself on the basis of its life-experience the identical subject-object, the subject of action; the 'we' of the genesis: namely the proletariat. [HCC, 148–49.]

It seems not unjustified to suppose that a certain fear roused Lukács to try to solve the classical paradoxes—a fear that his approach would not otherwise enjoy a telling critical force. Equating reification and objectification, Lukács tied the prospects for making good his *political* ideals to the chances for success of his *metaphysical* speculation. He could thus forgo the worst aspects of Hegelianism only if he abjured the best aspects of Marxism. To escape (or, more strictly, to finesse) this grim dilemma, we shall have to part ways with Lukács and reconceive the task of a political theory.

Second, much of the language and the categorial structure of *History and Class Consciousness* fits in all too neatly with traditional metaphysics, though in a politically charged fashion. When, for instance, Lukács decried the transformation of time into "an exactly delimited, quantifiable continuum" that "reduces space and time to a common denominator and degrades time to the dimension of space" (HCC, 90, 89), he accepted too unreservedly the idea of a sharp originary distinction between space and time that had somehow been expunged during the rise of the bourgeoisie. His concepts should have been made more patently dialectical; that is, he should have affirmed that the dimensions of time and space always interpenetrate totally as well as exclude each other totally.[37] Neither category can be reduced to the other one, since neither category can be reduced to itself.

An equally unfortunate choice of terms can be found in Lukács's central reliance on a contemplation/action dichotomy as a tool for understanding reified modes of life. Under capitalism, Lukács argued, human beings at every tier of social existence have declined into passive spectators: "The subject . . . becomes purely contemplative in the philosophical sense. . . . [T]he subject . . . assumes increasingly the attitude of the pure observe[r]" (HCC, 130, 131). Evocative as this vein of analysis may be, its conflation of metaphysics and politics will give rise to enormous difficulties when pushed too far. Not only does it work against many of Lukács's best insights, but it runs aground on some recent styles of thought that have put decisively into question any basis for marking off contemplative outlooks from active outlooks—which nonetheless remain wholly unassimilable.[38]

To be sure, the imperatives of the philosophical tradition can brook no absolute dissent. As was earlier suggested by a quotation from Derrida, we shall cease to think if we have refused to do so in the confines of Western metaphysics.[39] Nonetheless, though we cannot once and for all discard the metaphysical concepts, we can try to manipulate them to our advantage (even as we are manipulated *by* them). One need not relish the specific advice or the too empiricist tone of the following remarks by Fredric Jameson to agree with his underlying assumption—that strategic thinking must guide one's way as one chooses (and as one is thus chosen by) a theoretical framework:

> [I]t is certainly the case that a belief in the natural is ideological and that much of bourgeois art has worked to perpetuate such a belief. . . . Yet in different historical circumstances the idea of nature was once a subversive concept with a genuinely revolutionary function, and only the analysis of the concrete historical and cultural conjuncture can tell us whether, in the post-natural world of late capitalism, the categories of nature may not have acquired such a critical charge again.[40]

Jameson properly denies any immutable conjuncture linking metaphysics and politics, but his attitude toward the philosophical tradition seems far too sanguine. In the view which this chapter will be espousing, the chief determinant of the critical and strategic potency of a discourse is the tenacious vigor that it displays in upsetting and disorganizing conventional metaphysics. Resistance will "never be pure and absolute," and can at most strive to "transform concepts, to displace them, to turn them against their presuppositions, to reinscribe them in other chains, and little by little to modify the terrain of our work and thereby produce new configurations" (OG, 46; *Positions*, 24). Such resistance should not be lightly forgone, however, merely because one has to mount it on a "bottomless chessboard"[41] or merely because it somehow may be at odds with short-run political expedience. *Peut-être*, an attack on reification becomes more arduous once the philosophic integrity of certain concepts is placed in doubt. But, as will be explained in Part Two, there may be corresponding advantages for even the most committed revolutionary.

Finally, like Marx, Lukács never adequately considered the (im)possibility of his own standpoint, and ergo made himself too liable to charges of dogmatism and naiveté.[42] The poverty of his self-reflection shows up not only in the audacious belief that he had come upon a "site [i.e., the position of the proletariat] from which to resolve all [philosophical] problems" (HCC, 145), but as well in his tendency to treat use-value as historically and analytically prior to exchange-value (HCC, 92)—a move that seemed to endow his theory with a grounding in "hard fact"—and also in his failure to recognize just how problematic and self-subverting were the conditions of possibility of his overall project.

On the one hand, James Schmidt may very well be justified in contending that

> Lukács refuse[d] to give [his] theory a foundation which is somehow outside of the historical process and thus capable of reflecting on the process without in any way altering either the situation examined or its own foundation. Historical materialism must be applied to *itself*, and hence cannot claim to be a theory which is somehow free of the historical tensions surrounding class conflict. Thus theory itself is not a reflection on a Bildung process, but rather is an integral part of it. . . . The truth status of the theory of society can only be the degree to which it both enlightens and is enlightened by the growing consciousness of the revolutionary class.[43]

Indeed, Lukács proclaimed that "the Marxist method is . . . as much the product of class warfare as any other political or economic product."[44] Yet, on the other hand, the relativistic drive of Lukács's approach—like every relativistic drive—entails a diluted form of empiricism. At the very moments when Lukács tried to be most self-conscious in bringing out the transient validity and confined purview of Marxist thought, he was most dogmatic in proclaiming the truth of his critique *within its proper domain.*

> [P]roletarian consciousness of social reality, of its own class situation, of its own historical vocation and the materialist view of history are all products of this self-same process of evolution *which historical materialism understands adequately and for what it really is for the first time in history.*
>
> . . . In the same way, the evolution of the proletariat reflects the inner structure of the society *which it was the first to understand. . . .*
>
> . . . Historical materialism both can and must be applied to itself. But this must not be allowed to lead to total relativism, let alone to

> the conclusion that historical materialism is not the correct historical method. The substantive truths of historical materialism are of the same type as were the truths of classical economics in Marx's view: they are truths within a particular social order and system of production. As such, but only as such, their claim to validity is absolute.[45]

If we leave aside the teleological overtones of this quotation—which are especially pronounced in the first two sentences, and which militate against finding the degree of scrupulous self-reflection that Schmidt and others have found in Lukács—we see here a relinquishment of overweening pretensions to a transhistorical view, combined with foolhardy statements of conceptual mastery and uncritical claims of rigor. To reflect only on the *contingent* standing of one's ideas is utterly insufficient; the very *coherence* of one's thought must be placed in question unremittingly. That is, one must keep in view synchronic (as well as diachronic) aporias. To take synchronic coherency for granted is to accept a smug and naive historicism.[46] Once again we come across problems which surround the criteria, both implicit and explicit, that Lukács was relying upon when he assessed the value of any theory (his own included, of course). Even the vital step of defining truth as consequences will have become enfeebled by glaring difficulties when tethered to an empiricist approach. Derrida's exhortation that we "conceive of a play in which whoever loses wins, and in which one loses and wins on every turn" (MP, 20), though directed squarely against Hegelianism, should warn us also about a facile credence in verifiability—even contingent verifiability—as a new ground for theorizing. If we are adequately to take into account what Derrida has been saying, without being overwhelmed or disheartened by it, we shall have to evolve more "playful" ways of analyzing reification.

C. Bad Faith and Reification: Jean-Paul Sartre

Jean-Paul Sartre has figured at least as saliently in the intellectual background of the critical legal scholars as have Lukács and Marx. One need only inspect the recently published dialogue between Peter Gabel and Duncan Kennedy to be conscious of the extensive interaction between Sartrean thought and the ideas of some major critical legal writers.[47] The interaction has as one of its main effects—or as one of its main determinants—a wistful Romantic strain that has informed the work of those writers. Nowhere is this more striking than in the critical legal scholars' attacks on reification.

Sartre's critique of reification can most lucidly be approached through his analysis of "bad faith." This analysis preoccupied Sartre in several famous texts, but it was articulated most fully in *L'Être et Le Néant*.[48] Having begun his *magnum opus* by postulating an elemental rift between *l'être-en-soi* (being-in-itself, or matter) and *l'être-pour-soi* (being-for-itself, or sentience), and having offered a remarkably brief description of *l'être-en-soi*,[49] Sartre then proceeded to make out the elusive trail of the *être-pour-soi* of consciousness. In his view, a particularly fruitful means of investigation lay in inquiring: "What then must consciousness be . . . if man must be capable of bad faith?" (BN, 85 [EN, 84]; translation modified). By "bad faith" Sartre meant a specific type of behavior in which "consciousness instead of directing its negation outward turns it toward itself" (BN, 87). Such behavior is commonly disparaged as "lying to oneself," but Sartre was not entirely comfortable with this conventional designation.

> We shall willingly grant that bad faith is a lie to oneself, on condition that we distinguish the lie to oneself from lying in general. . . . [BN, 87.]
>
> [I]n bad faith it is from myself that I am hiding the truth. Thus the duality of the deceiver and the deceived does not exist here. Bad faith on the contrary implies in essence the unity of a *single* consciousness. [BN, 89; emphasis in original.]

Given Sartre's premise of the complete *translucidité* of consciousness, "lying to oneself" will perhaps seem an incoherent notion. To flee this predicament, we must turn to a distinction—made by Sartre near the very beginning of his book—between consciousness and knowledge. Consciousness, as Sartre described it, is the most basic level of awareness, which forms the inescapable mode of being of all types of experience and thought. "Every conscious existence exists as consciousness of existing" (BN, 13). This "consciousness of existing" amounts to an "immediate, non-cognitive relation of the self to itself" (BN, 12). Knowledge, on the other hand, is positional or divided rather than nonreflective and immediate; that is, the knowing subject has to have posited a known thing or event at some remove from the faculty of knowing. To be sure, the known object can be the subject's own consciousness. However, in such cases of self-reflection, "the reflecting consciousness posits the reflected consciousness as its object" (BN, 12 [EN, 19]; translation modified). (One should note, incidentally, that in Sartre's work the reflecting subject will perforce be excluded from a full reappropriation of self.[50]) Knowledge, then, must implicate consciousness, but the latter need not and often does not entail the former. Pre-reflective aspects of consciousness may quite easily escape the ken of one's knowledge.

Having made cognition merely one type of sentience, Sartre was able to accept the notion of lying-to-oneself, without "introducing into consciousness the subject-object dualism which is typical of knowledge." (BN, 12.) Lying-to-oneself—which, of course, is Sartrean "bad faith"—

occurs when someone lacks knowledge of the fundamental features of human consciousness (and therefore acts in ways that amount to a denial of her true power as a consciously choosing agent). As Fredric Jameson has argued:

> *Mauvaise foi* is an enterprise of self-mystification [in which we] persuade ourselves that the unpleasant facts in question do not exist, all the while that we are still dimly aware of being in the process of so persuading ourselves. It is a structure of self-deception which becomes ever more intricate as we attempt to maintain it in being, and may aptly be symbolized by the desperate and contradictory attempt to keep ourselves from thinking about something (which we have to think about in order to know what we want to avoid). Thus the notion of *mauvaise foi* provides a means whereby a given act may be seen as both containing and not containing an awareness of its own basic intention or conscious purpose.[51]

Thus, Sartre reached a point where he could answer the query that was his principal concern: what exactly *is* the nature of human consciousness that remains beyond the purview of someone acting in bad faith? Confronting this basic question, Sartre gave a seemingly paradoxical response. "[H]uman reality, in its most immediate being, in the intrastructure of the pre-reflective *cogito*, must be what it is not and not be what it is" (BN, 112). He here restated the conception of temporality that had been vividly captured in the ancient Greek myth of Cronos, who devoured his own children at the instant that they were born.[52] The dimension of *l'être-pour-soi* is time, and time flees constantly from itself. Human awareness will be forever throwing itself ahead and leaving itself behind. Save at death and in totally blank sleep, consciousness can never come to a standstill or coincide with itself, but must always make and remake itself throughout the continuum of temporality. Sartre phrased this point well in his discussion of the "intentional unity" of sadness:

> [S]hould we not say that being sad means first to make oneself sad? That may be, someone will say, but after all doesn't giving oneself the being of sadness mean to *receive* this being? It makes no difference from where I receive it. The fact is that a consciousness which affects itself with sadness is sad precisely for this reason. . . . If I make myself sad, I must continue to make myself sad from beginning to end. I can not treat my sadness as an impulse finally achieved and put it on file without re-creating it, nor can I carry it in the manner of an inert body which continues its movement after the initial shock. There is no inertia in consciousness. If I make myself sad, it is because I *am* not sad—the being of the sadness escapes me by and in the very act by which I affect myself with it. The being-in-itself of sadness perpetually haunts my consciousness (of) being sad, but it is as a value which I can not

> realize; it stands as a regulative meaning of my sadness, not as its constitutive modality. [BN, 104; emphasis in original.]

Now, from this vision of the metaphysical nature of being-for-itself, no ethical or political consequences spring ineluctably. Truthfulness does not *necessarily* attach either to "*tout comprendre, c'est tout pardonner*" or to any sort of negation of that maxim (i.e., its negation as a whole or in part). Nonetheless, *L'Être et Le Néant* translated its metaphysical premises into casuistic terms, as a somber discourse of "freedom" and "responsibility." Conscious beings are unalloyedly free within their respective situations, and are therefore responsible *in toto* for aims, activities, and beliefs they have taken up. Because there is no inertia within consciousness, people must *decide* at each moment—wittingly or unwittingly—what they are to become. "Whatever our being may be, it is a choice" (BN, 607).

This, of course, does not mean that any person *tout seul* creates the contexts wherein he or she lives. Sartre recognized that "[t]here can be a free for-itself only as engaged in a resisting world. Outside of this engagement the notions of freedom, of determinism, of necessity lose all meaning. . . . [T]here is freedom only in a *situation*, and there is a situation only through freedom. Human-reality everywhere encounters resistances and obstacles which it has not created" (BN, 621, 629; emphasis in original). However, to the absolute freedom of *l'être-pour-soi* the "situation" can pose no threat. A "resisting world" is indeed the necessary backdrop for an unconstrained being, but resistance will have *become* resistance only in the course of freely willed thoughts and actions:

> [T]he coefficient of adversity in things can not be an argument against our freedom, for it is *by us*—i.e., by the preliminary positing of an end—that this coefficient of adversity arises. A particular crag, which manifests a profound resistance if I wish to displace it, will be on the contrary a valuable aid if I want to climb upon it in order to look over the countryside. In itself—if one can even imagine what the crag can be in itself—it is neutral; that is, it waits to be illuminated by an end in order to manifest itself as adverse or helpful. . . .
>
> . . . What is an obstacle for me may not be so for another. There is no obstacle in an absolute sense, but the obstacle reveals its coefficient of adversity across freely invented and freely acquired techniques. The obstacle reveals this [co]efficient also in terms of the value of the end posited by freedom. The rock will not be an obstacle if I wish at any cost to arrive at the top of the mountain. On the other hand, it will discourage me if I have freely fixed limits to my desire of making the projected climb. Thus the world by coefficients of adversity reveals to me the way in which I stand in relation to the ends which I assign myself.[53]

Given this understanding of human freedom, Sartre's analysis of "bad faith" should not prompt any great surprise. Whenever a human agent tries to reduce herself to a thing—whenever someone tries to escape the anguish of temporality (and the choices it entails) for the comforts of clinging to a fixed essence—she is acting in bad faith. She is striving to *be* a clearly defined person in the way that an inkwell *is* a specific kind of inkwell. She excludes from her more reflective knowledge the one truth of which she *must* be aware at a pre-reflective level: *viz.*, the priority of her existence over her essence. She loses sight of that which disjoins people from the brute matter of *l'être-en-soi*.

In an important sense, bad faith is thoroughly self-defeating, for it is as much a choice as is every other type of action. As Mark Poster has observed: "When faced with the exigency of making a choice, a person in bad faith refuses to choose. Still, of course, there is a choice because human reality can never completely be thing-reality, although it is a mutilated choice since it denies the possibility of choice while making one."[54] As this quotation implies, what putatively distinguishes bad faith from "authentic" action is that within bad faith an agent does not know that her choices could have been made differently. In short, the agent apparently lacks knowledge that "choices" have been made here at all.

Sartre offered several vivid examples of *mauvaise foi*, the most renowned of them being the complaisant waiter who "applies himself to chaining his movements as if they were mechanisms, the one regulating the other; his gestures and even his voice seem to be mechanisms; he gives himself the quickness and pitiless rapidity of things. . . . [H]e is playing at *being* a waiter in a cafe" (BN, 101–102; emphasis in original). At times, exegetes have held some of Sartre's examples to be highlighting the facticity, rather than the freedom, of the individual *être-pour-soi*.[55] For instance, one leading analyst has taken exactly such a view when considering the example of the homosexual who refuses to call himself a "pederast." Seen in this light, attempts by the homosexual to dismiss the labels that are applied to him by his friends will smack of an untenable "identification of the self in terms of a pure freedom not really implicated in the world."[56] It would seem, however, that the example can more easily be construed as bearing a very different message. One can pronounce the homosexual to be in bad faith not because he dissociates himself too chirpily from his *past*, but because he blinds himself to the disseverability of the *future* from everything that has gone before. He declines to fix any labels to his past love affairs—though he has fully acknowledged each of them—because he fears that he then would be committing himself to a specific pattern of future conduct. Should he apply the label "pederast" to himself, he will (so he thinks) have dashed the possibility that he might in time alter his desires. Here, as elsewhere, lying-to-oneself consists not in *overestimating* one's freedom, but in *recoiling* from it.

> The homosexual recognizes his faults, but he struggles with all his strength against the crushing view that his mistakes constitute for him a *destiny*. . . . He would be right actually if he understood the phrase "I am not a paederast" in the sense of "I am not what I am." That is, if he declared to himself, "To the extent that a pattern of conduct is defined as the conduct of a paederast and to the extent that I have adopted this conduct, I am a paederast. But to the extent that human reality can not be finally defined by patterns of conduct, I am not one." But instead he slides surreptitiously toward a different connotation of the word "being." He understands "not being" in the sense of "not-being-in-itself." He lays claim to "not being a paederast" in the sense in which this table *is not* an inkwell. He is in bad faith. [BN, 107–108; emphasis in original.]

All instances of bad faith are marked by flight from Sartre's terrible admonitions: "I am condemned to exist forever beyond my essence, beyond the causes and motives of my act. I am condemned to be free. . . . [T]he for-itself . . . is the being which finds *no help, no pillar of support* in what it *was*" (BN, 567, 616; emphasis in original).

Key aspects of this discussion of bad faith were perspicaciously carried over to Sartre's subsequent work, most deftly to the *Critique of Dialectical Reason*.[57] The *Critique* is often read as the end point of the absorbing path that Sartre followed, going from the extreme atomism of *L'Être et Le Néant* to a richer grasp of the collective realities that subsume all projects of individual human beings. It has been maintained, for example, that "Sartre's development from his earlier existentialism to its later Marxist modification . . . is the most impressive example in contemporary philosophical anthropology of the achievement of . . . sociologically crucial insight" into the "social character of man's self-production."[58] This orthodox scheme of Sartre's "development" will have presupposed the general coherence of the first and last stages of his work, rather than have perceived each text as always already deconstructed (by itself as well as by other texts). Furthermore, even if one does not pursue the insights and rigor of a deconstructive approach, one should discern that the tidiness of the orthodox scheme—while perhaps not wholly unfair—is patently simplistic in two main ways: it has obscured arguments in the early writing that threw some glances at the social embeddedness of people, and it has overdrawn the *Critique*'s renouncement of metaphysical atomism. In fact, one observer has acidulously declared: "[T]he *Critique* . . . very much repeats the structure or problematic of *Being and Nothingness*. . . . And there are even some losses in the process that are not dialectically reappropriated."[59] Be that as it may, we can indeed find some parallels between Sartre's "eidetic of bad faith" and his subsequent attacks on reification. At the same time, it would be very foolish to disregard his efforts (in those attacks) to overturn and displace the humanism that inspired *Being and Nothingness*.

Most important among the similarities between Sartre's early work and his later work is a focus on the propensity of human beings to flee the bitterness and exhilaration of free choice. As much as ever before, Sartre in his later years saw a fundamental difference between human agency and brute matter. For example, in his *Search for a Method* he declared:

> [W]ithin this living universe, man occupies, for us, a privileged place . . . because he is able to be historical; that is, he can continually define himself by his own *praxis* by means of changes suffered or provoked and their internalization, and then by the very surpassing of the internalized relations. . . . [SM, 167; emphasis in original.]

> What must be the nature of human relations in order for these relations to be capable of appearing in certain definite societies as the relations of things to each other? If the reification of human relations is possible, it is because these relations, even if reified, are fundamentally distinct from the relations of things. [SM, 177.]

The distinctive ability of human agents to go beyond themselves—collectively or individually—remained the fundament of Sartre's theorizing. What elicited the *Critique* was the appalling failure of almost everyone to live up to being human; Sartre's social theory took great pains to explore how *praxis* so terribly falls short of uncabined self-renewal. (Once more, Sartre was confounding a metaphysical question and a political problem. From the view that people must always shape and reshape themselves, he wanted to deduce a specific value—i.e., the value of political and social unfixedness—that should guide the myriad projects of self-creation. Sartre's conflating of metaphysics and politics is on display nicely in his pronouncement that "relations between men are always the dialectical consequence of *their activity* to precisely the extent that they arise as a transcendence of *dominating* and institutionalised human relations" [CDR, 97; emphasis of "dominating" added]. A similarly unsound conflation by Gerald Frug will shortly be criticized, in the next Part.)

Why do people submit resignedly to oppression and to social arrangements that are both ossified and cold-heartedly atomistic? To this question the *Critique* furnished one overriding response: scarcity.

> [S]carcity as a univocal relation of each and of all to matter, finally becomes an objective social structure of the material environment, and

> in that way its inert finger points to every individual as both a cause and a victim of scarcity. And everyone interiorises this structure in that by his behaviour he makes himself *a man of scarcity.* His relation to the Other *in so far as* it comes from matter is a relation of exteriority: . . . because the Other is the pure (living but abstract) possibility of the destruction of the necessary product, so that he defines himself in exteriority as a threatening but contingent possibility inherent in the product itself, as an external object. . . .
>
> In pure reciprocity, that which is Other than me *is also the same.* But in reciprocity as *modified by scarcity,* the same appears to us as anti-human in so far as *this same man* appears as radically Other—that is to say, as threatening us with death. . . . Nothing—not even wild beasts or microbes—could be more terrifying for man than a species which is intelligent, carnivorous, and cruel, and which can understand and outwit human intelligence, and whose aim is precisely the destruction of man. This, however, is obviously our own species as perceived in others by each of its members in the context of scarcity.[60]

In conditions of scarcity, relationships among people are mediated through and through by the plight of their material circumstances; in the pursuit of jointly desired goods, the happiness of each person depends on the subordinating of others. Concerted action is inevitably unstable and exceptional (and, to a chilling extent, involuntary), for antagonism—rather than generosity—rules social existence. Given these circumstances, all attempts to refashion a society's underpinnings become hopelessly ambitious. Social structures congeal as human beings are rendered passive and isolated and thus incompetent to work together for change.

In accord with his other writings, Sartre filled many of the *Critique's* pages with incisive examples of his main themes, including reification. During one such example, he condemned the so-called free market as a milieu in which "an object in the practico-inert field is the unity-outside-themselves of inter-individual relations. . . . [T]he Other produces itself as the fleeting unity of all in so far as it appears in each as a necessary *alteration* of direct reciprocity" (CDR, 278; emphasis in original). Wielding this rather dense prose, Sartre conveyed the "logic" and involution of mass impotence. The market is in most ways the classic context for self-interested individuals chasing after scarce goods; here, in a pronounced form, we should be able to perceive "atomization," an omnipresent reality of the modern world.[61] And, indeed, once we start to probe activity within markets, atomization rears its head everywhere—for example, in the determination of prices:

> *[C]ollective objects* originate in social recurrence: they represent totalizations of impracticable operations. But they do not appear at first as an object of knowledge: above all, they are realities which we are subjected to and which we live, and we learn them, in their objectivity,

> through acts which we *have to do.* The price imposes itself on me, as a buyer, because it imposes itself on my neighbour; it imposes itself on him because it imposes itself on his neighbour, and so on. . . .
>
> . . . The competitive market can be conceived of as, at most, the radical atomisation (or massification) of human groups; the ponderous reality *of price,* fixed by common disagreement, is *the collective* (valid for everyone) *expression of the impossibility of a real unity,* of an organisation of buyers (or of sellers). It does not *connect:* rather, it is the consequence of separation, and a factor of new separation; in short, it is *realised separation.* [CDR, 288, 292; emphasis in original.]

Each market actor—be it an individual or an institution[62]—is utterly estranged from, *and* wholly governed by, the assemblage of other actors. On the one hand, alienation induced by scarcity leads people to be entirely self-absorbed and to expect comparable piggishness in their fellows:

> At the outset, everyone *yields* to the gathering; he already determines it (in alterity) by his expectations, and it already eludes him and determines him. Consequently, the market exists *through him* (in itself and for him) as an object of expectation and as the fleeting determination of his action. . . .
>
> . . . [E]veryone's expectations, in a market that is supposed to be competitive, depend on the hypothesis that atomisation will remain the typical social link at least for the duration of the exchange. Thus, the unity cannot be conceived as a unifying synthesis, but as a form of dispersal as such, when this dispersal is seen as a rule and means for action. (CDR, 286; emphasis in original.)

On the other hand, each actor is linked to fellow actors in medleys of relationships that are firm, inexorable, determinative, yet never simply present. Each agent encounters fellow agents only "fleetingly" (though decisively) (CDR, 280); interpersonal ties are grounded not in warm reciprocity, but in a shared obsession with material goods (that is, with the "practico-inert").

> The intelligibility of serial [i.e., alienated] action (that is to say, of serial unity as a negative totality) derives from the relation of concrete reciprocity which unites two practical organisms *in so far as* it produces itself as conditioned by its inability to act on all the others and in so far as each of the others has the same inability within a serial field whose structure is determined by an identical relation of everyone to the common object and to its demands. [CDR, 281; emphasis in original.]

Individuals who do not work together in a deliberate and cooperative fashion will end up doing so in a haphazard and inharmonious way, as they vie for access to a deficient number of goods. They have relinquished their power for collective mobilization to the control of the practico-inert, which unifies their relations in and through their egoistic antagonisms: "[M]aterial objects will be found to determine the serial order as the social reason for the separation of individuals. . . . The totality here is the practico-inert totalisation of the series of concrete negations of every totality. . . . The *collective object* is an *index of separation*."[63] In short, markets cause everyone to be "affected by an absent change, which always occurs elsewhere and which reflects to me the image of my impotence through atomisation" (CDR, 291).

As in the preceding sections on Marx and Lukács, I shall conclude here with some terse criticisms. As before, my remarks are not—not at all—meant as a thoroughgoing critique, but as pointers toward what a full critique might amount to. First, Sartre neglected to give free rein to his most brilliant analyses. Those analyses were profound and path-breaking; although the rampant humanism of Sartre's early work still left its hideous trail in one or two of his later pages, on the whole the author of the *Critique* displaced and reinscribed his former subjectivism—often splendidly so—into a dialectical interplay between *praxis* and inert matter. That is, subjectivism was not renounced, but was situated as a mere function within a paradoxical economy.[64] For one of the many instances of Sartre's heightened sophistication, we can again refer to his unsparing assessment of free markets:

> [T]he market is not the synthetic unity of a multiplicity, but the dispersive, real multiplication of its own unity. The unity of the market is not only the foundation of the operation which everyone tries to carry out, but also something which eludes him because the very action of this atomicity is *alienating*; and, finally, it is the fact that the centre of a market is *always elsewhere* as well as always present (as the place of the gathering or as all the information about prices); and it is this very contradiction which creates the social object. It is precisely this contradiction that enables the unity of the gathering to be not simply *transcended* by common action (as happens when there is a direct agreement between producers or consumers), or even by [individual] action, but on the contrary to present itself both as the common object of an action and as the rigid, external law of every particular action, that is to say, to exist in the manner of an instrumental object, 'to hand,' 'before one's eyes' and as an objective but alien necessity in every one of us.[65]

Sartre was not simply "rectifying" his early outlook by giving social entanglements their due. It was not a question, for him, of mixing some constraint and some leeway in a sophisticated balance or blend;[66] instead, he recognized, social theory must embrace both subjectivity and objectivity *pushed to their extreme limits*, each to the exclusion and each to the entailment of the other. For human subjects, everything will always already have been fixed, and everything will always have yet to be determined.

In light of these paradoxes, however, one must opine that Sartre failed to think through adequately the inconceivable disarticulation of his whole project. His underlying quest could "be formulated in the following terms: on what conditions is the knowledge *of a History* possible? To what extent can the connections brought to light be *necessary*?" (CDR, 40; emphasis in original). When one's aim is to "apprehend [the dialectic] as *the intelligibility* of the [historical] process in question" (CDR, 37; emphasis in original), one has not carried the dialectic far enough. Intelligibility itself must be situated and challenged—an imperative to which Sartre seemed curiously resistant:

> [M]an has to struggle not only against nature, and against the social environment which has produced him, and against other men, but also against his own action as it becomes other. This primitive type of alienation occurs within other forms of alienation, but it is independent of them, and, in fact, is their foundation. In other words, we shall reveal, through it, that a permanent anti-*praxis* is a new and necessary moment of *praxis*. If we do not try to define this moment, historical intelligibility—that is, certainty within the complexity of temporal development—loses one of its essential moments and is transformed into unintelligibility. [CDR, 124–25.]

By neglecting to follow through on his greatest insights, Sartre was much less daring in what he did (or in what he tried to do) than in what he said.

Second, throughout his life Sartre clung to his belief in a primal fissure between consciousness and insensate objects. This belief found expression so repeatedly in his works that it would be pointless to give quotation after quotation. Even in the *Critique*, he was endeavoring to establish "the heuristic value of the dialectical method when applied to the human sciences [as opposed to the natural sciences], and the necessity, with any fact, provided it is *human* [as opposed to natural], of reinserting it within the developing totalisation and understanding it on this basis" (CDR, 66; emphasis in original). Because this shortcoming of Sartre's work has been criticized elsewhere,[67] and because the spirit/nature dichotomy will receive careful attention in the next Part, we need not go into depth here. Suffice it to observe that at least two powerful methods of impugning such a dichotomy have gained salience in recent years: the deconstructive approach, favored in my critique of Hume, which shows that nature and spirit implicate and exclude each other in an irresolvable paradox; and the pragmatist approach, which relativizes the spirit/nature dualism by arguing that each of its two sides will always be already "under description."[68] With those approaches, one can spirit away the spirit/nature distinction into a more spirited line of thought.

Third, severe problems beset the role of "scarcity" throughout the *Critique*. Sartre's use of this concept was ambiguous and unconvincing. At a few points, he assigned "scarcity" *("rareté")* much the same status that Lacanians have ascribed to "lack" *("manque")*. (Note that the French word *"manque"* can refer to economic scarcity as well as to a more general lack.) That is, Sartre appeared at times to denote by "scarcity" what Lukács termed "objectification": the irreducible gap between a subject and the various objects of her desire, knowledge, and production. Under this definition, scarceness would amount to the unavoidability and centrality of difference (with a resultant lack of plenitude) that must thwart ultimate satisfaction or epistemological assuredness. It would loom as the inability of consciousness to close off its own movement and to leave its "unhappy" state (till death has parted it from itself). Between Eden and Judgment, totalizing *praxis* can but perpetuate itself through its own failure. Such, at any rate would appear to be the import of claims that "[s]carcity, as the lived relation of a practical multiplicity to surrounding materiality within that multiplicity itself, is the basis of the possibility of human history. . . . [T]o say that our History is a history of men is equivalent to saying that it is born and developed within the permanent framework of a field of tension produced by scarcity" (CDR, 125). If we read these statements as a Lacanian might, then Sartre's various examples of reified behavior and institutions would be results of a general process (of differentiation) that takes place everywhere at all times. Such a position would by no means be free of problems,[69] but it could serve as a vital moment within a deconstructive analysis.

It seems clear, however, that Sartre usually had in mind a different meaning of "scarcity." For the most part, he distinguished scarcity from objectification, and he argued that the former condition is determinate and contingent whereas the latter is inextirpable. Scarcity is coeval with history as we know it, but "[i]t is perfectly possible to conceive of a dialectical *praxis*, or even of labour, without scarcity" (CDR, 124). We can transcend scarcity, although objectification—or, as Sartre called it, "counter-finality"—would "still necessarily subsist."[70] According to this view, scarcity is shortage; more specifically, it is a remediable shortage of basic goods. Such goods, if available, would allow each person to satisfy her most pressing needs.

Now, even if we put to one side the problem of defining essential "needs," we have encountered a glaring weakness in Sartre's thought. Once scarcity is construed in relatively mundane terms, it cannot easily play its role as the "basic abstract matrix of every reification of human relations in any society" (CDR, 132). Sartre perceived scarceness as a contingent fact rather than as a structuring dynamic which subsumes all contingent facts and which has made such facts possible. Having defined scarcity in this fashion, as less than elemental, he could not—with any measure of plausibility—proceed to deduce from it the atomizing unhappiness of our modern life. His examples of reified behavior now seem like crude attempts at a quasi-functionalist social theory. It is utterly unconvincing to light upon one feature of past or present society and then educe from it all the other features; it is unconvincing, not because it cannot be done but because it *can* be done all too easily. As Michel Foucault argued, "[t]hese kinds of deduction are always possible. They are simultaneously correct and false. Above all they are too glib, because one can always do exactly the opposite" (P/K, 100). Little wonder is it that Sartre's theory has been reproached as facile and ethnocentric.[71]

Finally, Sartre endorsed a fiendishly problematic notion of time in both his early work and his later work (which can be demarcated as "early" writing and "later" writing only through such a notion of temporality). This shortcoming plagued the "dialectical *praxis*" of his *Critique* as much as the "existential choice" of *L'Être et Le Néant*. In each case, Sartre tried to keep the past and the future clearly separated. In *L'Être et Le Néant*, subjectivity was seen as an "instantaneous nucleus" (BN, 116), a nonbeing that—in its constant flight from itself—continuously divides sheer presence into a past that always is already receding and a future that always is already arriving. Along the same lines, the *Critique* saw human history as "an orientation towards the future and a totalizing preservation of the past."[72] Once more, Sartre declined to carry his own insights far enough or against themselves. Brilliantly, he reduced the present to a relationship between anteriority and posteriority, but he never came to terms with the paradoxical seesaws that accompanied this reduction. Symptomatic is his conservative scorn for the antinomies of motion put forth by Zeno of Elea (which I delineated in Chapter 1). Like Aristotle's *Physics*, *L'Être et Le Néant* construed Zeno's Paradox of the Arrow—which demonstrates that a flying arrow will never fly—as a failed disproof of the possibility of motion (BN, 286–90). Sartre in his text responded by emphasizing the continuous flow of time, which precludes any isolation of instants. As Zeno himself seemed to be aware, however,[73] his Arrow Paradox was more unnerving than Sartre would have us think. As was argued in my first chapter, Zeno had proved that holding time to be a continuum without moments is as inconceivable and self-disruptive as holding it to be discontinuous (i.e., composed of discrete moments, each of which is instantaneously present).[74] The incoherence of each of these conceptions of time will have imposed the other conception on us, which leads us back to the first conception and so forth, in never-ending reversals. Moreover, Zeno's paradox showed—through its deconstruction of "instants"—that the future, the present, and the past will have intertwined so uncannily as to overwhelm someone who purports to have made sense of historical unfolding (or of individual human lives). By linearizing time, Sartre cast his lot with "one of the deepest adherences [of modern philosophy] . . . to the history of classical ontology."[75] Even an apostle of individual freedom can be too uncritically a product of his environment.

D. Critical Legal Scholarship and Reification: Peter Gabel

Before moving to Part Two, this chapter briefly expounds "Reification in Legal Reasoning" by Peter Gabel. Gabel is important not just because he is a long-standing member of the critical legal studies movement—which has functioned (at least implicitly) as a target and backdrop for many arguments in this book, and which furnishes the direct context for Part Two of this chapter—but additionally because he weaves together some of the main ideas propounded by Marx, Lukács, and Sartre. To avoid tedious reiteration of points made earlier, I shall not conclude my summarizing of Gabel's work with brief critical remarks like those in the prior sections. This decidedly does not mean that Gabel's article is perceived here as beyond all reproof; indeed, his work displays the shortcomings of its theoretical forebears in an especially pronounced form.

Of the several dichotomies that structure "Reification in Legal Reasoning," the most important are "abstract/concrete," "imaginary/real," and "socially communicated/experiential." Each dualism acquires special force in the light of Gabel's prime starting point: "I take it as given at the outset of this essay that human relationships within contemporary capitalism are characterized by a traumatic absence of connectedness that does not wish to become conscious of itself" (RLR, 28). In Gabel's view, the felt reality of modern capitalism is rank impotence, isolation, and ennui. This stark reality is a basic experiential fact of which everyone has to be aware, at least at a prereflective level. However, despite being pre-reflectively in touch with their sorry state, most people have failed to recognize just how hellish their society is. They may share a "dim and intuitive comprehension that something is very wrong" (RLR, 27), but they have little or no knowledge about the rich possibilities of human life that they are forgoing. For this failure of understanding Gabel gives us a ready explanation: "[N]o one is normally aware of his or her sense of unconnectedness, passivity, impotence, and isolation, because this felt reality is *denied* by the socially communicated reality." People collectively play down the ghastliness of their lives by communicating to one another a reality that "substitutes a harmonious abstract world for the concrete alienation that characterizes . . . lived experience" (RLR,

28, 26; emphasis in original). The obscuring of felt realities by the socially communicated reality is brought about *en masse* through techniques of systematic and self-imposed delusion. Through these techniques we generate "an imaginary feeling of 'with-ness' by restoring the feeling of being-in-a-group in an imaginary way" (RLR, 45).

Chief among the patterns of discourse that have shaped imaginary cohesion is the reifying of abstract generalities plucked from concrete experience. Gabel detects such reification at the core of judicial reasoning; the bulk of his article is devoted to a "phenomenology of the legal opinion" (RLR, 29–42). Like everybody else, judges are passivized within roles that force them to carry out certain functions, and the distinctive function of the judiciary is "to give each of us the impression that the system operates according to a normative law. The law is a denial, at the level of social interpretation, of our collective experience of illegitimacy" (RLR, 29). When called upon for the task of healing disputes, a judge apprehends particular sets of data against the background of the entire social field: "[H]e has a sense of the whole culture all at once that he passivizes into the movement of a quasi-object, such that each discrete situation of facts reveals itself to his mind against the . . . total 'factual' context from which the law has emerged" (RLR, 31). A judge grasps the "total context" in line with its quotidian functioning as a system—a system that agrees with our common sense of what the world *is* and of what it *should* be. This "common sense" is the socially communicated reality of advanced capitalism; to repair disruptions in the communicated reality is the essential work of judicial reasoning.

When a judge calls to mind the "total factual context," she discerns—or, rather, takes as a given—myriad regularities of collective conduct. These regularities, which Gabel views as "intersubjective relations that have been mutated, through alienation, into relations of interlocking roles and functions" (RLR, 31), are reified and transformed by judges into movers and shakers of the social world. A judge "must abstract legitimizing concepts from the normal movement of the facts, concretize the abstractions, and then re-describe the facts with the aid of these abstractions. . . . [I]t will appear that the functioning of the system is simply the factual activity of the legitimating concepts, thereby representing the system itself as legitimate a priori" (RLR, 37, 38.) That is to say, notions such as "rights," "duties," and "privileges" are portrayed as causing the very patterns of conduct from which they grow. Though they are nothing more than abstractions drawn from regularized behavior, these rubrics tend to become the stars in a fantastical drama that has pushed real people offstage. In relying on these abstractions, judges bestow a normative veneer on their "common sense," and they grasp the social world "as if it . . . were an object, immutably moving according to its own internal dynamic. . . . What is presupposed is the inevitability of the system as it is in its normal movement" (RLR, 32, 35). Socially communicated reality, seen as functioning in compliance with laws in both a moral and a descriptive sense, has come to appear both necessary and desirable. As Gabel states:

> In order to legalize the normal movement of the social field, each party must be conceptualized as possessing certain universal normative "properties" signifying that the way people do function together normally is also the way people should function together normally. These properties are called "rights" and "duties." Within any fact-situation of whatever kind, each party is presumed to have a "right" to the other's normal functioning (e.g., prompt delivery of the goods, driving at normal speed), and each party is also presumed to have a "duty" to function normally toward the other. . . . [RLR, 39.]
>
> It follows from this that a "rule of law" is merely the normative reification of function—it is a way of describing a normal practice that has been generated by pressures within the system in a legitimating conceptual form. [RLR, 40.]

Within a structure that has been reified and exalted, each dispute appears as a threatening aberration from proper orderliness. Any disequilibrium in the normal operating of social life must be repaired at all costs, for—as Gabel repeatedly reminds us—our "common sense" of imaginary cohesion never can escape being imperiled by the dim "sense of illegitimacy that everyone feels in response to the system's normal functioning" (RLR, 32). We have arrived at the very heart of judicial reasoning:

> In order to grasp the way that the judge derives legal concepts from his apprehension of the social field, we must remember that his intention is to adjudicate a dispute in such a way that the system will be restored to a normal and legitimated equilibration in the realm of thought. . . . [RLR, 38.]
>
> The system is in disequilibration and the judge is asked to state its law, which, as we can now begin to see, is nothing more than the legitimating conceptual representation of its normal functioning. [RLR, 39.]

In the course of legitimizing the *status quo*, specific results will matter hardly at all; whoever wins or loses in a specific case, the capitalist system as a whole will be the ultimate victor.

> [T]he outcome is significant only in its effect on the collective imagination of the culture, because the outcome "is" nothing more than the signification of an image. . . . [I]t is but an incidental concrete aspect of the ritual through which law is brought into the world. In the "legal world" that is signified in the judge's opinion, the signification that

the buyer "wins" because her "right" has been "violated" is to express the necessary imaginary "outcome" of an imaginary interaction between essentially fictional characters. To the extent that people share in the judge's experience as it is signified in the opinion, they come to believe in a "legal order" that directs the concrete truth of daily life. [RLR, 41–42.]

Part Two

This Part builds on the themes and analytical postures summarized in Part One; those postures will be transvalued and rewritten, rather than be extended in a seemingly simple way. What follows is not so much an essay on deconstruction as an attempt to furnish a critique of reification that absorbs deconstructive insights. But this chapter does not propose to summon necessary political consequences from deconstructive methodologies. Such an enterprise would not pay due heed to the most vertiginous aspects of deconstructive thought.[76] Instead, this chapter will discuss reification in assorted ways designed to appeal to someone who values Derrida's work. That is, it takes for granted the principal ideas of deconstruction, and it inscribes many such ideas—explicitly and self-consciously—into discourses on reification and fetishism.

In rewriting the concepts that have been criticized heretofore, this Part does not undertake a "reconstruction" (at least as that term is commonly and naively understood). As this chapter has suggested already, reconstruction is but one moment in a deconstructive seesaw between negation and affirmation.[77] This seesaw should be incorporated explicitly rather than be dodged unsuccessfully; one should not aim to rid oneself of all weak spots by "surpassing" the deconstructionist movement, but to make one's vulnerable position less worrisome by exposing it systematically. A self-critical discourse can never be immune from future attacks, but it can anticipate them to some degree and thereby render them less destructive. As Nietzsche urged: "A very popular error: having the courage of one's convictions; rather it is a matter of having the courage for an *attack* on one's convictions!"[78] Deconstructive theory, as a result of anticipating countercritiques and noting its own problems of incoherence, will position itself to seize on problems of incoherence that ravage countercritiques. Its power is made perfect in weakness, its own weakness. Because all critiques become implicated in what they censure, and because careful deconstructionist writing will have stayed keenly alert to both the general dissemination of paradoxes by transference and the specific maelstroms of many of its own paradoxes, our anticipating countercritiques by helping them with their work may be the most adroit way to gain some leverage in deconstructing countercritiques. Complacent parries will highlight their own weak spots by fastening upon weak spots that have been highlighted in a deconstructionist discourse. At that point, where a deliberate nondefense has become the best defense, battles will be less over (in)coherency and illogic than over competing ways in which incoherency can articulate itself.

Analyses in this Part are not derived from close deconstructive readings of the thinkers discussed earlier. Such readings could nicely serve as a fruitful point of departure for a transformed view of reification, but they would extend this chapter unduly. It should be underscored once again that the brief critical comments in the sections on Marx, Lukács, and Sartre were intended only to hint at pathways that deconstructive readings might take; I most surely do not profess to have offered any detailed prescriptions for such readings. This Part, then, is not a *direct* critique of the works summarized in Part One. Though my argument will try to alter the ways we think about Marx and his successors, it will do so through a deferred engagement—through a diversionary attack that can displace the main battle front. By shifting the terms of battle, and by rewriting the classic views of reification, this fifth chapter will stake out what is left of critical jurisprudence once deconstructive methods gain currency. Along the way, it will have sought to transfigure one's conception of what a legal theory (or any theory) should be.

Hereafter, this Part will be divided into two sections. The first section puts forth some sweeping methodological considerations; whereas the second will concentrate on reification, as that phenomenon has been analyzed in Marxism and in critical legal studies. One should not make too much, however, of the discontinuity between these two major sections. Some of the most important threads of the argument emerge only in the detailed analyses of the second section.

A. General Methodology

In certain ways, the positions here advocated will resemble antifoundationalism and neo-pragmatism of the sort favored by Stanley Fish, Ludwig Wittgenstein, Richard Rorty, and others. These theorists affirm that all realities are shaped in contextualizing practices and procedures of social life. Things are defined socially, in the sense that they have to be encountered and grasped "under description," or through "interpretative assumptions," or in the course of a "language game." For the neo-pragmatists, "truth," "goodness," and other philosophic ideals are relativized and thrown into history; such ideals will hardly ever lack meanings, but each meaning will be specific to some context or other (which may, of course, be quite broad). "Brute facts" are seen as interpretations that are so widely shared and so unswervingly presupposed as to have been draped with "bruteness." Like all other things, such brute facts can be defined and categorized only through some contingent discoursive structure. Language's classifying schemes, then, are the unliftable "painted veil which those who live [c]all life."[79]

One scarcely should deny pragmatism's critical power. Yet one must be wary of adopting such a position wholesale, for it will lead to as many problems as it putatively clears up. More specifically, we can find a deep contradiction that upends and displaces pragmatism. This contradiction proves to be highly subtle, and does not stem flagrantly from what might be called the "self-refuting dynamic" of nihilistic versions of skepticism. Some critics have maintained, rather sophomorically, that the basic message of pragmatism is as inimical to itself as to the philosophies it attacks: if all truths are indeed relative, then so too must be the claim that "all truths are relative." But the pragmatist message is a relativistic one, and—as was underscored in my first chapter, which distinguished a nihilistic standpoint from a relativistic standpoint—the "problem" of self-embracement will *confirm* rather than *confute* relativistic species of skepticism. Hence, we discover that the issue of self-embracement has been skillfully handled by Richard Rorty and Stanley Fish. "The question of whether the Pragmatist view of truth [as 'what is good in the way of belief'] . . . is itself *true*," Rorty writes, "is thus a question about whether a post-Philosophical culture is a good thing to try for."[80] Fish likewise takes a position that does its utmost not to be a position:

> I have been saying that all arguments are made within assumptions and presuppositions that are themselves subject to challenge and change. Well, isn't that also an argument, and one therefore that is no more securely based than the arguments it seeks to dislodge? The answer, of course, is yes; but the answer is also "so what?" According to the position presented here, no one can claim privilege for the point of view he holds and therefore everyone is obliged to practice the art of persuasion. This includes me, and persuasion is the art that I have been trying to practice here. . . . Another way to put this is to say that the fact that I am subject to the same challenge I have put to my predecessors is not a weakness in my position but a restatement of it. The idea of a position that was invulnerable to challenge makes sense only if you believe in the possibility of a position innocent of assumptions; this of course is exactly what I do not believe and therefore the fact that my assumptions are capable of being dislodged does not refute my argument but confirms it, because it is an extension of it. [ITTC, 368.]

These retorts are hardly decisive, as they fail to include a self-encompassing clause; but they show that the playful dodging of neo-pragmatists is more subtle than their heavy-handed detractors seem to think. The "self-refuting dynamic" argument can therefore be put aside. Nor need we concern ourselves with the charge that pragmatism inevitably and *simply* collapses into immaterialism. Rorty has argued quite convincingly that a neo-pragmatist can and should remain an agnostic in the debate between realists and idealists, and that the best tactic for handling this debate is to flip between the two viewpoints undecidably.[81]

Of interest here is a somewhat different problem, a problem both of continuity and of genesis. To see this problem, we must turn pragmatist theses against themselves, albeit more subtly than in the "self-refuting dynamic" argument. Reality, so the neo-pragmatist thinks, can be regarded most usefully as a changing function of the discoursive networks and hermeneutic devices that come to be in place at a given time. This position (or nonposition) has left out an essential query: what is the status of the discoursive networks and the interpretive devices through which we grasp reality? How are they themselves grasped? Both the starting and the continuation of an interpretative group will have hinged on the ability of its members to hold a common set of beliefs. But how does someone "hold a set of beliefs"? If such beliefs arise only in a framework of antecedent beliefs, then pragmatists will be hurling toward an infinite regress, in which the moment of interpretation cannot arrive. Every clump of beliefs will have depended fully on a preceding clump of beliefs, *ad infinitum*. If, on the other hand, one's interpretive assumptions are deemed to be apprehended outside other beliefs, we shall be thrown back upon the unthinkability (of pre-interpreted knowledge) that had made pragmatism so tempting in the first place. Pragmatism leads straightaway into what it rules out, because it can supply the conditions of interpretation—which, in myriad forms, are held to make *all* knowledge interpretive—only by imputing to *them* the outlawed status of pre-interpretive knowledge. The start of interpretation will have to be its deferral, a deferral both originary and continuous.[82]

Thus, for example, every member of one of Stanley Fish's "interpretive communities" will be shaped and maintained as such by the texts she reads (and by the people to whom she talks). Apart from some miraculous inspiration, she has no *other* way of belonging to a hermeneutic community. At every point in time she must begin or renew contact with her assumptions, from an outlook that cannot presuppose those very assumptions—for if it does presuppose them, it cannot be used to establish them. If it incorporates them already, then *ipso facto* it will be emerging too late to *introduce* them (and to *reintroduce* them at each moment). To acknowledge this point, however, and to avert an infinite regress, Fish will have to renounce his primary insight that "strategies exist prior to the act of reading and therefore determine the shape of what is read rather than, as is usually assumed, the other way around" (ITTC, 14). Here, as elsewhere, the interpretive strategies cannot provide their own portal or their own grounding; they can never already be established before they have been established. Thus, every apparent "ground" of contextualization will itself need to be "grounded," and will ergo involve an endless vortex of ungraspable hermeneutic assumptions, or will require an acontextual stopping point—shorn of any hermeneutic assumptions—that Fish has stoutly and correctly proscribed. This blind spot will undo any pragmatist approach, for, strictly speaking, it renders pragmatism unthinkable.

That pragmatism has overturned itself does not mean that it can or should be discarded. To deconstruct the pragmatist view, one has to rely on it—which would suggest that pragmatism is not so much wrong as both completely wrong and completely right. Pragmatism must amount to a truly critical strategy that highlights its own impossible situation; anything more than this, *or anything less than this*, comes from evil. To be sure, as has been noted above, Rorty and his predecessors and followers have striven to disavow any programmatic intentions: "James, [for example,] when he said that 'the true is what is good in the way of belief' was simply trying to debunk epistemology; he was not offering a 'theory of truth'" (CP, 97). What pragmatism leaves out, nonetheless—*du moins* at a clearly thematized level—is the inconceivability of its demystifying crusades, even when they are put forth as a nonposition. The critical force of pragmatist philosophy is unthinkable, and it is this unthinkability which must be *thought out* and hence pushed audaciously to the fore. In the process (which will be a process of finding points of articulation between neo-pragmatism and deconstructive philosophy), we shall have to highlight questions that remain ancillary in the writings of neo-pragmatists: questions of strategy and struggle. Some of the major themes of pragmatism will have to be displaced into a more self-critical posture.

Thus, while exploring significant relations between neo-pragmatism and deconstructive philosophy, this section will bring out several important differences that forestall any neat conflation of the two modes of thought. But if we cannot assimilate them without aporias, neither can we turn pragmatism and deconstruction into a tidy dualism. Such a strategy "presupposes that the entities in question are fully homogeneous, identical to themselves in their antithesis."[83] If each position indeed differs from itself as much as it differs from the other standpoint, then the relationship between the two doctrines is more elusive than it may seem initially. We may conclude that pragmatism and deconstruction subvert themselves as they must subvert each other, but we should not deny that they proceed differently. Anyone who ventures to take account of the differences between these two modes of self-derangement—differences that should not be underestimated—will find that, to an irreducibly large extent, they always will remain to be analyzed.

One particularly useful strand of at least some versions of pragmatism is a full-scale challenge to the distinction between *Naturwissenschaften* and *Geisteswissenschaften*. As was pointed out earlier (in my critique of Sartre), pragmatists maintain that all natural objects are as much "under description" as are all sociocultural events; neither type of phenomenon will have made itself transparently present in unadorned immediacy. In this way, the Book of Nature is as much open to conflicting interpretations as is the Book of Job. No form of the spirit/nature distinction can withstand scrutiny, for no particular argot—scientific or otherwise—can enjoy solid metaphysical guarantees. At most, disciplines can be marked off by the salience of certain terms in their respective vocabularies. To hope for anything more than this, to think that a scientific language is more "objective" than other forms of discourse, is to fall prey to the "bad old metaphysical notion that the universe is made up [ontologically] of two kinds of things" (PMN, 351).

Now, as was briefly mentioned, a deconstructive approach to the spirit/nature dichotomy proceeds in a rather different fashion: it argues that each side of the dichotomy implicates and excludes the other in a relentless double bind. But a deconstructive critic could alternatively join hands with the neo-pragmatists, so long as the latter camp's position is suitably transformed. Not only must all types of phenomena be always "under description," but all descriptions (including those of pragmatism and deconstructionist texts) dismantle their own claims through the very feat of expressing them. Every theory—be it critical or apologetic, technical or exhortative, scientific or literary—can be shown to efface itself through the irresolvable paradoxes of its own arguments. No more than cultural or political texts, can scientific vocabularies escape the paradoxical dislocations of *différance*.[84] Given the basic themes of deconstruction—which have already been expounded and are here presupposed, and which are of course subject to their own critique—the spirit/nature dyad will not have vanished *tout court*, but each of its sides will be engulfed by antinomies.

One can make some broadly similar points about the split between facts and values. The pragmatist would regard such a dichotomy as contestable and variable—perhaps unavoidable and ubiquitous *in abstracto* (i.e., necessary in *some* form or another), but ascribable to agreement (rather than to imperatives of ontology) in its actualized contours. Like questions about "what *should* be," all questions about "what *is*" must be formulated and solved within a medley of hermeneutic conventions. Pragmatism's war against the "Myth of the Given" has induced, not surprisingly, an impatience with those theorists who yearn to step outside language to delve for brute facts. When William James defined "truth" as "whatever proves itself to be good in the way of belief," and when John Dewey defined "truth" as "warranted assertibility," they blurred and relativized the perceived split between facticity and ethics.[85] On the whole, they remade the value/fact diremption into a pair of concepts less fraught, or less naively fraught, with metaphysical implications: agreement versus disagreement. Issues that are well settled within a given community (whether they concern "what *is*" or "what *should* take place") will be deemed "factual"; issues that are more hotly disputed will be deemed "value-laden."[86]

Once again, deconstructive critics can follow pragmatists' lead. (Alternatively, of course, a deconstructor could show that the relationship between "facts" and "values" is one of total and irreducible co-inscription as well as mutual exclusion.) Factual propositions and happenings, as much as moral debates, will undergo deconstruction implicitly or explicitly at all times. "Nothing . . . is anywhere ever simply present or absent. There are only, everywhere, differences and traces of traces"—i.e., units that unravel their own identities, through the differentiation that amounts to their active source as well as their passive product (*Positions*, 26). One can have no reason to think that discourses on so-called facts will skirt the mind-gnarling paradoxes that accompany moral discourse. Facts and values alike are generated by "the systematic play of differences, of the traces of differences, of the *spacing* by means of which elements are related to each other. This spacing is the simultaneously active and passive . . . production of the intervals without which the 'full' terms would not signify, would not function" (*Positions*, 27). Whether this means we should concur with the pragmatists in their focusing anew on "agreement versus disagreement" is a more tangled problem, which will be posed in the next main section.

Another point on which deconstructive critics can side with neopragmatist thinkers is their impeaching of fixed dichotomies between theory and action (or discourse and production). Here the target takes many forms. Most notable is the tendency of Marxism to erect firm dividers between work and discoursive interaction. This shows up, for example, in a great many of the writings of Jurgen Habermas, and in a somewhat self-flagellatory pronouncement by Fredric Jameson:

> One cannot without intellectual dishonesty assimilate the "production" of texts (or in Althusser's version of this homology, the "production" of new and more scientific concepts) to the production of goods by factory workers: writing and thinking are not alienated labor in that sense, and it is surely fatuous for intellectuals to seek to glamorize their tasks—which can for the most part be subsumed under the rubric of the elaboration, reproduction, or critique of ideology—by assimilating them to real work on the assembly line and to the experience of the resistance of matter in genuine manual labor.[87]

For Marx himself, most of the time, the separateness of theory and action was *une donnée:*

> The question of whether objective truth can be attributed to human thinking is not a question of theory but is a *practical* question. Man must prove the truth, that is, the reality and power, the this-sidedness of his thinking in practice. The dispute over the reality or non-reality of thinking which is isolated from practice is a purely *scholastic* question. . . .
>
> The philosophers have only *interpreted* the world, in various ways; the point, however, is to *change* it.[88]

For the pragmatist and the deconstructive critic, a reinterpreting of the world *is* a changing of it, because interpretation defined narrowly is but one form of interpretation as it is understood here. We may extend "interpretation" to cover *all* kinds of social practices, natural phenomena, and individual actions; everything from physics to literary criticism to basket weaving should be construed as part of an amalgam of operations through which beings of every type—both outward things and our inner selves—have fixed and transformed their sundry interrelationships. In this way, the arrangement of people in a factory or the movement of celestial bodies will be as much a (self-)description or (self-)interpretation as will the series of words throughout a book. Phenomena in "real life" always unfold and gain their structure in ways that are essentially tantamount to the ways in which discourses develop. What we classify as "material production" will be one species of interpretation, not *fundamentally* distinguishable from other species. Though discourse and production can never *simply* or *finally* be collapsed into each other, they can be subsumed under our broad rubric of "interpretation." Michael Ryan has suggested this point: "[D]iscursive operations in texts cannot be declared an other to a real presence of substance in society; social life is itself constituted as a network of representations, relations, and discursive practices."[89] Showing even greater acuity, Thomas Heller has made an argument that blurs the distinction between natural phenomena and discourse:

> [T]he case for extending structuralism beyond language depends not on some attribution of consciousness to organic unities, but rather on a redefinition of the concept of subjectivity. The mediating institution need not be defined by its assertion of self-consciousness. If the subject is transfigured into the locus in which the structure is instantiated, there is no reason why such a locus must have a . . . biological character. The deconstruction of the natural or existential subject would permit the extension of structuralist analysis beyond linguistics.[90]

As one might very likely presume, a deconstructive writer subjects the pragmatist theses to a crucial displacement. When Derrida says that "[t]here is nothing outside the text" (OG, 158, 163), he is not merely stating pragmatist claims in highly colorful language.[91] His point, rather, is that all areas of existence—from literary texts to nuclear particles to political institutions—entail the sorts of uncanny oscillations that Derrida has highlighted in philosophical works. Every social practice (as well as every natural phenomenon) comprises myriad forms of categorization, and hence has always succumbed to a vertiginous interplay between samenesses and difference. Relationality and identity will forever constitute and subvert each other in "real life," just as much as in any discourse; the elements of specific circumstances in real life will have interknit and undone themselves through paradoxical dislocations, quite as much as the signifying elements of a text. Such dislocations should be regarded purely as epistemological (i.e., as bearing exclusively on conception and observation) and purely as ontological (i.e., as immanent in the world, whether perceived or not), and therefore as neither ontological nor epistemological. In *all* areas of existence, paradoxical interactions will have eluded and comprehended the breach between ontology and epistemology—a breach that emerges as reciprocal prioritization and complete interpenetration. For this illogical logic Derrida has come up with an array of terms: "*différance*," "textuality," "supplementarity," and so forth. To convey the fully generalized reach of presence/difference aporias and of structure/event antinomies, we may coin here the phrase "discoursive movement." What deconstructive critiques highlight is an uncanny logic, usually associated with discourse (that is, with *texts* in a narrow sense of the word), but also determining the movement of what we class as "non-discoursive" reality. Deconstruction "will provide itself the means with which to intervene in the field of oppositions that it criticizes, *which is also a field of nondiscursive forces*" (MP, 329; emphasis added). Paradoxes of differentiation and of structures-and-their-events must turn up everywhere.

That the fact/value and discourse/action dichotomies have been placed in doubt (though not once and for all obliterated) will not afford an unproblematic valence between metaphysics and politics. One's challenging and rewriting of the fact/value distinction for *some* purposes will not bar one from trading on it for *other* purposes. Indeed, efforts to collapse issues of politics and issues of metaphysics can lead to highly dubious arguments, as the following passage by Gerald Frug may indicate: "I use the ideal of participatory democracy . . . to refer to the process by which people create for themselves the form of organized existence within which they live. Only by creating these forms together can people confront the intersubjective nature of social life."[92] Here Frug combines a metaphysical usage and a political usage of the word "create." When he describes "democracy" as "the process by which people create for themselves the form of organized existence within which they live," he appears to envision people acting together in a fluid, egalitarian arrangement that promotes a high level of community-focused participation. (One might note, however, that the words "create for themselves" can be misread as pertaining to *all* forms of society, including the extremely hierarchical forms. Slaves, too, create the world in which they suffer from bondage.) But when Frug proceeds to argue that "[o]nly by creating these forms together can people confront the intersubjective nature of social life," he has shifted to a new meaning of "create." His contention here will hold up—though it will become clearly tautological—only if "create" is regarded as a general (metaphysical) term without a specific bearing on politics. If "create" is construed in a politically leftist sense, Frug's assertion will be invalid. Thus, in seeking to draw his democratic objectives from his neo-pragmatist theses (in a move profoundly religious, where intersubjectivity has replaced God), Frug has too hastily bridged the gap between metaphysics and politics, and has thus produced a non sequitur. He might endeavor to salvage his assertion by stipulating that to "confront the intersubjective nature of social life" is, precisely, to adopt democratic arrangements; but that would reduce his claim to an empty pleonasm—and a highly misleading one, at that. The turbulent waters in the passage that might join metaphysics and politics have claimed yet another shipwreck of someone trying to navigate them with ease.

Affinities between pragmatism and deconstruction again turn up when one tries to give an account of "easy cases." A pragmatist regards easy cases, whether they be judicial decisions or events in some other field, as flowing from widely credited assumptions. Easy cases do not enjoy a privileged metaphysical stature; they simply can be resolved posthaste within the hermeneutic conventions of a given society. They are easy *because* they will so quickly inspire agreement. They take place "within an agreed-upon set of conventions about what counts as a relevant contribution, what counts as answering a question, what counts as having a good argument for that answer or a good criticism of it" (PMN, 320).

This pragmatist view receives two jolts from a deconstructive analysis. First, the deconstructive critic should realize that explaining uncontroversial cases by positing the existence of widely shared beliefs is, by some standards, not truly an explanation at all; it is like tracing the soporific power of opium to its dormitive faculty. The obvious circularity of the neo-pragmatist view—which is recognized with composure by at least some pragmatists—should not be perceived as an unduly shuddersome and debilitating vice that ought to have been avoided, but should instead bring us to reformulate our ideas of what constitutes an adequate "explanation." One need not accept Hart's worry that a circular explanation is useless. Each of us may indeed be a "purveyor of truth," but, when made explicit, that can be an advantage even more than a disadvantage.[93]

Much the same might be said about another grave problem that confronts neo-pragmatists, the problem that was raised briefly near the beginning of this section: *viz.*, the daunting fact that a pragmatist depiction of easy cases' analytical contexts must fall prey to a charge of incoherence. Widely shared interpretive strategies must themselves be grasped at each moment, but any effort to grasp them will provoke an infinite regress or will demand a presupposition-free interpretive outlook that pragmatists themselves have so sharply put into question. But it would be rash to conclude that neo-pragmatism can be once and for all discarded. Rather, one might profitably conclude that pragmatism should more designedly situate its strategic force within deconstruction; that is, it should put itself to work against and within various philosophies even while it contests its power to do so. Self-criticism must play a leading role—to anticipate and defuse challenges from other perspectives, and to incorporate the resistless paradoxes that undermine those other perspectives (just as much as they foil one's own arguments). One must generalize the approach favored by Catharine MacKinnon: "Feminism affirms women's point of view by revealing, criticizing, and explaining its impossibility."[94] There is of course no pat strategy for interrogating one's own perspective, just as there is no magic formula for deconstructing other positions. Whatever may be the tactics, we shall have forced ourselves to impugn the very dichotomy between "other positions" and "one's own perspective."

Apart from the emphasis on self-reflection, a deconstructive account of "easy cases" will look quite different (in some characteristic ways) from the pragmatist understanding outlined above. Determinacy, for deconstructive critics, presents itself as a function or a moment in an unstoppable interweaving of fixed structures and free play. Determinacy and indeterminacy generate as well as exclude each other in a process that is itself both indeterminate and determinate. Amid the paradoxes that make up a general economy of *différance*, varied patterns of differentiation or self-subversion—which are generally not recognized as self-subversion, and which are actively structuring as well as passively structured—become more prominent than other such patterns, in an effect that we may call "highlighting." This effect, which is a condition of indeterminacy as well as of determinacy, has been described by Thomas Heller: "A case is easy when particular settled practices are reproduced across time without theoretical reexamination."[95] Derrida has made much the same point more strongly: "[T]he production of differences, *différance*, is not astructural: it produces systematic and regulated transformations which are able, at a certain point, to leave room for a structural science. The concept of *différance* even develops the most legitimate principled exigencies of 'structuralism'" (*Positions*, 28). That a structuralist approach can ultimately be shown to have deconstructed itself does not prevent it from functioning in an often routinized manner.

This description of "easy cases" will obviously share the problems that we uncovered in neo-pragmatism. To invoke "highlighting" as a way to account for the emerging of easy cases is manifestly circular (though perhaps evocative). And to write about settled patterns of differentiation is to call forth the specter of an infinite regress like the one that afflicted neo-pragmatism; in ascertaining what has become "settled," we shall confront exactly the same problem that a pragmatist will encounter when she tries to say how interpretive assumptions can ever be engaged. We must unceasingly interpret afresh the outcomes of cases studied heretofore—and hence their similarity to, or difference from, present cases. Yet this can happen only within a set of hermeneutic assumptions that have been shaped by one's past experience, including the bygone cases under scrutiny. One's procedures thus presuppose one's findings, every bit as much as *vice versa*. Pertinent here is this immensely thought-provoking remark by Wittgenstein: "One wants to say '*All* my experiences shew that it is so.' But how do they do that? For that proposition to which they point itself belongs to a particular interpretation of them."[96]

Indeterminacy indeed requires determinacy, but we are disqualified from *determining* which is which. The following sentences by Barbara Johnson make this point well, and boldly hoist themselves with their own petard: "If we could be sure of the difference between the determinable and the undeterminable, the undeterminable would be comprehended within the determinable. What is undecidable is whether a thing is decidable or not."[97] Moreover, as has been emphasized, a case that is easy will have undergone deconstructive paradoxes as unavoidably as a hard case. Through operations of highlighting, ancillary meanings within discoursive movement are subjugated but are never wiped out; a potential always exists, then, for the disrupting and overturning of what has been supposedly "settled."

At first glance, the paradoxes of deconstruction may seem demobilizing and burdensome. Infinite regresses and inescapable aporias are not—one may think—the stuff of which political progress can be made. When, for example, Paul de Man wrote that texts "compel us to choose while destroying the foundations of any choice" (AR, 245), he may have appeared to offer little comfort to those who strive for a better world. To see how misleading these initial impressions are, we must bring out an additional point of intersection between neo-pragmatism and deconstructive philosophy. We can begin here with the pragmatist focus on proliferating schemes of interpretation. Pragmatists' challenges to the "Myth of the Given" have ensued as much from their heightened consciousness of intellectual change as from their philosophical bag of tricks.[98] (Among other things, this heightened consciousness has thrown doubt upon the very divide between historical and philosophical explanations.) Though benefiting enormously from the work of Hegel and his disciples, neo-pragmatists have gained even more support from the embarrassing evanescence of analytical frameworks that have sought to defy time. "Pragmatists think that the history of attempts to isolate the True or the Good, or to define the word 'true' or 'good,' supports their suspicion that there is no interesting work to be done in this area."[99] It is not just the owl of Minerva, but also the remarkable frequency of that sage bird's flights, to which pragmatists have had recourse. To be sure, the frequency does not in itself amount to a vindication of neopragmatist views; after all, in the absence of a set of philosophical arguments for those views, the fleeting structures of intellectual life could be regarded as failures to attain the Truth which exists *tout de même.* But the transience of intellectual frameworks can indeed serve to foster moods of receptivity to the neopragmatist claims. A belief in the mutability and ephemerality of intellectual standpoints will not *per se* oblige anyone to join the neopragmatist thinkers in their relativism, but it very often encourages the sort of distrust that stokes the fire of relativistic theses.

Now, a person's relativistic acknowledgement of intellectual change will not automatically commit the person to hail a rapid turnover of disciplinary frameworks with good cheer. While affirming that current modes of intellectual discourse will prove ultimately ungrounded and thus impermanent, one can still endeavor to retain them as long as possible. (Moreover, someone who welcomes novelty in artistic or intellectual life will not *bon gré mal gré* have committed herself to the endorsement of fluxion in the realm of politics; intellectual daring and political quietism can happily coexist.) Nonetheless, in matters pertaining to the life of the mind—though not, for the most part, in political contexts—many devotees of neo-pragmatism have rivaled Paul's Athenian audience in their liking for what is new. They see the never-ending succession of predominant modes of thought as something to be acclaimed (or at least as something to be insouciantly acknowledged). They are willing to leave the dead to bury the dead, and they refuse to put new wine into old skins. Their distrust of metaphysical groundings is conjoined with their equanimity upon viewing the supplantment of one discoursive matrix after another. For pragmatists, controversies and categorial transformations are marks of health rather than of decline. One of the main *supports* of the neo-pragmatist point of view—the fluidity of conventions in an array of social practices—thus serves additionally as one of pragmatism's main *goals.* Rorty and his intellectual comrades strive to "perform the social function which Dewey called 'breaking the crust of social convention.'"[100]

Deconstructive critics applaud the pragmatists' questing for a dissemination of analytical schemes, but the approaches of the two camps diverge in several respects. First, deconstruction tends toward a far more wary view of historical analysis (even when the analysis favors discontinuity as its overriding motif). Deconstructors should hesitate to draw lessons from the past, for, as Derrida has observed, "[t]he metaphysical character of the concept of history is not only linked to linearity, but to an entire *system* of implications (teleology, eschatology, elevating and interiorizing accumulation of meaning, a certain type of traditionality, a certain concept of continuity, etc.)" (*Positions*, 57; emphasis in original). This is not to say that the pragmatists have been grossly naive in their reliance on history, nor is it to maintain—even more absurdly—that deconstruction has sought to do away altogether with the concept of "history." Within every analysis, an escape from "history" would be as futile and unthinkable as it would be imprudent.[101] Moreover, as Derrida makes clear, one should not seek to renounce the concept of "history," but to re-elaborate it (*Positions*, 49–50, 57–60). He writes:

> I have never believed that there were *metaphysical* concepts *in and of themselves*. No concept is by itself, and consequently in and of itself, metaphysical, outside all the textual work in which it is inscribed. This explains why, although I have formulated many reservations about the "metaphysical" concept of history, I very *often* use the word "history" in order to reinscribe its force and in order to produce another concept or conceptual chain of "history": in effect a "monumental, stratified, contradictory" history; a history that also implies a new logic of *repetition* and the *trace*, for it is difficult to see how there could be history without it. [*Positions*, 57.]

Nonetheless, as one might already have inferred from my critical attitude toward Sartre's treatment of temporality, deconstruction cannot invoke historical findings as uncritically as the pragmatists sometimes do. To be sure, historical data are no more vertiginously elusive and paradoxical than synchronic data,[102] but neither are they any less so. In accounting for "easy cases" of historical knowledge—which, as pragmatists underscore, relate frequently to discontinuousness—we shall have to put to work the concept of "highlighting," with its attendant self-criticism and circularity. On the one hand, we should agree that "[p]eriods differ from one another because there are different forms of heterogeneity [i.e., self-subversion]";[103] indeed, "different forms of self-subversion" can amount to a deconstructive translation of the pragmatist reference to "different forms of normal inquiry." What strikes a pragmatist as more or less coherent vocabularies will appear to a deconstructive critic as forms of disarticulation. On the other hand, we must acknowledge expressly that, in analyzing the differences among species of disarticulation, we undermine our own frame of reference. This, of course, does not mean that no distinctions can be persuasively drawn. While drawing them, however, an analyst will end up drawing and quartering himself.

Apart from undertaking rigorous self-criticism, deconstructive critiques transvalue neo-pragmatist thought by introducing an essential new term into the discourse: that of "strategy." For post-structuralists, proliferating discoursive networks (or forms of self-subversion) are not merely phenomena to be established and then transcended in due time. Rather, each system of interacting concepts will furnish a terrain for maneuvers—whether progressive or regressive cannot be finally determined—in strategies and struggles without finality. Though the importance of strategic thinking will be explored at length in the next section, we should here note some brief points that may avert facile remonstrances.

First, a discourse focused on strategy and struggles will not *have* to display a leftist slant in its politics; after all, a focus on struggles gained its most fervent and insightful expression in the work of Nietzsche.[104] This does not imply that a deconstructive approach is neutral or that it "leaves everything as it is." As Derrida maintains: "Why engage in a work of deconstruction, rather than leave things the way they are, etc.? Nothing, here, without a 'show of force' somewhere. Deconstruction, I have insisted, is not *neutral*. It *intervenes*" (*Positions*, 93; emphasis in original). Still less can one say that deconstructionist theories willy-nilly promote conservatism. But we should not smoothly map the struggles and fleeting triumphs of deconstruction onto political liberation movements. That is, we should assume that establishing a relationship between politics and deconstruction will itself be a constant struggle.[105]

Second, the crucial concept of "strategy" does not in itself promote a glib understanding of individual consciousness, devoid of self-criticism. One need not posit individual schemers behind the strategies (of resistance and domination) that extend through the social body. With all such strategies,

> the logic is perfectly clear, the aims decipherable, and yet it is often the case that no one is there to have invented them, and few who can be said to have formulated them. . . . Just as the network of power relations ends by forming a dense web that passes through apparatuses and institutions, without being exactly localized in them, so too the swarm of points of resistance traverses social stratifications and individual unities.[106]

Invocations of "strategy" thus amount to the highlighting of pivotal themes and patterns within discoursive movement (with the heavy self-criticism that such highlighting entails). In pragmatist terms, appeals to "strategy" will have formed a highly illuminating language in which various interactions can be portrayed.

To label sets of activities as "strategic" need imply no unchastened view about their source in any controlling subject. Moreover—and this brings us to yet a third point—even when we ascribe strategies to some individual or some group of individuals, we can situate and displace any vulgar humanism that perceives subjectivity as self-fashioned. This we can accomplish by laying stress on the expropriation of individuals through the very strategies they contrive as their means of coming effectively to grips with the world. Potent strategies and complete dispossession will have always entailed each other, for the individual is a pawn as well as a king. One loses mastery by virtue of gaining it:

> [Nietzsche's analytical writing] seems to end in a reassertion of the active performative function of language and it rehabilitates persuasion as the final outcome of the deconstruction of figural speech. This would allow for the reassuring conviction that it is legitimate to do just about anything with words, as long as we know that a rigorous mind, fully aware of the misleading power of tropes, pulls the strings. But if it turns out that this same mind does not even know whether it is doing or not doing something, then there are considerable grounds for suspicion that it does not know *what* it is doing.[107]

Since to *use* language is to *lose* oneself in it, any strategic outlook will displace its own centeredness in the very centering action of "pulling strings."

Fourth, strategies and struggles are "without finality," in the sense that they can and should be dislodged by ever new waves of struggles, and in the sense that they remain always susceptible to being deconstructed anew. One's strategies have no orienting goal that can stand outside the play of *différance;* one thus has to engage in "an operation that in the last analysis refuses to be governed by a teleo-eschatological horizon" (*Positions*, 71). To challenge teleological horizons, one must not only shift one's ground continually (MP, 7; OG, 70), but also interrogate the whole idea of "grounds." Deconstructive critiques will have explicitly focused inward as well as outward, and will hence be recuperative as well as aggressive. In the process, they blur all inside/outside distinctions. (OG, 24.) They involve choices and calculations, but these are "calculations without end" and choices within a "system that regularly change[s] transgressions into 'false exits'" (MP, 7, 135). As we turn here to think strategically about reification, we must know that the task awaiting us is at once interminable and always too late.

B. Notes on Reification

At the outset, it should once more be underlined that this section is not mounting an immanent critique of the works discussed in Part One. My aims will be rather different. This chapter is not trying to deconstruct past discourses on reification but is showing how deconstructionist critics might be engaged in them (in an active sense *and* a passive sense). It will ergo be necessary to reconceive and rewrite those discourses in language more suited to the "post-structuralist condition."

The works analyzed in Part One, along with some other writings from the critical legal studies movement, will form a context and a contrast for the remainder of this section. While, in certain respects, those writings have indeed marked the basic contours of the issues to be addressed here, they have done so along specific lines that I scout. Unquestionably, they serve as a background or a framework for my discussion; but they also serve as its targets. That these targets are approached indirectly (through a rewriting), rather than directly (through a close deconstructive reading), should only foster a sense of struggle and tension for an undertaking that hopes to scramble the direct/indirect alternative.[108]

Of course, some danger lies in sharpening differences between earlier critiques of reification and the perspectives that will here be advanced. Specifically, to contrast the later style of thought and the earlier style of thought is to disregard the contrasts within each style, and is thus to take for granted the self-identity and coherence of each. In extenuation of this possibility, two responses may be put forward. First, this section will concentrate on highlighting and favoring some unorthodox themes and tactics within its lines of critique; those themes and tactics, so it will be maintained, are especially explicit (and thus especially self-reflective) in their statements of the internal differences that prevent each line of critique from being adequate to itself.[109] Second, given the centrality of internal differences, the dichotomy *between* "within" and "between" cannot stay beyond all criticism. As Barbara Johnson has noted: "If . . . binary oppositions . . . play the role of the critical fall guy, it is not because one must try at all costs to go beyond them. The very impulse to 'go beyond' is an impulse structured by a binary opposition between oneself and what one attempts to leave behind." A self-critical theory focused on differences between two standpoints must serve as a wayward "bridge of translation, which paradoxically releases within each [standpoint] the subversive forces of its own foreignness."[110]

This section will be divided into three subsections, each of which will be plumping for a new phase—or at least for some selectivity—in accounts of reification. Certain ways of thinking about reification will be preferred to other ways that are arguably too shopworn. At the fore will lie strategic considerations; arguments will be framed in a vocabulary of "struggles," "tactics," "disruption," and "subversion," rather than "truth" (which is of course not to say that this last-mentioned philosopheme can be altogether discarded). Critical and strategic force at a particular juncture, not illusive veracity, is the touchstone that guides our choices.

As we give ourselves to strategically astute ways of describing reification, we must remain eager to shift our ground. As has been remarked, a process of choosing that is based on strategic factors will partake of no fewer problems than a logocentric pursuit of Truth. In a process of either broad type, we shall have to undergo a fatal disquietude, though admittedly in diverse forms. Critical power and tactical adroitness must serve as one's leading goals, but the game in which one is strategizing will go on endlessly. One must try—always with a considerable degree of failure—to attend carefully to the blindness that will be entailed by each of one's insights. In what follows, then, to be kept constantly in mind is a near-paralyzing tentativeness.

1. *Reification as False Determinateness*

At least within the critical legal studies movement, a common way to discuss reification is to attack the appearance of determinateness in a variety of decisions and institutions. In the play of discoursive movement, some regularities will have come to be highlighted, for reasons that do not ever dwell beyond the to-and-fro of such movement. These regular events, which must remain to be analyzed, account for the patterns of determinacy that are a product and a prerequisite of *in*determinacy within any given setting. What critical legal scholars maintain is that styles of discourse suited to areas of determinacy are invoked too often in less appropriate areas. This phenomenon can occur in many ways. For instance, Gerald Frug has averred that mainstream legal scholars treat highly open-ended abstractions—such as "interests," "needs," "goals," and "values"—as concrete things with readily ascertainable and fixed contents. In a like manner, Peter Gabel has again and again trumpeted that "the state" amounts to nothing but an *imaginary* union of people who are divided and powerless. In a not unrelated vein, Richard Parker has blasted open the conservative understanding of political life in present-day constitutional scholarship, by laying stress on the inequalities that belie images of a comfortably homogeneous republic. And, of course, almost all the critical legal writers have emulated the Legal Realists in pointing out the open-ended equivocalness of language in the texts of judicial opinions, statutes, and constitutional provisions. Conventional scholarship turns up closure and agreement where critical scholarship finds conflict and multiplicity.[111]

This first method of attacking reification—which was clearly harbingered by Lukács's lament over the reduction of time to space—can be taken up from several perspectives. Here it is proposed that, for a duration unspecifiable, we adopt one line of attack in preference to alternative lines. More specifically, perhaps the most fruitful and unconventional way of marking false determinateness is to distinguish what is settled from what is unsettled in a group of highlighted patterns. Reification then can be derided as an attempt by most people to blink unsettledness (through complacent discourse that takes determinacy for granted). As will be pointed out below, a settled/unsettled dualism breeds a host of grave difficulties, and therefore must be displaced eventually into a much less prominent role. Unlike Jeremiah's waistcloth, a set of terms will not spoil by being too soon abandoned but by being too long retained. *Pour le moment,* however, a vocabulary of "settledness" and "unsettledness" may furnish greater critical force than most alternative viewpoints. If we look, for instance, at Frug's dualism of "abstraction" and "concreteness," we face insufferable problems. Frug's terms, which are wholly simpatico with Gabel's "Reification in Legal Reasoning," will connect unguardedly—far too unguardedly—to traditions of Western metaphysics. Though such terms are not *inevitably* devoid of critical zest, they have become so tangled with the orthodox strands of most traditions that we should push them aside, at least temporarily.[112] Or, if they are not pushed aside (whence they would return, ineluctably, in an unforeseeable manner), they should be played down and cannily hedged about with (dis)qualifications. Above all else, one should not try to resolve aporias between the universal and the particular, or the abstract and the concrete, by privileging one term or the other. The ice we tread on is far too thin for such escapades.

Similar remarks may be brought to bear on Gabel's consignment of most groups to the outer darkness of the imaginary (where "the imaginary" is used in a non-Lacanian sense). It should be clear, from some of my observations in Part One, that such a consignment smacks of humanism; for it privileges subjectivity as the unique or primary agent in the constituting of social life, at least under "non-alienated" conditions. One can question Gabel's vocabulary on two grounds. First of all, by pronouncing on the spuriousness of current transindividual arrangements, Gabel implies—whatever his intention may be—that persons enjoy an ontological status which is free from the doubts that haunt the status of institutions. To a deconstructive critic such a view appears silly, because the paradoxes that have encompassed the life of an institution will be every bit as unsettling in the formation of individuals. With characteristic verve, Nietzsche offered a poignant way of thinking about the fissures in subjectivity: "'The subject' is the fiction that many similar states in us are the effect of one substratum: but it is we who first created the 'similarity' of these states; our adjusting them and making them similar is the fact, not their similarity" (WP, 269; sec. 485). Nietzsche's ironic use of "we" throws the human subject into an endless seesaw between its constituted and constituting states, each of which depends wholly on the other as its prerequisite. Uncritical myths of selfhood are here radically out of place.

Second, as has been emphasized throughout, a humanist frame of reference can but serve as one moment in a dialectical interplay between self and structure. Gabel's attempted dissolution of "the state" in the acid of its own factitiousness will inevitably founder, for such a move will necessarily raise the problems that it has to elide. For a strong statement of the contextuality that will enter into exchange with Gabel's humanism, we may look to Adorno:

> What shows up faithfully in the doctrine of the transcendental subject is the priority of the relations—abstractly rational ones, detached from the human individuals and their relationships—that have their model in exchange. If the exchange form is the standard social structure, its rationality constitutes people; what they are for themselves, what they seem to be to themselves, is secondary. . . .
>
> This alleged origin of all objects is objectified in rigid timelessness, quite in keeping with Kant's doctrine of the firm and immutable forms of transcendental consciousness. Its solidity and invariance, which according to transcendental philosophy bring forth all objects or at least prescribe their rule, are the reflective form of the reification of humans that has been objectively accomplished in the social relationship. . . . The philosophical problem of constitution has reversed into its mirror image; but in this very reversal, it tells us the truth about the historic[al] stage that has been reached—in a truth, of course, which a second Copernican turn might theoretically negate again. True, it has its positive aspect as well: society, as prior, keeps its members and itself alive. The particular individual has the universal to thank for the possibility of his existence—witness thought, which is a general relation, and thus a social one.[113]

To be sure, the paradoxical interlacing of subjectivity and its contexts will enfold all versions of social theory. Gabel's error—if such a word is still apposite—cannot be rectified in a way that would elude paradoxes; each of us must indeed submit. Nonetheless, insofar as we can create our modes of submission, we can still object to Gabel's pronouncements in an age that treats us to "the unceasing recitation of [humanist] discourse and its complements."[114]

A vocabulary of "settledness" and "unsettledness" can skirt some of the difficulties just mentioned. Such a vocabulary has not too often been highlighted in Western metaphysics, at least not to the same extent as the terms on which Frug and Gabel have relied. In that sense, it would perhaps come closer to "making antiphilosophical points in nonphilosophical language" (CP, xiv). Since it is not the aim here to give direct deconstructive readings of alternative standpoints—an aim that would have clearly rendered expedient the continued use of key terms (*Positions*, 71)—one is probably best advised, on strategic grounds, to champion relatively fresh terms without waiting to reinscribe those that have hitherto been dominating the field. We are seeking to transfigure a discourse by engaging in it and by extending it, and we should therefore not shrink from introducing a bit of rather unconventional language. (One must suppose that Derrida would agree, given his flair for brilliant neologisms.) Because my transformed critique of reification does not flow from a direct deconstruction of opposing critiques, a strategy of retaining important terms will too easily restrengthen the uncritical aspects of what it tries to disrupt. Though one must surely mount an "appropriation of a vocabulary turned against those who had once used it" (NGH, 154), part of the zestful violence of one's appropriation should lie in a foresighted relinquishment of some of the captured terms.

(One should feel unease over the too conventional dyads that have structured the argument above: direct/indirect, inside/outside, performance/criticism. Nonetheless, two brief observations can in some measure palliate this alignment with orthodoxy. First, deconstruction can never simply efface dichotomies on a route to some or another mode of undifferentiated presence. Dyadic contrasts are disassembled within aporias, but remain always available—and essential—for the crafting of any argument. Argumentation never works itself free of paradoxes, but it necessarily has to be articulated to reveal its own disarticulation. Moreover, Derrida himself uses the concept/name dyad to produce his convincing argument for the retention of key terms. If he can rely—with open self-criticism and determined irresolution—on *that* dyad as a vehicle for enunciating his own strategies, then one can feel justified in invoking other distinctions to *distinguish* one's strategies from his.)

Apart from some freshness and resultant vigorousness, the terminology advocated here will provide a major advantage: it will go some way toward finessing the subjectivity/objectivity problem that has plagued most critiques of reification. "Unsettledness" and "settledness" (or "predictability" and "unpredictability") waver between the structural and genetic sides of existence. That is, they can refer to both disputes *and* disputedness, to both the subjective state of disagreement or agreement *and* the objective state of regularity or irregularity. Thus, one should aspire to dance skillfully between these patterns of reference—so that one can avoid blatantly committing oneself to humanism or structuralism—whenever one tries to save indeterminacy from the reifying clutches of a determinate discourse.

Whatever be the advantages of assailing reification in the terms discussed here, recourse to a vocabulary of "settledness" and "unsettledness" (or "determinacy" and "indeterminacy") will by no means have qualified as "harmless."[115] My previous remarks on determinacy and indeterminacy ought to make clear that an assault on reification will not proceed quite as smoothly as the last few paragraphs might suggest. Decidability and undecidability are locked and unlocked in a relation of *différance*, as a result of which neither can amount to what each *must* amount to—i.e., a self-same condition. These phenomena become mutually exclusive only by being mutually inscribed; to salvage indeterminacy thus requires both the complete incorporation and the complete abandonment of determinacy. Any analysis that tries to separate these phenomena, like any analysis that tries to unify them, has always tumbled into the whirlpools of the mind-bending paradoxes that are highlighted by deconstructive readings. It is for this reason that Barbara Johnson writes: "The problem of difference can thus be seen both as an uncertainty over separability and as a drifting apart within identity. . . . There is, in other words, no position from which to judge that would be outside the lines of force involved in the object judged."[116]

A more specific problem relates to the supposed equivocality of the language that has just been defended. One of the virtues of that language is its marked ambiguity between objectivistic and humanistic standpoints. We may well find, however, that the language is much too closely akin to neo-pragmatist modes of discourse. Given the wide acceptance of pragmatism in legal theory and in philosophy, a critique of reification that amounts to rescuing unpredictability from predictability may collapse forthwith into pragmatism, with its goal of "breaking the crust of social convention." Of course, there exist some parallels between that objective and deconstruction's task of dissemination; each must affirm that truth is heterogeneous. But deconstructive theorists pursue their strategies with relentless self-criticism and with an acute knowledge of the ultimate incoherence of every strategy. They realize that the ideal of Truth will have continued to haunt their writing even when (or especially when) Truth appears to have been eliminated. As Derrida maintains, *différance* "transports and encloses the meaning of Being" even though it "no longer belongs to the horizon of Being" (MP, 22). Deconstructive theorists know, furthermore, that humanism and structuralism implicate as well as exclude each other in paradoxical disarrangements and interweavings that can never be mastered. Pragmatists, on the other hand, attempt to lean much too far toward humanism. In analyzing reification, for example, they would be very likely to transform "unsettledness" and "settledness" into "controversy" and "concord." Such a transformation (which cannot easily be avoided, given the closeness of my recommended vocabulary to the discourse of neo-pragmatism) would beckon us straightaway toward humanism, through a preoccupation with the beliefs and outlooks of human agents. This would leave accounts of reification far too vulnerable to deconstructive critiques. Though no account, no matter how self-critical, can exempt its claims from a deconstructive reading, one should not think that all accounts are equally valuable in strategic terms (OG, 139). One may expect, quite reasonably, to mobilize greater critical power with a set of terms that "designate rigorously their intimate relationship to the machine whose deconstruction they permit" (OG, 14) than with humanist discourses that attempt to lay aside their own necessary yet inconceivable dependence on structuralism. One should thus look with some concern on the possibility that one's critiques will too readily collapse into a smug neopragmatism.

The two problems that have just been sketched here are not disabling—or, rather, because they *do* most harshly disable us, they should be probed and taken into account as fully as possible. In that way, they lend force to one's overall critique rather than detract from it as an unseen menace. By emphasizing these problems, one can prefigure and thus situate some modes of attack to which one's analysis lies open. To be sure, not all lines of assault can be anticipated; every insight into one's failings will engender new blindness that ensures still further vulnerabilities. Though this may well merit despair, it equally warrants joy, for it confirms our approach exactly insofar as it undermines it. It should scarcely be cause for hand-wringing that our approach demonstrates its main message: the unstoppable play of deconstruction.

2. *Reification as False Necessity.*

Closely connected to the first way of analyzing reification—indeed, coinciding with it in large part though not *in toto*—are condemnations of "false necessity." This line of complaint has been by far the most common theme in texts that denounce reification, both for members of the critical legal studies movement and for their intellectual forebears. One can find it in the assault by Marx on the fetishism of commodities, in Lukács's disdain for capitalism's "second nature," and in Sartre's theory of "bad faith" and his later theory of collective inertia. Critical legal scholars, too, have devoted their energy to combating the rigidification of their surroundings. For instance, Duncan Kennedy has savaged the inclination of most people to act as if they had no control over their lives in numerous legal settings, from law schools to the analyses of the law-and-economics movement. Robert Gordon takes a similar view that the "process of allowing the structures we ourselves have built to mediate relations among us . . . is a way people have of manufacturing necessity." Gerald Frug joins in by denouncing the forms of legal rhetoric that persuade people to embrace their familiar patterns of everyday existence as the "equivalent of life itself." Karl Klare likewise maintains that, under capitalism, workers (including white-collar workers) "have no way to recall that the world in which they live has been created by themselves." David Trubek has summarized this tenacious criticism of false constraints:

> Critical scholars see social order as maintained by a system of beliefs. The belief systems that structure action and maintain order in capitalist societies present as eternal and necessary what is only the transitory and arbitrary interest of a dominant elite. This commonly accepted body of ideas justifies the unequal and unjust power of the dominant group. These systems of ideas are *reifications*, presenting as essential, necessary, and objective what is contingent, arbitrary, and subjective.[117]

As is suggested by the foregoing examples, the attacks by critical legal theorists on "false necessity" have often gone down humanist paths. If we are to continue venturing such attacks without giving in to humanism so quickly, we shall have to perform another rewriting. Once more, it is not a question of beginning from scratch; instead, some of the patterns of prevailing discourses will be highlighted and favored at the expense of other such patterns. The resulting approach will be divided into two main strands, one relating to the suppression of mutability, the other to the suppression of multiplicity. In both strands, we must resolve not only to controvert unfounded necessity (and thus to expand horizons), but also to present the strategically vital reasons for prosecuting such a campaign in unconventional terms—terms more unsettling than the language that has prevailed heretofore in critical legal studies.

Mutability becomes quashed through the self-fulfilling belief that little or nothing in the world can be very different from what it currently is (or from what most people think it currently is).[118] This belief will often hold sway in concert with the problem of determinacy and indeterminacy, though neither entails the other perforce. There are two main forms that can be assumed by the phenomenon of squelched mutability: either people fail altogether to imagine a way of life different from their humdrum routines, or they devise alternatives to what has become *vieux jeu* but then despair of ever putting them into practice (or even moving very far toward them).[119] Within either of these two main forms, the suppression of mutability can be effected in countless ways. Perhaps the most important of these is the "naturalizing" of contingent events and structures. Various conditions are deemed "natural" and are thus held to be impervious to all efforts at change, for nature is presumptively classified as unchanging.[120] Nature thus has stepped in to fill the role that was played at one time by God or gods: "[W]e can reinterpret [our] poverty into a necessity so that it no longer offends us when we see it and we no longer sulk at fate on its account. That is what a wise gardener does when he places the poor little stream in his garden in the arms of a nymph and thus finds a motive for its poverty; and who does not need nymphs as he does?" (GS, 90–91; sec. 17).

Before evaluating the strengths and weaknesses of the terminology just proposed, let us look *en passant* at the second major strand of the criticism of false necessity. Here the target is the submergence of multiplicity, a submergence which comes about as the widespread sharing of a belief that only one outcome or interpretation of some event is conceivable. Such an eventuality amounts to a classic instance of the "settledness/unsettledness" problem, and thus need not be dwelt on here. Most important to note is the oppressive air of inflexibility that emerges from "attempts to close off conversation by proposals for universal commensuration through the hypostatization of some privileged set of descriptions"

(PMN, 377). Like the squelching of mutability, the suppression of multiplicity tries to preordain choices by denuding them of their character as choices.

Analyzing false necessity through the dualisms of closure/openness and permanent/contingent, rather than through the concepts of "subjectivity" and "objectivity" (or "control" and "abdication"), would seem desirable for at least two reasons. First, a discoursive framework of "subjectivity" and "control" invites exactly the sort of humanism that has been a *bête noire* throughout this chapter. Myths of a subjectivity that has become alienated from itself are at once too hackneyed *and* too seductive to be of great strategic value for those who want change. Such myths garner assent too readily, and thus scotch careful self-criticism. In discouraging reflection, the advocates of these myths have to stake their hopes on evading deconstructive critiques, rather than on anticipating—and joining—some of the countless paths that a deconstructive challenge might take. Humanist myths, which are contained so easily by the metaphysical structures they purport to renounce, thus tend to be devastated (without being enriched greatly) when they are eventually deconstructed. A vocabulary of "openness" and "closure" should help to change devastation into enrichment, largely because its greater freshness carries more potential for self-reproving anticipation of deconstructive challenges. One can reduce one's vulnerability by drawing attention to it and by making a virtue of it.

Further, discourses of subjectivism are tied so closely to discourses of domination that we probably look in vain for a politically leftist impact from humanism. Now, in making this second point, one has to be careful not to claim too much. One will discover no necessary links between metaphysical individualism (i.e., a view of the individual agent as the primary source of meaning and action) and political individualism (i.e., a view that individual welfare is the foremost concern of politics). Nor will one discover a necessary tie between either sort of individualism and political domination. Moreover, humanism—that is, the prioritizing of subjectivity over structures—need not entail either of the types of individualism; the privileged subject can be perceived as transindividual or collective. Thus, for example, Marx's humanism can be construed as both metaphysically and politically collectivist.

In short, no necessary connection holds between a humanist vantage point and political domination; but problems of strategy do not deal with necessary connections. Inevitable relations do not exist, but strong contingent ones do. At least since the time of Bacon and Descartes, the linkage between political oppression and the embracement of subjectivity has been in general too close for comfort, notwithstanding the revolutionary part played by liberal individualism in the politics of the early modern age. This is not to argue that a focus on subjectivity must at present exclude all radicalism. Nor is it to claim that the undesirable consequences of humanism can be avoided through recourse to an objectivistic vocabulary. It should go without saying that the crimes perpetrated by those in thrall to objectivistic outlooks have been much more flagitious than atrocities carried out for the sake of humanist aspirations. (Indeed, it is not at all surprising that humanism and structuralism will have shared many weak points, given that—as has been repeatedly stressed—each of them gains its life from what it has condemned in the other.) My point here is not that humanism is *necessarily* promotive of domination, nor that we can devise a talismanic vocabulary that will prevent resistances from being derailed, but merely that subjectivist theorizing has turned so much into "an anemic apology for egotism" that it is unlikely to produce a bountiful left-wing harvest.[121] Close connections between such theorizing and entrenched modes of domination have virtually forced the prudent critic to aim to bypass the terminology of "control" and "self-determinedness." Those concepts should be displaced by the categories of "closure"/"openness" and "permanence"/"mutability." This is not because we should hope to have fled thereby into some political version of the Promised Land,[122] but because we may have thereby detached ourselves—to a considerable extent, though never entirely—from a focus on certain categories that have too often lit the iron furnaces of oppression. At the same time, we shall have introduced a flicker of novelty into a debate grown paralyzingly stale.

As might be expected, the vocabularies of "closure"/"openness" and "permanence"/"mutability" will have brought with them new problems even as they finesse some of the old ones. Any project that tries to rescue contingency must in due time yield to the claims of deconstruction, in a manner explored by Derrida at the end of his essay on the structuralism of Lévi-Strauss:

> There are thus two interpretations of interpretation, of structure, of signs, of play. The one seeks to decipher, dreams of deciphering a truth or an origin which escapes play and the order of the sign, and which lives the necessity of interpretation as an exile. The other, which is no longer turned toward the origin, affirms play and tries to pass beyond man and humanism, the name of man being the name of that being who, throughout the history of metaphysics or of ontotheology—in other words, throughout his entire history—has dreamed of full presence, the reassuring foundation, the origin and the end of play. . . .
>
> For my part, although these two interpretations must acknowledge and accentuate their difference and define their irreducibility, I do not believe that today there is any question of *choosing*—in the first place because here we are in a region (let us say, provisionally, a region

> of historicity) where the category of choice seems particularly trivial; and in the second, because we must first try to conceive of the common ground, and the *différance* of this irreducible difference.[123]

In reclaiming contingency, one will find that one cannot take a halfway measure; one's championing of mutability and interpretive openness will push one—wittingly or unwittingly—toward an affirmation of free play. But such an affirmation must thwart itself by being articulated, since "transgression of discourse (and consequently of law in general, for discourse establishes itself only by establishing normativity or the value of meaning, that is to say, the element of legality in general) must, in some fashion, and like every transgression, conserve or confirm that which it exceeds."[124] The two interpretations of interpretation are wholly irreconcilable but also mutually implicated and mutually determinative. An affirmation of free play will have hurtled into a dizzying seesaw (between unencumbered openness and absolute closure) from which escape has always already been impossible. If we try to "solve" this problem by moving to a discussion of "highlighting" within discoursive movement, and if we thereby seek to regard openness and mutability as an inverse function of the degree of rifeness and staying power achieved by dominant social patterns, we once more raise a host of attendant difficulties. On the one hand, analyses of "highlighting" would appear well suited to a narrative of "suppression" (i.e., suppression of mutability and multiplicity). Like "suppression," the term "highlighting" will have underscored—or highlighted—the precarious state of any dominant patterns. What seems marginal may indeed turn out to be central, and what is now in the background may inhabit the foreground. Suppression and highlighting will always leave room for overturning. On the other hand, as was noted in the preceding section, discourses on highlighting will confront a theorist with two cardinal problems: ineludible circularity and incompatible functions. Not only will such discourses beg whatever questions someone might put to them, but they force us to construe certain events—events bearing on the analysis, because of highlighting or because of suppression—as both the consequence and the precondition of any process of highlighting. This unnerving paradox, in which highlighted events must already *be* highlighted if they are to *become* so, should not deter us from wielding the vocabularies that have engulfed us in it. After all, one of the prime virtues of an approach that calls attention to mutability is that it points toward its own unfixedness and hence marks the need for its prospective demise. As has been argued more than once, a discourse informed by deconstruction can powerfully succeed in turning its vices into virtues by letting them act as proof of its main themes.

3. *Reification as Congealment*

A third way to attack reification is to single out the confinement of most areas of life within a desolatingly narrow set of potential forms. This line of assault—which obviously resembles Lukács's criticism of the objective side of reification, and which also should bring to mind the Sartrean theory of "inertia"—consorts with the above challenges to false necessity, but extends further to rigidification that may have very little to do with any conscious necessitarianism. In this sense, critiques of reification become critiques of all forms of stasis. Here, routinized social patterns evoke censure regardless of the subjectivity of the people who engage in them. In response to the suppression of novelty, the critical legal movement has sought to break the crust of social conventions and to keep society from congealing into a nightmare of tiresome ruts.

Roberto Unger has been one of the harshest critics of the suppression of novelty, denouncing the "repetitious quality of political life" as a "dismal, compulsive round of policy alternatives . . . that reduces even its most active and informed citizens to the condition of unresisting if not unknowing puppets." Mark Kelman appears to have in mind a roughly similar target when he complains that people have tended to rely on "fixed, reified entitlements as a shield against communitarian inquiry and dialogue on the justification for [their] claims against others." In a like vein, Karl Klare has pointed out that "all legal decisions are necessarily made within a context of assumptions . . . , and the historical tendency is for these underlying assumptions to become reified." Catharine MacKinnon highlights a commensurate process of rigidification in her critique of male dominance. She writes that male "objectivity is largely accurate to its/the/a world, which world is criticized; and . . . it becomes more accurate as the power it represents and extends becomes more total."[125]

The dyad of novelty and stasis should enjoy more resilient power, as a strategic wedge, than a distinction between subjectivity and objectivity (or humanity and brute things[126]), for reasons elaborated in the previous two subsections. It is a matter of bringing relatively fresh terms into one's theorizing, as opposed to the stale dichotomies that immure us in conventional metaphysics too uncritically. Familiar, too, are the types of blindness entailed by this unorthodox choice of terms. In differentiating between novelty and routinized patterns, we shall encounter once again the problems of incoherence and circularity that have impelled and disabled our entire project.

Aside from these advantages and these difficulties, the problem of suppressed novelty will have signaled an important qualification that has been implicit thus far—the incompleteness and bounded efficacy of all attacks on reification. While striving for greater social fluidity, the members of the critical legal studies movement do not expect that social configurations will become what Shelley at times yearned for: "one harmonious soul of many a soul, [w]hose nature is its own divine control."[127] As was emphasized in my discussions of Marx and Lukács, "divine (self-)control" is, sadly, not of this world. One ought not to perceive vulgar millenarianism in the premise that sundry discourses can be far more flexible than has been their norm. (This caution is directed both at the critical legal scholars and at their audience.) Indeed, the general arguments of this book should, on two levels, serve to warn us against all millenarianism, here defined as a mastery-of-fate-by-the-will arising from the utter plasticity of social life. First, throughout this volume we have observed that all discourses and all actions proceed by means of inevasible paradoxes—aporias that will pit heteronomy and control against each other in constant battles that each side loses by winning. Hence, total self-mastery is an unstable though necessary point in discoursive movement that always has already been deconstructed.

Second, even if we look at the patterns that are induced by highlighting, and gloss over the inconceivableness of such a look, we must have still further grounds for a jaundiced view of millenarianism. (The word "grounds," of course, is singularly inapposite.) Just as there can exist no indeterminacy without determinacy, there can occur no institutional transformations without *some* institutions, be they political, linguistic, or economic. When, for instance, Roberto Unger pursues "a social world less alien to a self that can always violate the generative rules of its own mental and social constructs and put other rules and other constructs in their place," he has affirmed the necessity of rules and constructs *in general* through his very appeal for the recurrent transcendence of *specific* constructs and rules.[128] If no structures have emerged to check transformation and to expropriate subjectivity, there will be neither transformation nor subjectivity, for each is made possible (and, indeed, necessitated) by precisely the structures that will have seemed to make it *im*possible.[129] Through an unyielding whirlpool of dislocations that resist being understood or contained, the interplay of totally free events and wholly decisive structures will continuously engender trails of highlighting, which embrace the structures and the events that make up everyday living. Neither of the poles in a quotidian dyad can dispense with the other pole, notwithstanding that each one of the poles is ineluctably driven toward its extreme counterpart in the truly fundamental dyad which was referred to in my last sentence—that is, the dyad of completely untrammeled agents and completely resistless structures, where the two poles will be extirpating each other (as well as calling each other forth *de tout temps*). Uninhibited self-creation and unimpeded newness therefore may best be viewed as fantasies, fantasies that are both imperative and unthinkable. As we learn at the beginning of *Genesis*, whatever lacks form is void.

Given this strong distrust of millenarianism, the attacks on reification by the critical legal scholars will derive from a certain air—both tragic and liberating—of fallenness. Gerald Frug has captured this nicely when he writes that "all forms of organization create forms of domination that need to be combatted," and when he vilipends "the very project of bureaucratic theorists—finding a structure that is necessary to promote and defend human freedom and relying on the device of reification to make such a structure intelligible" (IBAL, 1296, 1295). (For our purposes, the quest for a static bliss and the search for thoroughgoing plasticity will amount to the same thing, as each tries to expunge the difference between desire and structure. Note that, when millenarianism is defined as complete harmony instead of complete fluxion, it falls prey to the general theme of iterability—i.e., to Chapter 1's arguments that the possibility of *mal*functioning is an absolute condition of any *functioning*. Moreover, harmony and disharmony interfold each other in paradoxes of differentiation, wherein an act of total exclusion is perforce an act of total reliance.) Having given up hopes for the emergence of paradise, the critical legal scholars try to displace their social surroundings from one inevitably imperfect condition to another. In so doing, they have hoped to unsettle rigid structures of hierarchy to which most people submit with resignation. Critical legal scholars thus serve as what Michel Foucault denominated as "plebs"—those who have no more managed to step outside power than everybody else, but who attack the consolidation of the specific forms with which power has invested itself. Critical scholars launch resistances and counterattacks without pursuing a world in which complete flexibility would cause such measures to have become superfluous.

> [T]o the small extent that a man is incapable of yielding to considerations that either are official or are susceptible of becoming so, to the smaller extent that he is inclined to feel the attraction of a life devoted to the destruction of established authority, it is difficult to believe that a [fluid] world, conforming to his interests, could be for him anything other than a convenient illusion.[130]

In two ways, struggles will force themselves upon us: (1) every scheme of organization will exhaust only a small range of collective possibilities and will comprise "forms of domination that need to be combatted," and (2) each scheme will balk most efforts at transformation, and therefore will evoke struggles from anyone not inured to stasis. Critical legal scholars are thus condemned and privileged to wage numberless wars against the petrifaction of social life. Prosecuting such wars will enfold the critical legal theorists in paradoxes and vicious circularity. For all that, it may produce important effects. To be sure, critical insights will entail blindness; their effects will always remain to be accounted for. It may well turn out that upholding novelty against rigidified structures will promote stagnation far more than would a contrary tactic. That, however, seems a gamble worth taking.

Part Three. Conclusion

This chapter has studied the career of a basic theme in critical legal studies. Because attacks on reification have involved so many of the key problems addressed by critical legal writers, this chapter has aspired to be a far-reaching step in the revision of controversies and strategies for critical jurisprudence. It has carried out one type of analysis that should be performed if deconstructive insights are given currency. Along the way, it has generally presupposed those insights and has not rehearsed all the arguments in favor of them. Nor has this final chapter contained particular deconstructive readings of texts. The aim has been rather different. I have tried to show, at an abstract level and with a narrow focus, what remains of critical jurisprudence when deconstructive methodologies win esteem. Of course, the approach advocated here is but one set of ways of coming to terms with deconstruction. This approach, moreover, has been kept at a high degree of abstraction; rather than provide any detailed challenges to reification, I have tried merely to suggest the outlines that such attacks might gainfully take. Nonetheless, despite the abstraction and the deliberately narrow range of problems discussed, this chapter has constituted a plea for substantially rethinking the basic points of contention that have preoccupied the critical legal movement.

If there issues any dominant message from this chapter, it is that critical legal discourse needs to become much more aware of its unawarenesses. To be sure, self-criticism cannot manage to be exhaustive or free of double binds in a method that has put the dichotomy between self and other into question. As Derrida has noted: "[T]o state the difficulty is not . . . to surmount it."[131] But by watching for instances of self-subversion within the argumentative structure that allows watching to take place, one can situate and prefigure and thus absorb critiques to which one's position must be vulnerable. Such critiques are thereby defused—or, rather, their critical astuteness will be appropriated. They become continuations of our approach in the exact degree that they become its subversion. Even unanticipated critiques do not merely devastate the approach, but strengthen it as well. Lending great canniness and power to attacks on reification and other evils, a resistance to categories of traditional metaphysics can best be mounted through a highlighting of whatever makes resistance impossible. By laying stress on their paradoxical self-undoing, arguments can endeavor to be enriched, more than shattered, by deconstruction.[132] This chapter hence implores critical legal scholars to brace their movement by undermining and imperiling it.

Notes

PREFACE

1. Even sophisticated exponents of deconstruction have run aground on this point. See, e.g., J. Llewelyn, *Derrida on the Threshold of Sense* 46 (London: Macmillan, 1986).

2. In Dworkin's own terms, his theory is a mode of "external skepticism." For an insightful critique of Dworkin, see N. Simmonds, "Imperial Visions and Mundane Practices," 46 *Cambridge Law Journal* 465 (1987).

1. INTRODUCTION

1. See B. Johnson, *The Critical Difference* 105–107 (Baltimore: Johns Hopkins University Press, 1980).

2. For a general bibliography of critical legal writings up to the early 1980s, see "A Bibliography of Critical Legal Studies," 94 *Yale Law Journal* 461 (1984). I elaborate a wide-ranging network of strategies and ideas for critical legal scholarship in my book-in-progress, "Critical Legal Theory and the Challenge of Feminism."

3. See, e.g., J. Derrida, "Différance," in *Margins of Philosophy* 1 (Chicago: University of Chicago Press, 1982) (A. Bass trans.).

4. See G. Hegel, *The Phenomenology of Spirit* 9 (New York: Oxford University Press, 1977) (A. Miller trans.).

5. L. Wittgenstein, *On Certainty* 18 (Oxford: Basil Blackwell, 1979) (D. Paul and G. Anscombe trans.).

6. These last remarks will apply even to some theorists who have drawn upon Derrida's work. I especially have in mind the frequently stimulating texts of Dominick LaCapra. See, e.g., D. LaCapra, *A Preface to Sartre* (Ithaca: Cornell University Press, 1978); D. LaCapra, *Rethinking Intellectual History* (Ithaca: Cornell University Press, 1983).

7. Gerald Frug, "The Ideology of Bureaucracy in American Law," 97 *Harvard Law Review* 1277, 1289–90, 1292 (1984).

8. *Id.* at 1289.

9. *Id.* at 1291.

10. An otherwise splendid essay that fails to realize this point is R. Girard, "'To Entrap the Wisest': A Reading of *The Merchant of Venice*," in *Literature and Society* 100, 112–13 (Baltimore: Johns Hopkins University Press, 1980) (E. Said ed.).

11. G. Spivak, "Translator's Preface" to J. Derrida, *Of Grammatology* ix, xlv (Baltimore: Johns Hopkins University Press, 1976).

12. Because only a few fragments of Zeno's writings have survived—see K. Freeman, *Ancilla to the Pre-Socratic Philosophers* 47 (Cambridge: Harvard University Press, 1948)—it is necessary to (re)construct his paradoxes by way of Aristotle's frequently mordant summaries. One of the paradoxes is briefly analyzed in J. Culler, *On Deconstruction* 94 (Ithaca: Cornell University Press, 1982). All four of the paradoxes are taken up in W. Guthrie, *A History of Greek Philosophy: The Presocratic Tradition from Parmenides to Democritus* vol. II, 91–96 (Cambridge: Cambridge University Press, 1965). For a more extensive though frequently dogmatic appraisal, see J. Barnes, *The Presocratic Philosophers* 261–95 (rev. ed., London: Routledge & Kegan Paul, 1982).

13. M. Kramer, "The Metaphysics of the Delaney Clause," 15 *Capital University Law Review* 579, 589–91 (1986).

14. Aristotle, *Physics* 123 (Lincoln: University of Nebraska Press, 1961) (R. Hope trans.) (239b) [hereinafter cited as *Physics*]. In all my quotations from the *Physics*, the translator's index numbers have been deleted. I cite the page numbering of Immanuel Bekker's modern edition of the Greek text.

15. J. Barnes, *supra* note 12, at 266.

16. I have framed the Arrow Paradox this way in order to meet a curiously insubstantial objection raised by Jonathan Barnes. See J. Barnes, *supra* note 12, at 281–83.

17. The foremost work in the field is A. Grünbaum, *Modern Science and Zeno's Paradoxes* (London: George Allen & Unwin, 1968), despite its sometimes egregious begging of questions. For other pertinent essays, see *Zeno's Paradoxes* (Indianapolis: Bobbs-Merrill, 1970) (W. Salmon ed.). The most relevant piece of work by Georg Cantor is his "Über eine elementare Frage der Mannigfaltigkeitslehre," in *Gesammelte Abhandlungen mathematischen und philosophischen Inhalts* 278–80 (Berlin: Springer, 1932) (E. Zermelo ed.).

18. For fine expositions of Cantor's Theorem, see A. Fraenkel, *Abstract Set Theory* 50–53, 69–72 (2d ed., Amsterdam: North-Holland Publishing, 1961); D. Hofstadter, *Gödel, Escher, Bach* 421–24 (New York: Vintage Books, 1979); G. Hunter, *Metalogic: An Introduction to the Metatheory of Standard First Order Logic* 21–25 (Berkeley: University of California Press, 1971). On the relevance of the theorem to Zeno's paradoxes, see Salmon, "Introduction" to *Zeno's Paradoxes, supra* note 17, at 5; see especially *id.* at 15–16, 20–22.

19. Grünbaum, "Modern Science and Refutation of the Paradoxes of Zeno," in *Zeno's Paradoxes, supra* note 17, at 164, 168.

20. For a lengthier treatment of this problem, with citations to Wittgenstein, see *infra* pp. 76–78.

21. G. Hegel, *Logic* 37 (Oxford: Oxford University Press, 1975) (W. Wallace trans.). For more on the categories of universals and particulars, see *infra* chap. 5, note 112.

22. This view is implicit in B. Russell, *The Principles of Mathematics* 101–105, 523–28 (2d ed., London: George Allen & Unwin, 1937); and it is more explicitly stated in A. Fraenkel, Y. Bar-Hillel, and A. Levy, *Foundations of Set Theory* 11 (2d ed., Amsterdam: North-Holland Publishing, 1973) [hereinafter cited as *Foundations of Set Theory*]; D. Hofstadter, *supra* note 18, at 21; Snyder, "*Las Meninas* and the Mirror of the Prince," 11 *Critical Inquiry* 539, 546 (1985).

23. I initially came upon this second paradox, which is known as Grelling's Paradox, in *Foundations of Set Theory, supra* note 22, at 9; and in D. Hofstadter *supra* note 18, at 20–21.

24. See, e.g., L. Wittgenstein, *Philosophical Investigations* 39, 88 (New York: Macmillan, 1958) (G. Anscombe trans.) (Part I, secs. 84 and 240).

25. B. Johnson, *supra* note 1, at 108–109.

26. Juvenal, *The Sixteen Satires* 140 (Harmondsworth: Penguin Books, 1974) (P. Green trans.) (VI, l. 347).

27. See, e.g., Dahl, "On Removing Certain Impediments to Democracy in the United States," 92 *Political Science Quarterly* 1 (1977). I should note, incidentally, that my reason for taking the public/private dichotomy as a given is that I am discussing liberal theories of politics on their own terms. For a critique of the public/private distinction, see *infra* pp. 66–80.

28. See, e.g., A. Miller, "Reason of State and the Emergent Constitution of Control," 64 *Minnesota Law Review* 585 (1980).

29. Plato, *Theaetetus* 61–66 (Harmondsworth: Penguin Books, 1987) (R. Water-

field trans.) (169d–172b) [hereinafter cited as *Theaetetus*]. There are some resemblances between the remarks that follow and the analysis of disciplinary rules in H. Hart, "Self-Referring Laws," in *Essays in Jurisprudence and Philosophy* 170 (Oxford: Oxford University Press, 1983).

30. Countless critics of relativist views have failed to notice the distinction between their target and the much more easy target of nihilism. For two recent examples, see B. Johnson, "Teaching Deconstructively," in *Writing and Reading Differently* 140, 147–48 (Lawrence: University of Kansas Press, 1985) (G. D. Atkins and M. Johnson eds.); and J. H. Miller, "Mr. Carmichael and Lily Briscoe: The Rhythm of Creativity in *To the Lighthouse*," in *Modernism Reconsidered* 167, 188 (Cambridge: Harvard University Press, 1983) (R. Kiely ed.). For a good account of the shortcomings in Plato's argument, with citations to other commentaries, see Waterfield, "Essay," in *Theaetetus, supra* note 29, at 132, 172–76.

31. P. de Man, *Allegories of Reading* 277 (New Haven: Yale University Press, 1979).

32. For a citation to the main texts that have explored the theme of iterability in the ways that I shall here be describing, see *infra* chap. 5, note 98.

33. J. Derrida, *Speech and Phenomena And Other Essays on Husserl's Theory of Signs* 93 (Evanston: Northwestern University Press, 1973) (D. Allison trans.) (emphasis in original).

34. L. Wittgenstein, *supra* note 24, at 92.

35. J. Derrida, *Writing and Difference* 220 (Chicago: University of Chicago Press, 1978) (A. Bass trans.).

36. U. Eco, *A Theory of Semiotics* 7 (Bloomington: Indiana University Press, 1976) (emphasis in original). By showing that even outright tautologies can lie, I have gone a crucial step further than W. Quine, "Two Dogmas of Empiricism," in *From a Logical Point of View* 20 (2d ed., Cambridge, Mass.: Harvard University Press, 1961).

37. S. Knapp and W. Michaels, "Against Theory 2: Hermeneutics and Deconstruction," 14 *Critical Inquiry* 49, 62, 67 (1987).

38. J. Derrida, "Signature Event Context," in *Margins of Philosophy, supra* note 3, at 307 [hereinafter cited in text as "SEC"].

39. R. Rorty, *Consequences of Pragmatism* 99 (Minneapolis: University of Minnesota Press, 1982). For similar views, see, e.g., A. Feenberg, *Lukács, Marx, and the Sources of Critical Theory* 22 (New York: Oxford University Press, 1981); R. Bernstein, *Beyond Objectivism and Relativism* 202 (Philadelphia: University of Pennsylvania Press, 1983); "General Introduction" to *After Philosophy* 1 (Cambridge, Mass.: MIT Press, 1987) (K. Baynes, J. Bohman, and T. McCarthy eds.).

40. G. Hegel, *supra* note 21, at 133. For a Heideggerean-Derridean view of skeptical standpoints, see J. Derrida, *Margins of Philosophy, supra* note 3, at 38.

41. For some suggestive remarks along these lines, see J. Derrida, *supra* note 11, at 8–9; J. Derrida, *supra* note 35, at 227–29.

42. On this point, see A. Einstein, *Relativity: The Special and the General Theory* 44 (London: Methuen, 1962) (R. Lawson trans.); A. Einstein and L. Infeld, *The Evolution of Physics* 191–92 (New York: Simon & Schuster, 1966); R. Resnick and D. Halliday, *Basic Concepts in Relativity and Early Quantum Theory* 29 (2d ed., New York: John Wiley & Sons, 1985).

43. J. Derrida, *Positions* 90 (Chicago: University of Chicago Press, 1981) (A. Bass trans.).

44. J. Derrida, *supra* note 11, at lxxxix, 70, 97. For a somewhat different critique of "the example," see J. Derrida, *supra* note 35, at 169–75.

45. This complaint will be fleshed out in my interweaving of pragmatism

and deconstruction in Chapter 5. For a recent, sophisticated example of the one-sided attempts at syncretism, see H. Staten, *Wittgenstein and Derrida* (Lincoln: University of Nebraska Press, 1984).

46. P. de Man, "Introduction," 18 *Studies in Romanticism* 495, 498 (1979), quoted in J. Culler, *supra* note 12, at 242.

47. J. Derrida, *Margins of Philosophy, supra* note 3, at 12.

2. THE SPECTER OF COMMUNISM

1. The ties of Marxism to the heritage of the West—including many streams of that heritage which Marx had sought to abandon—can be discerned from many perspectives, a few of which I note here. For a pro-ecology view, see I. Balbus, *Marxism and Domination* (Princeton: Princeton University Press, 1982). Balbus maintains: "[T]he epistemological premise that underlies Marx's argument . . . not only militates against the discovery of the solution to the problem of a self-destructive Western culture, it is, in fact, precisely the expression of this problem itself." *Id.* at 260. For a Nietzschean view, see M. Foucault, "Two Lectures," in *Power/Knowledge* 78, 84–85 (New York: Pantheon, 1980) (C. Gordon ed.) (inveighing against those who are "straining to establish the scientificity of Marxism" and who are thereby "investing Marxist discourses and those who uphold them with the effects of a power which the West since medieval times has attributed to science and has reserved for those engaged in scientific discourse"). For a structuralist argument, see M. Foucault, *The Order of Things* 260–62 (New York: Vintage, 1970): "At the deepest level of Western knowledge, Marxism introduced no real discontinuity. . . . Marxism exists in nineteenth-century thought like a fish in water." For an anti-eschatological position, see K. Löwith, *Meaning in History* 33–51 (Chicago: University of Chicago Press, 1949): "Though perverted into secular prognostication, the *Communist Manifesto* still retains the basic features of a messianic faith: 'the assurance of things to be hoped for.'" *Cf.* A. MacIntyre, *Marxism and Christianity* 92 (London: Duckworth, 1968): "Marx's confidence that capitalism would be replaced by socialism . . . is a secularized version of a Christian virtue." See also M. H. Abrams, *Natural Supernaturalism* 313–16 (New York: Norton, 1971). Among the many feminist challenges to Marxism, one of the most convincing is C. MacKinnon, "Feminism, Marxism, Method, and the State: An Agenda for Theory," 7 *Signs* 515 (1982).

On Marx as an epigone of Hegel, see, e.g., H. Gadamer, *Hegel's Dialectic* 73 (New Haven: Yale University Press, 1976) (arguing that Marx's criticisms of Hegel had been forestalled by Hegel's own system); C. Taylor, *Hegel* 154–55, 270–71, 436–37 (Cambridge, England: Cambridge University Press, 1975) (noting some similarities between Marxian and Hegelian doctrines).

On Marxism as a doctrine of tyranny, see, e.g., J. Cohen, *Class and Civil Society: The Limits of Marxian Critical Theory* 108 (Amherst: University of Massachusetts Press, 1983): "Marx, against all his intentions, provides the basis for the anti-democratic single-party state penetrating all of civil society when he argues that civil liberties and democratic forms in bourgeois society are mere reflections of capitalist market relations that communism can well do without." See also L. Kolakowski, *Main Currents of Marxism* vol. III, 526 (Oxford: Oxford University Press, 1978): "Communism is not a mere 'degeneration' of Marxism but a possible interpretation of it, and even a well-founded one, though primitive and partial"; G. Lichtheim, *Marxism* 398 (London: Routledge & Kegan Paul, 1961): "[T]he Marxian scheme clearly lent itself to utilisation by revolutionaries in search of a system which validated their drive towards total reconstruction; and it did so because Marx's starting-point had been the all-inclusive rationalism of Hegel, with its conception of history as the realisation of liberty." Perhaps most revealing is the astonishing trenchancy with which one of Marx's foremost critics was able, in 1872, to predict the shape of Marxism in practice. See M. Bakunin, "The International and Karl Marx," in *Bakunin on Anarchism* 286, 315–19 (Montreal: Black Rose Books, 1980) (S. Dolgoff ed.).

On the linking of political ambitions to philosophical speculation, see *infra* p. 219. I am not suggesting that philosophical discourse can proceed outside politics. My only point is that causing one's political credo to hinge on the success of one's metaphysical speculation will usually result in bad speculation and even worse politics.

2. For Marx's best work, see K. Marx, "Economic and Philosophical Manuscripts," in *Early Writings* 61 (New York: McGraw-Hill, 1963) (T. Bottomore ed.). This, of course, is by no means the only text in Marx's *oeuvre* that I set store by; but it is, I think, the most consistently penetrating. For Adorno's thought, see especially T. Adorno, *Negative Dialectics* (New York: Continuum, 1973) (E. Ashton trans.); this book stands as arguably the greatest accomplishment of the Marxist tradition. For a discussion of Lukács, see *infra* pp. 212–22. For Marcuse's critique of technocratic oppression, see, e.g., H. Marcuse, *One-Dimensional Man* 9–18, 144–69 (Boston: Beacon Press, 1964). For a discussion of Sartre, see *infra* pp. 222–35. Despite an embattled tone, a "last-instance" economism, a baleful politics, and a problematic embrace of science, Althusser offers powerful insights into the dynamics of social institutions and Marxist theory. See especially L. Althusser, *For Marx* (London: Verso, 1977) (B. Brewster trans.); L. Althusser, "Marx's Immense Theoretical Revolution," in L. Althusser and E. Balibar, *Reading Capital* 182 (London: Verso, 1970) (B. Brewster trans.); L. Althusser, "Ideology and Ideological State Apparatuses (Notes towards an Investigation)," in *Lenin and Philosophy* 127 (New York: Monthly Review Press, 1971) (B. Brewster trans.).

3. I especially have in mind Adorno, whose later work has been denounced by one observer as "apolitical and impotent." W. Adamson, *Hegemony and Revolution* 245 (Berkeley: University of California Press, 1980). For a more sophisticated assessment, see S. Buck-Morss, *The Origin of Negative Dialectics* 61–62 (New York: Free Press, 1977): "If there were Marxist elements in Adorno's understanding of history, his was not Marx's understanding." For other valuable Marxist works that I have not yet mentioned, see, e.g., A. Gramsci, *Selections from the Prison Notebooks* (New York: International Publishers, 1971) (Q. Hoare and G. N. Smith trans.); M. Horkheimer, *Critical Theory* (New York: Continuum, 1982); F. Jameson, *The Political Unconscious* (Ithaca: Cornell University Press, 1981); K. Korsch, *Marxism and Philosophy* (New York: Monthly Review Press, 1970) (F. Halliday trans.); V. Volosinov, *Marxism and the Philosophy of Language* (New York: Seminar Press, 1973) (L. Matejka and I. Titunik trans.).

4. J. Derrida, *Positions* 62–64, 74–75 (Chicago: University of Chicago Press, 1981) (A. Bass trans.) [hereinafter cited as *Positions*]. For a similar view of Freudianism, see S. Felman, "Turning the Screw of Interpretation," in *Literature and Psychoanalysis* 94, 116 (Baltimore: Johns Hopkins University Press, 1982) (S. Felman ed.).

5. G. Cohen, *Karl Marx's Theory of History* (Princeton: Princeton University Press, 1978) [hereinafter cited as KMTH]. Other texts by Cohen that will be studied here are "Being, Consciousness and Roles: On the Foundations of Historical Materialism," in *Essays in Honour of E. H. Carr* 82 (Oxford: Oxford University Press, 1974) (C. Abramsky ed.) [hereinafter cited as "Roles"]; "Freedom, Justice and Capitalism," 126 *New Left Review* 3 (1981) [hereinafter cited as "Freedom"]; "Reconsidering Historical Materialism," 26 *Nomos* 227 (1983) [hereinafter cited

as "Materialism"]; "The Structure of Proletarian Unfreedom," 12 *Philosophy and Public Affairs* 3 (1983) [hereinafter cited as "Proletarian Unfreedom"].

6. R. Wokler, "Rousseau and Marx," in *The Nature of Political Theory* 219, 230 (Oxford: Oxford University Press, 1983) (D. Miller and L. Siedentrop eds.).

7. For praise of Cohen amid heavy criticism, see, e.g., *id.;* W. Adamson, "Review Essay," 19 *History & Theory* 186, 203 (1980): "Cohen has brought analytical philosophy to bear on Marx, and in some very stimulating ways"; J. Cohen, "Book Review," 79 *Journal of Philosophy* 253, 254 (1982) (praising Cohen's "substantial and often quite brilliant effort"); J. Elster, "Cohen on Marx's Theory of History," 28 *Political Studies* 121 (1980) (Cohen's book "sets a new standard for Marxist philosophy"); S. Lukes, "Can the Base be distinguished from the Superstructure?" in *The Nature of Political Theory, supra* note 6, at 103, 104 (Cohen's book is "the most coherent and analytically refined defence [which historical materialism] has yet received"); R. Miller, "Productive Forces and the Forces of Change: A Review of Gerald A. Cohen, *Karl Marx's Theory of History,*" 90 *Philosophical Review* 91 (1981): "Those with their own interpretations of Marx will find that their thinking about him is enriched, clarified, and stimulated, even if their final thought about Cohen's book is that it is deeply wrong"; D.-H. Ruben, "Review Article: Cohen, Marx, and the Primacy Thesis," 11 *British Journal of Political Science* 227 (1981): "Cohen's book is an extraordinarily rich one."

On the "brilliance" of Cohen's work, see, e.g., J. Cohen, *supra* note 7, at 254; R. Gordon, "Critical Legal Histories," 36 *Stanford Law Review* 57, 105 n. 109 (1984). On Cohen's "clarity," see, in addition to the foregoing sources, A. Gilbert, "Book Review," 74 *American Political Science Review* 156 (1980); G. Graham, "Book Review," 30 *Philosophical Quarterly* 274 (1980); K. Tribe, "Book Review," 31 *British Journal of Sociology* 304 (1980). On Cohen's "rigor," see—in addition to the foregoing sources—R. Atkinson, "Book Review," 55 *Philosophy* 416 (1980).

8. See KMTH, *supra* note 5, at 89, 138, 145. Equally condescending is the assertion that Marx "outgrew" Hegel. See *id.* at 22.

9. For treatment of these questions, see, e.g., Adamson, *supra* note 7 (arguing that Cohen has given only one possible interpretation of Marx and has ignored other possible readings); J. Elster, *Making Sense of Marx* 269–72 (Cambridge, England: Cambridge University Press, 1985); Miller, *supra* note 7.

10. See, e.g., J. Cohen, *supra* note 7, at 266–71; Elster, *supra* note 7, at 124 (observing that "the productive forces were largely static up to recent times"); D. Hodges and R. Gandy, "Varieties of Economic Determinism," 40 *Journal of Economic History* 373, 374 (1980): "In modern Western Europe we have, for the first time, an economically advancing society."

11. J. Derrida, *Of Grammatology* 163 (Baltimore: Johns Hopkins University Press, 1976) (G. Spivak trans.); Derrida, "Living On/Border Lines," in H. Bloom, P. de Man, J. Derrida, G. Hartman, and J. Miller, *Deconstruction and Criticism* 75, 84 (New York: Continuum, 1979).

12. For a distinction largely similar to Cohen's, see L. Althusser, "Ideology and Ideological State Apparatuses," *supra* note 2, at 138–40. See also L. Althusser, "A Letter on Art in Reply to André Daspre," in *Lenin and Philosophy, supra* note 2, at 221, 224 (drawing a distinction between "seeing" and "knowing").

13. J. Derrida, *supra* note 11, at 166.

14. See, e.g., F. Nietzsche, *The Will to Power* 339, 368 (New York: Vintage, 1967) (W. Kaufmann and R. Hollingdale trans.) (secs. 635, 689) (discussing quanta of force, whose "essence lies in their relation to all other quanta"). For a fine analysis, see G. Deleuze, *Nietzsche and Philosophy* 39–64 (New York: Columbia University Press, 1983) (H. Tomlinson trans.). As Deleuze notes: "We must remem-

ber that every force has an essential relation to other forces, that the essence of force is its quantitative difference from other forces and that this difference is expressed as the force's quality. Now, difference in quantity, understood in this way, necessarily reflects a differential element of related forces—which is also the genetic element of the qualities of these forces. This is what the will to power is; the genealogical element of force, both differential and genetic" (49–50).

15. K. Marx, *A Contribution to the Critique of Political Economy* 20 (London: Lawrence and Wishart, 1971) (S. Ryazanskaya trans.), quoted in KMTH, *supra* note 5, at 28.

16. Indeed, as Chapter 1 would suggest, I am understating my case; Wittgenstein would claim further that *all* conclusions are *ex silentio*. See L. Wittgenstein, *Philosophical Investigations* 56–88 (New York: Macmillan, 1958) (G. Anscombe trans.) (I, secs. 143–239). See especially *id.* at 75 (sec. 186).

17. The quoted terms are from KMTH, *supra* note 5, at 136, 225, 335, 343, 91, 136, 310, 308.

18. By far the longest account of this distinction is in K. Marx, *Theories of Surplus Value* vol. I, 152–304 (London: Lawrence and Wishart, 1969) (E. Burns trans.). For a good introduction, see I. Gough, "Marx's Theory of Productive and Unproductive Labour," 76 *New Left Review* 47 (1972).

19. In regard to the first reason, see, e.g., K. Marx, *supra* note 18, at 165. In regard to the second reason, see *id.* at 157: "Productive labour is here defined from the standpoint of capitalist production." In regard to the third reason, see Gough, *supra* note 18, at 60–61 (arguing that Marx's distinction is "inseparably linked . . . to the labour theory of value"). For Cohen's avoidance of the labor theory of value, see, e.g., KMTH, *supra* note 5, at 353. At times—especially in his fifth chapter and his first appendix—Cohen violates his disclaimers and falls back upon a labor theory of value.

20. For a similar point, see J. Elster, *supra* note 9, at 245–46.

21. See, e.g., G. Hegel, *Philosophy of Right* 89–90 (Oxford: Oxford University Press, 1952) (T. Knox trans.) (sec. 135). In speaking of "abstract" form, I am not criticizing any mere lack of detail. Accounts of the class positions may be very extensive and illuminating—as some of Cohen's are—but so long as they are seeking to define classes with no explicit mention of outlooks, they will be abstract in the important sense that they remove themselves from that which instantiates them and gives them effect. Such, at least, is the impossible aim of those who offer such accounts.

22. I shall not here take account of iterability—the potential for role playing without any accompanying intentionality. *Cf. supra* pp. 25–31. That phenomenon, though of great importance in general, will not bear on the present point of dispute.

23. KMTH, *supra* note 5, at 89. Lest Cohen seem racist or insensitive, I should point out that his example of Negro servitude is taken explicitly from Marx.

24. This is a point made in Van Parijs, "Marxism's central puzzle," in *After Marx* 88 (Cambridge, England: Cambridge University Press, 1984) (T. Ball & J. Farr eds.); and in J. Elster, *supra* note 9, at 269.

25. J. Cohen, *supra* note 7, at 257. See also J. Elster, *supra* note 9, at 286 note 4.

26. Elster, *supra* note 7, at 124.

27. See J. Cohen, *supra* note 7, at 257. G. A. Cohen has at last started to wrestle with this query. See G. A. Cohen and W. Kymlicka, "Human Nature

and Social Change in the Marxist Conception of History," 85 *Journal of Philosophy* 171 (1988).

28. KMTH, *supra* note 5, at 158. For critiques of the (il)logic of supplementarity, see J. Derrida, *supra* note 11, at 141–64; J. Derrida, *Writing and Difference* 289–90 (Chicago: University of Chicago Press, 1978) (A. Bass trans.). For an attack on necessitarian views like those held by Cohen, see M. Weber, *Economy and Society* vol. II, 1090–92 (Berkeley: University of California Press, 1978) (G. Roth and C. Wittich eds.). Unsurprisingly, Weber's critical thrusts retain quite a strong belief in necessitarianism. For another viewpoint opposed to Cohen's see Gordon, *supra* note 7. In the course of attacking functionalism in several ways, Gordon writes of "the myriad paths to capital accumulation" that "should at least make the functionalist hesitate" (*id.* at 78).

29. In KMTH, *supra* note 5, at 153, Cohen admits that his "argument [for the Development Thesis] has two large gaps."

30. These arguments are set forth in *id.* at 191–92. Cohen's best arguments are close to the one set forth in A. MacIntyre, *After Virtue* 100–101 (Notre Dame: University of Notre Dame Press, 1981).

31. On the unfreedom of free markets, see, e.g., Morris Cohen, "The Basis of Contract," 46 *Harvard Law Review* 553 (1933); Morris Cohen, "Property and Sovereignty," 13 *Cornell Law Quarterly* 8 (1927); R. Hale, "Bargaining, Duress, and Economic Liberty," 43 *Columbia Law Review* 603 (1943); R. Hale, "Coercion and Distribution in a Supposedly Non-Coercive State," 38 *Political Science Quarterly* 470 (1923). The harshness of restrictions on the mobility of workers under Stalin is described in G. Hosking, *A History of the Soviet Union* 157, 302–03 (London: Fontana, 1985). *Cf. id.* at 199–200 on devices used to "encourage" high productivity in the Soviet slave labor camps.

32. S. Hook, *Towards an Understanding of Karl Marx* 142–43 (New York: John Day Company, 1933). For a similar view regarding the base/superstructure relationship, see D. Kennedy, "The Role of Law in Economic Thought: Essays on the Fetishism of Commodities," 34 *American University Law Review* 939, 978–79 (1985).

33. KMTH, *supra* note 5, at 246. See also *id.* at 205. *Cf.* Adamson, *supra* note 7, at 195: "[N]ot only does [Cohen] deprive historical materialism of any implications for cultural and aesthetic theory, but he would seem to have to deny as well that Marx had any interest in cultural and aesthetic theory."

34. *Cf.* L. Althusser, "Preface to *Capital* Volume One," in *Lenin and Philosophy, supra* note 2, at 71, 104: "[L]egal relations and the relations of production must not be confused."

35. Cohen remarks, importantly, that "[t]his is not to say that the adjustment of the legal order to the economy is always carried out consciously" (KMTH, *supra* note 5, at 231).

36. *Id.* at 232. Cohen's analysis of law has been given wide attention. For examples of commendation, see Elster, *supra* note 7, at 125; Adamson, *supra* note 7, at 198: "This is a plausible interpretation of how Marx regarded the structure-superstructure relationship." Critiques have thus far been highly unsatisfactory. See, e.g., Lukes, *supra* note 7; H. Collins, *Marxism and Law* 81–90 (Oxford: Oxford University Press, 1982). For a rejoinder, see G. A. Cohen, "Base and Superstructure: A Reply to Hugh Collins," 9 *Oxford Journal of Legal Studies* 95 (1989). Collins and Lukes both restate parts of Cohen's theory as if they were presenting objections to it. Critical legal scholars who mention Cohen's book seem, alas, to have relied on the glib and futile critique by Collins. See, e.g., Gordon, *supra* note 7, at 105 n.109; M. Tushnet, "Marxism as Metaphor," 68 *Cornell Law Review* 281, 285–86 (1983).

37. I am here looking askance at the belief of J. Hillis Miller that deconstruction "gives the priority to the text, not to subjectivity." "Marxism and Deconstruction: Symposium at the Conference on Contemporary Genre Theory and the Yale School," in *Rhetoric and Form: Deconstruction at Yale* 75, 91 (Norman: University of Oklahoma Press, 1985) (R. Davis and R. Schleifer eds.) (comments by J. Hillis Miller). For someone of Miller's sophistication, this one-sidedness is rather bizarre. For a salutary response to similar views, see J. Derrida, *Memoires for Paul de Man* 123–24 (New York: Columbia University Press, 1986) (C. Lindsay, J. Culler, and E. Cadava trans.).

38. J. Derrida, *supra* note 28, at 283–84.

39. For an example of such use by a social scientist, see T. Lowi, *The End of Liberalism* 50 (New York: Norton, 1969).

40. "Freedom," *supra* note 5, at 5. *Cf.* Kennedy, *supra* note 32, at 997 note 62: "The firepower of the Pinkertons, like the fist of the battering husband, is a thoroughly mediated physicality, by which I mean that the social and social-psychological contexts exert all kinds of influences on both the aggressor and the victim, decreeing for example that the battered woman be untrained in self-defense, that the crowd of workers lack a secret arms cache." Of course, neither argument for discounting the law-morals connection would *necessarily* quash a view that legal propositions and moral claims are of the same form. Such a view of propositional form would not *perforce* lead one to a conclusion that "is" and "ought" must substantially overlap in legal systems, and it would hence not be rebutted by a critique that turned up discrepancies between "is" and "ought."

I accept, moreover, that a belief in natural law is not ineluctably conservative in itself; but it would become profoundly conservative if it were combined with the legal positivism that Cohen favors.

41. See M. Weber, *Economy and Society* vol. I, 212–301 (Berkeley: University of California Press, 1978) (G. Roth and C. Wittich eds.). I do not wish to ascribe any special soundness to the classificatory scheme that Weber put forth. The general direction of my approach cuts against the categories and the distinctions that Weber hoped to maintain.

42. *Id.* at 217; M. Weber, "The Social Psychology of the World Religions," in *From Max Weber* 267, 294–95 (New York: Oxford University Press, 1946) (H. Gerth and C. Mills eds.).

43. M. Weber, "Politics as a Vocation," in *From Max Weber, supra* note 42, at 77, 78.

44. For a critique of formalism, see G. Frug, "The Ideology of Bureaucracy in American Law," 97 *Harvard Law Review* 1276, 1297–1317 (1984). Frug limits himself by emphasizing a quasi-structuralist methodology.

45. KMTH, *supra* note 5, at 223 (emphasis added). *Cf.* "Proletarian Unfreedom," *supra* note 5, at 6–7: "[T]he structure of capitalism is not in all senses self-sustaining. It is sustained by a great deal of deliberate human action, notably on the part of the state."

46. M. Weber, *supra* note 43, at 80.

47. H. Hart, *The Concept of Law* 112 (Oxford: Oxford University Press, 1961). Strictly speaking, Hart here focuses not on intentionality but on rule-accepting behavior. My point relating to intentions would be agreeable to Hart *a fortiori*.

48. J. Derrida, *Margins of Philosophy* 326 (Chicago: University of Chicago Press, 1982) (A. Bass tran.).

49. I am especially worried that I may have sounded too much like M. Friedman, "The Methodology of Positive Economics," in *Essays in Positive Economics* 3 (Chicago: University of Chicago Press, 1953).

50. See J. Derrida, *supra* note 28, at 274–76. *Cf.* Romans 3:20, 4:15, 7:7.

51. K. Marx, *Grundrisse*, in *Selected Writings* 345, 349 (Oxford: Oxford University Press, 1977) (D. McLellan ed.). For an alternative translation, see K. Marx, *Grundrisse* 88 (New York: Vintage, 1973) (M. Nicolaus trans.). Cohen (mis)interprets the quoted phrase as if it were "law is also club law." See KMTH, *supra* note 5, at 225. I do not want to imply that such a transposition could never win our acceptance as a reading of Marx; if it were to do so, however, it would have to have been backed up with far more convincing arguments than the one Cohen puts forward. He will have to do more than say that his interpretation is "plainly" the correct one.

52. In addition to the articles cited *supra* note 31, see R. Hale, "Force and the State: A Comparison of 'Political' and 'Economic' Compulsion," 35 *Columbia Law Review* 149 (1935). For very good though brief summaries of the Realist challenge to public/private distinctions, see E. Mensch, "The History of Mainstream Legal Thought," in *The Politics of Law* 18, 28 (New York: Pantheon, 1982) (D. Kairys ed.); D. Kennedy, "The Stages of the Decline of the Public/Private Distinction," 130 *University of Pennsylvania Law Review* 1349, 1351–52 (1982). For overviews of Legal Realism, see, e.g., Note, "'Round and 'Round the Bramble Bush: From Legal Realism to Critical Legal Scholarship," 95 *Harvard Law Review* 1669 (1982); E. Purcell, *The Crisis of Democratic Theory* 74–94 (Lexington: University of Kentucky Press, 1973). See also K. Llewellyn, "Some Realism About Realism—Responding to Dean Pound," 44 *Harvard Law Review* 1222 (1931). I should note, by the way, that Morris Cohen was a strong critic of Legal Realism as well as a contributor to it.

53. These effects will become apparent in a variety of settings: schools, families, religious practices, and so forth. The settings themselves are of course structured by law, and those who propagate ideology within them can best be seen—in line with what the Realists maintained—as executing a delegated public function.

54. C. Dalton, "Book Review," 6 *Harvard Women's Law Journal* 229, 243 note 53 (1983) (reviewing *The Politics of Law*, *supra* note 52).

55. Closer to addressing this latter problem, of uncurbed violations, is a query by Gerald Gunther: "Can authorization be distinguished from mere tolerance, where the state has power to forbid private discrimination and does not exercise that power?" G. Gunther, *Constitutional Law: Cases and Materials* 987 (10th ed., Mineola: Foundation Press, 1980).

56. G. Frege, *Translations from the Philosophical Writings* 125–26 (Oxford: Blackwell, 1952) (P. Geach and M. Black eds.).

57. *Cf.* L. Wittgenstein, *supra* note 16, at 84 (sec. 211): "How can he *know* how he is to continue a pattern by himself—whatever instruction you give him?—Well, how do I know?—If that means 'Have I reasons?' the answer is: my reasons will soon give out. And then I shall act, without reasons."

58. One of the best statements of this view is in *id.* at 74–75 (sec. 185). See also *id.* at 84 (sec. 213): "If intuition is an inner voice—how do I know how I am to obey it? And how do I know that it doesn't mislead me? For if it can guide me right, it can also guide me wrong"; *id.* at 100 (sec. 292): "You . . . have to apply the rule in the particular case without guidance." Highly relevant here, of course, is Derrida's remarkable study of framing. See J. Derrida, "The Parergon," 9 *October* 3 (1979).

59. See, e.g., L. Wittgenstein, *On Certainty* 21 (Oxford: Basil Blackwell, 1969) (G. Anscombe and G. von Wright eds.) (sec. 139): "Not only rules but also examples are needed for establishing a practice. Our rules leave loop-holes open,

and the practice has to speak for itself." *Cf.* J. Derrida, *supra* note 28, at 26: "Structuralism lives within and on the difference between its promise and its practice."

60. On the significance of this last phrase (and its cognates), see *infra* chap. 5 note 26.

61. *Positions, supra* note 4, at 19.

62. I here reinstate the circle that Socrates evaded with characteristic sophisms. See Plato, "Euthyphro," in *Euthyphro, Apology, Crito* 1, 11–13 (Indianapolis: Bobbs-Merrill, 1956) (F. Church and R. Cumming trans.).

63. N. Simmonds, *Central Issues in Jurisprudence* 85 (London: Sweet & Maxwell, 1986).

64. One of Heidegger's best descriptions of this phenomenon occurs in the opening two pages of M. Heidegger, "The Origin of the Work of Art," in *Poetry, Language, Thought* 17 (New York: Harper & Row, 1971) (A. Hofstadter trans.). The hermeneutic circle was, of course, seen by Heidegger as both necessary and desirable. See, e.g., M. Heidegger, *Being and Time* 363 (Oxford: Basil Blackwell, 1962) (J. Macquarrie and E. Robinson trans.). For an account of the circle by a distinguished Heideggerian, see H. Gadamer, *Truth and Method* 235–67 (New York: Seabury Press, 1975) (G. Barden and J. Cumming trans.).

65. I leave aside further difficulties, such as the problem of self-dividing bounds—in our case, the bounds of concepts—that Derrida explores in so many of his essays. See, e.g., J. Derrida, "The Law of Genre," in *On Narrative* 51 (Chicago: University of Chicago Press, 1981) (W. Mitchell ed.).

66. See *Positions, supra* note 4, at 28: "*[D]ifférance* . . . produces systematic and regulated transformations which are able, at a certain point, to leave room for a structural science"; J. Derrida, *supra* note 48, at 327: "I will not conclude . . . that there is no effect of the performative, no effect of ordinary language, no effect of presence and of speech acts."

67. J. Derrida, *supra* note 28, at 285.

68. For some playful remarks on "*le propre*," see J. Derrida, *Spurs/Éperons* 108–19 (Chicago: University of Chicago Press, 1979) (B. Harlow trans.).

69. KMTH, *supra* note 5, at 292. Compare the view of a leading pragmatist: "To accept the contingency of starting points is to accept our inheritance from, and our conversation with, our fellow humans as our only source of guidance." R. Rorty, *Consequences of Pragmatism* 166 (Minneapolis: University of Minnesota Press, 1982).

70. For a good discussion, from a structuralist standpoint, of some of the codes that enter into the reading of literary texts, see J. Culler, "Convention and Naturalization," in *Structuralist Poetics* 131 (Ithaca: Cornell University Press, 1975). If literature can in any way be deemed distinctive, then the distinctiveness "consists perhaps only in the fact that [nonliterary discourse] is more likely to be blind to the way in which its own critical difference from itself makes it, in the final analysis, literary." B. Johnson, *The Critical Difference* 12 (Baltimore: Johns Hopkins University Press, 1980).

71. *Cf.* J. Derrida, *supra* note 28, at 32 (noting that "real life . . . may always be absent"); *Positions, supra* note 4, at 20 (proposing that "every signified is also in the position of a signifier"); J. Derrida, *supra* note 11, at 158; "Yet if reading must not be content with doubling the text, it cannot legitimately transgress the text toward something other than it, toward a referent (a reality that is metaphysical, historical, psychobiographical, etc.) or toward a signified outside the text whose content could take place, could have taken place outside of language, that is to say, in the sense that we give here to that word, outside

of writing in general." It should be re-emphasized that Derrida is by no means simply a pragmatist. See *supra* pp. 29–34; *infra* pp. 240–53.

72. See, e.g., N. Goodman, *Ways of Worldmaking* 1–22, 109–40 (Indianapolis: Hackett, 1978).

73. R. Rorty, *supra* note 69, at 94.

74. Johnson, "Taking Fidelity Philosophically," in *Difference in Translation* 142, 145 (Ithaca: Cornell University Press, 1985) (J. Graham ed.).

75. This seems as good a place as any to reprimand Isaac Balbus for arguing that substitution demands equality, rather than mere commensurability, of goods. See I. Balbus, "Commodity Form and Legal Form: An Essay on the 'Relative Autonomy' of the Law," 11 *Law and Society Review* 571 (1977). Balbus has not renounced this contention, despite his repudiation of Marxism. See I. Balbus, *supra* note 1, at 101–102. Mark Tushnet seems to endorse Balbus's elementary misstep (without actually citing Balbus's work). See Tushnet, *supra* note 36, at 288–90 (giving qualified support to a "commodity-exchange theory" of law).

76. A. Parker, "Futures for Marxism: An Appreciation of Althusser," *Diacritics*, Winter 1985, at 57, 66 (quoting K. Marx, *A Contribution to the Critique of Political Economy* 28 [New York: International Publishers, 1977] [M. Dobb ed.]).

77. K. Marx, *Capital* vol. I, 69, 114 (New York: International Publishers, 1967) (S. Moore and E. Aveling trans.).

78. For a very good critique of Marx, see Parker, *supra* note 76.

79. K. Marx, *supra* note 15, at 36.

80. Lukes, *supra* note 7, at 119. For an opposing view, see L. Althusser, "Ideology and Ideological State Apparatuses," *supra* note 2, at 134–36. But see L. Althusser, *Reading Capital*, *supra* note 2, at 26–27, for a more cautious view of spatial metaphors.

81. For an interesting though slightly wary account of anti-ocularcentrist strains in Michel Foucault's work, see Jay, "In the Empire of the Gaze: Foucault and the Denigration of Vision in Twentieth-Century French Thought," in *Foucault: A Critical Reader* 175 (Oxford: Basil Blackwell, 1986) (D. Hoy ed.). Jay discusses, with painful brevity, some of Foucault's predecessors. For a feminist treatment of vision-related discourse, see L. Irigaray, *Speculum of the Other Woman* (Ithaca: Cornell University Press, 1985) (G. Gill trans.). See especially *id.* at 47–48, 147–51.

82. J. Derrida, *supra* note 48, at 252. For Descartes's clarifying metaphors, see R. Descartes, "Meditations on First Philosophy," in *The Essential Descartes* 154, 179–80, 182–83 (New York: Mentor, 1969) (M. Wilson ed.). For a critique of Descartes, see J. Derrida, *supra* note 48, at 266–67.

83. J. Derrida, *supra* note 48, at 268.

84. If E. M. Forster's terms are to be followed, I should substitute "plots" for "stories." See E. Forster, *Aspects of the Novel* 86 (San Diego: Harcourt Brace Jovanovich, 1927). Nietzsche would have us speak of "myths." See F. Nietzsche, *Beyond Good and Evil* sec. 21 (New York: Vintage, 1966) (W. Kaufmann trans.). What one should keep in mind is that causal narratives disrupt their own workings. See M. Kramer, "The Metaphysics of the Delaney Clause," 15 *Capital University Law Review* 579 (1986).

For a sample of Nietzsche's tirades against causal discourse, see F. Nietzsche, *Twilight of the Idols* 48–52 (Harmondsworth: Penguin Books, 1968) (R. Hollingdale trans.); F. Nietzsche, *The Gay Science* secs. 112, 217 (New York: Vintage, 1974) (W. Kaufmann trans.). Hume's critique of causality can be found in D.

Hume, *An Enquiry Concerning Human Understanding*, in *Enquiries Concerning Human Understanding and Concerning the Principles of Morals* 26–79 (Oxford: Oxford University Press, 1975) (L. Selby-Bigge and P. Nidditch eds.) (secs. 4–7); D. Hume, *A Treatise of Human Nature* 69–176 (Oxford: Oxford University Press, 1978) (L. Selby-Bigge and P. Nidditch eds.) (pt. III, secs. 1–15). The great merit of these critiques is that, while they are wholly circular, they make plain that any kind of riposte—and thus any defense of causal language or of induction more generally—will be just as circular. The critiques rely, however, on deeply problematic appeals to the self-presence of subjectivity. Thus, at times, Nietzsche's discourse sounds more than slightly Kantian. For a critique of the subjectivist side of Nietzsche, see P. de Man, "Rhetoric of Persuasion," in *Allegories of Reading* 119 (New Haven: Yale University Press, 1979).

85. For a different view, see F. Nietzsche, *The Gay Science*, *supra* note 84, at sec. 205: "Need is considered the cause why something came to be; but in truth it is often merely an effect of what has come to be."

86. B. Johnson, *supra* note 70, at 129.

87. For a critique of this trope, see P. de Man, *supra* note 84, at 248–49; J. Derrida, *supra* note 28, at 282–84; J. Derrida, *supra* note 11, at 103–105.

88. *Cf.* J. Derrida, *supra* note 11, at 215: "What does Rousseau say without saying, see without seeing? That substitution has always already begun; that imitation, principle of art, has always already interrrupted natural plenitude; that, having to be a *discourse*, it has always already [breached] presence in differance; that in Nature it is always that which supplies Nature's lack, a voice that is substituted for the voice of Nature."

89. "Materialism," *supra* note 5, at 240. *Cf.* R. Barthes, *Mythologies* 101–102 (New York: Hill & Wang, 1972) (A. Lavers trans.). Also *cf.* S. Kierkegaard, *Concluding Unscientific Postscript* 273, 275 (Princeton: Princeton University Press, 1941) (D. Swenson and W. Lowrie trans.): "To think existence . . . in abstract terms is essentially to abrogate it. . . .

". . . [T]he Hegelian philosophy, by failing to define its relation to the existing individual, and by ignoring the ethical, confounds existence.

". . . To exist under the guidance of pure thought is like traveling in Denmark with the help of a small map of Europe, on which Denmark shows no larger than a steel pen-point—aye, it is still more impossible."

90. Were the priority merely temporal, Cohen could escape my critique. See KMTH, *supra* note 5, at 177, 179–80. For an example of the type of criticism that Cohen shows to be ill conceived, see I. Balbus, *supra* note 1, at 142 note 42.

91. Indeed, we could accept *arguendo* the power-based production relations that Cohen posits, without detracting from the point that I make here.

92. D. Kennedy, "Cost-Benefit Analysis of Entitlement Problems: A Critique," 33 *Stanford Law Review* 387, 422–44 (1981). The quotation is from *id.* at 422. For a critique similar to Kennedy's, see L. Bebchuk, "The Pursuit of a Bigger Pie: Can Everyone Expect a Bigger Slice?" 8 *Hofstra Law Review* 671 (1980).

93. L. Kornhauser, "The Great Image of Authority," 36 *Stanford Law Review* 349, 359 (1984). This is Kornhauser's summary of Mark Kelman's view, a view to which Kornhauser subscribes with an appropriate reservation: "[T]he endogenicity of preferences does not negate the usefulness of the neoclassical assumption of fixed preferences within certain bounds. That culture or economic structures may determine the preferences that individuals have does not imply that preferences are not fixed for most short-term or medium-term horizons. Capitalism

may have shaped the preferences that each of us has in some profound way, but it seems unlikely that even a dramatic shift in social organization would instantaneously (or even within the course of a single generation) dramatically alter individual preferences. After all, one suspects that preference formation is a very complex process mediated by many different parts of the social structure." *Id.* For a critique of preference-formation under a free-market regime, see C. E. Baker, "The Ideology of the Economic Analysis of Law," 5 *Philosophy & Public Affairs* 3, 34–40 (1975): "Any structure, but more specifically the market and consumer sovereignty, shapes tastes and distributions, organizes the processes of realizing values, and embodies a concept of value and man." Relevant also is M. Kelman, "Choice and Utility," 1979 *Wisconsin Law Review* 769, 781 note 25 and accompanying text, though Kelman's specific point would apply to increases in absolute wealth as much as to changes in distribution.

94. *Positions, supra* note 4, at 43 (emphasis in original). *Cf.* T. Adorno, *supra* note 2, at 136: "Once dialectics has become inescapable, however, it cannot stick to its principle like ontology and transcendental philosophy. It cannot be maintained as a structure that will stay basic no matter how it is modified. In criticizing ontology we do not aim at another ontology, not even at one of being nonontological. If that were our purpose we would be merely positing another downright 'first'—not absolute identity, this time, not the concept, not Being, but nonidentity, facticity, entity."

3. THE RULE OF MISRECOGNITION IN THE HART OF JURISPRUDENCE

1. On the frightful *ressentiment* of Dante, see, e.g., G. Steiner, *In Bluebeard's Castle* 54–55 (New Haven: Yale University Press, 1971).

2. See, e.g., F. Nietzsche, *The Gay Science* sec. 344 (New York: Vintage, 1974) (W. Kaufmann trans.). Nietzsche's remarks were specifically directed against science, but they forcefully apply to the whole era of liberalism.

3. J. Mill, *On Liberty* 56 (Indianapolis: Bobbs-Merrill, 1956) (C. Shields ed.) [hereinafter cited in text as OL]. For Mill's view of the pretensions of Christianity to truth, see *id.* at 58–63.

4. Indeed, Mill's view was prefigured to some extent in the writings of Locke and Milton. See, e.g., J. Locke, "A Letter Concerning Toleration," in *The Locke Reader* 245, 253 (Cambridge, England: Cambridge University Press, 1977) (J. Yolton ed.): "[E]very church is orthodox to itself; to others, erroneous or heretical. Whatsoever any church believes, it believes to be true; and the contrary thereunto it pronounces to be error. So that the controversy between these churches about the truth of their doctrines, and the purity of their worship, is on both sides equal; nor is there any judge, either at Constantinople, or elsewhere upon earth, by whose sentence it can be determined."

Milton's "Areopagitica" teems with splendid passages that anticipate Mill's view. See J. Milton, "Areopagitica," in *The Portable Milton* 151, 185–95 (Harmondsworth: Penguin, 1977) (D. Bush ed.). See especially *id.* at 194–95: "[T]here must be many schisms and many dissections made in the quarry and in the timber ere the house of God can be built. And when every stone is laid artfully together, it cannot be united into a continuity, it can but be contiguous in this world; neither can every piece of the building be of one form; nay rather, the perfection consists in this, that out of many moderate varieties and brotherly dissimilitudes that are not vastly disproportional, arises the goodly and graceful symmetry that commends the whole pile and structure."

To be sure, each of these early liberals had a more rigidly Christian sense of truth than did Mill (who was himself no relativist). Locke, for example, did not hesitate to regard central beliefs of Judaism, Catholicism, and paganism as "false and absurd" (J. Locke, *supra*, at 270), and he refused to put up with atheism at all. Milton went even further in his intolerance, arguing that "popery and open superstition . . . should be extirpate[d]" (J. Milton, *supra*, at 201).

I should remark, finally, that there are no necessary bonds joining relativist beliefs (or philosophical pluralism) and tolerance (or political pluralism); neither entails the other. Nor does a belief in metaphysical Truth prevent adherence to political pluralism (or *vice versa*). Nonetheless, many liberals did indeed base their advocacy of tolerance on their partial rejection of dogmatic limits to truth.

5. See, e.g., H. Hart, *Law, Liberty, and Morality* (Oxford: Oxford University Press, 1968). Were I to consider this book in depth, I should have to subject it to a critique informed by feminism.

6. H. Hart, *The Concept of Law* (Oxford: Oxford University Press, 1961) [hereinafter cited as *Concept*]. The two other texts to which I occasionally refer are H. Hart, *Essays on Bentham* (Oxford: Oxford University Press, 1982) [hereinafter cited as *Bentham*]; H. Hart, *Essays in Jurisprudence and Philosophy* (Oxford: Oxford University Press, 1983) [hereinafter cited as *Jurisprudence*].

7. *Concept*, *supra* note 6, at 144. Hart's comments on the "will theory"/ "objective theory" dispute are similar: "Plainly, each side to this dispute fastens on something important but exaggerates it. . . . The truths latent among the errors of the 'will' theory and the 'objective' theory can therefore be brought together." (*Jurisprudence*, *supra* note 6, at 96).

8. In this paragraph, as in the preceding two paragraphs, I have presented a deliberately pat reading of history. Not only have I excluded some important traditions—such as humanist republicanism, which both diverges from the liberal tradition and resembles it in certain respects—but I have ignored differences *within* liberalism and *within* Christianity that prevent neat contrasts *between* them (like those I have been elaborating). Having said that, I stand by the negative remarks that have been made here about Christianity.

9. *Concept*, *supra* note 6, at vi. *Pace* Hart, intertextuality is a leading motif of structuralism and post-structuralism. I limit myself to three examples from an enormously wide field: (1) "We now know that a text is not a line of words releasing a single 'theological' meaning (the 'message' of the Author-God) but a multi-dimensional space in which a variety of writings, none of them original, blend and clash. The text is a tissue of quotations drawn from the innumerable centres of culture." R. Barthes, "The Death of the Author," in *Image-Music-Text* 142, 146 (New York: Hill & Wang, 1977) (S. Heath trans.). (2) "Whether in the order of spoken or written discourse, no element can function as a sign without . . . being constituted on the basis of the trace within it of the other elements of the chain or system. This interweaving, this textile, is the *text* produced only in the transformation of another text." J. Derrida, *Positions* 26 (Chicago: University of Chicago Press, 1981) (A. Bass trans.). (3) "[B]ooks speak of books: it is as if they spoke among themselves. In the light of this reflection, the library seemed all the more disturbing to me. It was then the place of a long, centuries-old murmuring, an imperceptible dialogue between one parchment and another." U. Eco, *The Name of the Rose* 286 (New York: Harcourt Brace Jovanovich, 1983) (W. Weaver trans.).

10. "It is, I hope, evident how great a break Bentham made with his predecessors' habit of thought" (*Bentham*, *supra* note 6, at 2). "Bentham says that [in formulating a deontic logic] he had to make the tools he needed for his analysis

and to begin, as he puts it, *ab ovo*. His claims to be an innovator in this important matter are I think justified. . . . Bentham's articulation of [deontic logic] seems to have been quite without a forerunner" (*Id.* at 112).

11. To prepare for writing this chapter, I have read more than fifty articles and books relating to Hart's work. By and large, I agree with P. M. S. Hacker's observation that "most of these writings [are] of poör quality" (Hacker, "Hart's Philosophy of Law," in *Law, Morality, and Society* 1 [Oxford: Oxford University Press, 1977] [P. Hacker and J. Raz eds.]), though I do not feel that Hacker's essay contributes very much toward improving the situation. The best introduction to Hart's work is N. Simmonds, *Central Issues in Jurisprudence* 77–95 (London: Sweet & Maxwell, 1986). Also useful is R. Sartorius, "Hart's Concept of Law," in *More Essays in Legal Philosophy* 131 (Berkeley: University of California Press, 1971) (R. Summers ed.). Though I differ with Simmonds and Sartorius on many specific points—and even more on overall methodology—their assessments of Hart provide more valuable insights than any other writings that I have come across. Valuable, too, is P. Soper, *A Theory of Law*, chap. II (Cambridge: Harvard University Press, 1984). Often perceptive, but uneven, is N. MacCormick, *H. L. A. Hart* (Stanford: Stanford University Press, 1981) [hereinafter cited as *H. L. A. Hart*].

12. Austin's foremost theoretical work, containing most of the ideas that Hart outlines, is J. Austin, *The Province of Jurisprudence Determined*, in *The Province of Jurisprudence Determined and The Uses of the Study of Jurisprudence* (London: Weidenfeld & Nicolson, 1954) (H. Hart ed.). Hart's account of Austin's theory (with a few modifications) is in *Concept*, *supra* note 6, at 18–25.

13. W. Hohfeld, "Some Fundamental Legal Concepts as Applied in Judicial Reasoning," 23 *Yale Law Journal* 16, 44 (1913).

14. Hohfeld's differentiation between powers and rights is based on a more far-reaching split between juridical structures and social structures; the exercise of a power has its immediate effect in the juridical structure, whereas the exercise of a right has its immediate effect in the social structure. Yet, as I have attempted to show, this wider dualism turns out to be a great deal more problematic than it may initially seem. See *supra* pp. 66–80.

15. Thus, when P. M. S. Hacker states, with no argument whatsoever, that "primary rules [i.e., most duty-imposing rules] do not confer rights" (Hacker, *supra* note 11, at 19 note 22), he commits an absurdity, at least from a Hohfeldian point of view. Hacker does not indicate any other point of view from which his assertion might be judged more kindly. Perhaps, however, he is alluding to Hart, "Bentham on Legal Rights," in *Oxford Essays in Jurisprudence, 2nd Series* 171 (Oxford: Oxford University Press, 1973) (A. Simpson ed.), reprinted in *Bentham*, *supra* note 6, at 162. (My citations are to the reprinted version of the essay.) Therein Hart maintains that "if, to say that an individual has . . . a right means no more than that he is the intended beneficiary of a duty, then a 'right' in this sense may be an unnecessary, and perhaps confusing, term in the description of the law; since all that can be said in a terminology of such rights can be and indeed is best said in the indispensable terminology of duty" (*Id.* at 181–82). Unfortunately for Hart, his argument can be used, *mutatis mutandis*, against his own position. We can dismiss the "indispensable terminology of duty" by pointing out that "to say that an individual has [a duty] means no more than that he [or she] is [someone against whom someone else has a right]." If rights are "nothing more . . . than an alternative formulation of duties" (*id.* at 182), then the reverse is equally true, and Hart has supplied no reason for preferring one set of words to the alternative set (or to the use

of both sets). His choice of the "indispensable terminology of duty" partakes of arbitrariness.

In the same essay, Hart moves on to an argument—first put forth in Hart, "Are There Any Natural Rights?" 64 *Philosophical Review* 175, 180–81 (1955)—relating to third-party beneficiaries in contract law. Hart's argument seems, at most, to establish that one's qualifying as a contractual beneficiary is not *enough* to bestow rights. Two or more people may somehow benefit from a contract under which only some of them hold rights. Hart decidedly fails to show that benefits, albeit perhaps what he refers to as "secondary benefits"—a label, incidentally, that begs the pertinent questions—are not *necessary* to bestow rights. Be that as it may, his account of third-party interests need not here be evaluated. His argument in no way seeks to impugn the correlativity of rights and obligations; rather, it takes such correlativity for granted.

In the 1955 essay on natural rights, Hart propounds an odd argument concerning the Ten Commandments: "[I]t would be a surprising interpretation of [the Commandments] that treated them as conferring rights. In such an interpretation obedience to the Ten Commandments would have to be conceived as due to or owed to individuals, not merely to God, and disobedience not merely as wrong but as *a wrong to* (as well as harm to) individuals" (Hart, "Are There Any Natural Rights?" *supra*, at 182 [emphasis in original]). For just such a "surprising interpretation," see *Ecclesiasticus* 23:23. Now, even if one approves Hart's curious line of thought, one will have done nothing to challenge Hohfeld's doctrine—a doctrine both tautological and illuminating—that rights and duties entail each other. The Ten Commandments, in Hart's view, confer no rights; but neither do they place duties on people *vis-à-vis* one another. No one enjoys a right *against* anybody else, but similarly no one bears a duty *toward* anyone else (except to God, obviously). All duties are owed to God, under Hart's interpretation. Duties are not owed *to* people, and thus rights are not held *by* them. Hart's argument proves too much and hence proves nothing (at least in the sublunary vale of tears) against Hohfeld's position. Given the correlativity of rights and obligations, one would not expect to find rights where obligations do not exist; far from disproving Hohfeld's views, Hart's argument reaffirms them. (It is not at all clear what would be needed to disprove a tautology. Moreover, it seems quite likely that Hart does not have Hohfeld in mind here. However, his account of the Decalogue is often read—or, I think, misread—as a direct challenge to Hohfeldianism.)

16. *Concept, supra* note 6, at 31. For further discussion, see *id.* at 109–12.

17. The phrase "radical difference" can be found three times in Hart's discussion. See *id.* at 28, 31. The word "grotesque" can be found in *id.* at 31, and the word "distortion" in *id.* at 30.

18. Jonathan Cohen, Critical Notice, 71 *Mind 395, 405–06 (1962) (reviewing Concept, supra* note 6).

19. For a biblical version of this theme, see the well-known (though not typically Pauline) statement in *Romans* 1:20. *Cf. Wisdom of Solomon* 13:1–9; *Psalms* 19:1–4. Though Diotima's speech in Plato's *Symposium* evinces scant respect for the mundane world, it became the *locus classicus* for the development of the theme to which I advert. See Plato, *Symposium* 79–95 (Harmondsworth: Penguin, 1951) (W. Hamilton trans.). See also Plato, *Phaedrus* 92–101 (Cambridge, England: Cambridge University Press, 1952) (R. Hackforth trans.) (249d–253c). On the pervasiveness of neo-Platonism and the idea of "Platonic love" in Renaissance thought and culture, see P. Kristeller, *Renaissance Thought* 51–52, 63–65 (New York: Harper & Row, 1961). Many of the selections in *Philosophies of*

Art and Beauty (Chicago: University of Chicago Press, 1964) (A. Hofstadter and R. Kuhns eds.) underscore the access to the Creator that can be gained through the close examining of created beauty. See especially *id.* at 139–70, 203–76 (selections from Plotinus, Ficino, and Shaftesbury). The desire for such access also played a key role in Romantic aesthetics. For a sparkling critique, see P. de Man, "The Rhetoric of Temporality," in *Blindness and Insight* 187 (2d ed., Minneapolis: University of Minnesota Press, 1983). A modern, secularized version of the quest for the One by way of the Many is expressed in Jacob Bronowski's dialogue "The Abacus and the Rose," in J. Bronowski, *Science and Human Values* 79, 95 (rev. ed., New York: Harper & Row, 1965): "When the student sees that Ohm's law flows from the behavior of electrons, when he finds that it is part of, and that it expresses, the structure of matter itself, then he does have a profound experience. He knows that nature is one in all her expressions. And he knows that he is one with nature—he is one of her expressions." For a humorous portrayal of medieval Christianity's version of this quest, see U. Eco, *supra* note 9, at 143–45.

20. *Concept, supra* note 6, at 87–88. Hart's distinction, an offshoot of the distinction between explaining and understanding, bears only slight resemblance to the contrast between signals and signs drawn by Umberto Eco. *Cf.* U. Eco, *A Theory of Semiotics* 20–21 (Bloomington: Indiana University Press, 1976).

21. In *Concept, supra* note 6, at 90, 91, 92, Hart thrice refers to secondary rules as a "supplement" to primary rules. For a critique of supplementarity, see J. Derrida, *Of Grammatology* 141–64 (Baltimore: Johns Hopkins University Press, 1976) (G. Spivak trans.): "[T]he concept of the supplement and the theory of writing designate textuality itself . . . in an indefinitely multiplied structure—*en abyme*. . . . And we shall see that this abyss is not a happy or unhappy accident. An entire theory of the structural necessity of the abyss will be gradually constituted in our reading; the indefinite process of supplementarity has always already *infiltrated* presence, always already inscribed there the space of repetition and the splitting of the self" (*Id.* at 163; emphasis in original). See also J. Derrida, *supra* note 9, at 43: "[T]he *supplement* is neither a plus nor a minus, neither an outside nor the complement of an inside, neither accident nor essence. . . . Neither/nor, that is, *simultaneously* either *or*" (emphasis in original). *Cf.* J. Derrida, *Speech and Phenomena* 88 (Evanston: Northwestern University Press, 1973) (D. Allison trans.): "What is supplementary is in reality *différance*."

22. *Concept, supra* note 6, at 92. For critiques of "parasitism," see J. Miller, "The Critic as Host," in H. Bloom, P. de Man, J. Derrida, G. Hartman, and J. Miller, *Deconstruction and Criticism* 217 (New York: Continuum, 1979); J. Derrida, *Margins of Philosophy* 321–30 (Chicago: University of Chicago Press, 1982) (A. Bass trans.).

23. For a good discussion, see J. Raz, *The Authority of Law* 92–93 (Oxford: Oxford University Press, 1979), though I disagree with Raz's contention that "since the rule of recognition is a customary rule, it *must* be interpreted as duty-imposing" (*id.* at 93; emphasis added). Other duty-imposing rules that are perhaps secondary are discussed in *H. L. A. Hart, supra* note 11, at 106.

24. Hart repeatedly makes use of the damning epithet "blurred" to characterize the insights of Austin's theory of law. See, e.g., *Concept, supra* note 6, at 64, 74, 97. Even more frequent are the expressions of Hart's concern to dispel "obscurity." See, e.g., *id.* at 95 (aiming to dissipate "the obscurity which still lingers about [legal concepts]").

25. *Id.* at 109. It should be noted, incidentally, that Hart's opposition to command theories is, to a superficial extent, in line with Michel Foucault's

warning that "representation of power has remained under the spell of monarchy. In political thought and analysis, we still have not cut off the head of the king." M. Foucault, *The History of Sexuality* 88–89 (New York: Vintage, 1978) (R. Hurley trans.). However, Hart's basic view of the relation between law and individual conduct fits comfortably with what Foucault criticized as the "juridico-discursive" model of power. *Cf. id.* at 82.

26. J. Derrida, *Writing and Difference* 338 note 42 (Chicago: University of Chicago Press, 1978) (A. Bass trans.).

27. See, e.g., I. Duncanson, "The Strange World of English Jurisprudence," 30 *Northern Ireland Legal Quarterly* 207, 218–21 (1979); N. Simmonds, *supra* note 11, at 85. See also *H. L. A. Hart, supra* note 11, at 109–20; N. MacCormick, *Legal Reasoning and Legal Theory* 54–56 (Oxford: Oxford University Press, 1978) [hereinafter cited as *Reasoning*].

28. *Concept, supra* note 6, at 107 (emphasis added). See also *id.* at 97, 98, 104.

29. Hacker, *supra* note 11, at 23. See also J. Raz, *supra* note 23, at 92 note 23; Duncanson, *supra* note 27, at 219–20.

30. Hart occasionally stumbles in regard to this point. He writes, for example, that "[w]herever . . . a rule of recognition is accepted, both private persons and officials are provided with authoritative criteria for identifying primary rules of obligation" (*Concept, supra* note 6, at 97). This careless omission of the ascertainment of secondary rules can perhaps be traced to Hart's absorption in his misconceived efforts to stake off primitive modes of life (which ostensibly have primary rules only) from advanced modes of life (with their rules of recognition). In any case, Joseph Raz would appear to be on a solid footing when he contends that the "rule of recognition is a rule for the identification of *all* the other rules of the system" (J. Raz, *supra* note 23, at 91; emphasis added).

31. Duncanson, *supra* note 27, at 220.

32. J. Derrida, *Otobiographies* 21–22 (Paris: Éditions Galilée, 1984) (my translation; emphasis in original).

33. R. Rorty, "Philosophy Without Principles," 11 *Critical Inquiry* 459 (1985).

34. The quoted phrase, borrowed from Wilfrid Sellars, is one of Rorty's favorites. See, e.g., R. Rorty, *Consequences of Pragmatism* 29, 226 (Minneapolis: University of Minnesota Press, 1983).

35. P. de Man, "The Epistemology of Metaphor," in *Language and Politics* 195, 213 (New York: New York University Press, 1984) (M. Shapiro ed.). (This essay, first published in 1978, is not really deconstructive—except insofar as all analyses are.) Still the outstanding introductory survey of deconstruction and criticism, notwithstanding a few minor inadequacies, is J. Culler, *On Deconstruction* (Ithaca: Cornell University Press, 1982), which contains an excellent bibliography. Another useful introduction is W. Ray, *Literary Meaning* 141–49, 186–205 (Oxford: Basil Blackwell, 1984). Slightly more advanced is *The Yale Critics* (Minneapolis: University of Minnesota Press, 1983) (J. Arac, W. Godzich, and W. Martin eds.), which includes several fine essays. For a cogent argument that deconstructive literary critics have not lived up to the radically paradoxical insights of Derrida, see R. Gasché, "Deconstruction as Criticism," 6 *Glyph* 177 (1979).

36. On Zeno, *cf.* W. Salmon, "Introduction" to *Zeno's Paradoxes* 5, 42 (Indianapolis: Bobbs-Merrill, 1970) (W. Salmon ed.): "Zeno's paradoxes pose a compelling temptation for philosophers: few can resist the urge to comment upon them in some fashion. Those with a strong practical bent may try to dispose of such problems by getting up and walking around. . . . Such approaches are, of course,

totally irrelevant." For Descartes's comment on madness, see R. Descartes, *Meditations on First Philosophy*, in *The Essential Descartes* 154, 166 (New York: Mentor, 1969) (M. Wilson ed.). Descartes's gesture served as a pre-text for the debate several years ago between Jacques Derrida and Michel Foucault. See J. Derrida, *supra* note 26, at 31–63; Foucault. "My Body, This Paper, This Fire," *Oxford Literary Review*, Autumn 1979, at 9. For Locke's witticism, see J. Locke, *An Essay Concerning Human Understanding* 392 (New York: New American Library, 1964) (A. Woozley ed.) (bk. 4, ch. XI, sec. 8.) Johnson's kicks are recounted in J. Boswell, *The Life of Samuel Johnson* 129 (New York: Random House, 1965) (B. Evans ed.).

37. S. Fish, *Is There a Text in This Class?* 304 (Cambridge: Harvard University Press, 1980).

38. This theme, central to Nietzsche's brilliant diatribes against the "ascetic spirit," is powerfully explored in U. Eco, *supra* note 9. A bit further on, Hart does introduce some levity. See *Concept, supra*, note 6, at 230. For further evidence of Hart's flashes of humor, see *Jurisprudence, supra* note 6, at 287.

39. *Cf. Jurisprudence, supra* note 6, at 123: "American jurisprudence, that is, American speculative thought about the general nature of law, . . . is marked by a concentration, almost to the point of obsession, on the judicial process, that is, with what courts do and should do, how judges reason and should reason in deciding particular cases."

40. Duncanson, *supra* note 27, at 221 note 60.

41. Sartorius, *supra* note 11, at 159–60.

42. See, e.g., *H. L. A. Hart, supra* note 11, at 104: "[P]eople who have power to act as judges may also have duties in the role of judge concerning the way they are to exercise their powers."

43. It should be stressed that I am deliberately passing over the question of the modern public/private dichotomy. Unlike Hart, I consider it deeply problematic. See *supra* note 14.

44. *Concept, supra* note 6, at 98, 99. I am not necessarily accusing Hart of behaviorism.

45. For a clever analysis of repetition repeating itself in Locke's epistemology, see de Man, *supra* note 35, at 199–200.

46. See, e.g., *H. L. A. Hart, supra* note 11, at 22: "[I]t is sufficient that only governors and officials . . . accept [the rule of recognition]."

47. G. Lukács, *History and Class Consciousness* 143 (Cambridge, Mass.: MIT Press, 1971) (R. Livingstone trans.).

48. G. P. Baker, "Defeasibility and Meaning," in *Law, Society, and Morality, supra* note 11, at 26, 28.

49. See, e.g., *Law, Society, and Morality, supra* note 11. For a critical overview of work spawned by *The Concept of Law*, see W. Twining, "Academic Law and Legal Philosophy: The Significance of Herbert Hart," 95 *Law Quarterly Review* 557 (1979).

50. *Concept, supra* note 6, at 78. For some interesting remarks on "roots," see J. Derrida, *supra* note 21, at 101–102. I hope to show that the paradoxes of historical roots examined by Derrida are at work also in the structural roots that Hart wants to unearth.

51. The two best discussions of the basic norm are in H. Kelsen, *General Theory of Law and State* 110–22 (Cambridge: Harvard University Press, 1949) (A. Wedberg trans.) [hereinafter cited as *General Theory*]; H. Kelsen, *Pure Theory of Law* 193–221 (Berkeley: University of California Press, 1961) (M. Knight trans.) [hereinafter cited as *Pure Theory*].

52. See, e.g., G. Hughes, "Validity and the Basic Norm," 59 *California Law Review* 695 (1971).

53. See especially *General Theory, supra* note 51, at 115–16.

54. *Concept, supra* note 6, at 226. The prudence/morality distinction can obviously be displaced; every form of prudence is a form of morality, and every form of morality is a form of prudence. If, however, one temporarily grants the everyday split between prudential reasons and moral reasons, Hart seems correct in arguing that acceptance of a legal regime need not derive from moral considerations. For a sophisticated opposing view, see N. Simmonds, "The Nature of Propositions of Law," 15 *Rechtstheorie* 96 (1984); a similar but less subtle view is taken in McBride, "The Acceptance of a Legal System," 49 *Monist* 377 (1965). Hart's latest arguments on the topic—see *Bentham, supra* note 6, at 153–61; *Jurisprudence, supra* note 6, at 9–10—are not especially cogent, but his position can be stated more forcefully if we analogize legal systems to economic cartels. On the one hand, the members of a cartel might feel that they ought to abide by their agreement because transgressions would violate the Golden Rule (applied to themselves only). On the other hand, they might be motivated exclusively by the knowledge that their cartel will not work properly unless everyone keeps to the agreement. It seems possible that those in charge of a legal system will share a motive more or less like the second of the two motives just outlined: a concern with effective functioning. (Perhaps, for example, they will worry that an erratic implementation of the law may promote restiveness on the part of the general public, who would otherwise bow sullenly to official dictates.) And they could share this motive without ever giving any thought to the Golden Rule (applied to everyone), though of course the two motives could just as plausibly be combined.

55. I put this forward as an assertion that Hart might make, not as a thesis that I uphold. I find it puzzling that Hart completely ignores Freud in his whole discussion of the will to survive. Though one should sedulously contemn a vulgar, literalistic reading of Freud's work, one can still marvel at what texts such as S. Freud, *Beyond the Pleasure Principle* (New York: Norton, 1961) (J. Strachey trans.) and S. Freud, *The Ego and the Id* 30–37 (New York: Norton, 1960) (J. Strachey ed.) could do to displace the unity and the mastery of the individual subject in Hart's jurisprudence.

56. See, e.g., *H. L. A. Hart, supra* note 11, at 40–43; G. Hughes, "Rules, Policy and Decision Making," 77 *Yale Law Journal* 411, 419–24 (1968); H. Morris, Book Review, 75 *Harvard Law Review* 1452, 1455–57 (1962).

57. J. Derrida, *supra* note 22, at 21.

58. This phrasing should make clear that my argument is aimed at an infinite regression rather than at an infinite series. *Cf.* J. Passmore, *Philosophical Reasoning* 19–37 (London: Duckworth, 1961).

59. *Pure Theory, supra* note 51, at 193. Neil MacCormick seems to me justified in maintaining that—with regard to the is/ought dualism—"Hart is a Humean where Kelsen is a Kantian." *H. L. A. Hart, supra* note 11, at 26. However, one should not make too much, if anything, of this point.

60. These sentences may call to mind Sartre's dictum that "'Facticity' and 'Past' are two words to indicate one and the same thing." J.-P. Sartre, *Being and Nothingness* 173 (New York: Washington Square Press, 1966) (H. Barnes trans.). That my analysis smacks of Sartreanism is evidence of a deep complicity between humanism and positivism, which are also radically opposed.

61. J. Derrida, *supra* note 26, at 285.

62. See, e.g., *General Theory, supra* note 51, at 43: "Past and future are relative

to a certain moment in time." Hart's conception of time, implicit throughout his text, is perhaps most clearly at work in his discussion of the "continuity of law" (*Concept*, *supra* note 6, at 50–60), where Hart even maintains that the "acceptance of a rule by society at one moment does not *guarantee* its continued existence" (*Id.* at 58; emphasis in original). My use of the word "With" to begin the sentence in the text is supposed to capture at least two meanings. On the one hand, "With" can mean "Given," thereby making the first clause of the sentence into a condition for what follows. On the other hand, "With" can mean "Along with," thereby suggesting that the dynamic of self-elision, characteristic of Hart's theory of normativity, will also displace his view of temporality. It is this second meaning that is far more important: my critique is just as much a critique of Hart's assumptions about time as a critique of his conception of normativity. For more on temporality, see *supra* pp. 13–16; *infra* pp. 234–35.

4. NOTHING IN PARTICULAR

1. E. Burke, *Reflections on the Revolution in France* 152, 124 (Harmondsworth: Penguin, 1969) (C. O'Brien ed.).

2. M. Oakeshott, *Rationalism in Politics* 21 (London: Methuen, 1962). The title essay of Oakeshott's volume, from which I have here quoted, is a classic statement against rationalist abstraction.

3. R. Kirk, "Introduction" to *The Portable Conservative Reader* xviii (Harmondsworth: Penguin, 1982) (R. Kirk ed.).

4. D. Hume, "Of the Original Contract," in *Hume's Moral and Political Philosophy* 356, 358 (New York: Hafner, 1948) (H. Aiken ed.).

5. D. Hume, *A Treatise of Human Nature* 580 (Oxford: Oxford University Press, 1978) (L. Selby-Bigge and P. Nidditch eds.;) [hereinafter cited as *Treatise*]. *Cf. id.* at 273: "[W]e should yield to that propensity, which inclines us to be positive and certain in *particular points*, according to the light, in which we survey them in any *particular instant*."

6. D. Hume, *An Enquiry concerning the Principles of Morals*, in *Enquiries concerning Human Understanding and concerning the Principles of Morals* 169, 196 (Oxford: Oxford University Press, 1975) (L. Selby-Bigge and P. Nidditch eds.) [hereinafter cited as *Enquiries*].

7. Hume, *supra* note 4, at 364–65.

8. I have also treated this question in M. Kramer, "Book Review," 20 *New England Law Review* 599, 602 note 14, 624 note 84 (1984–85), and I consider it at some length in my book-in-progress, "Critical Legal Theory and the Challenge of Feminism." In regard to Hume's work, see, e.g., D. Miller, *Philosophy and Ideology in Hume's Political Thought* 13–14 (Oxford: Oxford University Press, 1981). Miller's own view is quite sophisticated, though it edges too close at times to seeing Hume's politics as a necessary result of his metaphysics. See, e.g., *id.* at 191, 203. In addition to the sources that Miller cites, those who have argued for an inherent correspondence between Hume's conservatism and his general philosophy include M. Grene, "Hume: Sceptic and Tory," 4 *Journal of the History of Ideas* 333 (1943); D. Livingston, *Hume's Philosophy of Common Life* (Chicago: University of Chicago Press, 1984); G. Postema, *Bentham and the Common Law Tradition* 133–34 (Oxford: Oxford University Press, 1986); R. Unger, *Knowledge and Politics* 129, 312 note 20 (New York: Free Press, 1975); S. Wolin, "Hume and Conservatism," in *Hume: A Re-evaluation* 239 (New York: Fordham University Press, 1976) (D. Livingston and J. King eds.). Of these, Wolin's position is the most subtle and ambiguous.

9. This point is made from the opposite direction by Philip Johnson in

"Do You Sincerely Want to Be Radical?" 36 *Stanford Law Review* 247, 261 note 42 (1984). For Bertrand Russell's view, see his "Reply to Criticisms," in *The Philosophy of Bertrand Russell* 681, 727 (Evanston: Northwestern University, 1944) (P. Schilpp ed.): "I have always maintained that there was no logical connection [between my views on social questions and my views on logic and epistemology], pointing to the example of Hume, with whom I agree so largely in abstract matters and disagree so totally in politics."

10. This was William Graham Sumner's position. See C. V. Woodward, *The Strange Career of Jim Crow* 102–105 (3d ed., New York: Oxford University Press, 1974).

11. See, e.g., D. Miller, *supra* note 8; N. K. Smith, *The Philosophy of David Hume* (London: Macmillan, 1941). See also P. Brownsey, "Hume and the Social Contract," 28 *Philosophical Quarterly* 132 (1978); T. Hearn, "'General Rules' in Hume's *Treatise*," 8 *Journal of the History of Philosophy* 405 (1970); D. Livingston, *supra* note 8. *Cf.* J. Derrida, *Margins of Philosophy* 111–13, 135 (Chicago: University of Chicago Press, 1982) (A. Bass trans.), where the categories of political life and metaphysical thought are rightly analogized.

12. 2 Timothy 2:14. *Cf.* 1 Timothy 6:4.

13. *Treatise*, *supra* note 5, at 262. This strand of Hume's thought receives the bulk of attention in D. Henze, "The Linguistic Aspect of Hume's Method," 30 *Journal of the History of Ideas* 116 (1969); and in M. Morrisroe, "Linguistic Analysis as Rhetorical Pattern in David Hume," in *Hume and the Enlightenment* 72 (Austin: University of Texas Press, 1974) (W. Todd ed.).

14. Henze, *supra* note 13, at 119.

15. This general devaluation of language has been tracked in diverse forms in post-structuralist and post-analytic texts. A good starting place is the criticism of Saussure in J. Derrida, *Positions* 19–25 (Chicago: University of Chicago Press, 1981) (A. Bass trans.). The following sentences from J. Derrida, *Of Grammatology* 167 (Baltimore: Johns Hopkins University Press, 1976) (G. Spivak trans.) provide an excellent summary: "[M]etaphysics consists of excluding non-presence by determining the supplement as *simple exteriority*, pure addition or pure absence. The work of exclusion operates within the structure of supplementarity. The paradox is that one annuls addition by considering it a pure addition. *What is added is nothing because it is added to a full presence to which it is exterior.* Speech comes to be added to intuitive presence (of the entity, of *essence*, of the *eidos*, of *ousia*, and so forth); writing comes to be added to living self-present speech."

16. Morrisroe, *supra* note 13, at 78–79.

17. D. Hume, *Dialogues Concerning Natural Religion* 80 (Indianapolis: Hackett, 1980) (R. Popkin ed.).

18. P. de Man, "The Epistemology of Metaphor," in *Language and Politics* 195, 197 (New York: New York University Press, 1984) (M. Shapiro ed.).

19. Flowery tropes perform a decisive part throughout J. Derrida, "White Mythology: Metaphor in the Text of Philosophy," in *Margins of Philosophy*, *supra* note 11, at 209–71.

20. See J. Derrida, *supra* note 11, at 124–34.

21. *Treatise*, *supra* note 5, at 121. *Cf. Enquiries*, *supra* note 6, at 222–23: "It is the business of poetry to bring every affection near to us by lively imagery and representation, and make it look like truth and reality."

22. Consider, for example, the following remark by Derrida on Foucault's history of madness: "[T]he silence of madness is not *said*, cannot be said in the logos of this book, but is indirectly, metaphorically, made present by its

pathos—taking this word in its best sense." J. Derrida, *Writing and Difference* 37 (Chicago: University of Chicago Press, 1978) (A. Bass trans.). For an insightful discussion of the madness-literature connection, see S. Felman, "Madness and Philosophy or Literature's Reason," 52 *Yale French Studies* 206 (1975). For a classic favorable treatment, see Plato, *Phaedrus* 57 (Cambridge: Cambridge University Press, 1952) (R. Hackforth trans.) (245a).

23. "Nor need we have recourse to the fictions of poets to learn this; but beside the reason of the thing, may discover the same truth by common experience and observation." *Treatise, supra* note 5, at 495.

24. A. Jardine, *Gynesis: Configurations of Woman and Modernity* 118 (Ithaca: Cornell University Press, 1985). An astute survey of some recent French thought on representation is contained in *id.* at 118–44. Critiques of representation are abundant in post-structuralism, feminism, Critical Theory, and neo-pragmatism, though I can here cite only a few works among the many that I have found to be stimulating. Most of Derrida's work is relevant. Indispensable, though laconic, is J. Derrida, "Sending: On Representation," 49 *Social Research* 294 (1982). More generally, see J. Derrida, *Of Grammatology, supra* note 15; and J. Derrida, *Speech and Phenomena* (Evanston: Northwestern University Press, 1973) (D. Allison trans.), which are filled with germane passages. Especially pertinent as well is J. Derrida, "Freud and the Scene of Writing," in *Writing and Difference, supra* note 22, at 196. A good survey of Foucault's work in this area is M. Jay, "In the Empire of the Gaze: Foucault and the Denigration of Vision in Twentieth-century French Thought," in *Foucault: A Critical Reader* 175 (Oxford: Basil Blackwell, 1986) (D. Hoy ed.). The best introduction to feminist critiques of representation that I have come across is C. Owens, "The Discourse of Others: Feminists and Postmodernism," in *The Anti-Aesthetic: Essays on Postmodern Culture* 57 (Port Townsend: Bay Press, 1983) (H. Foster ed.). Also invaluable are MacKinnon, "Feminism, Marxism, Method, and the State: An Agenda for Theory," 7 *Signs* 515 (1982); C. MacKinnon, "Feminism, Marxism, Method, and the State: Toward Feminist Jurisprudence," 8 *Signs* 635 (1983). Excellent, but considerably more difficult, is L. Irigaray, *Speculum of the Other Woman* (Ithaca: Cornell University Press, 1985) (G. Gill trans.). An important Marxist treatment of ideology-as-representation is L. Althusser, "Ideology and Ideological State Apparatuses (Notes towards an Investigation)," in *Lenin and Philosophy* 127, 162–83 (New York: Monthly Review Press, 1971) (B. Brewster trans.). A superb analysis of some of the main themes associated with critiques of representation is T. Adorno, *Negative Dialectics* 135–207 (New York: Continuum, 1973) (E. Ashton trans.). A recent volume, *Allegory and Representation* (Baltimore: Johns Hopkins University Press, 1981) (S. Greenblatt ed.), contains three especially thought-provoking essays: P. de Man, "Pascal's Allegory of Persuasion," in *id.* at 1; J. Fineman, "The Structure of Allegorical Desire," in *id.* at 26; and L. Bersani, "Representation and Its Discontents," in *id.* at 145.

25. Derrida, "Sending," *supra* note 24, at 304.

26. A critique of representation could proceed roughly along the lines of my short critique of pragmatism in Chapter 5. See *infra* pp. 240–42, 248, 249. For some brief remarks on representation, see *supra* p. 45.

27. *Treatise, supra* note 5, at 523–24 (emphasis added). For a virtually identical passage, see *Enquiries, supra* note 6, at 199 note 1.

28. *Enquiries, supra* note 6, at 214. For yet another passage, see *Treatise, supra* note 5, at 579.

29. *Enquiries, supra* note 6, at 229. In Hume's earlier *magnum opus*, the primary discussion of this theme is in *Treatise, supra* note 5, at 580–84.

30. *Enquiries, supra* note 6, at 229. Hume patently did not think that feelings

would accord with generalized language: "It is wisely ordained by nature, that private connexions should commonly prevail over universal views and considerations" (*id.* at 229 note 1).

31. *Id.* at 228. Immediately after the quoted lines, Hume introduced a note of representationalism—without, however, restoring sentiments to all their old privileges.

32. Aristotle, *Rhetoric* 1412a9–12, quoted in J. Derrida, *supra* note 11, at 238 note 41.

33. For a discussion of Condillac, see P. de Man, *supra* note 18, at 204–208. For Rousseau's view, see J.-J. Rousseau, *A Discourse on the Origin of Inequality*, in *The Social Contract and Discourses* 31, 67–68 (London: J. M. Dent, 1973) (G. Cole, J. Brumfitt, and J. Hall trans.). Nietzsche's position is expressed in F. Nietzsche, "On Truth and Lie in an Extra-Moral Sense," in *The Portable Nietzsche* 42, 46 (Harmondsworth: Penguin, 1954) (W. Kaufmann ed.). Wittgenstein's conception of overlapping "family resemblances" may be found in L. Wittgenstein, *Philosophical Investigations* secs. 65–71 (New York: Macmillan, 1958) (G. Anscombe trans.). *Cf. id.* at secs. 73–75.

34. Aristotle, *Poetics* 57 (Ann Arbor: University of Michigan Press, 1967) (G. Else trans.) (1457b).

35. On the acquisition of property by accession, see *Treatise, supra* note 5, at 509; and *Enquiries, supra* note 6, at 310 note 1. Hume's theory of narrative is contained mostly in a portion of the *Enquiry concerning Human Understanding* that was not included in the 1777 edition of that work. It is reproduced in D. Hume, *On Human Nature and the Understanding* 39–46 (New York: Macmillan, 1962) (A. Flew ed.). For the point made here about historical narratives, see *id.* at 40. On frustrated good intentions, see *Treatise, supra* note 5, at 584–85.

36. R. Jakobson, "Two Aspects of Language and Two Types of Aphasic Disturbance," in R. Jakobson and M. Halle, *Fundamentals of Language* 67, 90 (2d ed., The Hague: Mouton, 1971). Jakobson's reliance upon Saussure is made explicit in *id.* at 74–75. Jakobson's categories were powerfully developed by Jacques Lacan in J. Lacan, "The agency of the letter in the unconscious or reason since Freud," in *Écrits* 146 (New York: Norton, 1977) (A. Sheridan trans.). Jakobson had himself pointed out the relevance of his project for psychoanalytic theory. See R. Jakobson, *supra*, at 95.

37. R. Jakobson, *supra* note 36, at 94–95. Long after writing the current subsection, I came upon an analysis that resembles mine in seeing Hume's principles of psychology as principles of tropology. See J. H. Miller, *The Linguistic Moment* 278 (Princeton: Princeton University Press, 1985).

38. This paragraph should be read in light of the first two-thirds of J. Derrida, "The Supplement of Copula: Philosophy Before Linguistics," in *Margins of Philosophy, supra* note 11, at 175. See especially *id.* at 193 note 24.

39. See *Treatise, supra* note 5, at 477–84. For some useful analysis of these pages, see J. Harrison, *Hume's Theory of Justice* 1–13 (Oxford: Oxford University Press, 1981).

40. J. Christensen, *Practicing Enlightenment: Hume and the Formation of a Literary Career* 27 (Madison: University of Wisconsin Press, 1987) [hereinafter cited as PE].

41. For an interpretation that supports my analysis, see D. Forbes, *Hume's Philosophical Politics* 70–74 (Cambridge: Cambridge University Press, 1975).

42. PE, *supra* note 40, at 33. For similar views, see D. Forbes, *supra* note 41, at 70; J. Stewart, *The Moral and Political Philosophy of David Hume* 148–50 (New York: Columbia University Press, 1963).

43. *Treatise, supra* note 5, at 493. Even this quotation is not as damning

as it appears, for it may well refer only to the creation of familial units. See D. Forbes, *supra* note 41, at 74.

44. D. Forbes, *supra* note 41, at 70. I must here exclude Christensen, whose views are subtler than the views of more conventional critics (but are still clearly divergent from my own). My differences with him will be fleshed out shortly.

45. See L. Althusser, "Sur le Contrat Social," 8 *Cahiers pour l'Analyse* 5, 18–22 (1967).

46. See *supra* p. 196.

47. R. Derathé, *Jean-Jacques Rousseau et la Science Politique de Son Temps* 173 (Paris: Presses Universitaires de France, 1959) (my translation). For a good statement of this view in a critical discussion of Hobbes, see A. MacIntyre, *A Short History of Ethics* 136–37 (New York: Macmillan, 1966). My attention was called to Derathé's book by G. Bennington, "Reading Allegory," *Oxford Literary Review,* 1981 (no. 3), at 92 note 10.

48. See *Treatise, supra* note 5, at 539–41. For an exposition of Hume's view on this matter, see D. Deleule, *Hume et la naissance du libéralisme économique* 328 (Paris: Editions Aubier Montaigne, 1979). See also D. Forbes, *supra* note 41, at 73; G. Postema, *supra* note 8, at 122–23.

49. J. Mill, *Autobiography* 29 (Indianapolis: Bobbs-Merrill, 1957) (C. Shields ed.).

50. D. Hume, *supra* note 4, at 367–68.

51. See PE, *supra* note 40, at 27 note 8. *Cf. Enquiries, supra* note 6, at 191: "In many nations, the female sex are reduced to . . . slavery, and are rendered incapable of all property, in opposition to their lordly masters."

52. *Treatise, supra* note 5, at 490. (To the words "express" and "mutually express'd" the emphasis has been added; other emphases are in the original.)

53. See, e.g., *id.* at 93.

54. *Id.* at 602 (emphasis added). Hume had moral judgments in mind here, but he knew that his argument applied just as much to factual inferences. See *id.* at 603; *Enquiries, supra* note 6, at 227–28.

55. J. King, "The Place of the Language of Morals in Hume's Second *Enquiry,*" in *Hume: A Re-evaluation, supra* note 8, at 343 [hereinafter cited as PLM].

56. *Id.* at 357. In this connection, and in the light of J. Derrida, "The Ends of Man," in *Margins of Philosophy, supra* note 11, at 109, one would have to highlight King's unreflective use of various forms of the first-person plural pronoun. Derrida's remarks on this issue are most telling against Hegel and Heidegger. See *id.* at 120–21, 124–25.

57. D. Hume, "A Dialogue," in *Enquiries, supra* note 6, at 324, 334. The whole "Dialogue" is an exploration of moral relativity.

58. See, e.g., *Treatise, supra* note 5, at 547 note 1. For a like account of the rules of justice, see, e.g., *Enquiries, supra* note 6, at 203: "The convenience, or rather necessity, which leads to justice is so universal, *and everywhere points so much to the same rules,* that the habit takes place in all societies" (emphasis added).

59. *Treatise, supra* note 5, at 575. For less satisfying attempts to explain Hume's odd insistence, see D. Miller, *supra* note 8, at 53; A. Flew, *David Hume: Philosopher of Moral Science* 157 (Oxford: Basil Blackwell, 1986).

60. G. Hegel, *Logic* 64 (Oxford: Oxford University Press, 1975) (W. Wallace trans.).

61. J. Derrida, *supra* note 11, at 34.

62. *Treatise, supra* note 5, at 67 (emphasis added). For similar wording, see, e.g., *id.* at 197, 456.

63. Hearn, *supra* note 11, at 411. Hearn also identifies a corrective type of rule that does not concern us at present. This second type of rule was discussed earlier. See *supra* pp. 162–63.

64. For a telling deconstruction of Hume that focuses on this point, see K. Popper, *Conjectures and Refutations* 44–45 (4th ed., London: Routledge & Kegan Paul, 1972).

65. If Milton Friedman were to address himself to this problem, he would most likely endorse this style of explanation. See M. Friedman, "The Methodology of Positive Economics," in *Essays in Positive Economics* 3 (Chicago: University of Chicago Press, 1953).

66. I borrow the quoted phrase from R. P. Wolff, "Hume's Theory of Mental Activity," 69 *Philosophical Review* 289 (1960), though Wolff does not consider the problem I am discussing.

67. This point is made forcefully by Barry Stroud, among others. See B. Stroud, *Hume* 47–48 (London: Routledge & Kegan Paul, 1977).

68. *Treatise*, *supra* note 5, at 5–6. This passage was repeated almost verbatim in *Enquiries*, *supra* note 6, at 20–21.

69. J. Derrida, *supra* note 22, at 289.

5. NOTES ON REIFICATION AND CRITICAL LEGAL STUDIES

1. Gabel, "Reification in Legal Reasoning," 3 *Research in Law and Sociology* 25 (1980) [hereinafter cited as RLR].

2. J. Borges, "Kafka and His Precursors," in *Labyrinths* 199, 201 (New York: New Directions, 1964) (emphasis in original). Borges's next sentence will have made clear that interpretation is more unthinkably paradoxical than might be presumed from what I have quoted in the text: "His [i.e., a writer's] work modifies our conception of the past *as it will modify the future*" (*id.*, emphasis added). Past, present, and future must determine and preclude one another and thereby cause interpretation to be both absolutely imperative and wholly impossible. This paradox was elegantly captured by Walter Benjamin: "The historical materialist must abandon the epic element in history. For him history becomes the object of a construct *(Konstruktion)* which is not located in empty time but is constituted in a specific epoch, in a specific life, in a specific work. The historical materialist explodes the epoch out of its reified 'historical continuity,' and thereby lifts life out of this epoch, and the work out of the life work. Yet this construct results in simultaneous preservation and suspension *(Aufhebung)* of the life work in the work, of the epoch in the life work and of the course of history in the epoch." W. Benjamin, "Eduard Fuchs: Collector and Historian," in *The Essential Frankfurt School Reader* 225, 227 (New York: Continuum, 1982) (A. Arato and E. Gebhardt eds.). To be a poet, one has also to be a rabbi. *Cf.* J. Derrida, *Writing and Difference* 67 (Chicago: University of Chicago Press, 1978) (A. Bass trans.).

3. J. Derrida, *supra* note 2, at 267; J. Derrida, *Positions* 20 (Chicago: University of Chicago Press, 1981) (A. Bass trans.) [hereinafter cited as *Positions*]. Derrida is privileging difference over presence only as a tentative stroke in a broader deconstructive engagement. The dichotomy between presence and difference will be displaced and reinscribed into the so-called tissue of differences, which is the (dis)location of an unmasterable play between the two concepts.

A "transformation of one language by another" is Derrida's way of reconceiving translation. In undertaking any such transformation, we shall do well to keep in mind some remarks by Barbara Johnson: "It is . . . precisely the way in which the original text is always already an impossible translation that renders translation impossible. . . . In studying the *différance* of signification, Derrida follows the misfires, losses, and infelicities that prevent any given language from being one. Language, in fact, can only exist in the space of its own foreignness to itself." B. Johnson, "Taking Fidelity Philosophically," in *Difference in Translation* 142, 146 (Ithaca: Cornell University Press, 1985) (J. Graham ed.).

4. As I have stated, the *locus classicus* is K. Marx, *Capital* vol. I, 71–83 (New York: International Publishers, 1967) (S. Moore and E. Aveling trans.) [hereinafter cited as *Capital*, with volume and page number]. (I have checked all quotations with the German text in K. Marx, *Werke-Schriften-Briefe: Okonomische Schriften* vol. IV [Stuttgart: Cotta-Verlag, 1962] [H. Lieber and B. Kautsky eds.], and have found no need to modify the English translation.) Related passages appear intermittently in Marx's *Grundrisse* (New York: Vintage, 1973) (M. Nicolaus trans.) [hereinafter cited as *Grundrisse*]. See, e.g., *id.* at 156–65. Illuminating critiques of the fetishism of capital can be found in *Capital* III, 391–99, 826–31. The tone and substance of Marx's work on fetishism were to a large extent foreshadowed in the section of his "Economic and Philosophic Manuscripts" dealing with "alienated labor" *(die entfremdete arbeit)*. Particularly germane is the first half of that section, which discusses the worker's alienation from the products and processes of her labor. See K. Marx, "Economic and Philosophic Manuscripts," in *Early Writings* 63, 120–26 (New York: McGraw-Hill, 1963) (T. Bottomore ed.). Another highly relevant early work by Marx is "The German Ideology" (in *The Marx-Engels Reader* 146 [New York: Norton, 1978] [R. Tucker ed.]), in which he proclaimed: "This fixation of social activity, this consolidation of what we ourselves produce into an objective power above us, growing out of our control, thwarting our expectations, bringing to naught our calculations, is one of the chief factors in historical development up till now" (*id.* at 160). For a very good treatment of the section from Volume One of *Capital* cited *supra*, see D. Kennedy, "The Role of Law in Economic Thought: Essays on the Fetishism of Commodities," 34 *American University Law Review* 939, 968–988 (1985). A valuable account of the *Grundrisse*'s critique of the "externalization of social relations" is contained in C. Gould, *Marx's Social Ontology* 93–96 (Cambridge, Mass.: MIT Press, 1978). For an ingenious attempt to find a point of articulation between Marx's critique of the fetishism of capital and Derrida's critique of phenomenology, see M. Ryan, *Marxism and Deconstruction* 182–83 (Baltimore: Johns Hopkins University Press, 1982).

For a detailed look by an analytic philosopher at Marx's various attempts to formulate a labor theory of value, see J. Elster, "The Labor Theory of Value: A Reinterpretation of Marxist Economics," *Marxist Perspectives*, Fall 1978, at 70. As Elster notes, Marx's reliance on such a theory in the first volume of *Capital* amounted to "a deliberate simplification" rather than a mistake (*id.* at 77). Under the assumptions to which that volume adhered—assumptions of perfect competition and simple commodity production—the labor theory of value holds up. (Given perfect competition, the theory will hold up even in an economy with wage labor, as long as the ratio of direct and indirect labor is the same for every line of production). To avoid being confined to Marx's assumptions, I shall try to reconstruct his argument without appealing to any labor theory of value. His critique of fetishism does not simply lose all worth in the absence of a direct bond between the length of time needed to produce a commodity and the value of the finished commodity in relation to other objects of capitalist exchange.

5. C. Macpherson, *The Political Theory of Possessive Individualism* (Oxford:

Oxford University Press, 1962). Freud regarded fetishism as a perversion sprouting from "a very early impression of an abnormal instinctual trend or choice of object . . . to which the subject's libido [remains] attached all through his life. It is often impossible to say what it is that enabled this impression to exercise such an intense attraction on the libido." S. Freud, *Introductory Lectures on Psychoanalysis* 348 (New York: Norton, 1966) (J. Strachey trans.). (Freud considered the fetishized object to be a "substitute for the painfully missed, primordially postulated female penis." *The Letters of Sigmund Freud and Karl Abraham* 87 [New York: Basic Books, 1965] [B. Marsh and H. Abraham trans.], quoted in A. Bass, "On the History of a Mistranslation and the Psychoanalytic Movement," in *Difference in Translation*, *supra* note 3, at 102, 113. See also S. Freud, "Fetishism," in *Collected Papers* vol. V, 198 [London: Hogarth Press, 1950] [J. Strachey ed.].) The use of "fetish" to denote any type of preoccupation has become incorporated into everyday discourse, presumably in part owing to Freud's definition of the term. The older sense of the word—the sense in which Marx used it—has become relatively rare.

6. *Capital*, *supra* note 4, at I, 74; *id.* at III, 830. *Cf. id.* at III, 880: "[I]mplicit in the commodity, and even more so in the commodity as a product of capital, is the materialisation of the social features of production and the personification of the material foundations of production, which characterise the entire capitalist mode of production." *Cf.* R. Unger, *Knowledge and Politics* 136–37 (New York: Free Press, 1975). For a sometimes trenchant critique of metaleptic zigzags in Nietzsche's work, see P. de Man, "Rhetoric of Tropes (Nietzsche)," in *Allegories of Reading* 103 (New Haven: Yale University Press, 1979) [hereinafter cited as AR]. De Man's reading of Nietzsche's work could be a point of departure for a deconstructive reading of Marx.

7. *Capital*, *supra* note 4, at I, 71. See also *id.* at I, 178: "The soil . . . in the virgin state in which it supplies man with necessaries or the means of subsistence ready to hand, exists independently of him, and is the universal subject of human labour" (footnote omitted); K. Marx, "Critique of the Gotha Program," in *The Marx-Engels Reader*, *supra* note 4, at 525: "Labour is *not the source* of all wealth. *Nature* is just as much the source of use values . . . as labour, which itself is only the manifestation of a force of nature, human labour power" (emphases in original.)

What has just been said about Marx's view of Nature will apply also to his view of machines and other instruments. Marx was well aware that "[l]eaving out of consideration such ready-made means of subsistence as fruits, in gathering which a man's own limbs serve as the instruments of his labour, the first thing of which the labourer possesses himself is not the subject of labour but its instrument" (*Capital*, *supra* note 4, at I, 179). Indeed, Marx listed instruments as one of the three essential factors in any labor process (the other two being human labor itself and the material worked upon) (*id.* at I, 178).

8. A critic of Marx might broach here a vision of a fully automated economy (or sector of an economy). See, e.g., Elster, *supra* note 4, at 71. It seems that Marx could respond in at least two ways. First, he might note that if we push our etiological inquiry back far enough, we can attribute all the machines (and the consumer goods) of an automated economy to productive processes that include labor. Labor, that is, would be a necessary *indirect* factor—perhaps a *highly* indirect factor—in all lines of production. Second, and more important, Marx could rejoin that, even in a fully mechanized world, the key production decisions—decisions on what goods to produce and how to produce them—will be made through the more or less studied mental labor of human beings. Even

if such decisions are themselves rendered automatically (by computers), the embracement or the rejection of choices that have been made will in turn be reached through the mental and political work of human subjects. In a fully mechanized world, then, the role of human striving will have been merely displaced rather than excluded. One should not limit one's conception of labor to the visible transformation of materials.

9. As was discussed in Chapter 2, we cannot unproblematically separate production from distribution. Though we can never simply collapse these two dimensions of economic structures, we cannot effectively treat of one apart from the other. See sources cited *supra*, chap. 2, note 92. Marx's view was that distribution and production are "members of a totality, distinctions within a unity," and that "[m]utual interaction takes place between the different moments" (*Grundrisse, supra* note 4, at 99, 100). (This view had not really changed in 1875, when Marx denounced the Lasalleans for their failure to understand that "[a]ny distribution whatever of the means of consumption" is wholly shaped by "the mode of production itself" [K. Marx, *supra* note 7, at 531]. See also *Capital, supra* note 4, at III, 877–84. Even in the *Grundrisse*, Marx had declared that "[p]roduction predominates . . . over the other moments" [*Grundrisse, supra* note 4, at 99]; and, more important, even in 1875 Marx defined the "mode of production" in terms of "the *distribution* of the conditions of production" [K. Marx, *supra* note 7, at 531; emphasis added].) I separate production and distribution only as a makeshift device for clarifying Marx's critique of fetishism and for presenting it in its strongest form.

10. Quoted in R. Rorty, *Consequences of Pragmatism* 166 (Minneapolis: University of Minnesota Press, 1982) [hereinafter cited as CP].

11. *Capital, supra* note 4, at I, 78, 79, 82. There is an obvious parallel between this vision of a communist future and the yearning for "human emancipation" in Marx's "On the Jewish Question." At the end of the first part of "On the Jewish Question," for example, Marx urged that "[h]uman emancipation will only be complete . . . when [man] has recognized and organized his own powers (*forces propres*) as *social* powers so that he no longer separates this social power from himself as *political* power." K. Marx, "On the Jewish Question," in *Early Writings, supra* note 4, at 1, 31 (emphasis in original). Indeed, the analyses of political, religious, and economic institutions in "On the Jewish Question" are as important for understanding Marx's later critiques of fetishism as are the "Economic and Philosophic Manuscripts" and "The German Ideology."

12. My conception of "humanism" is basically the same as Sartre's in "Existentialism is a Humanism," reprinted in *Existentialism from Dostoevsky to Sartre* 345 (New York: Meridian, 1975) (W. Kaufmann ed.). Sartre equated humanism with existentialism, and he defined the latter as a general belief "that we must begin from the subjective" (*id.* at 348).

It cannot be emphasized here too strongly that Marx's work on fetishism was by no means univocal. Many passages could be cited against the interpretation that I am giving. See, e.g., *Capital, supra* note 4, at I, 73: "[T]he relations connecting the labour of one individual with that of the rest appear, not as direct social relations between individuals at work, but as what they really are, material relations between persons and social relations between things. . . . The two-fold social character of the labour of the individual appears to him, when reflected in his brain, only under those forms which are impressed upon that labour in every-day practice by the exchange of products"; *id.* at I, 76: "The categories of bourgeois economy . . . are forms of thought expressing with social validity the conditions and relations of a definite, historically determined mode of production"; *id.* at III, 830: "[I]t is . . . natural for the actual agents of production to feel completely at home in these estranged and irrational forms [of economic life] since these are precisely the forms of illusion in which they move about and find their daily occupation"; *Grundrisse, supra* note 4, at 156, discussing the transindividual creation of private interest, whose "content, as well as the form and means of its realization, is given by social conditions independent of all."

Indeed, even the passages on which I rely could be reinterpreted against my position. The complexity of this issue becomes apparent in the writings of two major contemporary Marxists: Louis Althusser and Fredric Jameson. Althusser, who has tended to play down the remaining humanism in Marx's mature work, openly makes concessions in a remarkable paragraph from *Reading Capital:* "We have proved that fetishism is not a subjective phenomenon related either to the illusions or to the perceptions of the agents of the economic process, that it cannot be reduced therefore to the *subjective effects* produced in the economic subjects by their place in the process, their site in the structure. But how many of Marx's texts present *fetishism as an 'appearance,'* an 'illusion' arising purely in 'consciousness,' show us the real, inner movement of the process *'appearing'* in a fetishized form to the 'consciousness' of the same subjects in the form of the apparent movement. And yet how many other texts of Marx's assure us that this appearance is not subjective at all, but, on the contrary, objective through and through, the 'illusion' of the 'consciousness' and perceptions being itself secondary, and dislocated by the structure of this primary, purely objective 'illusion.' At this point we see Marx most clearly struggling with reference concepts which are inadequate to their objects, now accepting, now rejecting them in a necessarily contradictory movement." Althusser, "Marx's Immense Theoretical Revolution," in L. Althusser and E. Balibar, *Reading Capital* 182, 191 (London: Verso, 1970) (B. Brewster trans.) (emphases in original).

Still more revealing is a curious vacillation in F. Jameson, *Marxism and Form* (Princeton: Princeton University Press, 1971). After quoting at length from Marx on fetishism, Jameson dissects capitalist life in terms of appearance and reality (*id.* at 296–97). Such an analysis indirectly bears out my own interpretation of Marx. Immediately afterward, however, Jameson argues that "Marxism . . . has at its disposal two alternate languages (or codes, to use the structuralist term) in which any given phenomenon can be described. Thus history can be written either subjectively, as the history of class struggle, or objectively, as the development of the economic modes of production and their evolution from their own internal contradictions" (*id.* at 297). He makes clear that the touchstones for deciding between these "languages" are strategic: "The notion of two codes also clarifies the question of basic or primary realities involved in each description; for this now becomes what I would like to call a question of rhetorical form and effect, and depends very much on the type of illusion a given description is called on to dispel. . . . In one sense, therefore, these two alternative Marxist languages, functioning as they do critically, that is, depending on the predetermined nature of the situation or context in which one or the other is to be used, must be evaluated with respect to the historical moment in which each has developed" (*id.* at 298). This interpretation of Marx's work as a continual fluctuation between differing rhetorical modes will tend to blunt many of the criticisms I am advancing here, and also comes very close to the positions developed in Part Two (*provided* we take into account the deconstruction of rhetoric that has figured importantly in the writings of Paul de Man, Barbara Johnson, and others).

13. Hertz, "Two Extravagant Teachings," 63 *Yale French Studies* 59, 63 (1982). We need not suppose that this interior difference always presents itself in a single form. As Marx observed: "The authority assumed by the capitalist as the personification of capital . . . is essentially different from the authority exercised on the basis of production by means of slaves, serfs, etc." (*Capital, supra* note 4, at III, 881). The fetishism of *commodities* may well prove a transitory state of affairs.

For a classic displacement of subjectivity, see J. Derrida, *Speech and Phenomena* 70–87 (Evanston: Northwestern University Press, 1973) (D. Allison trans.) (deconstructing the "pure auto-affection" of hearing oneself speak [*s'entendre parler*]). Critiques of self-presence have been a mainstay of Continental thought and of certain strains of Anglo-American philosophy. Rather than provide an unwieldy string of citations to the "primary" texts, I shall confine myself here to listing a few good "secondary" works that focus on the idea of self-expropriation. For a very brief but useful account of structuralism's war on the metaphysical sanctity of the self, see T. Heller, "Structuralism and Critique," 36 *Stanford Law Review* 127, 147–51, 163–64 (1984). For a more lengthy perusal of this theme in structuralist anthropology and psychology, see J. Mehlman, "The 'floating signifier': from Lévi-Strauss to Lacan," 48 *Yale French Studies* 10 (1972). For a generally reliable survey of Foucault's work on the constitution of individuals within apparatuses of power, see C. Gordon, "Birth of the Subject," *Radical Philosophy*, Summer 1977, at 15. A very good account of the displacing and reinscribing of self-presence by deconstructive philosophy is contained in Gasché, "Deconstruction as Criticism," 6 *Glyph* 177 (1979). For an admirably limpid overview of the anti-humanist strand of Critical Theory, see M. Jay, "The Frankfurt School's Critique of Marxist Humanism," 39 *Social Research* 285 (1972). For an interesting look at crucial "moments" in feminism that culminate in an explicit deconstruction of subjectivity, see J. Culler, *On Deconstruction* 43–64 (Ithaca: Cornell University Press, 1982). For a pragmatist recapitulation of the view that self-presence will have always been mediated through language, and that the incorrigibility of sincere first-person reports is "a sociological rather than a metaphysical concern," see R. Rorty, *Philosophy and the Mirror of Nature* 173–92, 218–19 (Princeton: Princeton University Press, 1979) [hereinafter cited as PMN].

14. *Cf.* J. Derrida, *Of Grammatology* 89 (Baltimore: Johns Hopkins University Press, 1976) (G. Spivak trans.) [hereinafter cited as OG], analyzing "the absolute hearing-itself-speak . . . as a function responding to an indestructible but relative necessity." See also J. Derrida, *Margins of Philosophy* 15–16 (Chicago: University of Chicago Press, 1982) (A. Bass trans.) [hereinafter cited as MP], situating the subject as a "determination or an effect within a system which is no longer that of presence but of *différance*."

The two sentences juxtaposed below provide a glimpse of the paradoxes that structure *Capital:*

"Since the producers [of commodities] do not come into social contact with each other until they exchange their products, the specific social character of each producer's labour does not show itself except in the act of exchange." (*Capital, supra* note 4, at I, 73).

"The characters that stamp products as commodities, and *whose establishment is a necessary preliminary to the circulation of commodities,* have . . . acquired the stability of natural, self-understood forms of social life" (*id.* at I, 75; emphasis added).

15. S. Avineri, *The Social and Political Thought of Karl Marx* 250–51 (Cambridge: Cambridge University Press, 1968). For a similar view, see R. Tucker, *Philosophy and Myth in Karl Marx* 152–54 (2d ed., Cambridge: Cambridge University Press, 1972). For a strongly opposing view, see F. Jameson, *The Political Unconscious* 50–52 (Ithaca: Cornell University Press, 1981). We need not dwell upon the nefarious implications of Marx's quest for an earthly paradise. Suffice it here to say that the furtherance of Stalin's despotic reign by Marx's utopian ideals, though not ineluctable, seems less than wholly coincidental. See sources on this point cited *supra*, chap. 2, note 1.

16. Marx asked that we "picture to ourselves, by way of change, a community of free individuals, carrying on their work with the means of production in common, in which the labour-power of all the different individuals is consciously applied as the combined labour-power of the community" (*Capital*, *supra* note 4, at I, 78). Nowhere in Chapter 1 of *Capital* did he explicitly state that such a community would emerge from the future ashes of bourgeois life. As I shall observe shortly, nonetheless, Marx was not so discreet in many of his other writings (including other parts of *Capital*).

Augustine's scathingly pessimistic view of mundane political life—as well as his ecstatic view of the felicity that awaits the fortunate souls who have been redeemed—was most brilliantly set forth in *The City of God* (Harmondsworth: Penguin, 1984) (H. Bettenson trans.). Many relevant excerpts are contained in *The Political Writings of St. Augustine* (South Bend: Gateway Editions, 1962) (H. Paolucci ed.).

17. Even if we forbear from criticizing the hortatory extremes of the *Communist Manifesto,* we can find instances of secular millenarianism throughout Marx's *oeuvre*. For some lengthy passages in point, see, e.g., *Capital, supra* note 4, at III, 819–20; "Economic and Philosophic Manuscripts," *supra* note 4, at 155; "The German Ideology," *supra* note 4, at 197–98. See also *Capital, supra* note 4, at I, 763: "[C]apitalist production begets, with the inexorability of a law of Nature, its own negation. It is the negation of negation [a Hegelian term for the absolute self-presence of Spirit]."

18. B. Johnson, "Translator's Introduction," in J. Derrida, *Dissemination* vii, xv (Chicago: University of Chicago Press, 1981). *Cf.* M. Foucault, "The Discourse on Language," in *The Archaeology of Knowledge and The Discourse on Language* 215, 219–20 (New York: Pantheon, 1972) (A. Sheridan Smith trans.): "True discourse . . . is incapable of recognising the will to truth which pervades it; and the will to truth, having imposed itself upon us for so long, is such that the truth it seeks to reveal cannot fail to mask it. . . . [W]e are unaware of the prodigious machinery of the will to truth, with its vocation of exclusion." As Foucault freely acknowledged, his critique of the "will to truth" was heavily indebted to Nietzsche. Throughout Nietzsche's work, disciplines that pursue truth (such as philosophy and the sciences) are portrayed as dangerous and delusive efforts to succeed where religion failed—in gaining access to the eternal. See, e.g., F. Nietzsche, *Beyond Good and Evil* 9–32 (New York: Vintage, 1962) (W. Kaufmann trans.). Particularly relevant, too, is F. Nietzsche, *The Gay Science* 280–81 (New York: Vintage, 1974) (W. Kaufmann trans.) (sec. 344) [hereinafter cited as GS].

The phrases "mystical veil," "illusions of the monetary system," and "mist-enveloped regions" are from *Capital, supra* note 4, at I, 80, 82, 72. Georges Van Den Abbeele has disclosed a like failure of self-criticism in Dean MacCannell's semiological study of tourism. See G. Van Den Abbeele, "Sightseers: The Tourist as Theorist," *diacritics*, December 1980, at 3, 12–13 (reviewing D. MacCannell, *The Tourist* [New York: Schocken, 1976]).

In *Capital*, *supra* note 4, at I, 74–75, political economy is three times referred to as "scientific." For an insightful challenge to the efforts by Marx and Marxists to clothe their theories with the prestige of "science," see M. Foucault, "Two Lectures," in *Power/Knowledge* 78, 83–87 (New York: Pantheon, 1980) (C. Gordon ed.) [hereinafter cited as P/K].

19. J. Derrida, *supra* note 2, at 285. See also *supra* pp. 23, 28–29, 32–34. *Cf.* G. Bennington, "Reading Allegory," *Oxford Literary Review*, 1981 (no. 3), at 83, 91–92: "It is assumed here that urbanity, seriousness and authority are not easily left behind, and that any attempt to step beyond their closure into a space of pure *jouissance* is meaningless." Richard Rorty has stumbled by directing this antinihilistic point at relativism. See CP, *supra* note 10, at 167. For a few citations to other writers who have committed Rorty's *faux pas*, see *supra*, chap. 1, note 30.

20. P. de Man, *Blindness and Insight* 106 (2d ed., Minneapolis: University of Minnesota Press, 1983). *Cf.* B. Johnson, *The Critical Difference* xii (Baltimore: Johns Hopkins University Press, 1980), arguing that "what is not known is . . . the unseen motivating force behind the very deployment of meaning." On this point, Frank Lentricchia sides with Johnson when he disparages "the Marxist confidence of Antonio Gramsci that *all* the traces of history that mark the interpreter can be inventoried." F. Lentricchia, *After the New Criticism* 209 (Chicago: University of Chicago Press, 1980) (emphasis in original). Derrida takes much the same view: "[T]he writer writes *in* a language and *in* a logic whose proper system, laws, and life his discourse by definition cannot dominate absolutely. He uses them only by letting himself, after a fashion and up to a point, be governed by the system. And the reading must always aim at a certain relationship, unperceived by the writer, between what he commands and what he does not command of the patterns of the language that he uses. This relationship is not a certain quantitative distribution of shadow and light, of weakness or of force, but a signifying structure that critical reading should *produce*" (OG, *supra* note 14, at 158). See also sources cited *supra* note 13.

21. J. Derrida, *supra* note 2, at 282. Together with Barbara Johnson, we should bring up the question that "must be asked of all . . . demystifications: to what structure of authority does the critique of authority belong?" B. Johnson, "Teaching Ignorance: *L'Ecole des Femmes*," 63 *Yale French Studies* 165, 176 (1982).

22. G. Lukács, *History and Class Consciousness* 83–222 (Cambridge, Mass.: MIT Press, 1971) (R. Livingstone trans.) [hereinafter cited as HCC]. The original edition of *Geschichte und Klassenbewusstsein* was published in 1923; it contained essays written between 1919 and 1922. In 1967, Lukács recalled that "the question of alienation, which . . . has its theoretical and methodological roots in the Hegelian dialectic[,] . . . was in the air" during the 1920s ("Preface to the New Edition," in *id.* at ix, xxii). For an overview of European philosophy in this period, emphasizing the renewed interest in Hegel, see M. Jay, *Marxism and Totality* 67–80 (Berkeley: University of California Press, 1984).

23. Though the following two articles do not directly address Lukács's prodigious claims, they typify the sardonic stance assumed by critical legal scholars when faced with quasi-religious millenarianism: P. Gabel and D. Kennedy, "Roll Over Beethoven," 36 *Stanford Law Review* 1 (1984), a dialogue in which Kennedy fleers the millenarian tendencies of Gabel; M. Kelman, "Trashing," 36 *Stanford Law Review* 293, 343–46 (1984), arguing that "theoretical utopian writing is

either empty or puzzling." Though these scornful attitudes are completely justified and convincing, an even more perceptive approach would be to inscribe yearnings for totality in the vertiginous oscillation of *différance*. See, e.g., MP, *supra* note 14, at 6, 22–23, stressing that *différance* "includes ontotheology, inscribing it and exceeding it."

24. Here, as in the section on Marx—though with a very different tone—one can justifiably refer to the great Bishop of Hippo. See the bloodcurdling defense of "*compelle intrare*" in *The Political Writings of St. Augustine*, *supra* note 16, at 190–207. Pertinent too is Nietzsche's insight that perfect bliss in the Christian heaven is based through and through on its differentiating itself from the torment of the damned. See F. Nietzsche, *The Genealogy of Morals* I, sec. 15, in *On the Genealogy of Morals and Ecce Homo* 48–52 (New York: Vintage, 1967) (W. Kaufmann and R. Hollingdale trans.). The dangers of any totalizing imperative were hauntingly adumbrated by Theodor Adorno in his assessment of the Holocaust: "Genocide is the absolute integration. It is on its way wherever men are leveled off—'polished off,' as the German military called it—until one exterminates them literally, as deviations from the concept of their total nullity. Auschwitz confirmed the philosopheme of pure [political] identity as death. The most far out dictum from Beckett's *End Game*, that there really is not so much to be feared any more, reacts to a practice whose first sample was given in the concentration camps, and in whose concept—venerable once upon a time—the destruction of nonidentity is ideologically lurking." T. Adorno, *Negative Dialectics* 362 (New York: Continuum, 1973) (E. Ashton trans.).

In fairness to Lukács, one should acknowledge that he distanced himself from Leninist orthodoxy "by emphasizing the cultural and pedagogical aspects of the party's mission." J. Miller, *History and Human Existence* 132 (Berkeley: University of California Press, 1979). Indeed, this maverick focus on educational functions was closely linked to the dialectical underpinnings of Lukács's methodology. See J. Schmidt, "The Concrete Totality and Lukács's Concept of Proletarian *Bildung*," 24 *Telos* 2, 36 (1975).

25. HCC, *supra* note 22, at 86. Examples of a humanist tone in Lukács's writing can easily be brought forth. See, e.g., *id.* at 93: "[T]he relations between men that lie hidden in the immediate commodity relation, as well as the relations between men and the objects that should really gratify their needs, have faded to the point where they can be neither recognized nor even perceived"; *id.* at 148, bemoaning the inability of Hegel and other leading philosophers to "break out of the limits imposed on formal and rationalistic (bourgeois, reified) thought *and thereby to restore a humanity destroyed by that reification*" (emphasis added); *id.* at 197: "[T]he only effective superiority of the proletariat, its only decisive weapon is its ability to see the social totality as a concrete historical totality; to see the reified forms as processes between men." All the same, Lukács cannot too readily be described as a humanist; his work abounds with structuralist moments. See, e.g., *id.* at 133, observing at length that "the capitalist as the incarnation of economic and technical progress, does not act but is acted upon." Indeed, it might seem bizarre to label as a humanist anyone who could make the following claim: "It is not the primacy of economic motives in historical explanation that constitutes the decisive difference between Marxism and bourgeois thought, but the point of view of totality. The category of totality, the all-pervasive supremacy of the whole over the parts is the essence of the method which Marx took over from Hegel and brilliantly transformed into the foundations of a wholly new science" (*id.* at 27). (One might even be induced to recall the strictures leveled against the quasi-religious holism that enthralled many

members of the structuralist camp. See, e.g., J. Starobinski, *Words Upon Words* 43 [New Haven: Yale University Press, 1979] [O. Emmet trans.], quoted in R. Young, "Post-Structuralism: An Introduction," in *Untying the Text* 1, 5 [Boston: Routledge Kegan Paul, 1981] [R. Young ed.], describing structuralism as a "theology of emanation." On this point, see also S. Fish, *Is There a Text in This Class?* 181 [Cambridge: Harvard University Press, 1980] [hereinafter cited as ITTC], which ill-advisedly conflates structuralism and post-structuralism.) Yet, as is underlined in the quotation above from HCC, *supra* note 22, at 197, Lukács's conception of "totality" can itself easily be regarded as humanistic.

We thus find that Lukács's writing tends to bear out Jameson's thesis in regard to the two discoursive "codes" of Marxism. See *supra* note 12. This becomes even more notable when we take into account the explicit paradoxes in Lukács's work—a few of which will be noted presently—that can best be described as both phenomenological *and* structuralist, neither phenomenological *nor* structuralist.

26. *Cf.* B. Johnson, *supra* note 20, at 111: "[I]n spite of the absence of mastery, there is no lack of effects of power." My resort to the phrase "for reasons that remain to be analyzed" is hardly accidental. This phrase recurs in Derrida's texts—see, e.g., *Positions, supra* note 3, at 52–53—and is here supposed to take on at least two meanings. On the one hand, it can highlight my frame of reference: i.e., the varied and continually shifting acts of exclusion that must site any discourse and rob it of its apparent purity. In this sense, the reasons will "remain to be analyzed" because I shall be focusing here on other questions. Alternatively, the phrase suggests that the reasons always *will* "remain to be analyzed"; under this view, no interpretation or theory will establish once and for all why some particular effects have prevailed. Like the Eiffel Tower, the reasons for the effects will generate, and be generated by, ceaseless exposition. *Cf.* R. Barthes, "The Eiffel Tower," in *A Barthes Reader* 236 (New York: Hill and Wang, 1982) (S. Sontag ed.).

27. HCC, *supra* note 22, at 87. Parentheses were again used to good effect several pages later: "The incomprehensibility and irrationality of crises is indeed a consequence of the class situation and interests of the bourgeoisie but it follows equally from their approach to economics. (There is no need to spell out the fact that for us these are both merely aspects of the same dialectical unity)" (*id.* at 105).

28. "Although deconstruction provides a justifying analysis of the global situation of reflection, it does not account for this situation without residues. If an account is a record of debit and credit to be balanced, deconstruction is precisely an operation which makes such a mastery impossible" (Gasché, *supra* note 13, at 213 note 62).

29. HCC, *supra* note 22, at 86, 128. As James Schmidt has pointed out, the phrase "second nature" was used by Lukács in *The Theory of the Novel,* which was written in 1914–15, before Lukács became a Marxist. Schmidt, *supra* note 24, at 21. See also A. Feenberg, "Reification and the Antinomies of Socialist Thought," 10 *Telos* 93, 100 (1971–72).

30. S. Coleridge, *Biographia Literaria* ch. XIV, in *The Portable Coleridge* 432, 518 (Harmondsworth: Penguin, 1950) (I. A. Richards ed.).

31. HCC, *supra* note 22, at 92. For a similar point, see *id.* at 213 n.32. Marx's view of context and consciousness is to be found at its most exquisite in his "Economic and Philosophic Manuscripts," *supra* note 4, at 157–59, where Marx concluded: "Thought and being are indeed *distinct* but they also form a unity." *Id.* at 158 (emphasis in original).

32. HCC, *supra* note 22, at 97. Lukács went on to say: "This is the source of the—apparently—paradoxical situation whereby the 'law' of primitive societies, which has scarcely altered in hundreds or sometimes even thousands of years, can be flexible and irrational in character, renewing itself with every new legal decision, while modern law, caught up in the continuous turmoil of change, should appear rigid, static and fixed. But the paradox dissolves when we realise that it arises only because the same situation has been regarded from two different points of view: on the one hand, from that of the historian (who stands 'outside' the actual process) and, on the other, from that of someone who experiences the effects of the social order in question upon his consciousness" (*id*). In my view, the contemporaneous "turmoil" and rigidity of our legal system are due less to differing standpoints from which to analyze bourgeois life than to the ability of a legal system to accommodate technological innovation while leaving an array of hierarchies essentially unchanged. In taking this view, one can reject Weber's formalism and functionalism, and one can also try to play down the focus on individual outcomes within a given legal regime.

33. Quoted in W. Spanos, "The Apollonian Investment of Modern Humanist Education: The Examples of Matthew Arnold, Irving Babbitt, and I. A. Richards," 1 *Cultural Critique* 7, 12 (1985). This is a free but admirably comprehensive translation of a fragment that is numbered 84b in H. Diels and W. Kranz, *Die Fragmente der Vorsakritiker* (6th ed., Berlin: Weidmannsche Verlagsbuchhandlung, 1951). For a translation that follows Diels's numbering, see K. Freeman, *Ancilla to the Pre-Socratic Philosophers* 30 (Cambridge: Harvard University Press, 1948). In a present-day translation by Charles Kahn, the fragment is numbered LIII. See C. Kahn, *The Art and Thought of Heraclitus* 52, 53 (Cambridge: Cambridge University Press, 1979). For a brief discussion of the fragment, see *id.* at 169–70. For a long critique of the fragmentation of American government into largely uncontrolled fiefdoms, see T. Lowi, *The End of Liberalism* (New York: Norton, 1969).

34. On the importance of this distinction, see HCC, *supra* note 22, at xxiii–xxiv. Lukács's failure to distinguish among these concepts is touched upon in Schmidt, *supra* note 24, at 37; and at greater length in A. Arato, "Lukács' Theory of Reification," 11 *Telos* 25, 33 note 33, 42–43 (1972).

In fact, the only distinction that Lukács amplified was between *alienation* and objectification. HCC, *supra* note 22, at xxiv, xxxvi. However, this need cause no serious problems, for "within the framework of capitalism alienation of individuals appears as the subjective side of reification." Arato, *supra*, at 33 note 33. Nor is it a matter for grave concern that Lukács viewed "objectification" as an act rather than a state—*viz.*, as the genetic rather than the objective side of the relation between structures and events. As Jan Kott has observed, if "*un coup de des n'abolira jamais le hazard,*" then it is equally true that "*le hazard n'abolira jamais le coup de des.*" *The Structuralist Controversy* 270 (Baltimore: Johns Hopkins University Press, 1972) (R. Macksey and E. Donato ed.) (a comment following the presentation [at a Baltimore symposium] of "Structure, Sign, and Play in the Discourse of the Human Sciences" by Jacques Derrida). A more important problem with Lukács's text is that, in staking off alienation from objectification, Lukács gave voice to a nostalgic utopianism: "Only when the objectified forms in society acquire functions that bring the essence of man into conflict with his existence, only when man's nature is subjugated, deformed and crippled can we speak of an objective societal condition of alienation and, as an inexorable consequence, of all the subjective marks of an internal alienation" (HCC, *supra* note 22, at xxiv).

35. Posing the matter in this way—though appropriate for my current purpose—is almost as misleading as it is helpful. To do justice to the paradoxical play between a structure and its events, we should realize that objectification will never be transcended *and* will always already have been transcended. Derrida's remarks concerning expressivism can be applied, *mutatis mutandis*, to objectification: "*On the one hand*, expressivism is never simply surpassable, because it is impossible to reduce the couple outside/inside as a simple structure of opposition. This couple is an effect of *différance*, as is the effect of language that impels language to represent itself as expressive re-presentation, a translation on the outside of what was constituted inside. . . . *On the other hand*, and inversely, I would say that if expressivism is not *simply and once and for all* surpassable, expressivity is in fact always already surpassed, whether one wishes it or not, whether one knows it or not" (*Positions*, *supra* note 3, at 33).

36. Schmidt, *supra* note 24, at 37. This is not to argue that Lukács's text was wholly univocal. For instance, in the following passage Lukács foresaw an end to all dualisms *against the force of his own insights*: "All earlier attempts to use dialectics [before Hegel] . . . do not involve the relativizing or the interpenetration of the subject and object themselves. But only if that were the case, only if 'the true [were understood] not only as substance but also as subject,' only if the subject (consciousness, thought) were both producer and product of the dialectical process, only if, as a result the subject moved in a self-created world of which it is the conscious form and only if the world imposed itself upon it in full objectivity, *only then can the problem of dialectics, and with it the abolition of the antitheses of subject and object, thought and existence, freedom and necessity, be held to be solved*" (HCC, *supra* note 22, at 142; emphasis added). The emphasized clause would appear to be a non-sequitur in relation to what precedes it. Or, at least, it draws out only one strand of what precedes it; it fails to maintain that all antitheses will not only have been effaced but will have also been re-entrenched (and will not simply have been transcended).

37. For a brilliant exploration of this theme, see J. Derrida, "*Ousia* and *Gramme*: Note on a Note from *Being and Time*," in MP, *supra* note 14, at 29.

38. Lukács was more sophisticatedly dialectical when he wrote that "even while 'acting' [a person under capitalism] remains the object and not the subject of events" (HCC, *supra* note 22, at 135). See also *id.* at 3, where, in one of his truly splendid passages, Lukács criticized Engels for omitting to "mention the most vital interaction, namely the *dialectical relation between subject and object in the historical process*, let alone give it the prominence it deserves. Yet without this factor dialectics ceases to be revolutionary, despite attempts (illusory in the last analysis) to retain 'fluid' concepts. For it implies a failure to recognise that in all metaphysics the object remains untouched and unaltered so that thought remains contemplative and fails to become practical; while for the dialectical method the central problem is to *change reality*" (emphases in original). Lukács's entire critical project can of course be seen as a struggle to break down the duality between contemplation and action; but that hardly affects my point that all too often for Lukács the dichotomy of action and contemplation is something which has yet to be overcome, rather than something which has yet to be overcome *and* which has always been overcome already.

For an extended attack on the distinction between knowing and doing, see J. Dewey, *The Quest for Certainty* (New York: Minton Balch, 1929). The claim here is not, of course, that there simply *is* no disjuncture between action and contemplation; such a claim would need to pass itself off as stemming from contemplation rather than from an active postulation, and thus would need to reintroduce the very disjuncture it purported to do away with. Rather, the claim is that all attempts to sunder action from contemplation must prove untenable—as must all attempts to *forbear* from sundering them.

39. *Cf.* J. Derrida, *supra* note 2, at 36: "The unsurpassable, unique, and imperial grandeur of the order of reason, that which makes it not just another actual order or structure (a determined historical structure, one structure among other possible ones), is that one cannot speak out against it except by being for it, that one can protest it only from within it; and within its domain, Reason leaves us only the recourse to stratagems and strategies. . . . Since the revolution against reason, from the moment it is articulated, can operate only *within* reason, it always has the limited scope of what is called, precisely in the language of a department of *internal* affairs, a disturbance." See also OG, *supra* note 14, at 139: "[T]he most radical discourse, the most inventive and systematic engineer are surprised and circumvented by a history, a language, etc., a *world* (for 'world' means nothing else) from which they must borrow their tools, if only to destroy the former machine."

40. F. Jameson, "Conclusion," in *Aesthetics and Politics* 207 (London: New Left Books, 1977) (F. Jameson ed.), quoted in G. Graff, "The Pseudo-Politics of Interpretation," in *The Politics of Interpretation* 145, 152 note 11 (Chicago: University of Chicago Press, 1983) (W. Mitchell ed.). See also the quotations from *Marxism and Form* in note 12 *supra*.

41. MP, *supra* note 14, at 22. Vincent Descombes provides a splendid account of deconstruction's "bottomless chessboard" (though he does not use the specific phrase): "Nobody can say whether dialectical identity and difference are the same thing or not. No Master can decide any longer. In this game at which 'whoever loses is the winner,' the player who calls 'identity' will immediately find it changed into difference; and if he calls 'difference,' it will be metamorphosed into identity. So much so that in the end Hegel's victory is also indistinguishable from his defeat. The outcome of the game is undecidable. His victory is his defeat, but his defeat is his victory. The game will be interminable." V. Descombes, *Modern French Philosophy* 152 (Cambridge: Cambridge University Press, 1980).

42. For instance, Andrew Arato writes that "we can no longer disregard the possibility that the whole problem of class analysis is solved rather dogmatically by Lukács. . . . This dogmatism is especially problematic when we remember that no unitary class analysis emerges from the work of Marx" (Arato, *supra* note 34, at 65). In my view, Lukács's "resolution" of the problem of class is but an extreme instance of his overall dearth of self-reflection.

43. Schmidt, *supra* note 24, at 25–26. As will shortly become clear, I am not persuaded that Schmidt is on a completely firm footing.

44. HCC, *supra* note 22, at 21. *Cf.* Foucault, "War in the Filigree of Peace: Course Summary," *Oxford Literary Review,* 1980 (no. 2), at 15, 17, describing the "biased and strategic truth" of seventeenth-century "historico-political discourse." See also M. Foucault, "Nietzsche, Genealogy, History," in *Language, Counter-Memory, Practice* 139, 156–57, 162–63 (Ithaca: Cornell University Press, 1977) (D. Bouchard ed.) [hereinafter cited as NGH], commending the "affirmation of knowledge as perspective."

I am using the word "empiricism" instead of "positivism," to avoid bringing in all the connotations of the latter word within the philosophy of history. See W. Walsh, *An Introduction to Philosophy of History* 45–47 (3d ed., New Jersey: Humanities Press, 1967). The allure that empiricism has held for pragmatists is clearly displayed in F. Cohen, "Transcendental Nonsense and the Functionalist Approach," 35 *Columbia Law Review* 809 (1935). Even John Dewey—who was arguably more sophisticated in this respect than was Peirce or James—gave in to the siren call of empiricism on more than one occasion. See R. Rorty, "Dewey's Metaphysics," in CP, *supra* note 10, at 72.

45. HCC, *supra* note 22, at 21, 228 (emphasis added). This modified empiricism has won support from nearly all pragmatists. For example, in literary theory one of the more astute pragmatists has written: "[T]here is a text in . . . every class if one means by the text the structure of meaning that is obvious *and inescapable* from the perspective of whatever interpretive assumptions happen to be in force. . . .

". . . The fact that a standard of truth is never available independently of a set of beliefs does not mean that we can never know for certain what is true but that we *always* know for certain what is true (because we are always in the grip of some belief or other)." ITTC, *supra* note 25, at vii, 365 (first emphasis added; second emphasis in original).

To Fish's claims we should counterpose Derrida's statement that "it is always something like an *opening* which will frustrate the structuralist project. What I can never understand, in a structure, is that by means of which it is not closed." J. Derrida, *supra* note 2, at 160 (emphasis in original).

46. The type of "scientific" historicism I have in mind was poignantly (if eccentrically) criticized by Walter Benjamin in several of his "Theses on the Philosophy of History," in W. Benjamin, *Illuminations* 253 (New York: Shocken, 1969) (H. Arendt ed.), most notably in Thesis VII, *id.* at 256–57. Pertinent here also are Derrida's remarks, in "Cogito and the History of Madness," regarding the vertiginous play between "hyperbole" (or unconditioned transcendence) and "*Weltanschauungen*" (or closed historical structures): "I believe that historicity in general would be impossible without a history of philosophy, and I believe that the latter would be impossible if we possessed only hyperbole, on the one hand, or, on the other, only determined historical structures, finite *Weltanschauungen*. The historicity proper to philosophy is located and constituted in the transition, the dialogue between hyperbole and the finite structure, between that which exceeds the totality and the closed totality, in the difference between history and historicity." (J. Derrida, *supra* note 2, at 60). In addition, the essay "Signature Event Context," though not directly discussing matters of historiography, can be read as challenging the ostensible rigor of historicism. See MP, *supra* note 14, at 307. Nietzsche's contempt for the "ascetic" ideal of written history as a "mirror" is forcefully conveyed in F. Nietzsche, *supra* note 24, at 157 (III, sec. 26). For a critique of Marx rather close to what I have just been saying about Lukács, see C. Colliot-Thélène, "Afterword," in I. Rubin, *The History of Economic Thought* 385, 426–29 (London: Ink Links, 1979).

47. Gabel and Kennedy, *supra* note 23. I have deliberately written here about "interaction" rather than about "influence," to avoid obscuring the paradox described in note 2 *supra*. Nonetheless, as Gayatri Spivak notes, even Derrida does not always keep himself from the "uncharacteristically positivist gesture" of tracing influences. G. Spivak, "Translator's Preface" to OG, *supra* note 14, at vii, lxiii.

48. J.-P. Sartre, *L'Être et Le Néant* (Paris: Éditions Gallimard, 1943) [hereinafter cited as EN], translated as *Being and Nothingness* (New York: Washington Square Press, 1966) (H. Barnes trans.) [hereinafter cited as BN]. All quoted passages are from the Barnes translation. I have occasionally found it best to modify the translation; whenever I have done so, I have included the relevant page numbers from the French edition.

49. Vincent Descombes has remarked, perhaps a wee bit too mordantly, that "of the 722 pages in [*L'Être et le Néant*], *things* are entitled to no more than four. . . . If four pages suffice to describe 'being in itself,' then there can hardly be very much to say about it. In fact, the reader cannot help feeling that even these are four too many." V. Descombes, *supra* note 41, at 50–51 (emphasis in original).

50. This point was developed masterfully by Maurice Merleau-Ponty. For an excellent discussion of his analysis, see Gasché, *supra* note 13, at 185–88. Apart from the inconceivability of *framing* a self-reflective discourse, one should note that the precondition for *starting* any such discourse would amount to its having been completed already: "If the experience of self-consciousness were a result of self-reflection, the following process would have to take place: the ego, still without cognition of itself, bends back on itself in an act of representation (*vorstellend*) and becomes there aware of: itself. However, how is it to cash in (*einlosen*) this insight if it did not already before have a conception of itself? For looking at something (even if it is *myself*) will never tell me about that particular quality of my object which consists in the fact that it is *I* that I am looking at. I must rather already have had this insight and now bring it into play." M. Frank, *Was ist Neostrukturalismus?* 251 (Frankfurt am Main: Suhrkamp Verlag, 1984), quoted in A. Bowie, "Individuality and Differance," 7 *Oxford Literary Review* 117, 121 (1985).

51. F. Jameson, *supra* note 12, at 226. Dominick LaCapra has pointed out that, as a means to escape Freudianism, Sartre's distinction between consciousness and knowledge is "related to his internal resistance to giving theoretical status to his own submerged tendencies, which radically place in question the idea of a pure and total freedom of man." D. LaCapra, *A Preface to Sartre* 133 (Ithaca: Cornell University Press, 1978).

52. I take some liberties here. Cronos was held to be identical with Chronos (or Time) probably by the later Greeks only. See R. Graves, *The Greek Myths* vol. I, 38 (Harmondsworth: Penguin, 1960). *Cf.* H. Rose, *A Handbook of Greek Mythology* 69 note 1 (6th ed., London: Methuen, 1958).

53. BN, *supra* note 48, at 620, 628 (emphasis in original). See also J.-P. Sartre, *Anti-Semite and Jew* 59–60 (New York: Schocken, 1965) (G. Becker trans.): "For us, man is defined first of all as a being 'in a situation.' . . . He cannot be distinguished from his situation, for it forms him and decides his possibilities; but, inversely, it is he who gives it meaning by making his choices within it and by it."

54. M. Poster, *Existential Marxism in Postwar France* 88 (Princeton: Princeton University Press, 1975).

55. See, e.g., R. Solomon, *From Rationalism to Existentialism* 293, 300–301 (Humanities Press, 1972). For a similar view, see P. Morris, "Self-deception: Sartre's Resolution of the Paradox," in *Jean-Paul Sartre: Contemporary Approaches to His Philosophy* 30, 37 (Pittsburgh: Duquesne University Press, 1980) (H. Silverman and F. Elliston eds.): "Other forms of self-deception involve the temporal elements of the self. For instance, without reflecting on my past series of temper outbursts, I can try to treat my present rage as something isolated, something wholly called forth by that other's present outrageous remark, and wholly isolated from my own past tendency to react violently to small provocations."

56. D. LaCapra, *supra* note 51, at 131. LaCapra ought to have given heed to Walter Kaufmann's advice that we pay "attention to this passage, toward the end of section II [of the chapter on 'bad faith']: 'there is a sincerity which

bears on the past and which does not concern us here. . . . Here our concern is only with the sincerity which aims at itself in present immanence.'" *Existentialism from Dostoevsky to Sartre, supra* note 12, at 280 (quoting BN, *supra* note 48, at 110). On this specific example, Solomon and Morris disagree with LaCapra. See R. Solomon, *supra* note 55, at 297–98; Morris, *supra* note 55, at 37. However, they fail to see that—from Sartre's point of view—their own examples will be at one (in all pertinent respects) with the case of the homosexual.

57. J.-P. Sartre, *Critique of Dialectical Reason* (London: Verso, 1976) (A. Sheridan-Smith trans.) [hereinafter cited as CDR].

58. P. Berger and T. Luckmann, *The Social Construction of Reality* 196 note 12 (New York: Doubleday, 1966). A similar view, in a more fully elaborated form, structures the argument of M. Poster, *supra* note 54.

59. D. LaCapra, *supra* note 51, at 150. See also J. Miller, *supra* note 24, at 177–78, 183. For an anticipation of the *Critique* in *Being and Nothingness*, see, e.g., BN, *supra* note 48, at 102, a remarkable account of the "many [social] precautions [that] imprison a man in what he is, as if we lived in perpetual fear that he might escape from it, that he might break away and suddenly elude his condition." Moreover, the concept of the "Third"—which played an essential role in the social theory of Sartre's later work—had been introduced in a section dealing with "us-objects" in *L'Être et Le Néant*. See *id.* at 537–47. See also D. LaCapra, *supra* note 51, at 137. *Cf.* H. Barnes, "Introduction" to J.-P. Sartre, *Search for a Method* vii, xxiii (New York: Vintage, 1963) (H. Barnes tran.) [hereinafter cited as SM], conceding that "Sartre prepared us for [the view that 'man finds himself to be the product of his own product'] in *Being and Nothingness*"; F. Jameson, *supra* note 12, at 249–52, taking account of Sartre's discussion of the "Third" in *L'Être et Le Néant*.

For the *Critique*'s retention of the earlier views, see, e.g., CDR, *supra* note 57, at 96, describing people as "initially separate objects." LaCapra has most fiercely condemned the individualistic leanings of the *Critique*. See especially D. LaCapra, *supra* note 51, at 165–66, characterizing the *Critique* as "militantly individualistic." For a more balanced (though perhaps too laudatory) discussion, see M. Poster, *supra* note 54, at 284–85.

On the undoing of historical schemes by deconstruction, see, e.g., J. H. Miller, *Fiction and Repetition* 22–23 (Cambridge: Harvard University Press, 1982), referring to literary history as "a series of nonprogressive variations" that are themselves incoherent.

60. CDR, *supra* note 57, at 131–32 (emphasis in original). Similar passages abound. See, e.g., *id.* at 735: "[T]he conditionings of antagonistic reciprocity are, as a whole, and *in the abstract*, based on the relation of the multiplicity of men to the field of action, that is, on scarcity. We have also seen that scarcity, as a mortal danger, produces everyone in a multiplicity as a mortal danger for the Other." I cannot here go into the many problems that surround the notion of scarcity in most parts of the *Critique*. (Near the end of this section, I shall make some comments.) Suffice it to say that I agree with Douglas Collins when he insists that Sartre distinguished carefully between objectification on the one hand and alienation derived from scarcity on the other, but I feel nonetheless that most of the *Critique*'s arguments will seem ludicrously bold until one abjures such a distinction. *Cf.* Collins, "Reply to LaCapra," 44 *Telos* 150, 151 (1980). I should also point out another curious zigzagging in *Marxism and Form* by Fredric Jameson. After distinguishing objectification from alienation in a useful way, Jameson then collapses the one into the other. Compare F. Jameson, *supra* note 12, at 239–40 with *id.* at 244–47.

61. This is not to say that the market should be construed as a "paradigm" of alienation. Any claim to "paradigmatic" import would disregard the attention lavished by Sartre on the distinctiveness of each one of his examples.

62. That some actors in any large-scale market are institutions should not be seen as a telling blow against Sartre's theory. Alienation, after all, is the very stuff of institutionalized groups. See, e.g., CDR, *supra* note 57, at 606: "In so far as the ossification of the ossified *praxis* which is the institution is due to our own impotence, it constitutes for each and for all a precise index of *reification*. This does not necessarily mean that we suffer it as a constraint, but rather that it is our own inorganic inertia in the social milieu." See generally *id.* at 576–663.

63. CDR, *supra* note 57, at 260, 280, 288 (emphasis in original). The first quoted sentence is from a critique of bus lines rather than from the section on free markets.

64. My use of "economy" is of course borrowed—at high interest—from Derrida. See, e.g., "From Restricted to General Economy: A Hegelianism Without Reserve," in J. Derrida, *supra* note 2, at 251. The "paradoxical economy" that I describe is a ceaseless shuttle between the discourse of independent subjectivity—which, to ensure independence, has to be all-embracing—and everything that subsumes and therefore undermines such a discourse.

For the lingering humanism in one of the later texts, see, e.g., SM, *supra* note 59, at 76–77: "We willingly grant that the *group* never has and never can have the type of metaphysical existence which people try to give to it. We repeat with Marxism: there are only men and real relations between men. From this point of view, the group is in one sense only a multiplicity of relations and of relations among those relations. . . . When we say there are only men and real relations between men (for Merleau-Ponty I add things also, and animals, etc.), we mean only that we must expect to find the support of collective objects in the concrete activity of individuals. We do not intend to *deny* the reality of these objects, but we claim that it is *parasitical*." In light of the final word of this passage, see the etymological critique of "parasites" in J. H. Miller, "The Critic as Host," in H. Bloom, P. de Man, J. Derrida, G. Hartman, and J. H. Miller, *Deconstruction and Criticism* 217–26 (New York: Continuum, 1979). See also MP, *supra* note 14, at 321–27 (arguing that what Austin dubbed "parasites" will lie at the heart of speech-act theory). For a splendid though terse critique of Sartre's humanism, see *id.* at 115–16.

65. CDR, *supra* note 57, at 287 (emphases in original). For other instances, see, e.g., *id.* at 35–36: "Dialectical rationality . . . must be seen as the permanent and dialectical unity of freedom and necessity. . . . [I]n a sense, man submits to the dialectic as to an enemy power; in another sense, he *creates it;* and if dialectical Reason is the Reason of History, this contradiction must itself be lived dialectically, which means that man must be controlled by the dialectic in so far as he *creates* it, and *create* it in so far as he is controlled by it"; *id.* at 238: "Everyone makes himself signify by interiorising, by a free choice, the signification with which material exigencies have produced him as a *signified being*"; *id.* at 737: "[C]onstraint does not eliminate freedom . . . ; it makes freedom its accomplice while allowing it no option but obedience."

66. *Cf. supra* p. 8. Wolfgang Iser has hoped for just such a blend in his conception of reading. For a good critical discussion of Iser's search, see J. Culler, *supra* note 13, at 75–76. Duncan Kennedy's recent writing often appears to move in a direction like that favored by Iser. See D. Kennedy, "Freedom and Constraint in Adjudication: A Critical Phenomenology," 36 *Journal of Legal Education* 518

(1986). However, a somewhat gracious reading would put Kennedy's work quite close to the positions and strategies that I commend in Part Two. In any case, even Sartre at times fell back from the dialectical rigor of his own insights. For example, in the following sentence he presumed to rein in the categorical freedom of subjectivity and the total closure of objectivity, by endowing individuals with a limited range of options: "It is obvious that . . . class-being does not prevent us from realising an individual destiny (each life is individual), but this realisation of our experience until death is only one of several possible ways (determined by the structured field of possibilities) of producing our class-being" (CDR, *supra* note 57, at 239). At such moments, we must read Sartre against himself.

67. See, e.g., C. Lévi-Strauss, *The Savage Mind* 246–47 (Chicago: University of Chicago Press, 1966); M. Poster, *supra* note 54, at 272–73; PMN, *supra* note 13, at 361 note 7. Alas, Poster seems to think that "humanity imposes itself upon nature"—and that "nature impinge[s] upon the human scene"—only in economic life (i.e., in production narrowly defined) (M. Poster, *supra* note 54, at 272). Even more objectionable and slack is the scientism of Lévi-Strauss, who calls for "the reintegration of culture in nature and finally of life within the whole of its physico-chemical conditions" (C. Lévi-Strauss, *supra*, at 247). Reductionism of this sort, *without a critical view of science*, is a cure worse than the disease.

68. See *supra* pp. 167–84. In the second Part of *Of Grammatology*, one of Derrida's chief concerns is to deconstruct the nature/culture division. See OG, *supra* note 14, at 97–316. For the pragmatist view, the *locus classicus* is PMN, *supra* note 13, at 343–56. Also important here is radical feminism, which holds that "the 'myth' of nature is a system of arbitrary signs which relies on a social consensus for meaning. Neither the concept of nature nor that of culture is 'given,' and they cannot be free from the biases of the culture in which the concepts were constructed." C. MacCormack, "Nature, Culture and Gender: A Critique," in *Nature, Culture and Gender* 6 (Cambridge, England: Cambridge University Press, 1980) (C. MacCormack and M. Strathern eds.), quoted in C. Greene and C. Kahn, "Feminist scholarship and the social construction of woman," in *Making a Difference: Feminist Literary Criticism* 1, 10 (London: Methuen, 1985) (C. Greene and C. Kahn eds.). See also C. MacKinnon, "Feminism, Marxism, Method, and the State: An Agenda for Theory," 7 *Signs* 515, 529 (1982) ("conceiving nature, law, the family, and roles as consequences, not foundations"). Too often, like pragmatism, the feminist critique has tried simply to invert nature/culture dyads—and has thus not perceived that its reversals will have reversed *themselves* without stop.

69. For a lengthy and caustic challenge to Lacanianism, see J. Derrida, "The Purveyor of Truth," 52 *Yale French Studies* 31 (1975). For a much more concise version of this critique, see *Positions*, *supra* note 3, at 107 note 44. For some helpful pages on Derrida's critique, see Spivak, *supra* note 47, at lxii–lxvii.

70. CDR, *supra* note 57, at 124. Oddly, Mark Poster views objectification as resulting from scarcity. See M. Poster, *supra* note 54, at 279–80, 286–87.

71. The most famous reproach along these lines is in C. Lévi-Strauss, *supra* note 67, at 248–50. See also D. LaCapra, *supra* note 51, at 166–67; J. Miller, *supra* note 24, at 187. Many types of functionalism are deftly criticized in R. Gordon, "Critical Legal Histories," 36 *Stanford Law Review* 57 (1984). To propound contrary arguments is, of course, to take only the first step in a critique of functionalism. One would then have to show that each of the antipodal viewpoints is the *différance* of the other—i.e., that each will have subverted itself along with the other viewpoint.

72. CDR, *supra* note 57, at 122. See also *id.* at 82, where *praxis* is defined as a "*temporal* relation between the future and the past, through the present" (emphasis in original). For a very good exposition of Sartre's treatment of temporality, see J. Fell, *Heidegger and Sartre* 83–87, 131–39 (New York: Columbia University Press, 1979).

73. This can be inferred from remarks imputed to Zeno in the *Parmenides* of Plato. See J. Barnes, *The Presocratic Philosophers* 235–36 (rev. ed., London: Routledge & Kegan Paul, 1982).

74. See MP, *supra* note 14, at 53–62. Most revealing is Sartre's tendency—at odds with some of his own assertions—to treat the past as a *quondam* present and the future as an *impending* present. See, e.g., BN, *supra* note 48, at 179 (EN, 168; translation modified): "As For-itself it has its being outside of it, ahead and behind. Behind, it *was* its past; and ahead, it *will be* its future"; *id.* at 281: "The For-itself can be presence to the *this* only as a presence which was. . . . [E]ach moment of the past is a 'having-been-present'"; *id.* at 289–90: "[I]n so far as [a moving object] is already at B, it is exterior to what it was at A and there is an annihilation of the [object]; but in so far as *it rediscovers itself* at C, beyond B, it is exterior to that very annihilation" (emphasis added).

75. OG, *supra* note 14, at 72. See also *id.* at 66–67. Another problem with Sartre's outlook is turned up brilliantly by Derrida in a critique of Heidegger, Aristotle, and Kant. Attempts to characterize time on the basis of its ontological standing will have presupposed an equation of pure being and presence. A doctrine that aims to reach the essence of temporality—and whose seeming ground lies in a specific view of ontology—will therefore have had to base itself on the very thing that was to be grounded. Incorporation of illegitimate starting points will have flowed from the unavoidable use of verbs and their tenses; there can be no "timeless" description that does not have to take for granted what it is purporting to ferret out (i.e., the relationship between being and time). As Derrida remarks: "[T]o state the no-thingness of time, one already has had to appeal to time, to a precomprehension of time, and, within discourse, to the self-evidence and functioning of the verb's tenses. Without *disclosing* it, one already has operated within the horizon of the meaning of time in order to think nonbeing as nonpresent, and being as present. Being has been determined temporally as being-present in order to determine time as nonpresent and nonbeing" (MP, *supra* note 14, at 50–51).

76. For a careful account of the complicated relation and nonrelation between deconstructionism and politics, see J. Culler, *supra* note 13, at 156–79. Even if *(mirabile dictu)* a clear relationship held, one then would encounter problems like those besetting Critical Theory. See, e.g., S. Buck-Morss, *The Origin of Negative Dialectics* 42 (New York: Free Press, 1977): "The fact of the matter is that Adorno's talk of the mediation between intellectual praxis and political praxis remained abstract and vague, with no explication of the social medium which might serve as a conduit for this mediation, once the role of the Party was rejected. The medium for Adorno's 'mediation' remained as mysterious as the medium between the spirits and the flesh of the world."

77. *Cf.* Gasché, *supra* note 13, at 212 note 29: "[S]peaking of deconstruction versus reconstruction turns deconstruction erroneously into a *moment* of the speculative process" (emphasis in original).

78. F. Nietzsche, *Gesammelte Werke, Musarionausgabe* vol. XVI, 318 (Munich: Musarion Verlag, 1927), quoted in GS, *supra* note 18, at 238 note 20 (translator's note).

79. P. Shelley, "Sonnet," in *Selected Poetry and Prose of Shelley* 117 (New York: New American Library, 1966) (H. Bloom ed.) [hereinafter cited as SPPS].

This metaphor was again used, almost verbatim, in "Prometheus Unbound." See *id.* at 190 (III. iv. 190). See also *id.* at 183 (III. iii. 113).

For some major texts of neo-pragmatism, see, e.g., ITTC, *supra* note 25; CP, *supra* note 10; PMN, *supra* note 13; L. Wittgenstein, *Philosophical Investigations* (New York: Macmillan, 1958) (G. Anscombe trans.). For texts closely akin to those just cited, see, e.g., R. Bernstein, *Beyond Objectivism and Relativism* (Philadelphia: University of Pennsylvania Press, 1983); J. Dewey, *supra* note 38; N. Goodman, *Ways of Worldmaking* 1-22, 71–140 (Indianapolis: Hackett, 1978); W. James, *Pragmatism* (New York: Longmans Green, 1947); T. Kuhn, *The Structure of Scientific Revolutions* (2d ed., Chicago: University of Chicago Press, 1970); A. MacIntyre, *After Virtue* (Notre Dame: University of Notre Dame Press, 1981).

80. CP, *supra* note 10, at xliii. For a more extended treatment, see PMN, *supra* note 13, at 371–72. For a largely similar view, see P. Feyerabend, *Science in a Free Society* 142–43 (London: Verso, 1982). For an example of the myriad anti-pragmatist onslaughts that confuse relativism with nihilism, see Graff, *supra* note 40, at 148: "Like the famous paradox of the liar, this line of argument [i.e., relativism] suffers from a built-in tendency to self-destruct."

81. See PMN, *supra* note 13, at 324–25, 344–45. See also CP, *supra* note 10, at xlvi note 31.

82. What I am saying is in many respects a version of the point made by Walter Benjamin in the passage that I included in note 2 *supra*. My argument also bears a certain resemblance to one strand of Derrida's critique of Freud. See J. Derrida, *supra* note 2, at 211–15.

83. A. Parker, "Futures for Marxism: An Appreciation of Althusser," *diacritics*, Winter 1985, at 57, 62.

84. *Différance*, which can fittingly be construed as dialectics without the *Aufhebung* (or, rather, as dialectics with the *Aufhebung* turned against itself), here amounts to the self-subverting "logic" that deconstruction finds (and produces) as the key operator in texts. It is what I called "paradoxes of differentiation" in Chapter 1. For an exhilarating account of Derrida's unaccountable term, see J. Derrida, "Differance," in MP, *supra* note 14, at 1. On the generalizability of deconstructionist methods, see, e.g., *id.* at 318: "I will extend [my methods] even to all 'experience' in general, if it is granted that there is no experience of pure presence, but only chains of differential marks" (emphasis in original).

85. W. James, *Pragmatism and the Meaning of Truth* (Cambridge: Harvard University Press, 1978), quoted in CP, *supra* note 10, at xxv; J. Dewey, *Logic: The Theory of Inquiry* 9 (New York: Henry Holt, 1938), quoted in R. Bernstein, *Praxis and Action* 218 (Philadelphia: University of Pennsylvania Press, 1971). The "Myth of the Given" is discussed in PMN, *supra* note 13, at 95–96 *passim*.

86. This view seems to have gained partial acceptance in the criminal law of Great Britain and the United States. A gross failure to understand the moral significance of one's deeds, just as much as a gross failure to understand the facts that constitute deeds, can warrant a finding of insanity. See generally S. Kadish and M. Paulsen, *Criminal Law and Its Processes* 584–635 (3d ed., Boston: Little, Brown, 1975).

87. F. Jameson, *supra* note 15, at 45. Relevant texts by Habermas include *Toward a Rational Society* 81–122 (Boston: Beacon Press, 1970) (J. Shapiro tran.) and *Theory and Practice* 253–82 (Boston: Beacon Press, 1973) (J. Viertel tran.). I have criticized Habermas elsewhere. See M. Kramer, "The Metaphysics of the Delaney Clause," 15 *Capital University Law Review* 579, 618–19 (1986).

88. K. Marx, "Theses on Feuerbach," in *The Marx-Engels Reader*, *supra* note 4, at 143, 144, 145. In his "Economic and Philosophic Manuscripts," Marx took

a more sophisticated position. See K. Marx, "Economic and Philosophic Manuscripts," *supra* note 4, at 157–58 (subsuming language and work under the category of "social activity").

89. M. Ryan, "The Marxism-Deconstruction Debate in Literary Theory," *New Orleans Review,* Spring 1984, at 29, 32, quoted in R. Terdiman, "Deconstructing Memory: On Representing the Past and Theorizing Culture in France Since the Revolution," *diacritics,* Winter 1985, at 13, 34. Having brought together discoursive and non-discoursive elements under the heading of "apparatuses," Michel Foucault declared: "[I]t doesn't much matter for my notion of the apparatus to be able to say that this is discursive and that isn't. If you take Gabriel's architectural plan for the Military School together with the actual construction of the School, how is one to say what is discursive and what institutional? . . . I don't think it's very important to be able to make that distinction." M. Foucault, "The Confession of the Flesh," in P/K, *supra* note 18, at 194, 198.

A towering figure in regard to this general theme is Claude Lévi-Strauss, much of whose work contends that "the different aspects of social life (including even art and religion) cannot only be studied by the methods of, and with the help of concepts similar to those employed in linguistics, but also . . . constitute phenomena whose inmost nature is the same as that of language." C. Lévi-Strauss, *Structural Anthropology* 62 (Harmondsworth: Penguin, 1972) (C. Jacobson and B. Schoepf trans.). Lévi-Strauss concludes: "[A]s soon as the various aspects of social life—economic, linguistic, etc.—are expressed as relationships, anthropology will become a general theory of relationships. Then it will be possible to analyze societies in terms of the differential features characteristic of the systems of relationships which define them" (*id.* at 95–96). One major shortcoming of the tack adopted by Lévi-Strauss is the confinement of his analyses to the social realm. As I argue, the social/natural divide will prove as untenable as the language/life divide. Of course, the failings of Lévi-Strauss reach far beyond this one point. See J. Derrida, *supra* note 2, at 278–93; OG, *supra* note 14, at 101–40.

90. Heller, *supra* note 13, at 147. *Cf.* Rorty, "Philosophy Without Principles," 11 *Critical Inquiry* 459, 460 (1985): "I would urge that anything—a wave pattern, an arrangement of stars, the spots on a rock—can be treated not only as language but as any given sentence of English if one can find some way to map its features onto the semantic and syntactic features of that sentence (and other actual and possible patterns or arrangements or spots on the other sentences of English)."

Also *cf.* CP, *supra* note 10, at 199: "If you can't figure out the relation between a person, the noises he makes, and other persons, then you won't know much about him. But one could equally well say that fossils wouldn't be fossils, would be merely rocks, if we couldn't grasp their relations to lots of other fossils. Fossils are constituted *as* fossils by a web of relationships to other fossils and to the speech of the paleontologists who describe such relationships."

See also *id.* at 200: "The relation, on my view, between actions and movements, noises and assertions, is that each is the other described in alternative jargon." Also *cf.* PMN, *supra* note 13, at 351: "The sense in which human beings alter themselves by redescribing themselves is no more metaphysically exciting or mysterious than the sense in which they alter themselves by changing their diet, their sexual partners, or their habitation. It is just the same sense; viz., new and more interesting sentences become true of them."

91. See *supra* pp. 29–34. I am sharply at odds with Rorty, who does his best to assimilate deconstruction to his own standpoint. See, e.g., R. Rorty, "Nineteenth-Century Idealism and Twentieth-Century Textualism," in CP, *supra*

note 10, at 139. The equation of pragmatism and deconstruction has become strikingly widespread.

92. G. Frug, "The Ideology of Bureaucracy in American Law," 97 *Harvard Law Review* 1276, 1296 (1984) [hereinafter cited as IBAL].

93. "The Purveyor of Truth" is the English title of Derrida's critique of Lacan. See Derrida, *supra* note 69. (The French title, "*Le Facteur de la Vérité*," might have been better rendered as "The Postman of Truth.") One of the main charges against Lacan is that he flagrantly begged the question as he carried out his approach. See, e.g., *id.* at 89: "If this demonstration is granted it will not be surprising to find it confirmed"; *id.* at 99 note 36, accusing Lacan's Seminar of "finding it(self there) in truth" when it analyzes Poe's short story. But, as Barbara Johnson argues persuasively, Lacan's begging of questions can be viewed as one of his greatest strengths precisely because it was performed with the utmost skill and deliberation. See B. Johnson, *supra* note 20, at 141–42: "But if the act of (psycho-)analysis has no identity apart from its status as a repetition of the structure it seeks to analyze (to untie), then Derrida's remarks against psychoanalysis as being always already *mise en abyme* in the text it studies and as being only capable of finding *itself*, are not objections to psychoanalysis but a profound insight into its very essence." In this sense, and in this sense only, I agree with Heidegger: "What is decisive is not to get out of the circle but to come into it in the right way." M. Heidegger, *Being and Time* 195 (Oxford: Basil Blackwell, 1962) (J. Macquarrie and E. Robinson trans.). See generally *id.* at 27, 194–95.

For a pragmatist who accepts circularity with aplomb, see Rorty, *supra* note 90, at 461: "[A]ll of us who debate these matters start out with . . . intuitions and then go round in circles, defending them in one guise by appealing to them in another." See also N. Goodman, *supra* note 79, at 17: "[A] version [of the world] is taken to be true when it offends no unyielding beliefs and none of its own precepts."

94. C. MacKinnon, "Feminism, Marxism, Method, and the State: Toward Feminist Jurisprudence," 8 *Signs* 635, 637 (1983).

95. Heller, *supra* note 13, at 173–74 note 81. For further citations to accounts—primarily neo-pragmatist accounts—of the networks within which easy cases take shape, see Kramer, *supra* note 87, at 611 note 123.

96. L. Wittgenstein, *On Certainty* 21 (Oxford: Basil Blackwell, 1979) (D. Paul and G. Anscombe trans.) (sec. 145).

97. B. Johnson, *supra* note 20, at 146. It is perhaps worth noting that my remarks on "explicit" self-reflection will have had to suppose at least a modicum of agreement on what counts as "explicitness." Hence, those remarks will have succumbed to difficulties analogous to the ones raised here; shared standards for evaluating explicitness will formally correspond to the networks that allow cases to be decided easily.

98. In CP, *supra* note 10, at xxiv, Rorty lists a few stratagems from the "philosophical bag of tricks" to which I refer. To his list I would add Hegel's questioning of sense certainty, Wittgenstein's attack on the idea of a private language, and Derrida's work on "iterability." See G. Hegel, *Phenomenology of Spirit* 58–66 (Oxford: Oxford University Press, 1977) (A. Miller trans.) (chap. I); L. Wittgenstein, *supra* note 79, at secs. 243–71, 288-304, 344–46; MP, *supra* note 14, at 309–30.

99. CP, *supra* note 10, at xiv. This especially holds for Kuhn, who declares: "The man who takes historic fact seriously must suspect that science does not

tend toward the ideal that our image of cumulativeness has suggested" (T. Kuhn, *supra* note 79, at 96). Indeed, Kuhn begins his book with a ringing proclamation: "History, if viewed as a repository for more than anecdote or chronology, could produce a decisive transformation in the image of science by which we are now possessed" (*id.* at 1).

On the importance of Hegel for the pragmatists, see, e.g., CP, *supra* note 10, at xli: "Hegel himself, to be sure, had his Philosophical moments, but the temporalization of rationality which he suggested was the single most important step in arriving at the pragmatist's distrust of Philosophy." Indeed, few philosophers can be said to have learned as much from Hegel as did John Dewey. In writings such as *The Quest for Certainty,* Dewey's terms are steeped in Hegelianism, though a pallid version thereof. In later years, Dewey recalled: "Hegel's treatment of human culture . . . had a special attraction for me. . . . I should never think of ignoring, much less denying, what an astute critic occasionally refers to as a novel discovery—that acquaintance with Hegel has left a permanent deposit in my thinking." J. Dewey, "From Absolutism to Experimentalism," in *The Philosophy of John Dewey* 1, 7, 8 (Chicago: University of Chicago Press, 1981) (J. McDermott ed.).

100. PMN, *supra* note 13, at 379. See also *id.* at 13, using similar language to describe the chief purpose of *Philosophy and the Mirror of Nature.* For pragmatism's ready insistence on the caducity of intellectual structures, see, e.g., T. Kuhn, *supra* note 79, at 206–207: "[T]he notion of a match between the ontology of a theory and its "real" counterpart in nature now seems to me illusive in principle. Besides, as a historian, I am impressed with the implausability [*sic*] of the view. . . . [If this] position be relativism, I cannot see that the relativist loses anything needed to account for the nature and development of the sciences." See also T. Kuhn, *The Essential Tension* 176–77 (Chicago: University of Chicago Press, 1977): "[E]very unanticipated discovery . . . demands, from those most concerned, the sorts of readjustment that, when they are more obvious, we equate with scientific revolutions." On the rejuvenating effects of controversy, see, e.g., A.MacIntyre, *supra* note 79, at 206: "Traditions, when vital, embody continuities of conflict. Indeed when a tradition becomes Burkean, it is always dying or dead."

101. See P. de Man, "Shelley Disfigured," in *Deconstruction and Criticism, supra* note 64, at 39, 69: "*The Triumph of Life* warns us that nothing, whether deed, word, thought or text, ever happens in relation, positive or negative, to anything that precedes, follows or exists elsewhere, but only as a random event whose power, like the power of death, is due to the randomness of its occurrence. It also warns us why and how these events then have to be reintegrated in a historical and aesthetic system of recuperation that repeats itself regardless of the exposure of its fallacy." For the sophistication of pragmatist views of history, see, e.g., PMN, *supra* note 13, at 344, referring to history as "Whiggish stories." But Rorty has sometimes strayed too close to empiricism; see, e.g., *id.* at 50 note 19, 51 note 21, speculating whether John Yolton's view of seventeenth-century philosophy is "correct."

102. Here I agree with Terry Eagleton, who has approached this issue from the opposite side: "It may well be that we can only know the past in terms of our present relationship to it; but then how else do we know anything? We do not tend to deny that our knowledge of tables and chairs is (in some suitably modest, workable sense of the term) objective, simply because it is ineluctably knowledge in terms of our relationship to them. Is the past in this sense ontologi-

cally different?" T. Eagleton, "Marxism and the Past," 68–69 *Salmagundi* 271, 279–80 (1985–86).

103. J. H. Miller, "Deconstructing the Deconstructors," *diacritics*, Summer 1975, at 24, 31.

104. For an example of Nietzsche's powerful highlighting of struggles, see F. Nietzsche, *The Will to Power* 299 (New York: Vintage, 1967) (W. Kaufmann and R. Hollingdale trans.) [hereinafter cited as WP] (sec. 552d): "All events, all motion, all becoming, as a determination of degrees and relations of force, as a *struggle*." I have been and shall be focused on the question of "strategy" as it appears in Derrida's work. Equally important, however, are Michel Foucault's genealogies of "struggles" and "domination." See, e.g., NGH, *supra* note 44, at 139, 148–52, advocating genealogical reconstruction of the "hazardous play of dominations"; M. Foucault, *supra* note 18, at 80–87, discussing "insurrections of subjugated knowledges"; M. Foucault, *The History of Sexuality* 92–102 (New York: Vintage, 1978) (R. Hurley trans.) [hereinafter cited as HS] (a remarkable account of Foucault's conception of power).

105. Much to his credit, Michael Ryan concedes that his "subject [i.e., the articulation of Marxism and deconstruction] is one that cannot be concluded" (M. Ryan, *supra* note 4, at xvi). Nonetheless, he is all too eager to assert that "there is a necessary relationship between conceptual apparatuses and political institutions. . . . [T]he deconstructive critique of absolutist concepts in the theory of meaning can be said to have a political-institutional corollary, which is the continuous revolutionary displacement of power toward radical egalitarianism and the plural defusion [*sic*] of all forms of macro- and microdomination" (*id.* at 8). This should be compared with J. Derrida, *supra* note 2, at 276: "It would be absurd for the transgression of the Book by writing to be legible only in a determined sense." Among other problems with Ryan's work is one that Jonathan Culler mentions: "Such projects [as Ryan's] . . . beg numerous questions about what is truly progressive and what is not" (J. Culler, *supra* note 13, at 158). For instance, Ryan gives his apparently unqualified endorsement to Edward Said's breathtakingly Manichean outlook on the tragedy of the Palestinians. See M. Ryan, *supra* note 4, at 153, 228 note 16. For a good though very brief criticism of Said's lack of balance, see A. Rabinbach, "Anti-Semitism Reconsidered: Reply to Piccone and Berman," 21 *new german critique* 129, 139 (1980).

106. HS, *supra* note 104, at 95, 96. Foucault made a very nice distinction between "strategies," which are non-localizable, and "tactics," which can be traced to persons or institutions. As I argue in my next point, however, and as Foucault was well aware, this duality—useful and inescapable though it is—cannot ultimately hold up, for each of its aspects must have pre-existed the other.

107. AR, *supra* note 2, at 131. *Cf. id.* at 19, describing our processes of reading "not as an emotive reaction to what language does, but as an emotive reaction to the impossibility of knowing what it might be up to"; *Positions, supra* note 3, at 82, maintaining that deconstructive strategy "is *made* in the general movement of the field, and is never exhausted by the conscious calculation of a 'subject'" (emphasis in original); M. Ryan, *supra* note 4, at 38: "The historical arena is too deeply sedimented and one is too unconsciously embedded in it to assume that what one wants or intends is what one effectuates or gets, or even is what is really going on." *Pace* Ryan, the problem here is decidedly not one of historical richness, but one of deconstructive play: "If totalization no longer has any meaning, it is not because the infiniteness of a field cannot be covered by a finite glance or a finite discourse, but because the nature of

the field—that is, language and a finite language—excludes totalization. This field is in effect that of *play*, that is to say, a field of infinite substitutions only because it is finite, that is to say, because instead of being an inexhaustible field, as in the classical hypothesis, instead of being too large, there is something missing from it: a center which arrests and grounds the play of substitutions." J. Derrida, *supra* note 2, at 289. Ryan himself acknowledges a partly related point. See M. Ryan, *supra* note 4, at 226 note 8: "For Derrida, the principle of undecidability, incompleteness, and the nonsaturability of contexts does not imply an infinite or inexhaustible richness, but rather a structural dilemma at the very heart of any axiomatic system that pretends to be exhaustive."

108. I am alluding here to phenomena known as "transference" and "intertextuality." Transferential displacements and intertextual seesaws will permit one to probe a given text through some other texts that—at the very most—can be seen as highly oblique (and often premature) commentaries. As Derrida states: "One text reads another. . . . And, among other things, vice versa. Each 'text' is a machine with multiple reading heads for other texts." J. Derrida, "Living On," in *Deconstruction and Criticism*, *supra* note 64, at 75, 107. The phrase "post-structuralist condition" is from P. Lewis, "The Post-Structuralist Condition," *diacritics*, Spring 1982, at 2.

109. *Cf.* B. Johnson, *supra* note 20, at 12: "[T]he difference between literature and criticism consists perhaps only in the fact that criticism is more likely to be blind to the way in which its own critical difference from itself makes it, in the final analysis, literary." It would be advisable to keep in view here my reservations about "explicitness" as a standard for appraising the rigor of one's self-reflection. See *supra* note 97.

110. B. Johnson, *supra* note 20, at xi; Johnson, *supra* note 3, at 148.

111. For Frug's outlook, see IBAL, *supra* note 92, at 1293–94. See also R. Unger, *supra* note 6, at 136–37. For Gabel's position, see, e.g., Gabel and Kennedy, *supra* note 23, at 28–29, 35. Ronald Dworkin takes the same view from the perspective of liberal individualism. See R. Dworkin, "Is Wealth a Value?" 9 *Journal of Legal Studies* 191, 204 (1980). But see R. Dworkin, *Law's Empire* 167–75 (London: Fontana, 1986). For Parker's assault on the complacent visions of harmony that enthrall the mainstream of constitutional theorizing, see R. Parker, "The Past of Constitutional Theory—And Its Future," 42 *Ohio State Law Journal* 223, 239–57 (1981). For the critical legal scholars' view of language, see, e.g., E. Mensch "The History of Mainstream Legal Thought," in *The Politics of Law* 18, 27–28 (New York: Pantheon, 1982) (D. Kairys ed.): "Words are created by people in history, and their definition inevitably varies with particular context and with the meaning brought to them by the judges who are asked to interpret them. That act of interpretation is, in every instance, an act of social choice."

112. Rorty makes a similar point in his discussion of the nature/culture dichotomy. See PMN, *supra* note 13, at 353. The "abstract/concrete" dualism has played an indispensable role in Western philosophy, in many guises (such as "form/matter" and "universal/particular"). Aristotle and Plato, not surprisingly, were among the earliest to conceive of this dyad in remarkably influential ways. See, e.g., Plato, *The Republic* 179–89 (New York: Oxford University Press, 1945) (F. Cornford trans.) (V.474B-480), delineating the doctrine of universal Forms; Aristotle, *Metaphysics* bk. VII (Ann Arbor: University of Michigan Press, 1960) (R. Hope trans.). During the Middle Ages, the division between universality and particularity preoccupied intellectuals everywhere. See, e.g., Boethius, *The Second Edition of the Commentaries on the Isagoge of Porphyry* bk. I, in *Selections from Medieval Philosophers* vol. I, 70, 91–98 (New York: Charles Scribner's Sons,

1929) (R. McKeon ed.). See also *id.* at 67–68 for editor's comments on the importance of Boethius's discussion for later medieval thought. In modern times, the problem of universals and particulars received its most brilliant scrutiny in the work of Hegel, whose treatment of the problem has been acclaimed by Roberto Unger as the "single greatest achievement of [Hegel's] philosophy." R. Unger, *supra* note 6, at 312 note 24, citing G. Hegel, *Wissenschaft der Logik*, in *Samtliche Werke* vol. V, 35–65 (Stuttgart: Fromman, 1928). (Unger, in my opinion, does not do justice in his own texts to the dialectical verve of Hegel's philosophizing.) In more recent times, this question was of supreme importance for many followers of the early pragmatist movement, who took roughly the same position as that of Frug. See, e.g., F. Cohen, "Transcendental Nonsense and the Functional Approach," 35 *Columbia Law Review* 809 (1935). For modern Anglo-American assessments of the universality/particularity problem, see *Universals and Particulars* (Garden City: Anchor Books, 1970) (M. Loux ed.). It presumably is because of this vast tradition that John Pocock has emphasized the universality/particularity dyad in his approach to republican political theory. See J. Pocock, *The Machiavellian Moment* 1-80 *passim* (Princeton: Princeton University Press, 1975).

113. T. Adorno, "Subject and Object," in *The Essential Frankfurt School Reader*, *supra* note 2, at 497, 501. For a very good account of the dialectical twists and turns of Adorno's views on reification, see M. Jay, *Adorno* 68–70 (Cambridge: Harvard University Press, 1984).

114. Heller, *supra* note 13, at 197 note 110.

115. But see Rorty, *supra* note 90, at 460, advocating a "harmless distinction between normal or familiar properties and abnormal or unfamiliar ones."

116. B. Johnson, *supra* note 20, at x, 107.

117. D. Trubek, "Where the Action Is: Critical Legal Studies and Empiricism," 36 *Stanford Law Review* 575, 606 (1984). Trubek is not entirely comfortable with this view. See *id.* at 610–15. The other quotations are from R. Gordon, "New Developments in Legal Theory," in *The Politics of Law*, *supra* note 111, at 281, 289; IBAL, *supra* note 92, at 1294; K. Klare, "Judicial Deradicalization of the Wagner Act and the Origins of Modern Legal Consciousness, 1937–1941," 62 *Minnesota Law Review* 265, 338 (1978). For Kennedy's view, see, e.g., D. Kennedy, "Legal Education and the Reproduction of Hierarchy," in *The Politics of Law*, *supra* note 111, at 40, 48, arguing that "law school teaching makes the choice of hierarchy and domination . . . look as though it flows from and is required by legal reasoning rather than being a matter of politics"; D. Kennedy, "Cost-Benefit Analysis of Entitlement Problems: A Critique," 33 *Stanford Law Review* 387, 411 note 75 (1981), labeling law and economics as "fetishism," because of its "belief that economic properties determine the relations between people."

For a further statement of Gordon's view, see Gordon, *supra* note 71, at 71: "We invent shorthand labels like 'modernization' as a way of summarizing what has happened in and trying to generalize about the history of particular societies. Then, by a trick of the mind, we suddenly reify our labels into a process that *had* to happen the way it did. The next thing you know, we start explaining the whole contingent miscellany of contemporary social practices (especially the nasty ones) as the *natural* outcome of the 'modernization process.'"

118. Suppression of mutability can occur also as the *approval* of what exists; in short, the *status quo* can seem thoroughly desirable. Such a state of affairs is very often conjoined with the effects of reification that are described here, but the two developments are not exactly the same. I focus on the latter because the former is customarily treated under the rubric of "ideology."

119. On the first form, see, e.g., Gordon, *supra* note 117, at 287: "[D]eeply held assumptions about politics, economics, hierarchy, work, leisure, and the nature of reality . . . are profoundly paralysis-inducing because they make it so hard for people (including the ruling classes themselves) even to *imagine* that life could be different and better" (emphasis in original). See also M. Horkheimer and T. Adorno, *Dialectic of Enlightenment* 41 (New York: Continuum, 1982) (J. Cumming trans.): "The mythic scientific respect of the peoples of the earth for the *status quo* that they themselves unceasingly produce, itself finally becomes positive fact: the oppressor's fortress in regard to which even revolutionary imagination despises itself as utopism and decays to the condition of pliable trust in the objective tendency of history."

On the second form of squelched mutability, see, e.g., F. Olsen, "The Family and the Market: A Study of Ideology and Legal Reform," 96 *Harvard Law Review* 1497, 1502–1507 (1983), for well-drawn examples of paralyzing modes of argumentation. Michel Foucault has criticized a radical version of the suppressing of mutability: "We readily believe that the least we can expect of experiences, actions, and strategies is that they take into account the 'whole of society.' This seems absolutely essential for their existence. But I believe that this is asking a great deal, that it means imposing impossible conditions on our actions because this notion functions in a manner that prohibits the actualization, success, and perpetuation of these projects." M. Foucault, "Revolutionary Action: 'Until Now,'" in *Language, Counter-Memory, Practice*, *supra* note 44, at 218, 233.

120. See, e.g., AR, *supra* note 2, at 249, probing Rousseau's concept of "nature," which repeatedly "presents itself as the sole and true order of things." *Cf.* R. Barthes, "Myth Today," in *Mythologies* 109 (New York: Hill & Wang, 1972) (A. Lavers trans.), arguing that the second-order semiological systems of bourgeois myths "transform history into nature." See also sources cited *supra* note 68.

121. Heller, *supra* note 13, at 149. Critical studies of the politically regressive side of subjectivistic vocabularies are legion. I mention here only four of the most insightful lines of attack. (1) Michel Foucault assailed humanistic standpoints throughout his work, perhaps most vividly in his sharp critique of discourses on sex. See, e.g., HS, *supra* note 104, at 58–70, viewing confessions as "the general standard governing the production of the true discourse on sex" from the Christian era to the modern-day forms of self-revelation. Foucault's challenge to those who plead for the liberation of concupiscent subjectivity is well summarized in *id.* at 34–35.

(2) Though Fredric Jameson can justifiably argue that the Frankfurt School strongly criticized the reification of subjectivity under capitalism—F. Jameson, "Imaginary and Symbolic in Lacan: Marxism, Psychoanalytic Criticism, and the Problem of the Subject," in *Literature and Psychoanalysis* 338, 390–93 (Baltimore: Johns Hopkins University Press, 1982) (S. Felman ed.)—Horkheimer and Adorno were well aware, perhaps *too* keenly aware, that a subjectivist outlook readily interacts with nefarious political goals. See, e.g., M. Horkheimer and T. Adorno, *supra* note 119, at 83: "The system the Enlightenment has in mind is the form of knowledge which copes most proficiently with the facts and supports the individual most effectively in the mastery of nature. Its principles are the principles of self-preservation. Immaturity is then the inability to survive. The burgher, in the successive forms of slaveowner, free entrepreneur, and administrator, is the logical subject of the Enlightenment." This passage is the more notable in that it occurs during a discussion of the systematizing power of bourgeois thought, by which "[e]verything—even the human individual, not to speak of the animal—is converted into the repeatable, replaceable process, into a mere example for the conceptual models of the system" (*id.* at 84).

(3) Though at times oversimplifying the closure of male dominance—which is open *by virtue* of its closure—feminists have illuminatingly drawn contingent links between discourses of subjectivity and the subordination of females. See, e.g., MacKinnon, *supra* note 68, at 538, 541: "Woman through male eyes is sex object, that by which man knows himself at once as man and as subject. . . . Sexual objectification is the primary process of the subjection of women. It unites act with word, construction with expression, perception with enforcement, myth with reality. Man fucks woman; subject verb object." *Cf.* L. Irigaray, *Speculum of the Other Woman* 133, 139–40 (Ithaca: Cornell University Press, 1985) (G. Gill trans.): "If there is no more 'earth' to press down/repress, to work, to represent, but also and always to desire (for one's own), no opaque matter which in theory does not know herself, then what pedestal remains for the ex-sistence of the 'subject'?" A highly interesting variant of Irigaray's view is offered in S. Bordo, "The Cartesian Masculinization of Thought," 11 *Signs* 439 (1986), where it is argued that the aggressive independence of human subjects (*vis-à-vis* nature) in Cartesian philosophy was a means of compensating for *angst* brought on by the erosion of medieval feelings of oneness with the (female) world. The glibness of some of Bordo's arguments should induce a certain degree of skepticism. Indeed, John Brenkman has adopted what is in many ways a strongly opposed stance. He maintains that the obscuring of femaleness in Plato's *Symposium* amounted to a suppression of the irreducible gap between subjectivity and objectivity. See J. Brenkman, "The Other and the One: Psychoanalysis, Reading, the *Symposium*," in *Literature and Psychoanalysis, supra*, at 396, 440–50. Favoring either Brenkman or Bordo is not an easy matter; one should not presuppose that the differences *between* them are more important than differences *within* each.

(4) For a scintillating critique of the non-necessary but strong relationships between "order in general" and the "order of reason" that endows subjects with mastery over objects, see M. Serres, "The Algebra of Literature: The Wolf's Game," in *Textual Strategies* 260 (Baltimore: Johns Hopkins University Press, 1979) (J. Harari ed.).

As has been noted, subjectivism *qua* metaphysical persuasion or *qua* political outlook can be put to radical uses. The subversive power of liberal individualism, in times past, has been recognized by critical legal scholars. See, e.g., Heller, *supra* note 13, at 164 note 67; D. Kennedy, "The Structure of Blackstone's Commentaries," 28 *Buffalo Law Review* 205, 218 (1979). (For a good conventional treatment of early liberalism, see I. Kramnick, *The Rage of Edmund Burke* 13–20 [New York: Basic Books, 1977].) To find a pairing of metaphysical humanism and political leftism, one need not look any further than to the critical legal studies movement, many of whose most prominent figures wield a humanist rhetoric with at least arguable appeal. See, e.g., R. Unger, "The Critical Legal Studies Movement," 96 *Harvard Law Review* 561, 584–87 (1983). Still, it seems not unlikely that the political goals of leftist scholars can be pursued more effectively without blatant humanism.

For an eloquent portrayal of the atrocities committed in the name of anti-subjectivistic creeds, see A. Koestler, *Darkness at Noon* (New York: Bantam, 1966) (D. Hardy trans.), where the Party's murderous "definition of the individual was: a multitude of one million divided by one million" (*id.* at 208). For a verbose attack (from a largely humanist point of view) on the baleful politics of structuralist Marxism, see E. Thompson, "The Poverty of Theory or An Orrery of Errors," in *The Poverty of Theory and Other Essays* 1 (New York: Monthly Review Press, 1978), where it is argued that "Althusserianism *is* Stalinism reduced to the paradigm of Theory. It is Stalinism at last, theorised as ideology" (*id.* at 182). For a much more penetrating, though also very unflattering, assessment of Althusserian Marxism, see J. Rancière, *La Leçon d'Althusser* (Paris: Gallimard, 1974).

122. Concerning the proposed stress on mutability, I think that one cannot lightly disregard Philip Johnson's fear that "police and mob terror" will be required to carry out Roberto Unger's suggestions for the remaking of institutional schemes and individual lives. P. Johnson "Do You Sincerely Want to be Radical?" 36 *Stanford Law Review* 247, 282 note 91 (1984). The language of "openness" can be impugned from the other end of the political spectrum. Herbert Marcuse argued, for example, that "inasmuch as [tolerance] refrains from taking sides . . . it actually protects the already established machinery of discrimination. . . . To tolerate propaganda for inhumanity vitiates the goals not only of liberalism but of every progressive political philosophy." H. Marcuse, "Repressive Tolerance," in R. Wolff, B. Moore, and H. Marcuse, *A Critique of Pure Tolerance* 81, 85, 120 (Boston: Beacon Press, 1969). For a similar view, see M. Horkheimer and T. Adorno, *supra* note 119, at 210. Marcuse's argument was inspired by a rather ugly Manichaeism, but (like Johnson's fears) it should not be disregarded completely. Indeed, his point becomes even more telling when we recall that the Legal Realists put into question the divide between the passive and active roles of state power. See *supra* pp. 66–80.

Ellen Rooney has taken the "critique of repressive tolerance" further—in a direction of which Marcuse was well aware: "The paradox of pluralist discourse is that it is a polemic for inclusion coupled with a programmatic commitment to exclusions. And as Barthes might observe, it is precisely at the moment of its greatest generosity, in its most *persuasive* mode, that pluralism 'reinforces this relation of exclusion.' The exclusion of marxist theory, for example, is *justified* by the charge that marxism itself is a discourse that insists on the necessity, indeed, the inevitability, of exclusions (sometimes by violence); but is *practiced* by means of a discursive strategy that theoretically excludes the possibility of exclusion." E. Rooney, "Who's Left Out? A Rose by Any Other Name is Still Red; Or, The Politics of Pluralism," 12 *Critical Inquiry* 550, 561 (1986). (Michael Ryan takes a similar view. See M. Ryan, *supra* note 4, at 121–22.)

Furthermore, we always must be concerned about cooptation. See Marcuse, *supra*, at 83–84, 111: "[W]ithin a repressive society, even progressive movements threaten to turn into their opposite to the degree to which they accept the rules of the game. To take a most controversial case: the exercise of political rights . . . in a society of total administration serves to strengthen this administration by testifying to the existence of democratic liberties which, in reality, have changed their content and lost their effectiveness. In such a case, freedom (of opinion, of assembly, of speech) becomes an instrument for absolving servitude." The gravity of this problem should by no means be underestimated, even by those (like me) who prefer being defused to being set upon by police dogs.

123. J. Derrida, *supra* note 2, at 292–93. It is perhaps worth noting that what Derrida means by "humanism" is not exactly the same as my own usage.

124. *Id.* at 274.

125. Unger, *supra* note 121, at 591; *id.* at 590, 591; Kelman, *supra* note 23, at 296 note 11; Klare, *supra* note 117, at 335 note 276; MacKinnon, *supra* note 94, at 638 note 6.

126. Not surprisingly, this latter distinction has achieved prominence in the work of critical legal scholars who look most favorably upon Sartre. See, e.g., Gabel and Kennedy, *supra* note 23, at 43–44: "There is an irreducible element

of the absurd and the free in people's choices to fit themselves into [reified patterns of behavior]. If there are no electrodes in their heads, it's always a choice to be patterned according to false consciousness.

"Now the whole critique of rights, the way we tend to develop it, denies that. It suggests that rights analysis (the bad thing) is like pneumonia. Once you've got it, you've got it, until you've gotten an antibiotic and been cured of it."

127. SPPS, *supra* note 79, at 205 (IV. 400–401). Nietzsche made fervent calls for an individualistic form of "divine control." See, e.g., F. Nietzsche, *Thus Spoke Zarathustra* 62–63 (Harmondsworth: Penguin, 1966) (W. Kaufmann trans.): "But do you want to go . . . the way to yourself? Then show me your right and your strength to do so. Are you a new strength and a new right? A first movement? A self-propelled wheel? Can you compel the very stars to revolve around you? . . .

"Can you give yourself your own evil and your own good and hang your own will over yourself as a law? Can you be your own judge and avenger of your law?"

128. Unger, *supra* note 121, at 602. *Cf.* R. Unger, *supra* note 6, at 222–26, developing a neo-Hegelian program of "concrete universality" that tries to allow each person's "life, in its limitations and in its brevity, to be an expression rather than a sacrifice of the many-sidedness he [or she] shares with [hu]mankind." Likewise, Nietzsche admitted that a desirable "brevity" of one's habits can emerge only if one keeps taking up habits that are to be transcended. See GS, *supra* note 18, at 237.

129. This may sound inordinately akin to Sartre's theory of "situations"; I should thus take note of an all-important difference between my standpoint and that of Sartre. At least in his early years, Sartre tried to escape the paradox of events and structures by allotting to subjectivity and objectivity their circumscribed shares in the producing and forming of experience. As I have noted, this "escape" will be doomed. See *supra* note 66. However, what I am trying here to show is that even if we join Sartre in looking at highlighted stabilities and dynamics of social life, we shall have no grounds to start waiting for divine redemption (or some secular equivalent thereof).

130. G. Bataille, "The Notion of Expenditure," in *Visions of Excess* 116, 117–18 (Minneapolis: University of Minnesota Press, 1985) (A. Stoekl ed.). For Foucault's notion of "plebs," see M. Foucault, "Power and Strategies," in *P/K*, *supra* note 18, at 134, 138. *Cf.* M. Foucault, "Truth and Power," in *id.* at 109, 133: "It's not a matter of emancipating truth from every system of power (which would be a chimera, for truth is already power) but of detaching the power of truth from the forms of hegemony, social, economic and cultural, within which it operates at the present time."

131. J. Derrida, *supra* note 2, at 37. In the first sentence of the paragraph in the text, I have followed Barbara Johnson: "If [*The Critical Difference*] has any overall preoccupation, it is perhaps the importance of the functioning of *what is not known* in literature or theory." B. Johnson, *supra* note 20, at xii (emphasis in original).

132. For example, in reading Barbara Johnson's critique of Derrida's critique of Lacan, one almost inevitably gains a heightened esteem for the self-critical strength and richness of Derrida's attack.

Topical Index

Name Index

MATTHEW KRAMER teaches jurisprudence at Cambridge University, where he is a Fellow of Darwin College. He has published articles in leading journals of legal theory and political theory.